D0082306

PERSONAL FINANCE

PERSONAL FINANCE

SECOND EDITION

JANE KING
MARY CAREY

OXFORD
UNIVERSITY PRESS

Great Clarendon Street, Oxford, OX2 6DP,
United Kingdom

Oxford University Press is a department of the University of Oxford.
It furthers the University's objective of excellence in research, scholarship,
and education by publishing worldwide. Oxford is a registered trade mark of
Oxford University Press in the UK and in certain other countries

First edition 2014

Impression: 1

Published in the United States of America by Oxford University Press
198 Madison Avenue, New York, NY 10016, United States of America

British Library Cataloguing in Publication Data
Data available

Library of Congress Control Number: 2017932762

ISBN 978-0-19-874877-9

Printed in Great Britain by
Ashford Colour Press Ltd, Gosport, Hampshire

To Richard, Sam, and JJ, with love.

Jane King

For Adrian, Sarah, Jon, Chris, and Maddy, with love.

Mary Carey

Foreword

Empowering young people to develop financial skills in preparation for work and life is crucial. The inclusion of financial education in the National Curriculum since 2014 was a positive step towards ensuring people are equipped with the knowledge, confidence, and skills to manage their money properly—vital skills for both the present day and the future.

As the UK's leading professional membership body, supporting over 147,000 chartered accountants around the world, we understand the important contribution financial literacy makes to our social and economic progress.

Financial capability is at the core of what our members do. They are the biggest source of business advice in the UK, reaching over 2m businesses. At the same time, unsustainable personal debt is a cost to growth and the UK's long-term economic stability. The ability to have the right finances in place and plan financial matters effectively is a skill for major events—whether planning for university, buying a house, or when starting a business.

Responsible financial management is required, not only in business, but also for governments and consumers.

We have seen the impact that having no financial education has on the most vulnerable in society, but people must learn to take responsibility for their finances or face being left behind. The introduction of universal credit, the reductions in, and changes to, housing benefit, and the continued increase in total household debt highlight the pressures people will have to face. In the face of such issues it quickly becomes clear how important it is to be financially literate; such consumers are therefore key to ambitions for a sustainable UK economy.

Financial education comes in many different forms. For example, ICAEW Chartered Accountants volunteer to promote sustainable financial education in schools. As an organization, we also work with community associations and vulnerable residents. We have found that simple tools can help to enhance the financial capability of those that need it most, to help them deal with everything from basic bank accounts to coping with debt.

Personal Finance takes the fear out of financial planning. Taking control of finances is both empowering and positive and these are life skills that will ensure that the best decisions are made from the cradle to the grave. Whether it is which bank account to choose, information on pensions, or deciding on a mortgage, we continue to be faced with personal finance decisions on a regular basis and this looks set to increase. Having the confidence to deal with these choices is key.

Michael Izza,
ICAEW Chief Executive

Preface

This book is targeted at students, particularly first and second year undergraduates, and other young people. Its principal goal is to equip them with a sound understanding of many key personal finance issues. The authors have many years of experience in delivering personal finance modules at Oxford Brookes University.

The book aims to help its readers develop confidence and ability in dealing with personal finances so that, both during their time as students and after graduating, they can take practical steps towards taking control of their personal finances. The book is intended to equip readers with the knowledge and confidence to make informed decisions regarding financial planning and products, including those relating to savings, mortgages, investments, and pensions.

Personal Finance hopes to make the subject clear and accessible, limiting the use of jargon and explaining it where necessary through the use of key terms. In addition, the text includes a number of case studies, used throughout the chapters, that are designed to illustrate the practical application of theory and bring the subject to life. Readers have the opportunity to use the knowledge and techniques learned to inform financial decisions in common real-life situations.

As a society we often lack confidence when dealing with our personal finances. Many people worry that the issues are too difficult to handle personally and prefer to hand over responsibility to someone else to make decisions on their behalf. Whilst financial advisers can be an extremely useful resource, it is important for individuals to understand the issues involved for themselves, so that they can consider any advice carefully and make informed choices. The history of financial product mis-selling in the United Kingdom shows how important it is to have a clear appreciation of personal finance issues. *Personal Finance* aims to help students develop their confidence and understanding in order to build up their personal financial literacy skills.

Brief contents

Detailed contents

Acknowledgements

The authors would like to thank Kat Rylance at Oxford University Press for her encouragement and support throughout the writing process.

We would like to thank the many reviewers drawn from friends, colleagues, and family who have helped us with their insightful comments, and in particular Richard Shuker.

We would like to thank everyone else who has read chapters and provided feedback and encouragement on a more informal basis.

Disclaimer

This book aims to inform and educate the reader on certain financial issues. Nothing in this book should be construed as specific advice and it should not be relied upon as a basis for any decision or action. It is sold with the understanding that neither the authors nor the publisher are engaged in rendering professional financial services. The authors and the publisher do not accept responsibility or legal liability for any errors in the text, for the misuse or misapplication of information in this work, or for any outcomes arising from its use.

Links to third party websites are provided by Oxford in good faith and for information only. Oxford does not accept any responsibility or legal liability for the materials contained in any third party website referenced in this work and your access and use of such services and materials is at your own risk.

All characters, companies, and settings depicted are fictitious, and any resemblance to real persons, living or dead, is purely coincidental.

How to use this book

 Learning Objectives

After studying this chapter, you should understand:

- The need for each individual to take responsibility for their pe
  finances
- The fundamental steps needed to control an individual's perso
  finances
- How inflation is measured and why it is important to consider

Learning objectives

A bulleted outline of the main concepts and ideas indicates what you can expect to learn from each chapter.

 Ponder point

How easy would it be for you to cope with a large unforeseen expend
replace your computer?

Planning for the unexpected is one of the keys to successful
finances. If there is a financial plan in place and a strategy
events, then it should be possible to weather some financial

Ponder points

Regular 'Ponder points' encourage you to stop, think, and check your understanding of the key ideas covered in the chapter.

 Key term

The **Financial Conduct Authority (FCA)** is the organization responsi
services in the UK, ensuring that financial markets and firms operate
are protected.

The FCA has a general objective to ensure that financial mar
ficiently and that consumers are protected. The organization

Key terms

Key terms boxes explain the technical terms you will encounter when dealing with your personal finances.

Case study—Oliver

Oliver graduated with a degree in drama studies a few years ago and ha
ber of acting jobs since that time. Each role that he has been cast for has
between two and eight months but he has also had similar periods whe
Oliver, who lives in London, is a very keen concert goer and he atte
mer music festivals as he can fit in. When he is not working, tickets fo
usually paid for by credit card.
Oliver has the following debts:

Case studies

Each chapter features a set of case studies and questions to work through, giving you the opportunity to apply the theory you have covered to a range of practical problems. Scenarios are built around recurring characters and are carefully placed within the text so that you have all of the necessary information to understand the cases as they appear.

Examples

Frequent and clear examples are used to illustrate key concepts and encourage you to consider these ideas as you learn.

Example 4.8

A homebuyer is considering two potential properties, one of which one is valued at £235,000. The homebuyer has saved a deposit of £3 be for each of the properties?

Property valued at £170,000: Loan = £170,000 – 35,000 = £135,0

$$LTV = \frac{135,000}{170,000} \times 100\% = 79\%$$

Practice questions

A variety of end-of-chapter questions presents the opportunity to check your understanding of the topic covered and to apply what you've learned to a range of problems. Answers to some of the questions are provided at the back of the book, but answers to those marked with an asterisk (*) are available only to your lecturers.

Question 2 Vikram

Vikram wants to check whether he has paid the right amount of incom He has gathered together all his paperwork and produced the followir income:

- Vikram's salary was £24,000 per annum on which he paid income ta
- He received interest on an ISA of £300 and interest from a savings a
- He received dividends of £480 during the year.

How to use the Online Resource Centre

www.oxfordtextbooks.co.uk/orc/king_carey2e/

The Online Resource Centre (ORC) comprises resources for both lecturers and students, including:

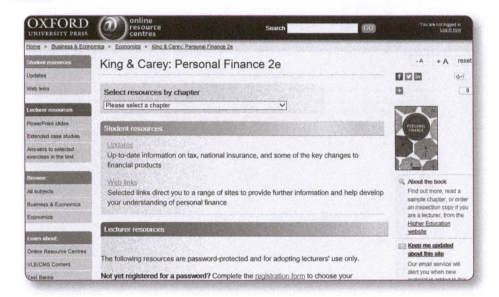

Student Resources
Free and open-access material available:

The website of the students loans company:
http://www.slc.co.uk

A website providing information on student loan
http://www.direct.gov.uk

This is a useful website for researching current

Links to relevant websites

Carefully selected links direct you to a range of sites to provide further information and help develop your understanding of personal finance.

Updates

Updates covering recent developments will
alerted when a new update is added by click
✉ Keep me updated

Online updates

Up-to-date information on tax, National
Insurance, and some of the key changes
to financial products keeps your text as
current as possible.

Lecturer Resources

Free for all registered adopters of the textbook:

Learning objectives

After studying this chapter, you should
understand:
- Reasons why it is important to have savings
- Risks associated with saving

PowerPoint slides

Each chapter is supported by a suite of
customizable slides to be used in lecture
presentations.

Solution 3 Chelsea

a) Table 2.8 Chelsea's monthly cash budget, first draft

	£
Income:	1,50
Net earnings (take home pay)	
Expenses:	
Rent, utilities, and food	4(

Solutions to selected questions in the text

Solutions to the asterisked (*) end-of-
chapter questions are available here,
allowing these to be used as assessments
or seminar questions.

Gavin Case Study

Gavin graduated ten years ago with a degree in mathematics b

since that time to training and competing as an international a

represented his country at the highest level culminating in rea

men's 110 metre hurdles final at the London Olympics. He de

Extended case studies

Two extended case studies and their
suggested solutions are available to help
develop student understanding of how
to apply theory to practical, real-world
problems.

Indicative rates

Writing a personal finance book is rather like shooting at a moving target. Rules, rates, and applicable dates are liable to change and this can occur with little warning. This book does not use exact figures for every allowance but rather uses indicative rates that give an indication of the size of a particular figure and are usually given as round sum amounts that make demonstrating the principles clearer and examples easier to follow.

This book aims to explain the key principles underpinning personal finance issues and once these are understood, the current rates and allowances can easily be referred to and inserted into any computation.

Whenever indicative rates are used, an (iR) symbol is used. In any chapter that uses such rates, references are given that will allow readers to find the current figures that apply.

(iR) Indicative rates

Table 1

Income tax Personal allowance and tax bands		
Personal allowance	£12,500 per annum	
	Income tax rate	Income tax rate for dividends
Personal Savings Allowance First £1,000 of savings income (available to basic rate taxpayers)	0%	—
Dividend Allowance First £5,000 of dividend income	—	0%
Tax bands		
First £32,000 of taxable income (Basic rate/Dividend ordinary rate)	20%	7.5%
Next £118,000 of taxable income (Higher rate/Dividend upper rate)	40%	32.5%
Above £150,000 of taxable income (Additional rate/Dividend additional rate)	45%	38.1%

Table 2

Car and fuel benefit		
CO$_2$ emissions (grams/kilometre)	Appropriate percentage (petrol car)	Appropriate percentage (diesel car)
From 0g/km to 50g/km	9%	12%
From 51g/km to 75 g/km	13%	16%
From 76g/km to 94g/km	17%	20%
100g/km to 104g/km	19%	22%
190g/km and above	37%	37%
Amount used for fuel benefit calculations	£22,500	£22,500

Table 3

National Insurance contributions Class 1—payable by employees	
	Earnings per month
Primary threshold	£700
Upper earnings limit	£3,700
	National Insurance contributions
On earnings between the primary threshold and the upper earnings limit	12%
On earnings above the upper earnings limit	2%

Table 4

National Insurance contributions Classes 2 and 4—payable by the self-employed	
Class 2 small profits threshold	£6,000
Class 2 rate	£3.00 per week
Class 4 lower profits limit	£8,000
Class 4 upper profits limit	£44,000
Class 4: rate on profits between lower and upper limit	9%
Class 4: rate on profits above upper limit	2%

Table 5

Capital gains tax Exemptions and bands	
Annual exemption amount	£12,000
Personal possessions exemption	£6,000
Taxable income band	**Capital gains tax rate**
Standard rate	10%
Standard rate residential property	18%
Higher rate	20%
Higher rate residential property	28%

Table 6

Inheritance tax Nil rate band and rate	
Band	**Inheritance tax rate %**
Nil rate band 0–£325,000	0
Main residence nil rate band Next £175,000	0
Remainder of estate	40
Gift exemptions—indicative amounts	
Exemption	**Amount**
Small gifts	£250 per person
Gift from parents	£5,000 on marriage
Annual exemption amount	£3,000
Indicative rates of tax on potentially exempt transfers (PETs)	
3–4 years	20% reduction in tax due on gift
4–5 years	40% reduction in tax due on gift
5–6 years	60% reduction in tax due on gift
6–7 years	80% reduction in tax due on gift
More than 7 years	100% reduction in tax due

Table 7

Student loans starting after 1 September 2012	
Maximum loans (full-time students)	
Tuition fees loan	£9,000
Maintenance loan (The maximum depends on whether the student lives at home or in London)	Variable
Interest on student loans	
During the course	RPI + 3%
On graduating, if earning less than £21k	RPI
On graduating, if earning between £21k and £41k	RPI + between 0 % and 3%, depending on income
On graduating, if earning more than £41k	RPI + 3%
Loan repayments	
On earnings over £21,000	9% of earnings over £21,000

Table 8

Annual ISA allowances	
Individual under 18 years old	Cash and/or shares Junior ISA Limit of £4,100
Individual aged 16–18 years of age (Can invest in a Junior ISA at same time)	Cash ISA Limit of £20,000
Individual aged over 18 years	Cash and/or shares ISA Limit of £20,000
Individual aged 18–40 years	Lifetime ISA £4,000 (subject to overall limit of £20,000 for all ISAs)
Individual aged over 16 years	Help to Buy ISA £2,400 (subject to overall limit of £20,000 for all ISAs)

Table 9

Financial Services Compensation Scheme
£75,000

Facing life decisions

 Learning Objectives

After studying this chapter, you should understand:

● The need for each individual to take responsibility for their personal finances

● The fundamental steps needed to control an individual's personal finances

● How inflation is measured and why it is important to consider its potential impact

Introduction

Most people appreciate that it is important to look after their health and fitness, and will accept that taking personal responsibility for this means having a healthy lifestyle throughout their life. Ensuring that your personal finances are in a similarly good condition will also mean that they need to be looked after continuously and from a young age.

There has been a great deal of attention drawn to the limited financial literacy skills that seem to be fairly prevalent in the population as a whole. Personal finance can seem to be inaccessible as the jargon used can act as a barrier to understanding. Sometimes, subjects that would be easy to understand remain unexplored because of this language barrier.

The demands of modern life frequently mean that people do not have the time to spend on issues that do not appear to be urgent. Drawing up a plan or researching financial products can easily be seen as something that can be done next week, next month, or next year, especially when the pressures of work and home life leave little free time to relax. There may be a temptation to consider that if, for example, an individual can afford to make his debt repayments, is making some pension contributions, and has no immediate financial concerns, that person does not need to engage in financial planning with any urgency. The fact that the debt may be attracting a high interest rate or that the pension savings are inadequate will go unnoticed, unless that individual takes the time to explore his personal financial situation.

Alongside this lack of financial literacy and reluctance to engage with personal finance issues, there have been huge advances in the information and data that can be accessed, thanks to the internet. Whilst the internet is undoubtedly very useful for research purposes, having a sound understanding of the product being researched is an essential prerequisite to any financial decision. Being able to find relevant and appropriate information and understanding what to look out for, has become ever more important as financial products can be presented in very appealing ways that do not necessarily highlight all pertinent information.

Background

A financially secure person is someone who is financially literate, is in control of their financial situation, and who takes the time to undertake a regular review of their finances and put their plans into action.

Gaining an understanding of the issues and the terminology involved in personal finance is essential in order to ensure that the right questions are asked and better decisions made. An individual who has the confidence to take control of their financial plans will feel empowered, in contrast to the situation where that control is lacking and the individual has no real understanding of their current or likely future financial position. They may not know, for example, whether they have any unnecessary insurance cover in place or whether they are making adequate savings to meet their ambitions.

The alternative to gaining control over personal finances is to fail to become informed and to neglect to undertake any kind of personal financial planning. The risks arising from this approach might include: personal goals not being achieved, inadequate savings being made, dependants not being adequately provided for, inappropriate lending being taken out, and ultimately there is the risk the individual may become financially dependent on the state and this will almost certainly lead to a constant struggle to cover day-to-day living costs.

Individuals who fail to plan will not experience the reassurance that can be achieved by knowing that you understand and control your finances.

Fundamentals of financial planning

Managing your personal finances needs time and commitment and the complexity involved will, in general, increase as you get older. The basic process of personal financial planning can be thought of as a five-step approach as illustrated by Figure 1.1.

Step 1: Set your objectives

A key aspect of planning is that it should be carried out with a view to enabling the person concerned to progress towards achieving their goals and meeting their ambitions.

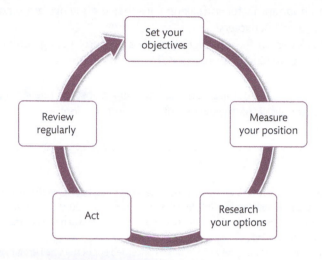

Figure 1.1 The personal financial planning process

Different people will have different goals and these will usually be influenced by age, background, and personal circumstances. There are some common personal goals, for example:

- To have enough savings to cover potential emergencies
- To buy your own home
- To ensure that your dependants would be financially secure if you were no longer able to earn an income
- To have a reasonable income in retirement

Once personal goals have been identified, then some attempt should be made to prioritize them, as it may not be possible to take action on all of them at any one time. Some goals may be short term and others may be much longer term. The fact that a goal is a long-term one does not reduce the need to start planning for it. Many long-term goals will only be achievable if action is taken over many years.

Step 2: Measure your position

A key part of any personal finance review will be to assess your current financial position by preparing a personal budget and gathering together details of all significant personal assets and debts.

A personal budget, where income and expenditure are compared, is a central part of the planning process. It is essential to prepare one in order to ascertain whether there are likely to be funds available for certain actions to be taken. In order to achieve many personal finance goals, it will be necessary to save and having a realistic financial budget is an important factor in making sure that the savings are made. Personal budgets are covered in Chapter 2.

An individual's personal assets might include a property, savings, and investments. The review process provides an opportunity to evaluate these assets and check whether the returns being earned on savings and investments are in line with expectations. This will involve looking at the numbers and also carrying out some relevant research into the types of asset held. If this review identifies a poorly performing asset, then actions may be considered to replace that asset.

Example 1.1

A woman carrying out a review of her personal assets finds that her home that she bought for £210,000 a year ago is now worth a little less than that, probably £205,000. She also discovers that her savings account is paying her interest at the rate of 0.1%, when she is aware that similar savings accounts are paying 2.5%.

After carrying out the review, the woman is not concerned about the small drop in her house price as she understands that property prices can vary over time and she hopes that in the long run its value will recover. To move home is a disruptive, expensive, and time-consuming business.

Having established that her savings are invested in a poorly performing savings account, she decides to act and to move those savings into an account paying a better rate of interest.

In addition to considering personal assets, it is essential to look in detail at all the debts that a person has.

 Ponder point

What do you consider are the most common types of debts that an individual might have?

Examples of common debts that individuals have include bank overdrafts, student debt, bank and finance loans, mortgages, credit card debts, and unpaid bills.

In addition to identifying the amount owed to the lender, note should also be made of the interest rates being charged and the repayments due. With this information, it is possible to assess whether it would be possible to reduce borrowing costs. Managing your debts is covered in Chapter 4.

 Ponder point

In drawing up the list of personal assets for financial planning purposes, do you think it would be appropriate to include any of the following items that a person owns: a car, a laptop computer, a mobile phone?

All of the above items will bring benefits to their owner but that does not necessarily mean they are assets that should be included in any personal financial planning exercise. The car is certainly an asset but it is a depreciating asset as it falls in value over time and with use. It will have been bought so that it can be used and unless it is a vintage car, any owner would expect to sell it for less than it cost. It is usually not relevant to include it in a personal finance exercise.

The mobile phone and the laptop may have cost a significant amount but, after a relatively short period of time, their value tends to fall sharply as technology changes. These devices, although very useful to the owner, would generally not be assets recognized for personal financial planning purposes. If any of these items were about to be sold, then the proceeds of any sale would be considered an asset.

Step 3: Research your options

Once you have a full understanding of your financial situation and have identified the goals you plan to pursue, you can start to identify the steps that need to be taken in order for progress to be made towards those goals. This will involve having an understanding of the issue, the factors to consider, the terminology used, the pitfalls to look out for, and, most importantly, the risks attaching to any financial product. The internet has made it very easy to research products but it is essential to understand the product you are researching and to be aware of the independence, or limitations, of any websites used. Understanding the terms used by financial products is essential in order to know what to look for, what questions to ask, and for appropriate options to be identified.

Step 4: Act

Once a decision has been made, then steps need to be taken to put the plan into action. For example, to move savings into an account that pays a good rate of interest or to start living within a clearly defined budget, so that savings can be built up to fund a gap year.

Step 5: Review regularly

The actions taken should be reviewed on a regular basis to ensure that progress is being made towards the desired outcome. The whole financial planning process should be revisited on a two to three yearly basis or when personal or economic circumstances change.

 Ponder point

In addition to regular reviews, there are certain life events that should probably trigger a review of a person's personal finances. Can you list some of these events?

The list of possible key events could include starting work, changing jobs, being made redundant, becoming self-employed, getting married, getting divorced, having a child, or facing health problems. In each of the above situations, there may be changes to expected income, changes to expected outgoings, changes to personal responsibilities, lump sums received, and hence there are likely to be changes to goals and plans.

Life decisions

There are many personal finance issues that will have to be faced by almost everyone at some point in their lives. The most common concerns that people are likely to face include:

- How to balance their personal budget?
- When to take on debt and how to manage it?
- How much to save so as to have cash available for unforeseen problems?
- What taxes will have to be paid and how much will have to be paid?
- Whether to buy or rent their home?
- Whether property represents a good investment?
- How much to save and when to start saving for retirement?
- Which types of insurance to take out?
- When and how to make a will?

Most of the above concerns cannot be considered in isolation, as there are often links between them. For example, buying your own home would require you to draw up a budget and then make significant savings in order to afford the deposit. When the property is purchased and a mortgage is taken out, this would significantly increase your level of debt. Owning your own home raises the prospect of having a major asset, the property, to insure.

The above concerns are typical of the type of issues that will be considered when a personal financial review is carried out, but there are many more factors that may arise. Every individual will have their own unique circumstances, individual aims, and be at a different point in their overall financial lifecycle.

Typical patterns of income, debt, and savings

Every person is unique; individuals are influenced by their own personal circumstances, their goals and ambitions, the opportunities that they are presented with, and their individual capabilities. Throughout each person's adult life, their income will vary and their debts and savings will increase and decrease in response to behaviours and events. There are certain key events that will have a big influence on an individual's financial situation, such as going to university or buying a house. Recognizing that there is a pattern of income, debts, and savings that will be followed over an adult's lifetime can be useful to reflect on. The individual elements are sometimes interrelated and understanding where someone is in that lifecycle pattern will help to clarify their existing financial position and where they aim to be in the future. The details will vary hugely according to the individual concerned.

Example 1.2

Luke is thirty-five years old and has just purchased his first home. Being financially literate, he manages his finances carefully and using all his available savings to buy his own home has caused him to reflect on the likely pattern of income, debt, and savings that he may experience over his lifetime. Using some actual and some predicted figures, based on his plans, he draws up three graphs. Figure 1.2 shows his anticipated income over his adult life, Figure 1.3 shows his expected levels of debt over his adult life, and Figure 1.4 shows his expected level of savings.

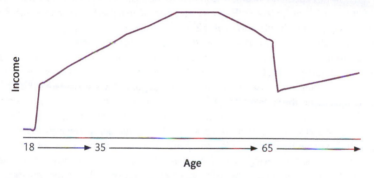

Figure 1.2 Luke: profile of income over his adult life

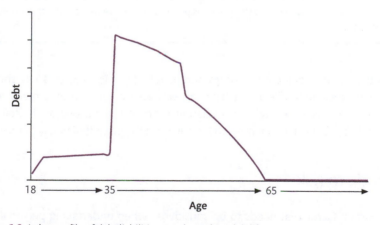

Figure 1.3 Luke: profile of debt liabilities owed over his adult life

(continued...)

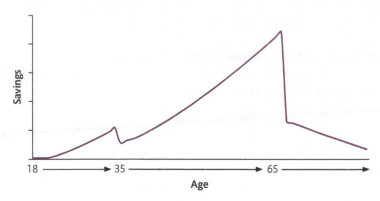

Figure 1.4 Luke: profile of savings held, including pension savings, over his adult life

The income graph shows how Luke's income increased steadily during the years after graduation and how he expects his income to continue to increase in the years up to around the age
of fifty, after which time it plateaus. He expects his income to fall as he approaches retirement
and at sixty-eight, when he plans to retire, his income will decrease sharply.

The debt graph shows how Luke's student debt led to significant levels of debt in his early
twenties, which continues to increase slightly as his loan repayments do not cover the interest
charged on his student debt. Luke anticipates that he will still have some student debt thirty
years after graduating and this will be written off at that point. The big increase in his debt, at
age thirty-four, marks the large mortgage taken out to buy his home that is to be repaid over
thirty years. By the age of sixty-five, he hopes to have no debts outstanding.

The savings graph shows how Luke has been building up his savings since graduation.
Some of those savings have been made into a pension fund and some savings were made for
a deposit to buy a home. Making the property purchase has used up those savings and he
anticipates that his savings may increase less steeply for a few years due to the demands of
paying a mortgage and establishing a home. By the time the age of forty is reached, Luke plans
to be saving increasing amounts in order to secure a comfortable retirement. When he retires
the graph shows his savings drop sharply as his pension savings are converted into an annual
pension income.

Clearly these graphs of income, savings, and debt (Figures 1.2, 1.3, and 1.4), show one
individual's expected profile but each person will have a different profile, many very different to the graphs shown. When considering personal financial issues, it is useful to reflect on what your profiles are likely to look like and the point that you are currently at.

Attitude to risk

An important factor that needs to be considered when undertaking personal financial planning, is an individual's attitude to risk. A general principle is that the riskier a

financial product, the greater the potential rate of return it will offer. The more secure a product, the lower the rate of return it will offer. Some people are risk-takers, others are risk averse, and most are somewhere between the two.

There are questionnaires that enable people to assess their personal attitude to risk. A typical question might be as follows:

Example 1.3

In order to assess your personal attitude to risk, consider the following scenario.

There are five investment choices available to you and for £1,000 invested the expected paybacks after one year are shown in Table 1.1.

Table 1.1 Attitude to risk: which option would you take?

Option	Possible outcomes	Average payback
1	The investment is certain to produce a payback of £1,040.	£1,040
2	There is an 80% chance that the investment will payback £1,100 and a 20% chance that it will payback £950.	£1,070
3	There is an 80% chance that the investment will payback £1,200 and a 20% chance that it will payback £850.	£1,130
4	There is an 80% chance that the investment will payback £1,330 and a 20% chance that it will payback £650.	£1,194
5	There is an 80% chance that the investment will payback £1,500 and a 20% chance that it will payback £500.	£1,300

Which of the above choices would you make?

Option 1 is the risk-free option but offers the lowest rate of return and a person selecting that option would be categorized as strongly risk averse. Option 2 carries some risk of incurring a small loss and would be a low risk option. A person selecting that option might be known as an individual prepared to take modest risks. Option 3 carries a moderate level of risk and Option 4 is higher risk. Option 5 carries the highest average payback but anyone choosing it would be prepared to accept a high level of risk. There is a 20% chance that the value of their investment will fall by a half over the course of the year and an 80% chance that they will get a return of 50% over that year. Any individual choosing that option would be categorized as having a very high risk tolerance.

Attitudes to risk are partly linked to personality but age and personal circumstances also play a part. Where financial products involve an element of risk, it is very important for the individual to consider the risk involved and only to choose a product with which they will be comfortable because it offers an acceptable level of risk.

Risks

There are numerous types of risk attached to personal finance products. Many of these risks will be discussed in the chapters where they are most relevant but it is important to have an overall understanding of the general types of risk that can impact on an individual's finances:

- There is the risk posed by inflation. Over time inflation can erode the value of savings and investments. It may also impact positively on borrowers but this will depend on the circumstances of each case. The impact of inflation is discussed below.

- There is the risk that there could be an unexpected change in interest rates and this would impact on many products: interest paid on borrowings, interest earned on savings, the value of some pensions and investments, and more.

- There is political risk as governments change and policies change; this can have a very significant impact on individuals, businesses, and economic prospects, which in turn can impact on the value of personal savings, property, and investments.

- Market risk is where the market for one type of asset is affected by particular circumstances and the value of all the assets in that market will be liable to change in a similar way. This can be witnessed on days where nearly all listed share prices show an increase or a day when they nearly all show a decrease.

The risk posed by inflation needs to be clearly understood before personal finance issues are considered. Even relatively low levels of inflation have a very significant impact on the real value of savings, other assets, and debt.

Inflation

Inflation describes the situation when the cost of goods and services that households buy, increases. This means that the purchasing power of money will fall.

 Key term

Inflation describes the situation when the costs of goods and services are rising; it is measured in percentage terms.

Example 1.4

An individual stores her savings of £5,000 under her mattress. If inflation is running at 5% per annum, then one year after the money is tucked away, the £5,000 will not buy as many goods and services as it would have done at the beginning of the year. In real terms, it will be worth £5,000 × 0.95 = £4,750 at the end of the year.

If the money was left undisturbed for five years and over that time inflation continued to run at 5% per annum, then the purchasing power of those savings would have fallen to £3,869 (£5,000 × 0.95^5) by the end of the five years.

Example 1.4 demonstrates how inflation can quickly erode the real value of savings if nothing is done to protect them. The rate of inflation is a crucial measure in many areas of financial planning. Inflation lowers the purchasing power of money and this makes it crucial to factor the impact of inflation into any financial decision. It is not enough to know by how much a savings account will grow when the most meaningful measure would involve considering the purchasing power or 'real value' of those savings.

Some financial products have in the past been protected from the effects of inflation. The interest paid on some National Savings certificates was linked to the rate of inflation, which was particularly attractive to investors when inflation rates were fluctuating and relatively high. The government has not issued any in recent years but may do so again in the future. Some pensions and state benefits are linked to the rate of inflation although it is possible that, in the future, governments may make changes to this link.

Lower inflation means greater financial stability and provides a much more predictable environment preferred by government, business, and most individuals.

Example 1.5

A borrower took out a loan for £40,000. If inflation meant that the purchasing power of that loan six years later was £32,000, then the amount that borrower owed in real terms would have fallen.

The borrower may be better off as a result as long as his income has kept pace with inflation. Another factor that may impact on this borrower is that the interest payable on a loan will usually be greater when inflation is higher.

 ### Key terms

CPI (Consumer Prices Index) is a measure of inflation based on the change in price of an average basket of goods and services on which a household spends money but, unlike RPI, it excludes a number of housing costs including mortgage interest, council tax, and house depreciation.

RPI (Retail Prices Index) is a measure of inflation based on the change in price of an average basket of goods and services that a household spends money on.

The government has two measures for inflation, both of which are quite similar but one, the consumer prices index (CPI), usually leads to a lower measure of inflation. The retail prices index (RPI) and the CPI both measure the change in price of a representative basket of goods and services bought by a typical household. The RPI and the CPI both take into account the relative significance of each item in the basket.

The CPI's average basket of goods and services is different from the RPI's average basket because the CPI excludes a number of housing costs including mortgage interest, council tax, and house depreciation. The actual index amount of the CPI or RPI is not of particular note; it is the change in that index that measures the rate of inflation. The change is computed over twelve months and is quoted as an annual figure.

Example 1.6

The CPI index is 130 in August. One year later, the CPI index is 135.
The rate of inflation for the year as measured by the CPI would be

$$\frac{(135-130)}{130} \times 100 = 3.8\%.$$

Example 1.7

The RPI index is 250 in August. One year later, the RPI index is 260.
The rate of inflation for the year as measured by the RPI would be

$$\frac{(260-250)}{250} \times 100 = 4.0\%.$$

 Ponder point

A saver has money in a deposit account opened many years ago that is paying interest at the rate of 0.3% per annum, whilst inflation as measured by the CPI stands at 4.0%. What will be the impact on the saver?

If savings yield 0.3% per annum whilst inflation is running at 4.0%, the real value of the savings will be falling year by year. If this situation continued for a few years, the real value of the savings would be severely depleted.

 Key term

The **real rate of return** earned on a financial product is the return earned after the effect of inflation is taken into account.

This book uses five different case studies, covering a range of individuals and couples, to provide a variety of scenarios that can be employed as a basis for applying knowledge and skills in a practical setting. The various cases are introduced below and as you go through the text, you will become more familiar with their financial situation and the issues that they face.

Case study—Oliver

Oliver graduated from university with a degree in drama studies two years ago. His one ambition is to act and, since graduating, he has shared a rented flat in London with a friend, worked part-time, and attended auditions on a regular basis. He has just been offered a role in a touring production that will tour the UK for six months. He plans to take his guitar and laptop with him, neither of which is insured.

Oliver has no savings but does have a large amount of student debt, an overdraft, and credit card debts.

Required:

Identify three personal finance goals that are likely to be important to Oliver.

Case study—Rachel

Rachel joined a large retail chain on graduating and as an organized and ambitious young person, she immediately set herself some personal finance objectives:

- To pay off her overdraft
- To buy her own property in a few years
- To save as much as she can

Rachel is now aged twenty-five and has paid off her overdraft and saved a substantial sum towards a deposit on a property. She continues to rent a small flat. She has been regularly promoted by her employer throughout her years with the firm and is now a store manager.

Required:

a) **What sort of actions might Rachel have taken in order to have met her initial objectives?**

b) **Can you think of some personal finance objectives that Rachel may now wish to consider?**

Case study—Imran

Imran, aged twenty-six, is a lawyer living and working in London. He has a well-paid job but he spends most of what he earns. He rents a modern flat in a central location, enjoys eating out regularly, and has a lively and expensive social life. He belongs to a luxurious gym where he works out once a week. Imran also enjoys travelling to more unusual destinations for his holidays.

Imran is paid a bonus from time to time and he has managed to save most of the bonuses he has received. He has student debt outstanding.

Imran has an ambition to own his own home. He has not yet made any pension contributions and states that he is reluctant to do so as his uncle had a bad experience when he lost most of his pension savings.

Imran recognizes that he is in a fortunate position and very much enjoys his lifestyle. He is financially literate and understands many financial products. He is confident that he can

(continued...)

manage his personal finances and does not feel the need to set aside time in his busy life to carry out a financial planning exercise, especially at what he considers to be an early stage in his working life.

Required:

Discuss Imran's situation and whether you consider Imran would benefit from carrying out a personal financial planning review.

Case study—Theo and Kate

Theo, aged forty, and his wife Kate have three young children and together they are buying their own home. Theo works in the public sector and has been a member of his employer's pension scheme for the last fifteen years. Kate runs a small business from home that generates an income for her of £500 each month.

Theo and Kate have a large mortgage, owe significant sums on their credit cards, and have a large overdraft. Theo has never considered undertaking any kind of personal financial planning. His view is as follows:

Given my current financial predicament, I have absolutely no choices to make as I have no spare cash to consider investing. Personal financial planning is for people with money to save.

Required:

a) **Do you consider that Theo's view is right and that personal financial planning is not relevant to him?**

b) **Describe some of the benefits that personal financial planning could offer to Theo and Kate.**

Case study—Tian and Brian

Tian and Brian are a married couple in their fifties who have, over the last thirty years, periodically set time aside to review their personal finances and plan for the future. They have three grown-up children who are financially independent. The couple own and run their own business selling organic pies to shops and cafes and have recently received an offer of £1.2 million for the business, which they plan to accept and then, possibly, retire.

The couple's main assets are their shareholdings in the business, their jointly owned house, on which there is no outstanding mortgage, a small amount of other savings and investments, and a very modest amount saved in a pension scheme.

There are a number of issues that might form the focus for Tian and Brian's financial planning at this point in their lives, including:

- How to invest the proceeds from the sale of business?
- What will be the tax implications of the business sale?
- What pension is predicted from recent projections? Should they consider investing more into a pension scheme?
- What other investments might they consider in order to ensure a reliable retirement income?
- Check that their will is up to date and consider inheritance tax planning.

Conclusion

Personal financial planning is not easy and will never be an exact science as nobody can predict the future. This should never be a reason to delay starting to engage in financial planning as the younger people are when they start planning, the better.

Every individual will have different circumstances, different attitudes to risk, different priorities, and, ultimately, different goals. There are, however, certain common life decisions that most people will face. This book aims to cover each of these decisions by explaining the main principles that underpin a topic and the key considerations that need to be taken into account when reaching a decision.

The discipline of carrying out a regular review of your personal finances is one that should be adopted from adulthood onwards. As well as doing this on a regular cycle every two to three years, it will also be necessary to revisit plans when significant personal or economic events occur. Being in control of your finances is both liberating and empowering. It should help to ensure that the most is made of any savings opportunities, that adequate savings are built up, and the best rates and deals are identified. It should also enable debts to be managed sensibly and steps taken to ensure that an adequate retirement income is built up over a person's working life.

The alternative to taking control of your personal finances is to leave the future to chance, manage month to month and hope that all will be well. This is highly likely to lead to inadequate savings being made, missed opportunities to respond to changing circumstances, and failure to benefit from good deals when they arise. With no plans in place, personal goals have little chance of being achieved and it is likely to lead to an inability to respond to a crisis when it arises. Ultimately it may lead to problems with debt and possibly a retirement spent living on a low income.

Useful websites

To assess your attitude to risk:
http://www.standardlife.co.uk

The official website for information on how inflation is calculated and for details of current and historic inflation rates:
http://www.ons.gov.uk

Practice Question

Question 1 Quick Questions TRUE OR FALSE?

1.1 Personal financial planning is a process that should be carried out on a regular five-yearly basis.

1.2 It is far more important for older people to engage with personal financial planning, than younger people.

1.3 Someone who is said to be risk averse prefers not to take risks.

1.4   Someone with a very high risk tolerance will be prepared to accept high levels of risk in exchange for potentially receiving high returns.

1.5   Political risk would include the risk that a government changes its policy regarding the age at which the state pension is payable.

1.6   The RPI and the CPI indices are both measures of inflation.

1.7   If the RPI is greater than the CPI at a particular time, then this means that inflation is rising.

1.8   If inflation is measured at 3% per annum and a savings account is paying interest at 3% per annum, the buying power of the savings made will remain unchanged.

1.9   If inflation is measured at 3% per annum and a savings account is paying interest at 1% per annum, the buying power of the savings will fall.

1.10   If you do not take control of your finances and end up in financial difficulty, state benefits will help you maintain your lifestyle.

 Visit the Online Resource Centre that accompanies this book for additional material: **www.oxfordtextbooks.co.uk/orc/king_carey2e/**

2 Balancing your personal budget

 Learning Objectives

After studying this chapter, you should understand:

- The importance of budgeting as a personal finance tool
- How to prepare a personal cash budget
- How to use a budget to gain control over your finances and meet objectives

Introduction

Budgeting is a fundamental tool that enables individuals to understand their pattern of income and expenses and provides an opportunity for them to regulate their spending and take control of their finances. A budget is a financial plan that compares an individual's expected future income and expenditure. Preparing one is a practical and straightforward process that is based on 'common-sense' principles. Often personal budgets are only used if someone runs into financial difficulties, when their regular use might have avoided a financial crisis arising in the first place.

There are many reasons to budget and for one individual some or all of the following objectives might apply:

- To ensure that personal expenditure does not exceed income
- To help start a savings plan, perhaps to save for a deposit on a property
- To work out how to afford a big budget item, such as a car or major holiday
- To build up a reserve to cover expenses that may arise from unexpected future events
- To pay off debts

This chapter mainly focuses on the first objective of ensuring that expenditure does not exceed income, to illustrate the usefulness of cash budgets when taking control of personal finances.

In many ways it is easier not to budget and some people live their lives hoping to make ends meet. They may run into unplanned overdrafts, buy things using increasing credit card debt to fund their purchases, and struggle to cope with financial crises as they occur. Young people may have access to some form of family backup that they can turn to in an emergency to ask for help, but all independent adults should take responsibility for their own finances and be able to live within their means. They should be able to cope with financial setbacks, such as a major car repair, needing a new washing machine, or more fundamental problems such as being made redundant or facing a serious illness. In order to handle these crises it is important to have a financial strategy and a plan in place, to ensure there are sufficient resources available to deal with such situations.

 Ponder point

How easy would it be for you to cope with a large unforeseen expenditure, such as having to replace your computer?

Planning for the unexpected is one of the keys to successful management of personal finances. If there is a financial plan in place and a strategy to cope with unforeseen events, then it should be possible to weather some financial storms without resorting to increased credit card use, overdrafts, or expensive short-term loans. These emergency sources are uncertain and some can prove very expensive. Preparing a cash budget is the first step towards meeting the objective of building up savings to provide a reserve to cover unexpected situations.

The cash budget

Spreadsheets are the perfect tool for preparing a cash budget. There are many different websites, apps, and personal budgeting packages available to help create a personal financial plan, but a simple spreadsheet can meet the needs of most people. The main point of a budget is for a person to gain a clear picture of their income and expenditure in order to develop a plan of how to achieve their objectives. Generally a monthly budget will be the most useful, but a weekly budget can also be helpful.

Apart from the very wealthy, the majority of people would benefit from preparing a budget and as a result, gaining a clearer understanding of their personal finances. It should enable them to ensure that they live within their means. The penalty of not living within their means is often getting into debt, which generates further costs and financial difficulty. It is better to prepare a cash budget and take control of spending, rather than waiting for the bank to give the bad news at the end of month, showing an unexpected overdraft position.

If a person's objective is to ensure that their expenditure does not exceed their income, preparing a cash budget enables them to measure their position. If they are not currently achieving their objective then they should be able to consider different options to bring the budget into balance and take appropriate action. The budget should be regularly reviewed and updated to maintain control.

Preparing a cash budget

The starting point when preparing a cash budget is to predict, as accurately as possible, expected income and expenditure. To start with, it will be useful to refer to a number of sources of information including payslips, receipts, credit card statements, bills, cash withdrawals, and bank statements. These documents provide a record of past income and expenses although not always in much detail.

 Ponder point

How might you arrive at a clear understanding of how you currently spend your money?

Keeping a log of all money spent over a few weeks can be a very illuminating process. Whilst certain key expenses will be predictable and known, many costs may be met using cash where no record is normally kept. Keeping a detailed log of everything spent is probably the best way of clearly understanding where your money goes. There are several smartphone and computer apps that provide a tool for creating such a log.

These records showing where money is being spent should enable the preparer to identify all the expenses that he incurs. It can also be useful to refer to a pro-forma budget to ensure that all items of income and expenditure have been considered. The current amounts should then be adjusted for any known or anticipated changes in the future. Having collected together the relevant information, the figures can be inserted into a spreadsheet, app, or set out on paper.

Example 2.1

An example of a cash budget is shown in Table 2.1 for a student whose objective is to keep control of her financial position and live within her budget.

Table 2.1 Cash budget for one month—student (Figures for illustration only)

	Per month £
Income:	
Earnings (after any deductions)	250
Student loan	300
Parental contribution	100
Total income	**650**
Expenditure:	
Regular outgoings:	
Rent/hall fees	320
Mobile phone	30

(continued...)

Table 2.1 (*continued*)

	Per month £
Everyday expenses:	
Food/drink	90
Clothes	40
Eating out/takeaways	20
Going out/entertainment	80
Travel/petrol	40
Toiletries	10
Textbooks	30
Occasional expenses:	
Holidays, birthdays, or other	30
Total expenditure	**690**
Net expenditure	
(Total income–total expenditure)	**(40)**

If the student for whom the budget in Example 2.1 was prepared had started the month with £100 in the bank, then she would expect to have £60 in the bank by the end of the month, as her net expenditure for the month amounts to £40.

Having prepared the cash budget for one month, it is then possible to consider how it might look over the next few months. This requires the balance from the end of the current month to be carried forward to become the starting balance for the next month.

Example 2.2

If the student in Example 2.1 expects to have the same income and expenses over the next three months, then her cash budget for those months would be as set out in Table 2.2.
(Income and expenses are shown in total, rather than giving the details again.)

Table 2.2 Cash budget for three months–student

	Month 1 £	Month 2 £	Month 3 £
Total income	650	650	650
Total expenditure	690	690	690
Net expenditure	(40)	(40)	(40)
Balance at beginning of the month	100	60	20
Balance at the end of the month	60	20	(20)

In Example 2.2 each month's income and expenditure is compared to arrive at the net income or expenditure for that month. There is £40 net expenditure each month and as a result the bank balance falls by this amount. The expected bank balance is £60 at the end of the first month, £20 at the end of the second month, and £20 overdrawn at the end of the third month. The arrows show how one month's closing balance becomes the next month's opening balance.

Balancing the budget

As part of their financial planning, individuals should take responsibility for managing their personal finances and balancing their own budgets. When taking control of personal finances, it is useful to prepare a cash budget for the next three to six months, then consideration should be given to reviewing any months where expenditure is expected to exceed income and what might be done about it. The different options should be researched before taking action.

 Ponder point

Where a person's expenditure is greater than their income, what might be done about it?

When expenditure is expected to exceed income, there are a few key steps that can be taken, including looking carefully at all expected expenditure and distinguishing between essential and non-essential expenditure. Essential expenditure is that which is necessary to continue day-to-day activities and includes housing, utility bills, food, and transport. Non-essential expenditure would be all other expenses. Having distinguished between the two types of expenditure, there are three possibilities:

1. Reduce expenditure: a critical review of the expenditure included in the budget might reveal opportunities to cut back on expenditure, particularly on non-essential items.

2. Increase income: this might involve working extra hours or withdrawing some savings where there are some available.

3. Borrow to cover the shortfall.

Case study—Imran

Imran is a commercial lawyer, living and working in London. His current salary, net of all deductions, is £1,800 per month. In February he expects to receive a bonus of £4,000 net of deductions.

Imran pays rent of £870 per month, utilities of £80 per month, and his travel costs amount to £180 per month as he often uses taxis to get home from work. Each month he spends

(continued...)

£200 on groceries and toiletries, £40 on a mobile phone contract, £250 on entertainment and eating out, and £75 on gym membership. He is planning a skiing trip, costing £850, that will have to be paid for in January and he expects to spend £400 whilst he is on the trip in March. (He will only spend £130 on travel costs that month but all other expenses will stay the same.)

He is planning to take advantage of the January sales in order to buy a new work suit. He hopes to pay approximately £300 for the suit. In other months, he will spend on average £60 per month on clothes.

At the beginning of January, he will have £400 in his current account and he also has some savings and investments.

Required:

a) **Prepare Imran's cash budget for the four months from January to the end of April.**

b) **Imran's short-term objective is to avoid any overdrafts arising over the four-month period. Suggest actions that Imran could take to avoid an overdraft arising during the period.**

c) **Imran's longer-term objective is to buy a property but he is not saving as much as he hoped, despite earning a good salary and receiving an annual bonus. What changes would you suggest that he makes to his lifestyle in order to save more?**

Case study—Oliver

Oliver is twenty-four and lives in London. Oliver is an actor whose income fluctuates considerably and he is aware that he should be budgeting in order to manage his finances. His objective is to be able to live within his means. For some months he has had temporary work in a restaurant for a few shifts a week whilst he waits to start touring in April in a production of *As You Like It*. The tour is due to last for six months. He is looking forward to going on tour because it is relatively well paid and he will be able to enjoy spending money again.

He has just realized that he might not be able to pay his January rent bill of £600 or meet his living expenses for that month as his bank will not extend his overdraft that currently stands at £1,000. He cannot use his credit card because it has reached its credit limit and his income from the restaurant will not cover his essential living expenses. He asks his parents for help and they agree to step in, but only on the understanding that a proper budget is prepared and a repayment schedule organized for when Oliver goes on tour.

He has found a friend to move into his flat whilst he is away, which will cover the rent. He will have to pay £450 per month for theatrical lodgings whilst on tour.

Oliver's parents ask him to work out his income and expenditure for the next six months, assuming that they loan him £4,500: £2,000 to pay off his credit card debt and £2,500 to pay into his current account to get rid of his overdraft of £1,000 and to enable him to cover his costs over the next three months.

Oliver measures his position by preparing his cash budget for the six months to the end of June, shown in Table 2.3.

Table 2.3 Oliver's cash budget to 30 June—first draft

	Jan £	Feb £	Mar £	Apr £	May £	June £
Income:						
Net earnings (take home pay)	800	800	800	2,500	2,500	2,500
Loan from parents	4,500					
Total income	**5,300**	**800**	**800**	**2,500**	**2,500**	**2,500**
Expenditure:						
Rent/theatrical lodgings	600	600	600	450	450	450
Utilities	150	150	150	–	–	–
Phone	35	35	35	35	35	35
Travel	120	120	120	100	100	100
Food	300	300	300	300	300	300
Entertainment	100	100	100	200	200	200
Clothes	30	30	30	100	100	100
Sundry	70	70	70	70	70	70
Pay off credit card	2,000					
Loan repayment to parents				500	500	500
Total expenditure	**3,405**	**1,405**	**1,405**	**1,755**	**1,755**	**1,755**
Net income/(expenditure)	**1,895**	**(605)**	**(605)**	**745**	**745**	**745**
Balance at beginning of month	(1,000)	895	290	(315)	430	1,175
Balance at end of month	**895**	**290**	**(315)**	**430**	**1,175**	**1,920**

Oliver's parents review his budget. They ask him to:

- reduce his non-essential spending whilst he is in financial difficulties by not increasing his entertainment expenditure whilst he is on tour, and by limiting his clothes budget to £75 per month from April onwards
- increase his shifts at the restaurant for the next three months, to earn an extra £200 per month
- start to save £600 each month whenever he is on tour.

Required:

a) **Prepare Oliver's budget for the nine-month period from 1 January to the end of the tour, based on his original budget in Table 2.3, taking into account his parents' requirements.**

b) **Consider whether Oliver could repay his parents' loan at a faster rate.**

c) **Do you think that Oliver should have a separate account into which he transfers his monthly savings?**

> **? Ponder point**
>
> Do you consider that Oliver's cash budget should be very ambitious and expect him to save more?

It is important for the budget to be as realistic as possible including sensible estimates of income and expenditure. It must also be a budget that Oliver thinks he can stick to. An overly ambitious budget will not motivate Oliver to try and meet the targets set. The more realistic the estimates are, the more useful the budget will be. If Oliver does not consider the budget to be achievable, then he will be unlikely to stick to it.

The preparation of a cash budget may highlight the need to reduce expenditure, increase income, or in some cases find a source of borrowing to cover a short-term deficit, in order to ensure that income covers expenditure.

Reducing expenditure

The division between essential and non-essential expenditure is a useful distinction when analysing personal spending. In general, essential expenses will have to be paid but there may be ways of reducing the amount spent. For example, utility bills may be reduced if a better deal can be found from an alternative utility supplier.

Non-essential expenditure should be the main focus for anyone wishing to reduce their spending. By its very nature, the spending can be avoided. A common example of this is a daily take away coffee and lunch bought from the sandwich shop. With a coffee and lunch, daily spending might easily amount to £5. This equates to £25 for a working week or £1,200 for a year, which could be saved quite easily with forward planning and some time set aside to prepare a sandwich at home.

People are often subject to pressure to have the latest gadget, branded clothing, or goods. It is wise to stand back before making purchasing decisions and consider if the premium price demanded for these goods really represents value for money.

Money saving websites have plenty of suggestions for reducing expenditure on essentials and non-essentials. Money is hard earned, so it is worth taking the time to ensure that it is spent wisely and carefully. Perhaps one of the most useful maxims to bear in mind is that you have choices as to how you spend your money, but you can only ever spend it once.

Increasing income

There may be some possibilities for increasing income to cover a short-term deficit but this is often harder to achieve than cutting costs. It might be possible to increase earnings by taking on extra shifts at work or working overtime. It may be possible to take on an evening or weekend job, or to undertake some freelance work. A homeowner may consider renting out a room in their house. Selling off unwanted items on an internet selling site can yield useful cash from goods that are no longer required.

Borrowing to cover short-term cash deficits

If it is really not possible to balance a budget then there are several alternative sources of funds that might be available to meet a short-term cash deficit. However, these should only be considered after all other options have been explored because they all create a debt that will have to be repaid at some point. They include the following options.

A bank overdraft is a useful facility to cover a cash deficit in the short term. When money is withdrawn from a bank and the balance goes below zero, the account is overdrawn. Some bank accounts provide an automatic overdraft facility, up to a specified limit. Alternatively, individuals can arrange an overdraft limit with their bank and this represents the extent to which they are permitted to go overdrawn and if they stay within this limit, it is known as an arranged overdraft.

The overdraft may be interest-free or carry an agreed rate of interest. If the agreed limit of the overdraft is exceeded then unarranged overdraft fees and a higher rate of interest are likely to be charged. If someone is constantly overdrawn, an overdraft is no longer acting as a temporary solution. Instead, the overdraft will have become a longer-term financial necessity. In this situation an individual should consider replacing the overdraft with a personal loan, which is likely to have lower rates of interest.

A personal loan may be either secured or unsecured. Usually secured loans are only available to homeowners as the bank requires property as security for the loan. If the person defaults on the loan then the bank is able to sell the property to recover the loan. An unsecured loan has no such backing and is therefore usually more expensive. However, it is usually cheaper to borrow using a personal loan rather than an overdraft. Secured personal loans usually carry interest rates less than half those available for overdrafts. If an overdraft has become a permanent feature of a person's finances, then it would be better to replace the overdraft with a personal loan. It is important to be wary of consolidation loans, which wrap up several different types of borrowing into one loan, as these can prove to be very expensive in the long term and carry certain risks. Discussion of this type of loan can be found in Chapter 14.

Family might possibly be able to help out with a temporary loan to see an individual through a difficult financial period, but this is not an option available to everyone. It can also cause tensions between family members, so should not be seen as a permanent solution to a financial problem.

Payday loans are usually small, very short-term loans that will help an individual to cover their essential costs until their next payday. The rates of interest for very short periods of borrowing are usually exceptionally high compared to other longer-term forms of borrowing. For this reason, payday loans should be seen as a last resort. If resorting to a payday loan was a one-off situation, then it might be an acceptable short-term solution to an emergency, but one payday loan often leads to another the next month, with increasing costs and rising debt levels. Whilst they may seem to provide an easy solution to money problems, in reality they can prove to be a very expensive option and a path to ever-increasing debt.

Peer-to-peer lending websites are a relatively new concept in borrowing and lending. These sites enable individual savers to lend to individual borrowers and earn a higher rate of interest than they would on a cash deposit account. Borrowers have comparatively easy access to funds at reasonable rates of interest. The rate of interest offered depends on the riskiness of the borrower. The more risky the borrower, the higher the rate of interest that will be charged. Personal lenders may be much more willing to lend to individuals in difficult circumstances than the high street banks, so they can be a useful resource.

If an individual finds that they need to resort to borrowing to cover a short-term cash deficit, they should consider all of the potential sources and their relative costs before making any decision on which source to use. There are significant differences in cost between the different sources of short-term borrowing and a person resorting to short-term borrowing should seek the lowest cost funds available to them.

Level of savings

Most financial advisers suggest that savings equivalent to between three and six months' income should be kept readily accessible to cope with an emergency. Depending on the level of earnings, three to six months' income can be quite a considerable sum. Many people do not have savings at this sort of level and certainly not as readily available cash. If a person's objective is to build up such a sum, then preparing and using a cash budget can help to achieve this aim.

 Ponder point

What sort of circumstance might give rise to the need for this level of savings?

The sort of circumstance referred to here might arise if you are made redundant, you or your partner take long-term leave to look after babies or young children, or if you suffer a serious health problem. Other possible situations could be if you need to buy or replace a car or pay for a significant household repair.

Monitoring the budget

Having drawn up a cash budget, it is important to keep track of how actual income and expenditure compare to the budget. There may be differences that occur because of factors outside an individual's control. For example, inflation might cause the price of certain items to rise more steeply than anticipated. There may also have been unforeseen payments that had to be made. Alternatively, differences between budgeted and actual figures may arise due to a lack of discipline on the individual's part.

Once the cause of any difference is known, then action can be taken. Spending habits may need to change if future budgets are to be achieved.

In some ways taking control of your finances has many similarities to going on a diet. There is a period of significant control and reduction that should have the desired effect of getting you into financial shape. On the way you need to continually check your progress and see how you are measuring up against the plan. Once the immediate goals have been achieved it is important to stay in control of personal spending. So it is necessary to prepare a plan and keep checking on performance, similar to hopping onto the weighing scales.

Conclusion

Being able to prepare a cash budget is a key skill in taking control of personal finances and achieving financial objectives. It is important to recognize the need for a cash budget, to be able to prepare and use one, and to undertake regular reviews of the plan.

Cash budgets are not the preserve of those individuals who are in financial difficulty. Budgets enable an individual to fully understand where their money goes and to gain some control over it. Using a budget to establish regular savings plans can be a useful outcome of a budget. If an individual has debts, it should be possible to work out a way of managing those debts with the help of a cash budget. If income is not expected to cover expenditure then it will be necessary to find ways of increasing income or reducing expenditure, or perhaps both.

Once a budget has been prepared it should be reviewed regularly, amended where necessary, and, if the budget is achievable, it should strongly motivate the individual to live within their means and achieve their financial objectives.

 Useful websites

These two websites have useful personal budgeting tools:
http://citizensadvice.org.uk
http://moneysavingexpert.com

 Practice Questions

Question 1 Quick Questions TRUE OR FALSE?

2.1   Preparing a cash budget is only useful if you are in debt.

2.2   A budget can be prepared on a weekly, monthly, or annual basis.

2.3   The only way to prepare a budget is to use a spreadsheet.

2.4   A monthly budget will allow you to predict your bank balance at the end of each month.

2.5   A budget does not need to be accurate, rough estimates are sufficient.

2.6   In order to encourage saving, a person should draw up an exceptionally tight budget.

2.7   Once a budget has been made it should be monitored and revised regularly.

2.8   Unarranged overdrafts are a cheap form of borrowing in an emergency.

2.9   The only way to cover a shortfall in a budget is to cut back on expenditure.

2.10   Peer-to-peer lending websites would be a better form of short-term borrowing than a payday loan.

Question 2 Sam

Sam is thinking about buying a flat. He has no debt and limited savings amounting to £5,000 but he knows he will need approximately £20,000 for his deposit. His take home pay is £1,766 per month, after tax, National Insurance contributions, and student loan repayments have been deducted. He currently spends £500 per month on rent. He has a mobile phone contract for £35 per month. He runs a car, which costs £2,000 per year in tax, insurance, and servicing and petrol costs £100 per month. It would be possible for him to cycle or get the bus to work. His main leisure activity is going to the theatre and opera and he often spends £150 per month on this. His food costs amount to £250 per month and he spends a further £80 on beer and wine. Each month he puts £200 into a holiday fund. His utilities, excluding the mobile phone, cost £100 per month. Clothes and shoes cost him £50 per month and he spends a further £50 on buying lunches and coffees. His current account balance at the end of the current month is £150.

Required:

a) **Identify Sam's essential and non-essential expenditure.**

b) **Prepare a cash budget for Sam for the next three months using the information he has provided.**

c) **Suggest changes that Sam could make to enable him to save £15,000 over the next twenty-four months and prepare a revised three-month budget accordingly.**

Question 3 Chelsea

Chelsea has been working for six months, in her first job after leaving university, and she is eagerly anticipating a holiday. It is December and she is hoping to go to Greece in June, which would cost £1,800 for a two-week all-inclusive holiday. She has no savings and at the moment is spending everything she earns. After income tax and National Insurance she takes home £1,500 per month. She is currently living at home and pays £400 a month towards rent, bills, and food. She runs a car, meeting all of its costs, and has a mobile phone contract costing £35 per month. Her petrol costs are £150 per month and the car costs £2,400 a year to run. When asked about her spending habits, Chelsea admits that she enjoys clothes and shoes, spending £300 a month on these and £200 per month on nights out. She estimates spending £100 per month on cosmetics, hair, and beauty treatments. She spends £40 per month on gifts and donations to charities. Anything left each month is spent on sundry items too small to identify.

Required:

a) Based on the above information set out an estimated monthly cash budget for Chelsea, distinguishing between essential and non-essential expenditure.

b) Revise the budget by reducing non-essential expenditure to show how Chelsea might achieve her goal of saving £1,800 by May, when the holiday must be paid for.

Question 4 Henry

Henry finds himself in debt, as each month his income is £1,300 but his spending is £1,500 and he has set himself the objective of gaining control over his finances. He has a credit card but it has reached its maximum credit limit of £2,700 and he is not paying the balance off each month. He has a small mortgage which costs him £600 per month and he lives on his own in a two-bedroom flat in central London. His bank overdraft is at its maximum limit of £1,600 and he has no plans to pay it off. He owes his sister £500 and his best friend £200. He has some outstanding utility bills of £400. Henry has never prepared a budget and he has no idea where to start as he is never quite sure where all of his income is spent.

Required:

Outline the steps that Henry could take in order to achieve his objective of gaining control of his finances.

Visit the Online Resource Centre that accompanies this book for additional material:
www.oxfordtextbooks.co.uk/orc/king_carey2e/

3

Appreciating the limitations of financial regulation

◎ Learning Objectives

After studying this chapter, you should understand:

- Some of the recent history of financial regulation that operates in the UK and the background to the changes introduced in 2013
- The central elements of the system of financial regulation introduced in 2013
- The limitations of financial regulation
- The importance of developing your own personal financial capability

Introduction

Financial regulation is the system of supervision and control imposed upon financial services and financial institutions. The financial services industry and financial institutions form a key part of the British economy and it has become increasingly important to ensure that the activities of the sector are properly regulated. Financial institutions include banks, building societies, insurance companies, pension funds, and financial services providers.

According to the Bank of England's website:

> A stable financial system is a key ingredient for a healthy and successful economy. People need to have confidence that the system is safe and stable, and functions properly to provide critical services to the wider economy. It is important that problems in particular areas do not lead to disruption across the financial system.
>
> (Bank of England)

Prior to the 1980s, financial services were subject to piecemeal regulation in the UK, but since 1986 financial institutions have been subject to increasing regulation through a combination of Acts of Parliament, government departments, including the Treasury and the Department of Trade and Industry, the Bank of England, the Financial Services

Authority, and the Office of Fair Trading. It might be expected that with so much regulation in place, a consumer of financial services would be well protected and could feel confident in buying a product from a regulated provider. Unfortunately that has not always been the case and history provides us with many examples where financial regulation has not been able to protect consumers, either from fraud or mis-selling.

The system of financial regulation has been subject to enormous changes in recent decades. The amount of financial regulation legislation since the 1980s has been significant. The aim of this chapter is not to provide a detailed listing of all the past legislation, regulatory authorities, and their duties; rather it is to give a flavour of the various means of financial regulation since the 1980s, culminating in the 2013 regulatory organizations, whilst at the same time indicating that a flood of regulation will not protect a consumer from a determined fraudster or unethical salesperson. There is a well-known Latin phrase, 'caveat emptor' which means that a buyer should beware. This is an important principle in personal finance; despite the existence of regulation to protect consumers, any buyer of financial products and services should still exercise caution.

Background

Indicative rates

This chapter uses indicative rates that give an indication of the size of certain rates and allowances. Reference should always be made to any suggested websites in order to ascertain the current figures that apply.

Financial regulation includes both the regulatory regime applied to the banking sector and the regime that monitors financial services and products. At certain times banks and financial services have been regulated together and at other times they have had different regulatory statutes and bodies. This chapter will concentrate on financial regulation as it has been applied to financial services; banking regulation will only be covered where it has an impact on personal finance.

In order to understand the system of financial regulation that operates in the United Kingdom, it is useful to have a brief look at the historical events that have brought the regulatory system to this position.

The Great Depression began in America in 1929 with the stock market crash and its effects continued to be felt until the Second World War. In response to this major financial disaster, strong regulatory systems were set up in both the United States and the United Kingdom and financial institutions, particularly banks, were subject to rigorous controls. In particular, US legislation made a distinction between investment and retail banking and the two activities were kept separate in the US by the Glass–Steagall Act of 1933; the same principles were applied in the UK, but specific legislation was not considered necessary.

During the decades immediately after the Second World War, the Bank of England administered financial regulation of the banking sector. Regulation began to change with increasing wealth, the development of the financial services sector, and the creation of more sophisticated financial products for the consumer. The Banking Act of 1979 was the first piece of legislation to put banking regulation onto a statutory footing; meanwhile, regulation in the area of financial services began to develop in a piecemeal fashion, with self-regulation playing a key part.

The recent history of financial regulation can be divided into four separate and distinct periods:

1. Self-regulation of financial services between 1970 and 1986.
2. The early days of more formal regulation, between 1986 and 1997 combined with deregulation of the City of London.
3. The era of the Financial Services Authority (FSA) from 1997 to 2013.
4. The regulatory framework since 2013.

Any description of the regulatory framework is in danger of becoming submerged under a deluge of acronyms or initials used extensively as shorthand to refer to the many and varied regulatory bodies. As far as possible the use of such acronyms will be kept to a minimum in this chapter.

Self-regulation of financial services: 1970–1986

 Key term

Financial services are the services provided by financial institutions that relate to money. The term includes the provision of bank accounts, insurance policies, investment advice and management, pension funds, loans and mortgages, and financial advice.

Self-regulation is the regulation of an industry by its own members, usually by means of a committee that issues guidance and sets standards that it then enforces. Self-regulation relies on a voluntary code of conduct that establishes rules, monitors compliance by its members with those rules, and carries out investigations.

During the 1970s and 1980s the UK financial services industry was developing and changing and financial products and services were becoming more intricate and sophisticated. At this time the industry was self-regulating through a complex combination of a variety of organizations. Financial advisers were mainly governed by the Financial Intermediaries Managers and Brokers Regulatory Association, known as FIMBRA. However, there were many other self-regulatory bodies in existence at the same time, each playing a part in the self-regulation of financial services in specific areas.

The purpose of self-regulation of financial services was to assess and monitor firms to maintain market confidence, develop public awareness of financial goods and services, protect consumers, and reduce financial crime.

There is a risk arising from self-regulation that is the risk of a conflict of interest, where the regulatory body falls somewhere between a trade association representing its members' interests and a regulatory body enforcing rules. There is a further risk, if it is not a legal requirement for organizations to be a member of a regulatory body, that firms can choose to operate outside the system of self-regulation. Many people would argue in favour of self-regulation on the grounds that it is more flexible and cheaper than government regulation, but others would argue that 'self-regulation is no regulation'.

 Ponder point

Is it possible for an industry to regulate itself based on a voluntary code that member organizations sign up to?

It is possible for an industry to regulate itself up to a certain point, with member organizations appreciating the benefits if all firms sign up to a particular code of conduct and practice. However there is always a danger that self-interest can take over and supersede the group interest, allowing certain firms and individuals to work against the benefit of the industry as a whole. It can also be difficult for a self-regulating authority to act as an enforcement agent against its own members. There is also the possibility that not all firms will necessarily join the regulatory association and will choose to operate outside the system of self-regulation altogether. Furthermore it is often the case that the penalties for non-compliance with the rules set by a self-regulatory organization are not sufficiently strong enough to act as a deterrent.

Deregulation in the City of London: 1986

At the same time as the financial services industry was developing its self-regulatory structures, a completely contradictory action was about to take place in the financial markets. The City of London as a financial market was falling behind its international competitors and in order to give the City greater opportunity to compete internationally, the financial markets were deregulated. Deregulation was enacted on 27 October 1986 and later became known as the 'Big Bang'. It was the end of the principle that established a division between investment and retail banking operations. An important consequence of deregulation of the financial markets was that London once again became a major financial centre. This led to an increase in the power of the City of London and in personal wealth and also to an increase in a bonus culture in some financial institutions. Many commentators believe that this drove bankers to take ever greater levels of risk to achieve higher returns and that the ultimate result of the Big Bang was the near collapse of several high street banks. They believe that deregulation was a significant factor contributing to the severe global financial crisis that started in 2007. In 2011 Terry Smith, stockbroker, author, and financial commentator wrote:

> It may seem inconceivable that any of the Big Bang reforms will ever be repealed but until they are I think we will be condemned to suffer the sort of mistakes, malpractice and calamities which helped to cause the current financial crisis.
>
> (Smith, 2011)

The phrase 'Big Bang' referred to the increase in market activity arising from the regulatory changes. These included the abolition of fixed commission charges and the removal of any distinction between market-makers and dealers. The market-makers were stockjobbers, restricted to making prices for the buying and selling of shares and the dealers were stockbrokers acting on behalf of clients buying and selling shares. This had been an artificial distinction that was partly responsible for holding back activity and growth in the London Stock Exchange and limiting its position as a major international financial centre. At the same time, electronic trading was introduced, removing the need for a physical trading floor or market place where prices for the buying and selling of shares could be determined and replacing it with electronic screen-based trading.

The beginning of financial services regulation: 1986–1997

During the 1980s self-regulation of financial services continued until 1984 when a small bank called Johnson Matthey Bankers was subject to a significant fraud (Hansard, 1985). The bank's activities were overseen by the Bank of England, but this did not prevent Johnson Matthey Bankers from making a series of high risk loans. The loans grew to such a size that they threatened the bank's continued existence. In the end the Bank of England stepped in, purchased the Johnson Matthey Bank for £1, and took over its activities to prevent the bank from collapsing and thereby undermining faith in the banking sector (Lawson, 2008). The Johnson Matthey Bank case prompted the change from the self-regulation of financial services to independent supervision.

New regulatory powers were consolidated in an organization called the Securities and Investment Board (SIB), formed in 1985. In 1986 the Financial Services Act gave the Board a statutory regulatory role in monitoring the financial services industry. At this time there was a two-tier system, with the Securities and Investment Board overseeing regulation, whilst the self-regulatory bodies remained in existence and continued to regulate the activities of their members. FIMBRA carried out its self-regulatory role until 1994 when its activities were taken over by the newly established Personal Investment Authority (PIA), an independent regulatory body.

The banks were subject to separate monitoring and regulation by the Bank of England and there was a separate Banking Act in 1987. Despite these major changes to regulation, the developments were followed by some significant regulatory failures involving banks and financial services.

The first major financial scandal to affect the newly formed Securities and Investment Board was the collapse of Barlow Clowes in 1988. Barlow Clowes was a regulated investment firm that nonetheless failed to follow the regulations. The firm appeared to offer a return on government securities that was above the level of return that would normally be expected for the low level of risk associated with such investments (Dalton, 2011). It was highly recommended by some financial advisers to people approaching retirement as a way of boosting their retirement income. In the end it turned out that the fund had not simply invested in government securities but had also invested in many different kinds of risky investments, including a Welsh brewery. A substantial amount of money was lost and the directors were prosecuted.

Another scandal followed in 1991 when it was discovered that Robert Maxwell had taken the employees' pension funds of the Mirror Group Newspapers and Maxwell Communications Corporation in order to prop up the companies' falling share prices (Ringshaw, 2001). The pension funds were severely depleted and many employees lost their entire pension savings.

In 1991, the Bank of Credit and Commerce International (BCCI) collapsed as a result of major fraudulent activity (BBC, 1991). In 1995 Barings Bank almost collapsed following the disastrous trading activity of one of its traders in the Far East (Chua-Eoan, 2007). In 2000 Equitable Life, a major pension provider to the professions, announced that it was unable to meet its obligations and had to close to new business (Parliamentary and Health Service Ombudsman, 2007).

At the same time, some parts of the financial services industry were involved in several mis-selling scandals whereby consumers were sold inappropriate or unsuitable products based on misleading advice. Many financial advisers did not charge a fee for the financial advice they provided, but instead earned their income through commissions paid by the providers of the financial products that they were selling. The commission basis was often opaque and consumers were under the misapprehension that the advice they received was free, not appreciating that the commission was paid for out of any returns generated by their investments.

 Ponder point

Do you consider that there is a potential conflict of interest between providing financial advice and selling financial products on a commission basis?

Before 2012 it was often difficult for commission-based financial advisers to be truly objective and independent when providing financial advice to their clients, because their income was substantially based on the commissions they received on the products that they sold. The higher the commission available on a product, the greater the incentive to promote that particular insurance policy, investment trust, or pension fund whether or not it was the best product for the client. Of course not all financial advisers were influenced in this way and many financial advisers preferred to charge their clients a fee for their advice rather than rely on commission. Since 1 January 2013, following the Retail Distribution Review, discussed later in the chapter, it is no longer possible to provide financial advice based on commission.

Between April 1988 and June 1994 many individuals were advised to change to personal pension plans when they were already members of, or had access to, an occupational defined-benefit pension scheme (Hansard, 1996). Pension schemes are discussed in some detail in Chapter 12, but a defined-benefit pension scheme is usually of great value and difficult to improve upon in terms of providing retirement income. Certainly, moving from a defined-benefit scheme to a personal pension plan was unlikely to increase a person's retirement income and may have caused a significant decrease in expected income.

As the regulator, many commentators argued that the Securities and Investment Board should take some responsibility for failing to prevent the mis-selling (Hansard, 1996). Eventually the firms which had been involved in this activity were ordered to compensate those affected for any financial loss suffered.

Despite the order for compensation, there continued to be some poor sales practices in the financial services industry. Further compensation was ordered for those who, having been sold an endowment plan as a means of repaying a mortgage, found that it would fail to generate enough growth to do so.

The era of the Financial Services Authority (FSA): 1997–2013

 Key term

The **Financial Services Authority (FSA)** was the regulatory body responsible for monitoring financial services and banking from 1997 to 2013.

It was against this background of some significant regulatory failures that regulation was amended again in 1997,with the decision to merge banking supervision and investment services regulation into a single powerful regulatory authority to be known as the Financial Services Authority (FSA).

In May 2000 the FSA became the UK Listing Authority taking over responsibility from the London Stock Exchange for maintaining the official list of stocks and shares traded on UK regulated markets. The Financial Services and Markets Act 2000 significantly increased the regulatory powers of the FSA, which became the organization responsible for regulating banks, insurance companies, financial advisers, and mortgage business, up until April 2013. The FSA took on the responsibilities of several of the self-regulatory organizations.

The responsibilities of the FSA included contributing to the protection and enhancement of the UK financial system. During the time of its operation, the FSA had four very specific goals, set out in law, that were to:

- maintain market confidence
- ensure consumer protection
- contribute to the protection and enhancement of the stability of the UK financial system
- target and reduce financial crimes (FSA, 2012a).

Initially the FSA was also responsible for improving the financial capability of the general population, in order to reduce instances of mis-selling (FSA, 2012a). This responsibility was later transferred to the Money Advice Service, which has since been abolished.

Despite this increase in regulation, the new regulatory framework was unable to protect consumers in all cases from incidents of mis-selling and poor advice provided by some members of the financial services industry and the banks. One of the most significant issues was that of payment protection insurance. The problem arose mainly through the high street banks mis-selling payment protection insurance on mortgages, loans, credit cards, or credit agreements to individuals who would never be able to claim against the policy. The idea of payment protection insurance is that it should cover any debt repayments for a period of time if the policyholder is unable to work through unemployment or illness. Unfortunately a large number of these policies were mis-sold to individuals who would never be able to make a claim on the policy. Many individuals taking out loans or credit cards were under the misapprehension that the cover was compulsory or a legal requirement. Many were not clearly advised of the true costs of the policy and many did not understand what they were buying. The banks have paid and continue to pay compensation to those to whom the policies were mis-sold.

Ponder point

What measures might have prevented the mis-selling of financial products and services to consumers?

The mis-selling of financial products was often driven by commission-based selling of these products. It might have been possible to reduce the incentives for mis-selling if the regulatory authorities had banned commission at an earlier stage. It would also have helped if consumers were more knowledgeable about their finances and more careful about the advice they accepted and the financial products they bought. An improvement in financial education might have made a difference.

The FSA was in operation from 1997 to 2013. It was funded by the companies that it regulated through a mixture of fines, fees, and compulsory levies. The firms that were regulated passed the costs of regulation onto the consumer who effectively paid the final bill for the regulatory body.

There was some criticism of the FSA for not preventing certain personal finance issues and banking problems. Andrew Tyrie MP, Chair of the Treasury Committee that published a parliamentary report into financial regulation, said:

> We need a fresh approach to regulation. The plain fact is that the FSA did not succeed in protecting consumers from spectacular regulatory failures. The mis-selling of PPI and endowment mortgages are just two examples. The FSA is not only expensive, for which the consumer always pays, but many have told us that it has also become bureaucratic.
>
> (Treasury Committee Report, 2012)

Other commentators would argue that the FSA provided a regulatory framework that protected consumers during a time of ever-increasing intricacy when complex and opaque financial instruments made regulation difficult. It may be that with hindsight it is possible to say that the aims and objectives of the FSA were too far-reaching and ambitious—expecting a single organization to be responsible for the entire regulatory framework.

The Bank of England

The Bank of England was responsible for monitoring banking until those powers were transferred to the FSA in 1997. In 2009 the powers were transferred back to the Bank of England together with a statutory objective to contribute to protecting and enhancing the stability of the financial systems of the UK.

Retail Distribution Review

As part of its financial regulation and in order to improve financial services, the FSA introduced the Retail Distribution Review. This led to changes in the way financial advisers could charge for the financial advice they provided. Previously many financial advisers had not charged clients directly for their services but were paid via commission from the financial products that they recommended. This could, on occasion, lead to a conflict of interest where a financial adviser might be tempted to recommend a product paying a high commission, rather than recommending the most suitable product for the client.

Since 31 December 2012, instead of receiving commission on new investments, an adviser must clearly explain how much the advice will cost and agree with a client how the fees will be paid. This could be a set fee paid upfront or the client may agree with the adviser that the fee can be taken from the sum invested. This should ensure that individuals will know exactly what they are paying and that the advice they receive is not influenced by how much an adviser could earn from the choice of product.

Financial advisers are divided into those that offer:

- independent advice across the whole of the market and on all types of financial products
- restricted advice, that may be limited to certain providers, certain products, or both.

Financial advisers who provide independent advice are able to advise on all types of financial products from a wide variety of firms across the market. An adviser that has chosen to offer restricted advice will only consider limited products, and/or only a certain number of providers. They might only offer products from one company or they might be able to advise on just one type of product. An adviser must clearly explain what they are able to advise their clients upon, as illustrated in Example 3.1.

Example 3.1

An ethical consumer is seeking some financial advice with regard to her pension requirements; she finds the following financial advisers advertising locally:

Top Marks Independent Financial Advisers who state: as an independent adviser we will draw our recommendations from an analysis of products and investments from the whole of the market, so you can be comfortable the solutions we recommend are the best available to suit your requirements. Our advice will be based on a comprehensive and fair analysis of the relevant market and will be unbiased and unrestricted.

Top Table Financial Advisers who state: we specialize in providing ethical and socially responsible investment advice. We will advise and make a recommendation for you after we have assessed your needs. We offer restricted advice on a limited number of products and providers but you can be sure that we are expert in our knowledge of the products that we offer, ensuring that the financial products satisfy your ethical and socially responsible requirements.

Top Brass Financial Advisers who state: we specialize in providing advice on pensions, annuities, and retirement income so you can be sure of receiving specialist advice from an expert in the field. We offer restricted advice that is limited to this field but we will make our recommendations based on our analysis of the whole of the market for this type of financial product.

The ethical consumer considers the different information on the three advisers and decides that the most important criterion is the ethical dimension. In this case, taking into account her impressions of the different firms and the cost of advice from the different providers, she chooses to visit Top Table Financial Advisers to discuss her pension requirements.

Regulation since 2013

 Key term

Systemic risk is the risk posed to the entire financial system or the economy rather than the risk to an investor. It is the risk that exists within a system.

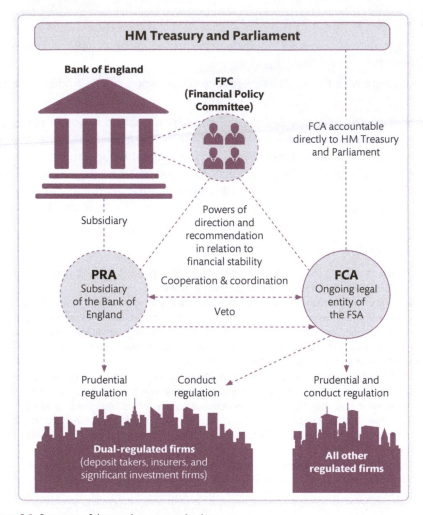

Figure 3.1 Structure of the regulatory organizations

Source: http://www.fca.org.uk, Journey to the FCA. © The Financial Conduct Authority.

The regulatory framework changed again in 2013 with the creation of the Financial Conduct Authority (FCA) and the Prudential Regulation Authority (PRA). These bodies took over the work of the Financial Services Authority (FSA) in regulating financial products and services. Banking is regulated via the independent Financial Policy Committee (FPC) at the Bank of England and also the Prudential Regulation Authority (PRA) as a subsidiary of the Bank. A diagram of the structure of the regulatory organizations is set out in Figure 3.1.

The Financial Policy Committee (FPC)

Part of the role of the FPC is to contribute to the Bank of England's financial stability objective by taking action to remove or reduce systemic risks with a view to protecting and enhancing the resilience of the UK's financial system as a whole.

The Prudential Regulation Authority (PRA)

The PRA has a general objective to promote the safety and soundness of the firms that are regulated, including banks, insurance companies, and certain investment firms. The PRA also has a specific objective to secure an appropriate degree of protection for insurance policyholders. The regulatory model is based on forward-looking judgements about the key risks to regulated firms, and seeks to ensure that, in the event of their failure, firms can be wound up in an orderly way.

The Financial Conduct Authority (FCA)

 Key term

The **Financial Conduct Authority (FCA)** is the organization responsible for regulating financial services in the UK, ensuring that financial markets and firms operate fairly and that consumers are protected.

The FCA has a general objective to ensure that financial markets operate fairly and efficiently and that consumers are protected. The organization is responsible for regulating financial services, markets, and exchanges.

In view of the fact that the FCA has more specific powers than the FSA, it has the potential to be a more effective regulator. In particular, if the FCA determines that there is a problem it is able to:

- take quick action to ban products for a year without consultation, whilst it decides on a permanent solution
- ban misleading marketing
- promote competition so no one firm dominates the market
- devote resources to analysing risks.

The FCA will continue to do much of the work that was previously undertaken by the FSA, such as preventing unauthorized firms taking advantage of consumers by taking enforcement action against such firms (FSA, 2012b).

Martin Wheatley, the chief executive of the new body, said:

> The FCA offers a huge opportunity for the regulator and firms to start afresh and work in partnership to reset how we deal with conduct in financial services. We see it as the role of the regulator to not only make the markets work but also to help firms put their customers at the heart of business.
>
> (FSA, 2012b)

 Ponder point

Do you consider that it is likely that the Financial Conduct Authority will prove a more effective regulator than the Financial Services Authority?

The abolition of commission-based selling should reduce the amount of mis-selling in financial services. The power of the FCA to ban products and misleading marketing may help to make it a stronger force than its predecessor. It has a more limited role in regulating the banking industry, restricted to conduct regulation, and it may be that the FCA is able to focus more on its core aims including analysing and reducing risk. Certainly the Treasury Report issued in 2012 was optimistic about the prospects for the new Authority.

The Treasury Report 2012

In January 2012 a committee of MPs commented that the new system of financial regulation must help consumers by promoting competition and better communication so it does not repeat the failings of the FSA. The Treasury Committee said that the FSA was 'dominated by a box-ticking culture' and had been unsuccessful in protecting people from 'spectacular' regulatory failures such as the mis-selling of payment protection insurance. The Committee strongly believed that the FCA is an opportunity to create something better than its predecessor. The Committee believed that the new Authority must minimize any adverse effects arising on competition from its activities and facilitate competition within the UK financial services sector to the benefit of the consumer. The Committee suggested that the FCA must have more reliable estimates of its own cost-effectiveness and be more accountable to Parliament, as well as communicating better with the financial services industry (Treasury Committee Report, 2012).

 Ponder point

In view of the existence of financial regulation, can investors rely on the regulators to protect them from a poor investment?

Regulation may have improved the provision of financial services in some areas, but as we have seen in the past it has not always been able to protect the consumer and the primary purpose of regulation is not to prevent a bad investment, rather it is to ensure that the consumer is treated fairly. However, where regulation has not managed to protect the consumer from fraud or mis-selling and financial loss has been suffered, the existence of regulation has often meant that compensation has been paid. This may not have always been adequate compensation, but compensation nonetheless. The principle of 'buyer beware' in financial products and services remains strong.

Financial capability

Whatever regulatory system is in place, it remains essential for individuals to develop financial capability and to take all possible steps to protect themselves against becoming the victim of financial scams and scandals.

Key term

Financial capability means having the knowledge and skills to manage personal finances and includes the ability to budget, save, plan for retirement and other life events, and choose appropriate financial products.

Financial capability includes having the motivation to efficiently manage finances and make changes. A financially capable person would be able to carry out day-to-day management of their finances, for example, effective budgeting and use of a bank account. It includes planning ahead for retirement, other life events, and unexpected events. A person with financial capability should be able to understand financial products and select appropriate ones, for example, by comparing repayment costs before taking out a loan. They should know where and how to find appropriate financial advice.

Financial ombudsman service

 Key term

An **ombudsman** is a person or organization that investigates complaints.

If an individual has a complaint about the financial services industry they can go to court and seek redress through the legal system. Such a course of action may be expensive and time-consuming. There is an alternative, free option, which is to register the complaint with the financial ombudsman. The financial ombudsman service was set up in 2001 to resolve individual complaints between consumers and financial businesses. It is a service provided by independent experts that is free to consumers. The service can look at complaints about a wide range of financial matters, from insurance and mortgages to savings and credit. They answer over a million enquiries a year and deal with more than 250,000 disputes (Financial Ombudsman).

 Ponder point

A million enquiries a year and 250,000 disputes seems like rather a lot of enquiries and disputes. What sort of action by the consumer might prevent the need for a complaint to the financial ombudsman?

The principle of 'buyer beware' is particularly important in financial services. The consumer should generally avoid products where the return seems too good to be true and avoid products that the consumer does not understand. It cannot be assumed that regulatory approval is equivalent to a mark of safety.

The ombudsman service was set up to be completely independent and impartial. In considering complaints, they look carefully at both sides of the story and weigh up all the facts. If they decide a business has in fact treated the consumer fairly, they will explain how they have arrived at their decision, but if they decide that the complaint is valid and the consumer has suffered a financial loss, they can order compensation to be paid. The length of time it takes to resolve a case depends on its complexity and can take many months to complete. Individuals do not have to accept the decision of the ombudsman and remain free to seek redress through the courts. However, if an ombudsman's decision is accepted, it is binding for both parties.

The pensions ombudsman and pensions advisory service

There is a specialist ombudsman for pension schemes, known as the pensions ombudsman. This ombudsman offers a similar free service to that of the financial ombudsman for people who have a complaint about the way in which their pension scheme has been run. There is also a service known as the pensions advisory service that provides free and independent advice to a person in connection with their pension.

Financial Services Compensation Scheme (FSCS)

Indicative amount

Maximum amount covered by financial services scheme	£75,000

The FSCS provides very valuable reassurance for individuals choosing a whole range of financial products, including savings accounts, insurance policies, and pension policies. The FSCS provides protection for an individual dealing with banks or building societies, credit unions, insurance companies, mortgage lenders, and investment and pension firms. As long as a firm is authorized by the regulator, the Financial Conduct Authority, the scheme will provide a level of cover for an individual. The cover is similar to an insurance policy, providing cover in cases where the firm goes out of business and the consumer suffers a financial loss. In that situation the scheme would be able to pay compensation up to a maximum of £75,000 for a bank or building society account. Lower limits apply for other types of business and the scheme's website should be checked for up-to-date compensation limits, at http://www.fscs.org.uk.

According to the organization's website:

The FSCS is the UK's compensation fund of last resort for customers of authorised financial services firms. We may pay compensation if a firm is unable, or likely to be unable, to pay claims against it. This is usually because it has stopped trading or has been declared in default.

(FSCS)

This means that up to £75,000 of personal savings is guaranteed by the British government should a bank, building society, or even a credit union fail. The £75,000 limit is per person and per financial institution; so wealthy savers may consider limiting their savings to £75,000 per institution if they wish to ensure that each of their deposits is effectively guaranteed by the British government. The limit for a joint account is doubled, so cover is increased to £150,000 where an account is held in joint names.

It is important to note that the £75,000 limit is per institution and to be aware that in the UK the same institution often owns several different brands. For example, RBS and NatWest are both part of the Royal Bank of Scotland Group and therefore the scheme would only cover up to £75,000 placed with that institution as a whole. It is also important to note that the deposit guarantee scheme does not cover savings held in the Channel Islands or the Isle of Man.

Example 3.2

If an individual placed £150,000 in a deposit account with a high street bank in the UK and the bank failed, then the saver would only be compensated for a loss of £75,000. If instead the saver put £75,000 into two separate deposit accounts with two different institutions in the UK, then the whole amount would be guaranteed under the Financial Services Compensation Scheme.

Example 3.3

Insurance claims are covered by the FSCS up to 90% of the value of a claim. If an individual takes out an insurance policy in the UK, makes a claim on the policy for £10,000 and the insurance company fails, then the policyholder would be compensated by up to £9,000 (90% of the value of the claim).

 Ponder point

Does the existence of the Financial Services Compensation Scheme remove the need for consumers of financial services and products to exercise care?

Although the FSCS provides a safety net underpinning transactions carried out with an authorized business, it is a fund of last resort and will only be able to provide compensation in the event that the business ceases to trade and the consumer has suffered a financial loss. It does not remove the need for the individual to exercise due care when entering into financial transactions. It cannot compensate an individual for poor financial decision-making.

 Ponder point

Who pays for financial compensation?

In the end the consumer pays for financial compensation, as the cost of contributing to the compensation fund is built into the cost of products provided by financial services firms.

Case study—Tian and Brian

Tian and Brian are financially secure; they own a large property and run their own successful business. From time to time Tian and Brian have bought various financial products and services. In 1988 they were moving house and increasing the size of their mortgage. A mortgage broker suggested that they take out an interest-only mortgage together with a low cost endowment policy. The broker explained that each month they would pay only the interest on their mortgage and at the same time make a payment into their endowment policy which was a combination of life assurance policy and savings plan. The endowment policy would be invested on the stock market and after twenty-five years when the mortgage came to an end the endowment policy would have grown to a sum large enough to repay the mortgage and provide a lump sum. Brian looked at the amounts he would put into the endowment and the growth projections and agreed that it seemed like a good idea. He would not have been able to afford a repayment mortgage for the amount of the loan.

In 2005 Tian and Brian were surprised to receive a letter advising them that their endowment policy was unlikely to grow to an amount sufficient to repay the mortgage. It was apparent that they would need to take some action in order to be able to repay the mortgage.

Required:

a) **What should Tian and Brian have considered in 1988 when they took out the interest-only mortgage together with the endowment policy?**

b) **What possible actions could Tian and Brian have taken in 2005 when they learned about the potential shortfall in their endowment policy?**

Conclusion

Financial regulation has been changing and developing rapidly in the UK since the 1970s. It began with self-regulatory organizations and moved on to statutory authorities with powers conferred upon them by legislation. At times the financial services and banks have been jointly regulated and at other times their regulation has been separate. For much of the period under consideration the Financial Services Authority has been the key regulatory body, working with the Bank of England and the Treasury. Despite the considerable amount of regulation in place, there have been a number of notable financial scandals; some of these have been spectacular failures of financial organizations and others have been mis-selling, such as the mis-selling of payment protection insurance.

Culpable firms have been ordered to pay compensation to those who have suffered financial loss. The financial ombudsman service exists to provide individuals with free and impartial arbitration as an alternative to the courts, where there is a financial grievance.

It is most likely that financial regulation will continue to increase and change but the final responsibility for the purchase of any investment or financial product remains with the consumer. Being financially capable and able to understand and assess products will always be the best way that consumers can protect themselves.

 ## Useful websites

Information on the Financial Services Compensation Scheme:
http://www.fscs.org.uk

The financial ombudsman service:
http://www.financial-ombudsman.org.uk

The pensions ombudsman:
http://www.pensions-ombudsman.org.uk

The pensions advisory service:
http://www.pensionsadvisoryservice.org.uk

 ## References

Bank of England *The Bank's Financial Stability Role.* Available at: http://www.bankofengland.co.uk/financialstability/Pages/default.aspx (accessed 28.10.2012)

BBC (1991) *Bank Collapse Cost Taxpayers Millions.* Available at: http://news.bbc.co.uk/onthisday/hi/dates/stories/july/9/newsid_2498000/2498975.stm (accessed 30.4.2013)

Chua-Eoan, H (2007) *The Collapse of Barings Bank 1995.* Available at: http://www.time.com/time/specials/packages/article/0,28804,1937349_1937350_1937488,00.html (accessed 30.4.2013)

Dalton, R (2011) *Barlow Clowes Scandal Remembered.* Available at: http://www.ifaonline.co.uk/ifaonline/feature/2077828/barlow-clowes-scandal-remembered (accessed 30.4.2013)

Financial Ombudsman *About Us.* Available at: http://www.financial-ombudsman.org.uk (accessed 20.4.2013)

FSA (Financial Services Authority) (2012a) *Statutory Objectives.* Available at: http://www.fsa.gov.uk/about/aims/statutory (accessed 24.3.2013)

FSA (Financial Services Authority) (2012b) *Launch of the Journey to the FCA.* Available at: http://www.fsa.gov.uk/library/communication/speeches/2012/1016-mw.shtml (accessed 24.3.2013)

FSCS (Financial Services Compensation Scheme) *About Us.* Available at: http://www.fscs.org.uk/what-we-cover/about-us (accessed 4.11.2012)

Hansard (1985) *Johnson Matthey Bankers.* Available at: http://hansard.millbanksystems.com/commons/1985/jul/26/johnson-matthey-bankers (accessed 30.4.2013)

Hansard (1996) *Mis-sold Personal Pensions etc.* Available at: http://hansard.millbanksystems.com/commons/1996/jan/25/mis-sold-personal-pensions-etc (accessed 30.4.2013)

Lawson, N (2008) *Failure After Failure.* Available at: http://www.time.com/time/magazine/article/0,9171,1715136,00.html (accessed 27.4.2013)

Parliamentary and Health Service Ombudsman (2007) *A Decade of Regulatory Failure.* Available at: http://www.ombudsman.org.uk/improving-public-service/reports-and-consultations/reports/parliamentary/equitable-life-a-decade-of-regulatory-failure-pt-1 (accessed 30.4.2013)

Ringshaw, G (2001) *Mirror Pension Warnings Ignored.* Available at: http://www.telegraph.co.uk/finance/4487800/Mirror-pension-warnings-ignored.html (accessed 30.4.2013)

Smith, T (2011) *Terry Smith Straight Talking.*
Available at: http://www.terrysmithblog.
com/straight-talking/2011/10/big-bang.html
(accessed 28.5.2013)

Treasury Committee Report (2012) *Parliamentary
Business.* Available at: http://www.parliament.
uk/business/committees/committees-a-z/

commons-select/treasury-committee/news/
financial-conduct-authoritys-objectives-
should-be-rewritten-to-include-duty-
to-promote-competition-for-benefit-of-
consumer-says-treasury-committee-report
(accessed 4.11.2012)

 ## Practice Questions

Question 1 Quick Questions TRUE OR FALSE?

3.1   During the 1970s and 1980s, the UK financial services industry relied upon a system of self-regulation through a variety of organizations.

3.2   The term 'financial services' refers only to the services provided by the high street banks.

3.3   Deregulation of the City of London was enacted in October 1986 and became known as the 'Big Bang'.

3.4   During the time that the Financial Services Authority (FSA) was the regulatory body responsible for monitoring financial services and banking, there were no instances of mis-selling of financial products and services.

3.5   Financial capability means having the knowledge and skills to manage personal finances and includes the ability to budget, save, plan for retirement and other life events, and choose appropriate financial products.

3.6   The existence of the Financial Services Compensation Scheme does not remove the need for consumers of financial services and products to exercise care.

3.7   The pensions advisory service will provide independent advice to a person in connection with their pension, at a reasonable cost.

3.8   Since the beginning of 2013 a consumer must pay an upfront fee for any financial advice.

3.9   Since 2013 the Financial Conduct Authority (FCA) is the organization responsible for regulating financial services in the UK, ensuring that financial markets and firms operate fairly and that consumers are protected.

3.10   The Financial Services Compensation Scheme will pay compensation up to a specified amount to a consumer, if they suffer a financial loss as a result of an authorized firm, a bank, or building society ceasing to trade.

Question 2 Financial Regulation

In 2013 the system of financial regulation changed substantially in the UK.

Required:

Describe the bodies that took over financial regulation in 2013, together with their responsibilities.

Question 3 Retail Distribution Review

The Retail Distribution Review changed the way in which financial advisers charge for advice and the way in which they must describe the services they offer.

Required:

Explain the way in which advisers charge for financial advice and describe the different categories of financial advisers and what they can advise upon.

 Visit the Online Resource Centre that accompanies this book for additional material: **www.oxfordtextbooks.co.uk/orc/king_carey2e/**

4 Managing your debt

 Learning Objectives

After studying this chapter, you should understand:

- The wide variety of lending products available
- The relative cost of different forms of borrowing
- The different circumstances when borrowing might be considered appropriate or inappropriate

Introduction

Debt is an integral part of most people's lives. Throughout your adult life, there will be many occasions when debt is taken out to finance a particular event or purchase. The decision to borrow money may be taken intentionally, as occurs when student debt is built up over the period of a university course, or a loan, known as a mortgage, is taken out in order to buy your own home. Sometimes, debt can build up in a more ad hoc fashion, when credit card bills accumulate and cannot be paid off or bank overdrafts are taken out.

Being in debt may therefore arise from any number of personal circumstances and borrowing for appropriate purposes from carefully researched lenders will be a necessity for most people. Unfortunately, some people will also find that they end up with unintentional debts where the choice of lender can be limited and the debts become a real problem for that person and their immediate family. Understanding sources of borrowing and measuring the relative cost of debt are therefore a fundamental part of managing personal finances.

 ## Indicative rates

This chapter uses indicative rates that give an indication of the size of permitted student loans, interest rates, and repayment terms. You should refer to the Student Loans Company website (http://www.slc.co.uk) or the government website (http://www.gov.uk) for details of current terms.

Background

Following the financial crisis of 2007, the level of household debt in the UK fell when lenders became less willing to make new loans and people were feeling insecure about their jobs and economic conditions in general. By 2015, levels of household debt had stopped falling as consumer confidence returned. Figures and graphs produced as part of the Office for Public Responsibility's Economic and Fiscal Outlook in July 2015, show that they expect levels of household debt to rise significantly up to 2020 with households expected to take out bigger mortgages and other debts. This is shown in Figure 4.1.

Banks, building societies, and finance companies are the main lenders and the range of products is huge and constantly changing. Common forms of personal borrowing include:

- bank overdrafts
- personal loans
- student loans
- mortgages
- credit cards.

Individuals may also owe money where bills have not been paid, for example for council tax, utilities, etc. This type of debt is outside the scope of this chapter as these debts arise from problems in managing personal budgets and, as such, are considered in Chapter 14.

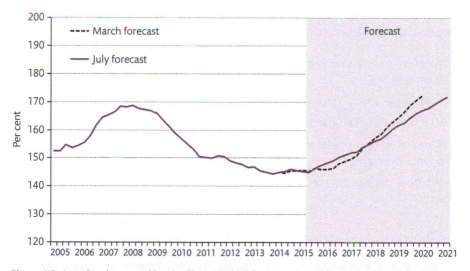

Figure 4.1 Actual and expected levels of household debt. Contains public sector information licensed under the Open Government Licence v3.0

Credit

 Key term

Credit arises when an individual is provided with cash, goods, or services in advance of when the payment is required. The individual is said to have been granted credit.

When an individual is granted credit, this is a way of describing that they have been allowed to owe money to a person or organization. This credit might arise because they have been given a credit card that they have used. Another example of granting credit would be where an individual is approved to take out a mortgage or a personal loan. In essence, if you are allowed credit, this entitles you to borrow a certain amount.

Credit ratings

 Key term

A **credit rating** or **credit score** is a measure of how risky it might be to allow credit to a specific individual.

When you apply for credit in any form, the lender that you approach will refer to your credit rating or credit score. There are a number of organizations that will provide a credit score for each person and they base your score on a wide range of data to which they have access, including the following:

- Whether you are a homeowner or not and how long you have been in your current home
- Whether you are on the electoral roll
- Whether you have dependants
- Whether you have or have had credit cards and loans and whether you made payments on time
- Whether you have any county court judgments against you

 Key term

A **county court judgment** is a court order, obtained by a creditor, stating what must be paid towards a debt.

Ponder point

By considering the list of factors on which a credit score is based, can you identify steps that an individual might be able to take in order to optimize their credit rating and hence their chances of being granted credit?

The steps that an individual could take include: not moving home too often and certainly not moving home just before applying for credit, having a credit card and managing it well, and making sure that they are on the electoral roll. It goes without saying that avoiding a county court judgment is wise for many reasons.

The official interest rate

In the UK, the Bank of England is responsible for setting the official rate of interest, known as the base rate. A decision is taken monthly to determine whether the rate will stay the same or be changed. When this rate varies, it is usually only a matter of time before interest rates on lending change in a similar direction. Historically, the base rate fluctuated considerably over time; throughout the late 1980s and early 1990s, it remained at over 10% but more recently has been kept at much lower levels for some years.

Annual percentage rate (APR)

 Key term

The **annual percentage rate (APR)** of a loan aims to measure the annual cost of borrowing by taking into account the interest charged and any unavoidable costs that the borrower will have to meet.

When money is borrowed, the borrower will expect to pay interest on the amount borrowed. The lender may also make certain other charges, for example arrangement fees or annual charges. The annual percentage rate (APR) takes into account the interest that would be charged on debt plus any unavoidable costs the borrower will incur and expresses the result as an annual percentage, the APR. When an arrangement fee or annual charge is made, this can have a disproportionate effect on the APR if the loan is for a relatively small amount, as demonstrated by Example 4.1.

(Calculating APR involves the use of complex formulae and an Excel spreadsheet function can be used to find a simple APR. There are APR calculators available online.)

Example 4.1

If £10,000 is borrowed on a three-year loan at an interest rate of 7% per annum and an arrangement fee of £500 is charged, then the APR would be 11%.

If a loan of £2,000 is taken out, at the same rate of interest, repayable over three years, and with the same £500 arrangement fee, then the APR would be 31%. The steep increase in the APR is caused by the size of the arrangement fee relative to the amount borrowed.

Source: http://money-saving-calculators.prudentminds.com

The aim is to provide a measure of the cost of the debt that can be used for comparative purposes and lenders are required to disclose the APR on any credit products they offer. In general, the lower the APR, the cheaper the debt but any potential borrower should check on the other costs that might arise on their borrowing. There may, for example, be charges made if the loan is repaid early or if a loan repayment is missed.

Student loans

 Key term

Student loans are long-term loans made to students to cover college or university fees and to contribute towards living costs whilst a course is being taken.

One of the first debts that many young people take on is a student loan and most students can expect to build up significant amounts of debt over the period of their course. The subject of university funding and how students are financed whilst studying for their qualifications remains the subject of a great deal of debate.

This chapter will deal with the rules as they would apply to full-time students on courses that started after 1 September 2012.

Courses that started before 1 September 2012 had very different terms relating to the level of student loans that could be taken out, the interest the debt attracted, and the way the loans were to be repaid. More information on these terms can be found on the website of the Student Loans Company: http://www.slc.co.uk

Student loans are administered by the Student Loans Company (SLC) on behalf of the government. Students can apply for loans to cover tuition fees and maintenance costs. Loans are available to cover tuition fees and to cover living costs, known as the maintenance loan. The amount students can apply for varies as university fees and living costs change. Typical amounts are shown in Table 4.1.

Table 4.1 Student loans

Maximum loans (full-time students)	
Tuition fees loan	£9,000
Maintenance loan (the maximum depends on factors, including whether the student lives at home or in London)	Variable
Interest on student loans	
During the course and up to April after graduation	RPI + 3%
From April after graduating, if earning less than £21k	RPI
From April after graduating, if earning between £21k and £41k	RPI + between 0% and 3%, depending on income
From April after graduating, if earning more than £41k	RPI + 3%
Loan repayments	
On earnings over £21,000	9% of earnings over £21,000

Key term

RPI (Retail Prices Index) is a measure of inflation based on the change in price of an average basket of goods and services that a household spends money on.

A typical undergraduate course lasts three years and the loans can be taken out each year. As soon as the loans are taken out, they start to attract interest and will continue to do so until either the loans are fully repaid or they are eventually written off after thirty years. The rate of interest is linked to the RPI (the retail prices index) and varies as shown in Table 4.1.

If a student borrows their full loan entitlement, then at the end of a three-year course, their debt is likely to amount to more than £40,000, with the exact amount depending on loan limits throughout their course and the RPI.

Once students have graduated, they are required to start making repayments on their loans beginning from the April after they graduate if their income exceeds a set amount, currently £21,000. The loans are repayable at the rate of 9% on earnings over £21,000.

Example 4.2

Three students graduate in June 2017, each with total student debt of £44,000. In the year after graduation they are all in employment but have very different levels of earnings. Graduate A earns £20,000, graduate B earns £23,000, and graduate C earns £45,000.

(continued...)

Assuming their salaries remain unchanged for at least the first two years after graduation, the amount that each student would have to repay between 1 April 2018 and 31 March 2019, would be:

		Loan repayments 2016/17
Graduate A	Earnings less than £21,000	£nil
Graduate B	(£23,000 – 21,000) × 9%	£180
Graduate C	(£45,000 – 21,000) × 9%	£2,160

Example 4.3

What amount would these three students have to repay in 2018/19 if they had each graduated with student debt of £25,000?

The answer is that they would have to repay exactly the same amounts as shown in Example 4.2. The amount to be repaid depends upon their level of income and not on the size of the debt.

Student loans attract interest and, depending on income, repayments are made each year. Any student debt remaining unpaid thirty years after graduation will be written off.

 Ponder point

Do you think that most graduates with student loans will repay these loans within thirty years?

Levels of student debt are subject to a number of very unpredictable factors. As interest rates are linked to RPI and future salaries can only be guessed at, no one can accurately predict exactly what will happen in the future. It is certainly the case that student loans will be very long-term debts for the majority of graduates. It seems likely that a proportion of graduates will still have some student debt outstanding after thirty years because they will have built up a large amount of student debt by graduation and interest will be charged throughout the life of the loan. In many of the early years of the loan, the repayments made will be less than the interest charged. Graduates who are not well paid may be making loan repayments for thirty years and have their remaining debt written off at the end of that time.

Student loans can be paid off early and no penalty will arise as a result. Compared to other debts student loans carry a relatively low rate of interest.

Example 4.4

A student graduating with £42,000 owing in student loans, takes a job on graduation that pays £26,000 per annum. Using the following assumptions:

- his starting salary will increase by 5% per annum throughout his working life
- the loan attracts interest at 3% per annum, throughout its term.

Table 4.2 shows the balance remaining on the loan over a twenty-six-year period, when it is paid off.

Table 4.2 Student debt repayment

	Student debt remaining
At graduation	£42,000
5 years after graduation	£45,000
15 years after graduation	£40,000
20 years after graduation	£27,000
26 years after graduation	£nil

Over the twenty-six years that the student debt took to repay, the graduate would have paid interest of £27,000 and repaid a total amount of £69,000 to the Student Loans Company.

Note that Example 4.4 was based on generous assumptions regarding the graduate's annual salary rise and the low level of interest that the loan would attract.

Collection of student loan repayments

A graduate who moves into employment will make their student loan repayments via the Pay As You Earn (PAYE) system. This means that their employer will deduct the loan repayments from salaries paid, in the same way that income tax and National Insurance contributions are deducted. (The PAYE system that collects these deductions is discussed in Chapter 5.) The employee receives the net amount due to them, after all the deductions, and does not have to make any payments directly to the Student Loans Company. Once a year, the Student Loans Company sends out a statement to all those with loans outstanding showing interest charged, repayments made during the year, and the balance owing. As with any statement, it is sensible practice for the recipient to check it.

If a graduate is self-employed, then the repayments are made once a year via the self-assessment system. This is the system that is used for self-employed people to notify Her Majesty's Revenue and Customs (HMRC) of their income and to pay over the amount of income tax and National Insurance that is payable.

Bank overdrafts

 Key terms

An **overdraft** arises when an individual withdraws funds from a bank or building society current account and causes the balance to fall below zero.

An **arranged overdraft limit** is the amount agreed by a bank for each customer which represents the amount by which their bank account is permitted to go overdrawn.

A bank overdraft is the amount borrowed from a bank or building society current account. Individuals can arrange an overdraft limit with their bank and this represents the extent to which they are permitted to go overdrawn. Some accounts allow customers to create a very small overdraft without specifically agreeing it with the bank. If a customer's overdraft remains within its limit, it is known as an arranged overdraft and if it exceeds this amount, the overdraft is known as an unarranged overdraft. If no overdraft limit is agreed, then any negative balance on the account will represent an unarranged overdraft.

A small number of overdrafts are offered that are free from interest and charges as long as the agreed limit is adhered to. Many student bank accounts offer interest-free overdrafts for the period of the course. Some graduate bank accounts also offer interest-free overdrafts for a limited time after graduation. The limits vary from year to year and need to be carefully noted.

If a payment was to be made from an account such that it would put the account into an unarranged overdraft position, or increase the amount of such an overdraft, then the bank may choose not to honour the payment and to return the item unpaid. The bank's decision on whether or not to meet the payment would depend on the individual concerned, the amounts involved, and the bank's attitude to unforeseen overdrafts. A bounced cheque or a declined direct debit could be rather embarrassing for the individual concerned and may cause a great deal of inconvenience for them and for the expected recipient. In addition, the bank will usually charge a fee for any returned payments.

Banks and building societies make various charges on overdrawn accounts:

- Interest is payable on overdrawn balances and the rates of interest charged on overdrafts tends to be relatively high, typically between 15% and 20% per annum. Some banks charge higher rates on unarranged overdrafts.

- Some accounts carry daily or monthly overdraft usage fees and these fees increase when the overdraft exceeds the arranged amount. Monthly usage fees can range from £0 to £8 per month and the customer is charged if the account becomes overdrawn, albeit within the agreed limit, at any time in the month.

- Banks usually charge customers for every payment that is made whilst the overdraft limit is exceeded and if the bank declines to make the payment, a charge is also levied.

A key point about bank overdrafts is that they are repayable on demand and overdraft limits can be changed with little notice.

Example 4.5

A third-year student opened her student bank account at the start of her course. Each year the agreed overdraft limit has been increasing and the terms that apply to her final year, are as follows:

a) Interest-free overdraft limit of £2,000.

b) Overdrawn balances in excess of this amount, will be charged interest at the rate of 1.6% per month, an equivalent of 21.0% per annum.

c) There is an account charge of 50 pence per day for every day that the account exceeds its arranged overdraft limit.

d) The bank makes a charge of £8 for every payment made whilst the account exceeds its arranged overdraft limit.

e) If the bank refuses a payment because the overdraft limit is exceeded, then a charge of £10 is levied.

At the start of her final year, the student had an overdraft of £1,400 and by eleven months into her final year, her overdrawn balance stood at £2,000. During the final month of the academic year, June, she made eight payments. The bank met seven of these but returned one of the cheques (for her graduation ceremony tickets) unpaid. Her average overdraft during the month was £2,210.

Table 4.3 gives a breakdown of the estimated cost, to the nearest pound, of the bank charges and interest that this student will have to pay for the month of June.

Table 4.3 Cost of an unarranged overdraft (one month)

Interest payable	(£2,210 − 2,000) = £210 over the limit × 1.6%	£3
Bank charges—daily charge	50 pence per day × 30 days	£15
Bank charges—unarranged payments	7 payments × £8	£56
Bank charges—returned payment		£10
Total interest and charges		£84

The total interest and charges that this student would incur as a result of exceeding her overdraft limit are very high indeed, relative to the £210 average by which she exceeded her interest-free overdraft limit in the last month of her course. In addition, the cheque for her graduation tickets was declined which at best would be embarrassing and possibly means that she misses the opportunity to attend the event.

 Ponder point

Do you consider that bank overdrafts are a useful means of short-term borrowing for individuals?

As a means of short-term borrowing, bank overdrafts can be an appropriate way of fulfilling a short-term need for extra cash. However, because the interest rates and bank charges that overdrafts attract are relatively high, overdrafts are certainly not appropriate for longer-term use. The one exception to this would be interest-free overdrafts. However, any borrower with an interest-free overdraft should be aware that at some point the overdraft is likely to attract interest and all overdrafts represent debt that at some point will have to be repaid.

Personal loans

 Key term

A **personal loan** is a loan made by a bank or building society to an individual that is usually repayable over a number of years.

Bank and building society loans can be a useful way of borrowing money for a defined project for a specified period of time. Some loans are specifically targeted at common personal financial issues including paying for a car or funding home improvements.

Personal loans can typically be arranged for sums ranging from £1,000 to £25,000 and for repayment over varying periods of time. Loans are usually repayable over a three- to fifteen-year period, and repayments are set such that equal monthly amounts are paid to the lender over the course of the loan; the total of these payments repays the amount borrowed plus interest.

The bank or lender will grant a loan and determine an appropriate interest rate to charge based on the base rate, the risk that the borrower poses, the period of the loan, and, sometimes, on the purpose of the loan. To assess the risk of the borrower, the bank will consider their credit rating, the age of the borrower, their income, the stability of that income, their other debts, and whether they are a homeowner.

Interest rates charged on personal loans are usually significantly less than the rate charged on overdrafts. When overdraft interest rates range between 15% and 20%, interest rates on personal loans typically range from 8% to 13%.

Example 4.6

A personal loan for £8,000 is taken out which will be repayable over eight years. The loan carries interest at 12%.

Monthly repayments under such a loan would be £130 per month. (This figure can be found from an online loan calculator or by using an Excel function.)

The amount of interest that the borrower will pay on this loan can be found:

	£
The total amount of the repayments made (£130 × 96 payments)	12,480
Amount borrowed	8,000
Total interest paid	4,480

Credit cards

 Key term

A **credit card** can be used to pay for goods or services, instead of using cash or a debit card, and each month the cardholder is sent a statement showing the total amount owing on the card. The full balance or a proportion of that amount may be paid off each month.

A credit card can be used to pay for goods or services instead of using cash or a debit card. The cardholder is then sent a monthly statement showing the total amount owing to the credit card company. The full balance or a proportion of that amount may be paid off each month. Credit cards can be very useful to those people who use them wisely and a passage to increasing debt, for those who do not.

Credit cards are operated by a variety of providers including banks, building societies, finance companies, and some large retailers and supermarkets. Credit cards allow customers to buy now, pay later. They can be used to pay for goods or services and each month the credit card company issues a statement to the user showing the following:

- The total amount owed to the credit card company.
- The minimum repayment that the customer must make, usually a relatively small amount, and the date by which that payment must be made.
- The credit limit that is set for the customer based on their credit rating. The credit limit represents the maximum debt that a user can build up on a credit card. The credit limit is not an indication of an advisable amount of debt for the individual concerned.

If a credit card customer times the usage of their card to optimum effect, they can end up with up to fifty-six days between using the card to purchase goods or a service and having to settle their credit card bill. This is clearly advantageous to the credit card user as that credit period is given to them interest-free, providing the balance is paid off in full each month.

Trouble arises when the user can no longer afford to repay the whole balance owing and opts to pay a portion of the balance, possibly the minimum repayment due. This minimum repayment is typically the greater of £5 or between 2% to 3% of the balance. The outstanding balance remaining will attract interest at a relatively high rate.

If credit card users make late payments to their credit card company, additional charges will become payable.

Example 4.7

A consumer with a credit card debt of £3,000 decides to make the minimum monthly repayment to her credit card company.

- The minumum monthly repayment is 3% of the balance outstanding or £5, whichever is the greater.
- The balance outstanding attracts interest at the rate of 1.6% each month.

Assuming that the credit card is not used for any further transactions, and working to the nearest pound, Table 4.4 shows the credit card-holder's remaining debt after one month, two months, five years, and ten years:

Table 4.4 Credit card repayments: effect on balance of making minimum monthly payments

	Opening balance	Repayment	Interest	Closing balance
At the end of month 1:	£3,000	£3,000 × 3% = £90	£2,910 × 1.6% = £47	£2,957
At the end of month 2:	£2,957	£2,957 × 3% = £89	£2,868 × 1.6% = £46	£2,914
After 5 years:	£1,269	£38	£8	£1,250
After 10 years:	£529	£16	£8	£521

During the first two months shown above, the balance outstanding is reduced by a very small amount and if this continued, then after five years there would be a balance of £1,250 owing and after ten years £521 would still be owing. It would take the credit card-holder a very long time to pay off the outstanding balance. She would end up paying a substantial amount of interest.

Although credit card companies offer a minimum monthly repayment to their customers, using this facility will end up costing the user a large amount in interest. If holders continue to use their cards and increase their borrowings whilst making minimum monthly repayments, it could lead to the user building up substantial credit card debts. They would be enjoying the purchases and services now and paying for them over many years into the future.

Interest rates on credit cards are amongst the highest rates charged on debt and are usually greater than overdraft interest rates. Typical interest rates on credit card debts might range from 7% to 20%.

Other charges

- Some credit cards require holders to pay an annual fee for the use of their card.
- Credit cards can be used to make cash withdrawals but such withdrawals will usually attract interest from the day they are made and may attract a handling charge.
- Charges are often made for transactions made overseas and on balances transferred from other credit cards.
- There is a huge variety of administration and handling charges that credit card companies may levy but most of these only arise if the credit limit is exceeded or the monthly payment is not made by the due date.

 Ponder point

What sort of customer is the most valuable to credit card companies?

Customers who take full advantage of the interest-free period and pay off their balance in full will never provide much income to credit card companies. However, the user who runs up increasing debts on their card and pays off the minimum, or close to the mini-mum, monthly repayment will end up paying large amounts of interest and possibly some charges. It is this type of customer who will be the most valuable to credit card companies.

Store cards

There are many types of cards that department stores, fashion chains, and supermar-kets offer. Some cards, although containing a store's branding, are simply credit cards that can be used in the same way as a credit card provided by a bank or building society.

Store cards are cards that can only be used in specific stores or stores that form part of a group. Consumers may be tempted to take on a card as a result of a generous dis-count on goods purchased using the card, the first time it is used. Typically, many store cards will carry higher rates of interest than other credit cards.

 Ponder point

Would you advise an individual to take on a store card rather than a credit card? Can you think of any circumstance when using a store card might be beneficial?

As well as carrying higher rates of interest, store cards can only be used in specified shops or groups of shops. The only benefit is likely to be an introductory discount on goods purchased when the card is taken on, and occasional other discounts offered.

There is probably one occasion when a store card might be useful and that would be when someone is purchasing a relatively expensive household item. The consumer could take on a store card, take advantage of the discount, pay off the balance when it is due, and not use the card again.

Credit card balance transfers

In order to attract valuable customers, credit card companies frequently offer zero per cent interest rate deals on balances transferred from other credit card companies. The interest-free period may typically range from twelve to thirty-six months, at the end of which time the outstanding balance will again attract the full rate of interest. If the new credit card is used for purchases after a balance has been transferred to the account, the new liabilities arising will not be covered by the interest-free arrangement. If the minimum monthly re-payments are not made, then the zero rate interest deal will be lost. Credit card companies often charge balance transfer fees ranging from 1% to 3% of the balance transferred.

The possibility of moving credit card debts so that they no longer attract interest pro-vides a valuable opportunity to people who have built up large credit card liabilities and want to pay them off. During the interest-free period, all of the payments they make will go towards reducing their transferred liability. At the end of the interest-free period, they may find another similar deal with a different credit card provider. The debt can be moved from company to company, and the balance will be reduced at a much faster rate due to the absence of interest being charged. However, when an individual has done this a few times, they could find that their application for a balance transfer deal is declined.

Case study—Oliver

Oliver graduated with a degree in drama studies a few years ago and has managed to find a num-ber of acting jobs since that time. Each role that he has been cast for has been for varying periods of between two and eight months but he has also had similar periods when he has had no paid work.

Oliver, who lives in London, is a very keen concert goer and he attends as many of the sum-mer music festivals as he can fit in. When he is not working, tickets for concerts and festivals are usually paid for by credit card.

Oliver has the following debts:

- He has student loans that currently amount to £30,000.
- When Oliver is working, he does not use an overdraft but when he is out of work, his bank overdraft is frequently close to, and at times exceeds, his arranged limit of £1,000.
- Oliver has credit card debts of £2,000 on which he makes the minimum monthly repay-ments when he is not in work.

Oliver's average annual income is around £20,000 and he is unconcerned about his debts as he knows that if he can find work for more than six months continuously, he can pay off his overdraft and credit card debt.

Required:

Advise Oliver on the relative cost of his debts and the steps he should consider taking in order to manage his debts in the future.

Mortgages

The debt that virtually all homeowners need to take on in order to purchase their own home is a mortgage. It will usually be the largest amount most individuals ever borrow in their lifetime.

Mortgages are long-term loans taken out from a bank or building society, secured on the property that the homebuyer is buying. This security means that if the home-buyer fails to meet their mortgage payments, then after a period of time, the lender can repossess the property and arrange to sell it in order to try and recoup the amount they are owed.

Mortgage lenders will usually require the would-be homebuyer to pay a deposit of at least 5% of the property's value and hence the mortgage would be for 95% or less of the property's value. One way of measuring the relative size of the deposit is known as the loan to value ratio:

$$\text{Loan to value ratio (LTV)} = \frac{\text{Amount borrowed}}{\text{Property value}} \times 100\%$$

The greater the deposit made by the borrower, the lower the LTV ratio. Mortgage lenders offer lower rates of interest on mortgage loans with lower LTV ratios where a greater proportion of the property cost has been met by the deposit.

Example 4.8

A homebuyer is considering two potential properties, one of which is valued at £170,000 and one is valued at £235,000. The homebuyer has saved a deposit of £35,000. What would the LTV be for each of the properties?

Property valued at £170,000: Loan = £170,000 – 35,000 = £135,000

$$LTV = \frac{135,000}{170,000} \times 100\% = 79\%$$

Property valued at £235,000: Loan = £235,000 – 35,000 = £200,000

$$LTV = \frac{200,000}{235,000} \times 100\% = 85\%$$

 Ponder point

Mortgage interest rates are usually low relative to other forms of debt and the lower the LTV, the lower the interest rate charged. Why do you think this is so?

Because mortgage lenders have security for their debts, they do not take on very much risk when a mortgage loan is made, especially when the LTV is low. If a borrower does not keep up their mortgage repayments, then the lender can recoup the amount owed to them by repossessing and selling the property. If property prices have fallen, then they could possibly risk not raising enough to cover the amount owed, but with low LTVs the property value would have to fall substantially for the lender to face a shortfall. Hence mortgage interest rates are lower than for most other forms of debt and, in general, lower interest rates are offered for lower LTV loans.

There are many different types of mortgage and the main types of mortgage loan available are discussed in detail in Chapter 9.

Case study—Rachel and her partner

Rachel is twenty-five years old and is a manager with a large retail company. Her current salary is £45,000 per annum. Since Rachel started work, she has diligently saved, paid off her student overdraft, and is currently in the process of buying her first home with her partner. The building society is prepared to loan her and her partner £210,000 towards the purchase of a house that is valued at £240,000.

Rachel's student loans currently amount to £28,000 and she has a bank loan of £4,500 she took out to buy a car two years ago. (It was originally a four-year loan.)

Rachel is concerned about her overall level of borrowing especially once the mortgage is in place. She believes that her well-paid job is secure for the foreseeable future.

Required:

a) **Prepare a schedule of Rachel's borrowings, listing them in order of increasing APR.**

b) **Discuss the likely terms of Rachel's various loans and whether she should be concerned about her overall level of indebtedness.**

Credit unions

Credit unions are not-for-profit organizations, owned and controlled by their members. Historically, credit union members had to share a common bond, for example living in the same area or working for the same employer but this is no longer a requirement for all credit union membership.

Members join together to pool their savings and members can apply to borrow funds from the credit union when they need to do so. The interest rates offered to borrowers will depend on a number of factors, including the purpose and the amount of the loan. Such loans do not usually carry any charges and they often allow individuals who might struggle to get a bank loan to borrow at reasonable rates.

Peer-to-peer lending

 Key term

Peer-to-peer lending allows individuals to borrow money from other individuals via a dedicated website. The interest rate charged depends on the riskiness of the borrower and is usually lower than high street banks and building societies can offer.

Peer-to-peer lending is a relatively recent addition to the borrowing and lending options available to individuals. The peer-to-peer arrangement is made via a website. People can apply to borrow relatively small amounts of money and then to repay the amount borrowed, typically over two to five years. Individuals who have savings they are prepared to lend out, provide the money. In principle, both sides should benefit from the arrangement. The savers usually receive a better rate than they would if the savings were deposited in a bank or building society savings account.

Borrowers usually pay a lower rate of interest on their loan than would be charged if the funds were borrowed from a bank or building society. The rate of interest that a borrower will be required to pay will be dependent on their credit rating, the size of the loan, and the period of the loan.

Hire purchase

 Key term

A **hire purchase** arrangement provides finance for the purchase of consumer goods, whereby hire purchase payments are made over an agreed term and the ownership of the item usually only transfers when the final payment is made.

Hire purchase arrangements are most commonly entered into for the purchase of consumer goods or cars. With hire purchase, the item being acquired is paid for over many months and is not owned by the purchaser until the final hire purchase payment is made. Up to that point, the purchaser is renting the product.

When consumer goods are advertised that can be paid for over a period of time, this often involves the purchaser entering into a hire purchase agreement. The price frequently reflects the fact that the purchaser can pay over many months or years. It may be described as interest-free finance but the reality is that the cost of providing that finance to customers will be built into the price of the product.

Example 4.9

A consumer keen to replace a sofa sees their ideal sofa advertised for sale as follows: 'Sofa for sale—£2,400. Buy now, pay later, interest-free credit available.' The customer is aware that he could buy an almost identical sofa now for £2,000.

(continued...)

Is the credit really interest-free?

The credit terms being offered on the sofa are not without a cost. By buying the sofa on the credit terms offered, the customer will pay a total of £400 more over the course of the loan. This represents the true cost of interest charged if this 'interest-free credit deal' is used.

Payday loans

 Key term

Payday loans are very high interest loans to individuals to enable them to meet their outgoings until their next payday at which point the loan has to be repaid.

Payday loans are a very expensive form of short-term loan. They are aimed at individuals who run short of cash during one month and need a loan to let them to meet their living costs until the next payday comes around. These loans are targeted at individuals who do not have credit cards or overdraft facilities to use to help fund their temporary cash crisis.

The loans available are typically for between £100 and £1,000 and the amount to be re-paid will be set such that APRs of between 1,000% to 1,500% are not uncommon. If a payday loan is used as a one-off means of funding a cash shortfall, then it could perhaps be con-sidered a useful, if very expensive, means of providing funds. The danger is that if a payday loan is needed in one month, the borrower may find that they need to take one out in sub-sequent months. As a result the borrower will end up with increasing amounts of debt that have been greatly exacerbated by the very high interest charges made on the payday loans.

Because payday loans are an extremely expensive way of raising funds, they should be avoided if at all possible. All other possibilities should be explored first: borrowing money from family members, selling some assets on internet trading sites, eliminating any non-essential expenditure, increasing an overdraft, using a credit card, etc. Only if every other possible means of raising funds has been explored, should a payday loan even be considered and then only for absolutely essential expenditure.

When an individual finds they are using payday loans on a regular basis, then every possible effort should be made to improve their financial circumstances. This would be likely to involve making major changes to the way they live. Steps that might help include moving to a cheaper home, taking on a second job or extra hours, and seeking advice from reputable debt advisory services. Options for dealing with debt problems are discussed further in Chapter 14.

Example 4.10

A couple with two young children, both earning modest incomes, find that every month they run out of money and have to live off a minimum amount during the last week before payday. The couple are very keen to get all the family some new bikes at a total cost of £300.

They have seen an advert for payday loans that are easy to set up and let you have the money in five minutes, so they decide to take one out for the sum required.

The loan is due for repayment on 30 June but the couple do not take any steps in June to put aside the repayment of £396 that is due. The payday loan company offers to roll over the loan such that it is due for repayment on 31 July and the full repayment due then amounts to £522. They realize that they are in trouble as they cannot possibly repay £522. If the loan is rolled over for a third and final month, they would owe £690 by the end of August.

The family could not afford to buy new bikes and borrowing from a payday lender has left them with a debt they cannot afford to repay and the actual cost of the bikes to the family is far greater than their cost of £300.

There are very few circumstances when a payday loan is likely to be helpful. It is an extremely expensive form of borrowing and one that is most likely to attract customers who are unable to access cheaper forms of borrowing.

 Ponder point

Can you think of some situations where you would consider borrowing to be an appropriate course of action?

Whilst every individual debt decision will be different, it is possible to identify, in general terms, the type of circumstances where borrowing is likely to be an appropriate course of action to take. Examples include student debt taken out to finance a degree, a mortgage taken out to finance the purchase of a property, or to extend or improve a property. In these situations the borrower would be making an investment either in themselves, using student debt, or in a substantial asset, using a mortgage. Other circumstances where borrowing is appropriate include the use of credit cards to allow people a short period of interest-free credit, or the use of interest-free overdrafts. There is no definitive list and you may have identified other situations where borrowing is an appropriate action to take.

Debt advice

An internet search for 'debt advisers' will yield a wide range of organizations prepared to offer advice on debt management. Anyone wanting unbiased independent advice will need to choose carefully as some of the debt advisers listed are likely to be agencies looking to generate fees either from arranging further lending or from arranging personal bankruptcies or individual voluntary arrangements. These arrangements are discussed in Chapter 14.

There are a number of not-for-profit organizations that have a great deal of experience in providing independent unbiased advice on managing personal debt. The list of useful websites at the end of this chapter and Chapter 14 contains links to some reputable organizations.

Conclusion

Most people will take on significant amounts of debt at various points during their lifetime. Where debt is understood and managed, it can be a means of achieving ambitions that could not be contemplated without the support of some form of borrowing. Student loans, mortgages, and many personal loans are examples of debt taken on for a valuable purpose.

Student loans are essential for almost all young people to enable them to study at university, gain a degree, and help launch them on their future career. They are repaid over a very long period of time at a rate dependent on the individual's income.

Mortgages are loans taken out to enable people to buy their own home. Personal loans can enable individuals to borrow money for a specific purpose, such as buying a car, and these are usually repayable over several years. Peer-to-peer lending is a potential source of personal unsecured loans.

Payday loans are a very expensive form of borrowing and should be avoided in almost all circumstances.

When borrowing is entered into in a less controlled way, it can lead to problems. Balances run up as a result of credit card spending attract high levels of interest, sometimes making it more difficult for individuals to repay the balance owing. Credit cards used wisely are a useful form of free credit but if used to fund purchases the cardholder cannot afford, then they are likely to lead to problem debt.

 Useful websites

The website of the Student Loans Company:
http://www.slc.co.uk
A website providing information on student loans and grants and how they are repaid:
http://www.gov.uk
This is a useful website for researching current deals that may be available on most types of borrowing:
http://www.moneysupermarket.com
A useful website that provides up-to-date information on good and bad credit deals, including current 0% credit card deals:
http://www.moneysavingexpert.com
This is an example of a peer-to-peer lending website:
http://www.zopa.com
The website run by the Citizens Advice has useful advice on borrowing money and borrowers' rights:
http://www.citizensadvice.org.uk

A website for calculating loan repayments and APRs:
http://www.money-saving-calculators.prudentminds.com

? Practice Questions

Question 1 Quick Questions TRUE OR FALSE?

4.1   Becoming a homeowner will generally improve a person's credit rating.

4.2   The APR is a useful measure for comparing the cost of two similar loans.

4.3   For graduates who are employees, their employers collect their student loan repayments as part of the PAYE system.

4.4   Graduates who are self-employed make repayments directly to the Student Loans Company.

4.5   Any student loans remaining unpaid twenty-five years after graduation will be written off.

4.6   Personal loans usually carry a higher rate of interest than bank overdrafts.

4.7   An arranged bank overdraft will usually be interest-free.

4.8   When an asset is bought on hire purchase, the ownership of the item usually transfers when the final payment is made.

4.9   Peer-to-peer lending could be an appropriate way of funding the purchase of a new car.

4.10   The limit set on a credit card is an indication of the amount it is wise to borrow on that card.

Question 2 Robin

Robin is about to graduate with a degree in zoology and he has built up student debts that amount to £46,000. He is planning to take a two-year research placement studying warthogs in Africa. He will be paid £10,000 per annum for the work. After the two years, Robin hopes to get a job as a research assistant that is likely to pay him £15,000 per annum but will allow him to study for his PhD at the same time. He hopes that the World Warthog Fund will fund his PhD and he expects to complete it in three years.

Assume that the RPI is 3%.

Required:

a) **Estimate the amount of Robin's student debt five years after graduating.**

b) **Advise Robin as to whether he should be alarmed by the size of his student debt and whether he should take steps to reduce it voluntarily.**

Question 3 Ulrika

Ulrika has recently separated from her partner and, wanting a fresh start, has moved to a different part of the country, where she is renting a flat. She has found herself a new job but needs to have a reliable car in order to carry out her new role. She has looked at various options and identified a particular car that costs £7,000.

Ulrika has some small credit card balances owing and no other debts. She has savings of £2,000 that she considers to be her 'rainy day' savings in case any unforeseen emergencies arise. She has been told that her credit rating is rather low and that this means she will be charged higher interest rates than other borrowers.

Ulrika has identified various options available to her to finance the purchase of her car:

i. The garage can provide finance to enable her to purchase the car. She would be required to repay £159 per month over five years. The loan has an APR of 13%.

ii. Ulrika could use her rainy day savings and borrow £5,000 using a bank loan. The bank would be prepared to loan the money to her at an APR of 10%. This loan would be repayable at £161 per month over three years.

iii. The bank would be prepared to loan £7,000 to her at an APR of 11%. This loan would be repayable at £229 per month over three years.

iv. A work colleague has suggested that she could use her savings plus use her two credit cards, each of which has a £2,000 limit, and use her bank overdraft facility to fund the remaining £1,000. He pointed out that this would enable Ulrika to repay her borrowings as quickly as she can, rather than being tied to a loan repayment schedule.

The credit cards both have APRs of 20% and the overdraft has an APR of 15%.

Required

a) Calculate the total interest that Ulrika would pay on the loans in options (i) to (iii) above.

b) Assess each of the options (i) to (iv) that Ulrika is considering and advise Ulrika on which option(s) deserve further consideration.

c) Suggest one other possible lender that she could consider using.

d) Ulrika was surprised that her credit rating was not perfect, as she has never failed to pay any bills in the past. Advise Ulrika as to the steps she might consider taking in order to improve her credit rating in the future.

*Question 4 Appropriate vs Inappropriate Borrowing

There are many forms of borrowing that an individual might take on at various times during their life. Below are a series of individual circumstances where individuals have borrowed money:

i. Student debt taken out to finance a degree course.

ii. Credit card debts that have built up as an individual has spent more on their cards than they can afford to repay.

iii. A mortgage taken out to fund the purchase of a home.

iv. A loan taken out to fund the cost of installing double glazing in a home.

v. Money owed to a landlord for rent that has not been paid.

vi. A peer-to-peer loan taken out to purchase a new computer that will be used to enable the borrower to work from home.

vii. A payday loan taken out to in order to repay the previous month's payday loan.

viii. A bank loan taken out to pay for a luxury holiday.

Required:

For each of the above circumstances, discuss whether it appears that the borrowing is being used appropriately or inappropriately. Make any assumptions that are necessary and explain your answer in each case.

* Question 5 Caitlin

Caitlin is a twenty-four year old who is buying her own home, a small flat in Leeds. She wants to install some new wooden flooring in her flat and a national firm is offering to do this at a cost of £2,000 on a three-years' interest-free credit deal.

Caitlin has the following debts:

- A five-year fixed rate repayment mortgage of £105,000 that she took out last year.
- An interest-free overdraft close to £1,000. The interest-free deal will come to an end in two months' time in line with the terms on her graduate account.
- Credit card debts that total £800, on which she usually makes the minimum monthly repayment.
- Student loans outstanding of £35,000.

Required:

a) Rank Caitlin's debts according to the likely interest rate that each attracts.

b) What actions would you recommend she takes in relation to her existing debts?

c) Advise Caitlin on the interest-free deal available on the wooden flooring.

 Visit the Online Resource Centre that accompanies this book for additional material: www.oxfordtextbooks.co.uk/orc/king_carey2e/

5 Understanding income tax and National Insurance

Learning Objectives

After studying this chapter, you should understand:

- Who is liable to pay income tax and make National Insurance contributions
- How income tax is charged on income arising in the UK
- The way to prepare a simple income tax computation
- How the PAYE (Pay As You Earn) system works
- How National Insurance contributions are calculated

Introduction

For people resident in the UK there are many taxes that will affect them. Some of these taxes are quite well hidden such as the VAT payable on most goods and services purchased. Some are much more obvious. Many UK taxpayers have some idea of how much income tax or National Insurance contributions they have paid during a tax year whereas they would be very unlikely to know how much VAT they have paid. Income tax is a direct form of taxation, based on earnings, whilst VAT is an indirect form of taxation, based on expenditure.

In the UK, the two main taxes that are levied on a person's income are income tax and National Insurance and both are charged on income arising from employment and self-employment. Although income tax and National Insurance contributions apply different rules to arrive at the amount payable, both are, in essence, taxes. Savings income, dividends, and property income are also subject to income tax and it is always important to consider the tax implications before any personal financial decision is made.

This chapter will outline the main principles relating to how income tax and National Insurance contributions are computed but it does not attempt to cover all the detailed rules that exist.

Indicative rates (iR)

This chapter uses indicative rates that give an indication of the size of certain rates and allowances. When carrying out a real-life computation, you should refer to the Gov.uk website (http://www.gov.uk) for details of current tax rates and allowances.

> ### 🔑 Key term
>
> The **tax year** for income tax purposes runs from 6 April in one year to 5 April in the next. When referring to a particular 'tax year' both calendar years are referred to; for example, the tax year 2017/18 runs from 6 April 2017 to 5 April 2018.

Background

Income tax is payable by anyone resident in the UK for a tax year on all of the income they receive. The tax year runs from 6 April in one year to 5 April in the subsequent year. Some forms of income are exempt from income tax: income arising within ISAs (individual savings accounts) is exempt from income tax and this is a benefit that many taxpayers take advantage of.

For income tax purposes, income is classified according to how it has arisen. The most common categories are as follows:

- employment income
- self-employed income
- interest
- dividends
- property income.

Each category of income has its own specific rules that apply when calculating the amount that is taxable.

The personal allowance

Each tax year, almost every taxpayer is entitled to have the benefit of a personal allowance. This is the amount of income that the taxpayer can receive before any income tax becomes payable. If a taxpayer does not use all or part of their allowance in a tax year, then that allowance is lost forever. However, the taxpayer would receive a new personal allowance for the subsequent tax year.

The amount of the personal allowance varies from tax year to tax year. In order to demonstrate the mechanism for preparing tax computations, this text will assume an indicative personal allowance of £12,500 per annum. When carrying out a real-life computation, it would be necessary to refer to the Gov.uk website to determine the current amount of the personal allowance.

 Key term

A **personal allowance** is the amount of income an individual can receive tax-free in a tax year, before the remainder of their income becomes liable to income tax.

Individuals earning more than £100,000 per annum start to lose their personal allowance.

Taxable income

Earnings from employment are a common type of taxable income and for many people, it will be their main source of income. In preparing an individual's tax computation for a tax year, employment earnings along with other taxable income are added together to arrive at the individual's total income. From this, the individual's personal allowance is deducted to arrive at their taxable income for the year. This is the income that is subject to income tax.

Income tax bands

Table 5.1 summarizes the indicative personal allowance and tax bands that are used throughout this book. For many UK taxpayers, the majority of their income will be taxed at the basic rate of 20%.

Table 5.1 Income tax: personal allowance and tax bands

Personal allowance	£12,500 per annum
Tax bands	**Income tax rate**
First £32,000 of taxable income (Basic rate)	20%
Next £118,000 of taxable income (Higher rate)	40%
Above £150,000 of taxable income (Additional rate)	45%

Once a person's taxable income exceeds £32,000, then the higher rate of tax is payable on the taxable income that exceeds the basic rate band. At even higher levels of taxable income, income tax is charged at an even higher rate, known as the additional rate.

Key terms

A **basic rate taxpayer** is a taxpayer whose entire taxable income falls into the basic rate band.
A **higher rate taxpayer** is a taxpayer whose taxable income exceeds the basic rate band and
hence some of their income falls into the higher rate band. (Their income is not so large that
their taxable income takes them into the additional rate band.)

Example 5.1

If an individual earns employment income of £35,000 in a tax year and has no other income,
the tax computation is shown in Table 5.2.

Table 5.2 Income tax computation

	£
Employment income	35,000
Less: personal allowance	(12,500)
Taxable income	22,500
Income tax liability:	
£22,500 @ 20%	4,500

This individual would be liable to pay £4,500 income tax on their income of £35,000 giving
them a net income after tax of £30,500. This person's income is all taxed at the basic rate and
they would be known as a basic rate taxpayer.

Example 5.2

For an individual earning employment income of £75,000 in a tax year and having no other
income, the tax computation is shown in Table 5.3.

Table 5.3 Income tax computation

	£
Employment income	75,000
Less: personal allowance	(12,500)
Taxable income	62,500
Income tax liability:	
32,000 @ 20%	6,400
30,500 @ 40%	12,200
Income tax liability	18,600

In the computation shown in Table 5.3, note that taxable income is £62,500 and this exceeds the basic rate band. The first part of the taxable income is taxed at the 20% basic rate and then the remaining taxable income of £30,500 is taxed at the higher rate of 40%. This individual would be liable to pay £18,600 income tax on their income of £75,000 giving them a net income after tax of £56,400.

Interest received

Interest received from banks, building societies, and other financial institutions is liable to income tax. However, every basic rate taxpayer is entitled to a Personal Savings Allowance (PSA) of £1,000 interest per annum on which they pay no tax. Higher rate taxpayers are entitled to a Personal Savings Allowance of £500 per annum. These allowances mean that a significant proportion of taxpayers do not have to pay any tax on interest received.

Example 5.3

A woman had employment earnings of £25,000 and received £200 interest during a tax year. She had no other forms of income.

This woman would be a basic rate taxpayer as her taxable income would be £12,700 (£25,200 – £12,500) and would fall into the basic rate band.

As a basic rate taxpayer, she would be entitled to a PSA of £1,000. She would therefore not have to pay any income tax on the interest she had received.

A second woman earns £100,000 per annum and hence will be a higher rate taxpayer. As such, she would be entitled to a Personal Savings Allowance of £500. If she receives interest of £800 during the tax year, there would no tax to be paid on the first £500 (the Personal Savings Allowance) and she would pay tax on the remaining £300.

Example 5.4

A man had self-employed earnings of £38,000 and received £3,000 interest during a tax year. He had no other forms of income. To determine whether he would be a basic or a higher rate taxpayer, a calculation is shown in Table 5.4:

Table 5.4   Determining whether basic or higher rate taxpayer

	£
Self-employed earnings	38,000
Interest	3,000
Total income	**41,000**
Less: personal allowance	(12,500)
Taxable income	**28,500**

The taxable income figure is less than the basic rate band of £32,000 and hence this person would be a basic rate taxpayer. He would be entitled to receive the full £1,000 Personal Savings Allowance.

The interest received of £3,000 would be taxed as follows: £1,000 of interest would be taxed at 0% (the Personal Savings Allowance) and £2,000 taxed at the basic rate.

Dividend income

Dividends received by shareholders are also subject to income tax. However, the Dividend Allowance (DA) which is available to all taxpayers, allows the first £5,000 of dividend income to be received free of income tax. Where taxpayers receive total dividends that exceed the Dividend Allowance (DA) then the rates of income tax attaching to those dividends are different from the rates applied to other income sources. Table 5.5 shows indicative tax bands and rates for dividend income.

Table 5.5 Income tax: tax bands for dividend income

Tax bands	Income tax rate
Dividend Allowance (DA)	
First £5,000 of dividend income	0%
Dividend income falling into the basic rate band (Dividend ordinary rate)	7.5%
Dividend income falling into the higher rate band (Dividend upper rate)	32.5%
Above £150,000 of taxable income (Dividend additional rate)	38.1%

Example 5.5

If a person has employment income of £25,000 and receives dividends of £3,000 during a tax year, then the dividends would be covered by the Dividend Allowance and would be taxed at 0%. This is because every taxpayer is entitled to a Dividend Allowance of £5,000.

Even if a taxpayer has employment income of £90,000 and receives dividends of £3,000 during a tax year, then these dividends would also be covered by the Dividend Allowance and taxed at 0%.

Individual savings accounts, known as ISAs, are tax-free savings accounts and any interest or dividend income generated in them is exempt from income tax.

All income, (interest and dividends), generated in ISAs does not need to be included in an individual's tax computation.

Example 5.6

In a tax year, a person had employment income of £34,000, and dividend income of £7,000 of which £3,000 was earned within an ISA.

The dividends earned in the ISA can be left out of any tax computation, as they are exempt from tax. The remaining dividends of £4,000 would be covered by the Dividend Allowance and would not give rise to any tax liability.

Table 5.6 shows how the individual's taxable income for the year would be calculated.

Table 5.6 Income tax computation

	Total £	Earned income £	Dividends £
Employment income (gross)	38,000	34,000	
Dividend			4,000
Less: personal allowance	(12,500)	(12,500)	
Taxable income	25,500	21,500	4,000
Income tax liability:			
Earned income	4,300		
(21,500 × 20%)			
Dividends	—		
(4,000 × 0%) DA			
Total tax liability	4,300		

There are a few things to note about the way that the tax computation in Table 5.6 has been constructed:

- All of the taxpayer's income for the year has been included. Employment income has been included at the gross amount received, that is the amount before any income tax has been deducted.

- Because the taxpayer has received income from a variety of sources, the computation has been laid out such that earned income and dividend income are recorded in separate columns.

- The personal allowance has been deducted from the total income to arrive at taxable income of £25,500 and set against earned income.

- Dividends earned in the ISA are not included in the tax computation.

- As taxable income is less than £32,000, it all falls into the basic rate band. Taxable employment income is then taxed at the basic rate of 20% and the dividends (being less than the DA) are taxed at 0%.

Preparing an income tax computation

We have already shown how some tax computations are carried out. There are systematic steps that need to be taken to prepare an income tax computation for a taxpayer. Depending on the taxpayer's income streams, the following steps may need to be taken:

1. **Calculate the individual's total income**

   All of the individual's taxable income for the tax year needs to be included in the computation and each income stream should be included at the gross amount. (The gross amount of employment earnings is the amount before any income tax has been deducted.) The total of these amounts is known as the taxpayer's total income.

2. **Separate income into different income streams**

   In the tax computation, it is necessary to use separate columns to separate the income streams into:

   ● Earned income—this includes income from employment and self-employment

   ● Interest received

   ● Dividend income

3. **Calculate taxable income**

   The personal allowance is then deducted from total income to arrive at taxable income.

   In the columns, the personal allowance should be deducted from earned income.

   If it is not fully offset against earned income, it should be deducted from interest and then dividend income, in that order.

4. **Determine if the individual is a basic rate or a higher rate taxpayer**

   ● If the taxable income is less than the basic rate band, then that person will be a basic rate taxpayer and entitled to a PSA of £1,000. (iR)

   ● If the taxable income is greater than the basic rate band, then that person will be a higher rate taxpayer and entitled to a PSA of £500. (iR)

5. **Calculate tax liability on individual income streams**

   Earned income is taxed first, followed by interest, and then dividend income. This is because different tax rates apply to interest and dividend income.

   (For the purposes of the tax computation, dividends are treated as if they are the last slice of income the taxpayer has received.)

6. **Calculate whether any income tax has to be paid, or a refund is due**

   This is found by comparing the tax liability for the year with any income tax paid during the year. Income tax will usually have been paid on employment earnings.

Example 5.7

In a tax year, an individual receives the following income: employment income of £26,000 (gross), interest of £1,000, and dividends of £1,500. Income tax of £3,000 was deducted on her employment income.

The individual's tax computation for the year is shown in Table 5.7.

Table 5.7 Income tax computation

This person is clearly a basic rate taxpayer as their taxable income will all fall into the basic rate band. She will be entitled to the PSA of £1,000.

	Total £	Earned income £	Interest £	Dividends £
Employment income (gross)	26,000	26,000		
Interest received	1,000		1,000	
Dividends	1,500			1,500
Total income	28,500	26,000	1,000	1,500
Less: personal allowance	(12,500)	(12,500)		
Taxable income	16,000	13,500	1,000	1,500
Income tax liability:				£
Earned income: 13,500 × 20%				2,700
Interest: 1,000 × 0% (PSA)				−
Dividends: 1,500 × 0% (DA)				−
Total tax liability				2,700
Less tax paid—employment income				3,000
Income tax refund due				300

Case study—Rachel (1)

Rachel is twenty-five years old and after joining a large retail company as a graduate trainee, she has risen to the position of manager of the food hall in one of their bigger stores. She currently earns £45,000 per annum, on which she has paid tax of £6,500. She has been saving regularly since she started work and receives interest and dividend income.

In the last tax year she received interest of £400 from Bing Building Society and received interest on an ISA with Leaf Bank of £250. She also received dividends of £200 from Olypoly plc.

Required:

a) Identify which of Rachel's incomes will be subject to income tax.
b) Will Rachel be classified as a basic rate taxpayer or a higher rate taxpayer?
c) How much Personal Savings Allowance will Rachel be entitled to receive and how much Dividend Allowance?
d) Carry out a tax computation for Rachel to determine her total income tax liability for the year.
e) Does Rachel have any further tax to pay or is she due a refund?

Employment income

Individuals in employment are liable to income tax on their employment earnings. In addition to any salary received, they will be liable to pay income tax on any bonuses, commission, or tips that they receive as a result of their employment. Sometimes employees receive non-cash benefits (known as benefits in kind) from their employers.

 Ponder point

Can you think of any benefits that an employer might provide for an employee?

One of the benefits most commonly provided to employees is a company car. As well as being able to use it for business purposes, the employee can also use it for private journeys. Sometimes the employer will pay for all of the fuel costs including fuel used on private journeys. Other benefits offered can include private medical insurance, making pension contributions on the employee's behalf, or offering a staff canteen, staff gym, or staff nursery at discounted rates, or for free.

Non-taxable benefits

A number of benefits are exempt from income tax including:

● pension contributions made on the employee's behalf

● subsidized meals in a staff canteen as long as the canteen is open to all employees

● a subsidized workplace nursery

● a subsidized workplace gym

● an interest-free loan where the loan is less than £10,000 throughout the tax year.

 Key term

A **benefit in kind** is something provided by an employer to an employee that is not cash, for example, a company car or private medical insurance.

Taxable benefits

The value of any taxable benefits is included in a tax computation as part of the taxpayer's total income for the year. Taxable benefits therefore have to be valued in some way and taken into account as part of an employee's employment income. Taxable benefits will increase a taxpayer's taxable income and hence their tax liability for the year.

The general rule that is applied in deciding how a benefit should be 'valued', is 'the cost to the employer' of providing the benefit. For example, if it costs the employer £350 per person to provide private medical cover, then an employee receiving private medical cover as a benefit, would have the £350 benefit included in their employment income for the year.

Car and fuel benefits have very specific rules that have to be applied.

Car benefit

Provision of a company car that can be used for personal journeys is a taxable benefit. So too is fuel provided to the employee for private use. For income tax purposes, the amount of the taxable benefit that attaches to a company car is based on the car's carbon dioxide (CO_2) emissions and its cost, measured by its list price. Tables are available to determine for each level of CO_2 emissions, the percentage that should be applied to the list price of the car. Indicative rates are given in Table 5.8.

By referring to Table 5.8, it can be seen that if a petrol driven car has CO_2 emissions of 75g/km, then the taxable benefit will be the list price of the car multiplied by 13%, known as the appropriate percentage. If the petrol driven car has CO_2 emissions of 76g/km, the appropriate percentage rises to 17%.

Table 5.8 Car and fuel benefit

CO_2 emissions (grams/kilometre)	Appropriate percentage (petrol car)	Appropriate percentage (diesel car)
From 0g/km to 50g/km	9%	12%
From 51g/km to 75g/km	13%	16%
From 76g/km to 94g/km	17%	20%
From 100g/km to 104g/km	19%	22%
190g/km and above	37%	37%
Amount used for fuel benefit calculations	£22,500	£22,500

Note that an electric car making zero emissions would attract the lowest appropriate percentage at 9% and that the highest appropriate percentage that can be used for any car, is 37%.

Example 5.8

An employee is choosing between two possible company cars both of which have a list price of £15,000. Car A has CO_2 emissions of 65g/km and car B has CO_2 emissions of 200g/km. Both cars are petrol driven. What will be the amount of the taxable benefit for each of these cars?

Chargeable car benefit:

Car A: Car benefit amount = £15,000 × 13% = £1,950
Car B: Car benefit amount = £15,000 × 37% = £5,550

If the employee chooses car A, his taxable income for the year will increase by £1,950. If he chooses car B, it will increase by a much greater sum, £5,550, as it has far higher CO_2 emissions.

Fuel benefit

If an employer provides fuel for the employees' private journeys, then a fuel benefit arises in addition to the car benefit. This is calculated by using the appropriate percentage, based on the CO_2 emissions and applying it to a set figure for each tax year. Table 5.8 shows indicative figures for appropriate percentages and for the fuel benefit.

If the company car is electric, then no fuel benefit arises as electricity is not a road fuel.

Example 5.9

The employee in Example 5.8, who is choosing between two possible company cars, learns that his employer will pay for all petrol used by the vehicle including any private mileage. What will be the amount of the chargeable fuel benefit for each of these cars and what will be the total car and fuel benefit for each of these cars?

Chargeable fuel benefit:

Car A: Fuel benefit amount = £22,500 × 13% = £2,925

Car B: Fuel benefit amount = £22,500 × 37% = £8,325

Total car and fuel benefit:

Car A: Car and fuel benefit amount = £1,950 + £2,925 = £4,875

Car B: Car and fuel benefit amount = £5,550 + £8,325 = £13,875

 Ponder point

Why do you think that the car and fuel benefits are calculated in this way?

By basing the taxable benefit on the CO_2 emissions of the car, the government is clearly signalling to taxpayers and their employers that if they want to reduce their tax liability, then they should choose a car with lower emissions that will be more environmentally friendly.

Example 5.10

In one tax year, an engineer earns a salary of £28,000 and is provided with a diesel car (list price £24,000) by her employer. The car emits CO_2 at the rate of 75g/km and all fuel, both for business and private purposes, is paid for by her employer. Table 5.9 shows the engineer's income tax computation assuming she had no other income.

(continued...)

Table 5.9 Income tax computation

	£
Employment income	28,000
Car benefit (24,000 × 16%)	3,840
Fuel benefit (22,500 × 16%)	3,600
Total income	**35,440**
Less: personal allowance	(12,500)
Taxable income	**22,940**
Income tax liability: 22,940 × 20%	4,588

Case study—Imran

Imran is a commercial lawyer who currently earns £40,000 per annum, together with an annual bonus of £6,000. He has been provided with the following benefits:

- a small company car that is mainly used for business purposes. The car, which is petrol driven, has a list price of £21,000 and emits 100g of CO_2 per kilometre. His employer pays all the fuel costs for the car
- a subsidized staff restaurant that is open to all staff
- private medical insurance that costs his employer £900 per employee.

During the year, Imran also received interest of £3,100.

Required:

a) **Identify which of Imran's benefits are liable to income tax.**

b) **Calculate the taxable amount for each of the benefits.**

c) **Would Imran be described as a higher rate taxpayer?**

d) **Carry out a tax computation for Imran to determine his total income tax liability for the year.**

e) **Imran lives in central London and very rarely uses his car for private purposes. Advise Imran on whether to continue using the car very occasionally for personal use.**

PAYE (Pay As You Earn)

Employers collect income tax and National Insurance (NI) contributions under the PAYE (Pay As You Earn) scheme. This is designed so that employees should have the correct amount of income tax and NI contributions deducted from each salary they receive. Each employee is paid the net amount due to them after the deductions have been made. The employer then pays over to HMRC the total amount of deductions taken from all their employees.

Key term

PAYE (Pay As You Earn) is the system whereby employers deduct income tax and National Insurance contributions from their employees' salaries, paying the employees the net amount after those deductions have been made. The employer then pays to HMRC the total tax and National Insurance contributions deducted from all employees.

In order that employers can make the correct deductions, each taxpayer is issued with a tax code that should take into account their personal allowance, the benefits they receive, and any other relevant factors. For example, if a taxpayer is expected to earn interest in excess of their PSA or dividends in excess of the DA, then the tax code can be set to take this into account, so that the correct amount of tax is deducted.

PAYE is operated on a cumulative basis such that employers using suitable payroll software will calculate and deduct tax on a monthly basis from their employees, ensuring that the tax allowances are spread throughout the tax year. For example, the benefit of the personal allowance is spread over the entire tax year and not just applied to the first months of the tax year.

When issued with a tax code, a taxpayer should always check it and even more importantly, prepare their own tax computation when a tax year has finished, to ensure that they have paid the right amount of income tax for the year.

 Ponder point

If a basic rate taxpayer is in employment and receives a small amount of bank interest and dividend income during a tax year, how would their income tax liability be settled?

A basic rate taxpayer should meet their income tax obligations as follows:

- Their employer would deduct income tax on their salary under the PAYE system
- Interest received will not be taxable if the interest is covered by the Personal Savings Allowance which is £1,000 for a basic rate taxpayer
- Dividends will not be taxable as long as the total received during the year is less than £5,000

If a person earns interest in excess of their Personal Savings Allowance, then their tax code will be altered by HMRC so that the right amount of tax is collected. It is the responsibility of the individual to make sure that they pay the right amount of tax in any tax year.

If a person receives dividends in excess of the Dividend Allowance, then they need to inform HMRC, so that the right amount of tax can be collected.

Many taxpayers who exceed the limits for the PSA and the DA will be taxed under self-assessment, whereby they complete an annual tax return detailing all their income for the tax year. This system is discussed later in the chapter.

Two important PAYE forms that taxpayers should be aware of:

P60

This form is given to employees at the end of each tax year and it shows the employee's gross pay and the total income tax and NI contributions deducted. Employees should retain their copy of this as evidence of their pay and deductions.

P45

This form is given to employees when they leave their employment and it shows the employee's gross pay received during that tax year up to the leaving date, and the income tax and NI contributions deducted during that period. It also shows the employee's tax code. When the taxpayer starts a new job, they should give a copy of this form to their new employer. This will allow their new employer to deduct the correct amount of tax.

Income from self-employment

Taxpayers who are self-employed are liable to pay income tax on the profits made by their business. A self-employed person can choose their business's accounting date, which is the date their accounts are made up to. (For example, the accounting date could be 31 March or 30 June.)

In arriving at the business's taxable profits, only allowable expenses can be deducted. To decide on whether an expense can be deducted in arriving at the taxable profit, the overall principle applied is that for expenses to be allowable, they must have been incurred *wholly and exclusively for the purposes of the business.*

 Key terms

An **allowable expense** is an expense that can be deducted in arriving at taxable income for tax purposes.
A **disallowable expense** is an expense that cannot be deducted in arriving at taxable income for tax purposes.

Example 5.11

Using the above *wholly and exclusively for the purposes of the business* principle, which of the following expenses are likely to be allowable for a window cleaner who runs his business using a camper van to travel from area to area.

a) The cost of window cleaning products

b) The cost of cloths and sponges used for cleaning

c) A salary paid to his wife who does not work in the business

d) A salary paid to his assistant who works part-time in the business

e) Insurance for the camper van (it is used for business and private purposes)

Expenses (a), (b), and (d) meet the criteria as being wholly and exclusively for the purposes of the business and would be allowable. Those expenses could be deducted in arriving at the taxable profit.

Expense (c) is not incurred for the purposes of the business and would not be allowable. Expense (e) would be partly allowable and partly disallowable depending on the extent to which the camper van is used for business and for private purposes.

Once the profits assessable to tax have been determined, there is then the issue of which tax year they are assessed in. The rule is that they are included in the income tax computation for the tax year in which the accounting year ends. For example, if a business had chosen 30 June as its accounting date, then its profits would be assessed as follows:

Profits to:	Tax year in which profits are assessed
accounting year end 30 June 2016	2016/17
accounting year end 30 June 2017	2017/18
accounting year end 30 June 2018	2018/19

If another business had chosen 31 March as its accounting date, then its profits would be assessed as follows:

Profits to:	Tax year in which profits are assessed
accounting year end 31 March 2016	2015/16
accounting year end 31 March 2017	2016/17
accounting year end 31 March 2018	2017/18

Self-assessment

If a taxpayer is in employment, then income tax and NI contributions payable will be calculated and deducted from their salary by their employer, under the PAYE system. As most interest received is covered by the PSA, the majority of taxpayers will have no tax to pay on interest received. Likewise, the majority of taxpayers who receive dividends will have no tax to pay on those dividends as a result of the Dividend Allowance.

Ponder point

Can you think of circumstances where a taxpayer will not have met their income tax liabilities through the PAYE system?

When a taxpayer receives very large amounts of interest or dividends, well in excess of the relevant allowances, then they will not necessarily have met all of their tax liabilities through the PAYE system. Also taxpayers who have other sources of income, for example, rental income may not necessarily have met all of their tax liabilities through PAYE. These taxpayers are required to submit a self-assessment tax return. A tax return has to be completed by the taxpayer giving details of all the income that they have received during the tax year, plus details of relevant expenses and pension contributions.

Taxpayers are given many months to complete and submit the return. Those individuals who submit online are allowed up to 31 January following the end of the tax year as their deadline for submission. Late submission and late payment of tax give rise to penalties and interest charges that can quickly build up to significant amounts.

 Ponder point

If a taxpayer is aware that they will have to complete a tax return, what sort of documents would you advise them to file carefully during and after the tax year?

Any taxpayer who is required to submit a tax return should keep all documents relating to their income received during the tax year: any P60 received if the taxpayer is in employment, any interest certificates received from banks and building societies, and any dividend vouchers received. They should also keep invoices for any relevant expenses. If the taxpayer is self-employed, then accounts will have to be drawn up in order for the taxable profit to be calculated.

National Insurance (NI) contributions

In addition to any income tax that is payable, National Insurance contributions are payable by anyone in employment or self-employment who is between the ages of sixteen and retirement age. National Insurance contributions are calculated separately from income tax and the rules surrounding the amount payable are different.

Payment of National Insurance contributions is required in order for an individual to qualify for certain state benefits, including a state pension.

National Insurance is divided into various classes as shown in Table 5.10:

Table 5.10 National Insurance

Individual earnings	National Insurance class
In employment	Class 1 NI contributions payable
Self-employed	Class 2 and class 4 NI contributions payable

Class 1—employee NI contributions

Class 1 contributions are based on an individual's gross salary, before any tax is deducted. They are calculated on income received during a 'contribution period', usually a month. The amount of NI contributions payable will depend on the salary received in a particular month and will not be affected by any amounts received in previous months. Table 5.11 shows indicative rates for class 1 NI contributions.

Table 5.11 National Insurance contributions: class 1—payable by employees

	Earnings per month
Primary threshold	£700
Upper earnings limit	£3,700
	National Insurance contributions
On earnings between the primary threshold and the upper earnings limit	12%
On earnings above the upper earnings limit	2%

Example 5.12

Three brothers earn the following salaries per annum:

Brother 1	£5,100
Brother 2	£24,000
Brother 3	£60,000

Table 5.12 shows how much each of them will pay per month in NI contributions.

Table 5.12 National Insurance contributions for the three brothers

	Annual salary £	Monthly salary £	National Insurance contributions per month (Class 1) £
Brother 1	5,100	425	Earnings less than £700 per month Class 1 NI contributions = £0
Brother 2	24,000	2,000	First £700: £nil Next £1,300: £1,300 × 12% = £156 Total Class 1 NI contributions = £156
Brother 3	60,000	5,000	First £700: £nil Next £3,000: £3,000 × 12% = £360 Next £1,300: £1,300 × 2% = £26 Total Class 1 NI contributions = £386

> **? Ponder point**
>
> Do you consider that National Insurance is a tax?

Many people would argue that National Insurance is a tax in that it has to be paid on employment earnings and self-employed earnings. It has different rates and rules to income tax but the impact on a basic rate taxpayer, such as Brother 2 in Example 5.12, is that in total he will pay 'taxes' of 32% on his taxable income, after the personal allowance and the National Insurance primary threshold, have been taken into account. He will be liable to pay 20% income tax on his taxable income and 12% NI contributions on income in excess of the primary threshold.

Class 2 and class 4—self-employed NI contributions

At present, self-employed people have to pay two classes of National Insurance contributions: class 2 and class 4 contributions. The government is planning to abolish class 2 and to reform class 4 contributions. The exact way that this will work is still under consideration and so this book will refer to the current system in place for the self-employed:

- Class 2 contributions are payable at a fixed amount known as the flat rate, as long as the individual's taxable income is above a certain amount, known as the small profits threshold.
- Class 4 NI contributions are payable at a certain percentage of the taxable profits for the year, in excess of a lower profits limit. If profits are below this limit, then no class 4 contributions are payable.

Class 2 and class 4 contributions are collected by self-assessment at the same time as income tax on profits is calculated and paid. The indicative rates for class 2 and class 4 National Insurance contributions are shown in Table 5.13.

Table 5.13 National Insurance contributions: classes 2 and 4—payable by the self-employed

Class 2	
Class 2 small profits threshold	£6,000
Class 2 rate	£3.00 per week
Class 4	
Class 4 lower profits limit	£8,000
Class 4 upper profits limit	£44,000
Class 4 rate on profits between lower and upper limit	9%
Class 4 rate on profits above upper limit	2%

Example 5.13

During the most recent tax year, two self-employed architects made taxable profits as follows: Architect 1 made taxable profits of £28,000 and Architect 2 made taxable profits of £60,000. Table 5.14 shows how the amount of class 2 and class 4 NI contributions payable by these two architects, is calculated.

Table 5.14 National Insurance contributions: Architects 1 and 2

Architect 1 National Insurance contributions		
Class 2	£3.00 × 52 weeks	£156
Class 4	(£28,000 – 8,000) × 9%	£1,800
Total Classes 2 and 4 NI contributions		£1,956
Architect 2 National Insurance contributions		
Class 2	£3.00 × 52 weeks	£156
Class 4	(£44,000 – 8,000) × 9%	£3,240
	(£60,000 – 44,000) × 2%	£320
Total Classes 2 and 4 NI contributions		£3,716

Case study—Rachel (2)

Rachel works for a retail company and earned £45,000 in the last tax year. She expects to be paid £48,000 in the next tax year. Other income in the next tax year is likely to consist of interest received of £620 in an ISA held with Leaf Bank and she also expects to receive £220 of dividends from Olypoly plc.

Using the indicative tax tables and tables for NI contributions provided in this chapter:

Required:

a) Calculate Rachel's expected total taxable income for next year.

b) How much income tax will be payable on her taxable income?

c) What class of NI contributions will Rachel have to pay?

d) Calculate the total amount of NI contributions that she will have to pay during the next tax year.

Case study—Kate

Kate set up her own graphic design business a few years ago. It has enabled her to work from home whilst she had a young family. During the current tax year, she anticipates her business will generate taxable profits of £15,000. Kate has no other source of income.

Required:

a) Prepare Kate's income tax computation and compute her expected total liability for income tax.

b) Compute the amount of class 2 and class 4 NI contributions that Kate will have to pay.

c) How will her income tax and NI liabilities be collected?

d) Kate is finding that running her own business and caring for her children is great fun but very time-consuming. Her view on her tax situation is as follows:

'When I was working, I paid my taxes every month. Now I am self-employed and the business is so small, I cannot believe that I have to complete a self-assessment tax return every year. I would prefer to leave it for a few years and then submit tax returns for a few years all at the same time.'

Advise Kate on the wisdom of this plan.

Conclusion

Income tax is payable by UK residents on their total income arising from employment, self-employment, property, interest, and dividends. (Tax on property income is covered in Chapter 10.) Every individual is taxed separately and most are entitled to receive a personal allowance that allows them to receive a certain amount of income free from tax each tax year. In a tax computation, a taxpayer's total income is computed and from this the personal allowance is deducted to arrive at their taxable income.

Each income stream is then taxed in a specific order—earned income is taxed first, then interest, and finally, dividend income.

Most individuals are entitled to receive a Personal Savings Allowance whereby some, if not all, of their interest is taxed at 0%. Any remaining interest is taxed at a rate determined by the band they fall into: basic, higher, or additional rate band. The PSA means that most taxpayers do not have to pay tax on the interest they receive.

All individuals are entitled to receive a Dividend Allowance whereby some, if not all, of their dividend income is taxed at 0%. Any remaining dividends are taxed at a rate determined by the band they fall into. The tax rates that apply to dividend income are different from those that apply to other forms of income. The DA means that most taxpayers do not have to pay tax on the dividends they receive.

Interest and dividends arising in an ISA are not subject to income tax.

National Insurance contributions are like a tax in all but name and are payable by people in employment or self-employment. Eligibility for certain state benefits depends on NI contributions having been paid. Unlike income tax that is computed for a whole tax year, NI contributions are calculated on income received during a contribution period, usually a month. Employees are required to pay class 1 contributions on their income and the self-employed pay class 2 and class 4 contributions.

🖥 Useful websites

A website with clear and straightforward information on income tax and National Insurance:
http://www.gov.uk

❓ Practice Questions

Question 1 Quick Questions TRUE OR FALSE?

5.1   Every individual is entitled to have the benefit of a tax-free personal allowance, as long as their income is less than £100,000.

5.2   If an individual does not use all of their personal allowance in one tax year, they can add it to the following year's allowance.

5.3   Only basic rate taxpayers are entitled to receive the full Personal Savings Allowance.

5.4   Employment income included in a tax computation should be stated as the gross amount.

5.5   Dividend income, in excess of the Dividend Allowance, is taxed at different rates to employment income or interest received.

5.6   Employers operate a PAYE system to collect tax and National Insurance contributions from employees.

5.7   Every taxpayer has to complete a self-assessment tax return.

5.8   A P45 is a given to employees when they leave an employment.

5.9   Class 1 National Insurance contributions are based on an individual's net income after income tax has been deducted.

5.10   Class 4 National Insurance contributions are payable by self-employed people based on their profits for the year.

Question 2 Vikram

Vikram wants to check whether he has paid the right amount of income tax in the last year. He has gathered together all his paperwork and produced the following summary of his income:

● Vikram's salary was £24,000 per annum on which he paid income tax of £2,300.

● He received interest on an ISA of £300 and interest from a savings account of £500.

● He received dividends of £480 during the year.

● He has access to a free workplace gym, that is available to all staff. This costs his employer £1,000 per annum per person.

Required:

a) **Identify which of Vikram's incomes and benefits will be subject to income tax.**

b) **Carry out a tax computation for Vikram to determine his total income tax liability for the year.**

c) **Has Vikram paid the right amount of tax?**

* Question 3 Matilda

Matilda is a marketing manager earning an annual salary of £38,000, plus a bonus of £4,000. Matilda receives a small amount of interest from ISAs. Matilda has been offered the opportunity to have a company car and the company would provide all the fuel whether for work or private use. Matilda is very excited at the prospect of a new car and has looked at the choices available to her. She is tempted to choose one of the following cars:

- Car 1 is a diesel car. It has a list price of £18,000 and CO_2 emissions of 100 g/km.
- Car 2 is a petrol driven car, costs £18,000, and has CO_2 emissions of 200 g/km.

Matilda currently runs her own car which she estimates costs her £3,500 per annum including petrol, servicing, repairs, and depreciation.

Required:
a) Prepare Matilda's income tax computation for the year, assuming that she chooses option 1 as her company car. What will be her total tax liability for the year?

b) What would Matilda's total tax liability be if she chooses option 2? Comment on your findings.

c) Summarize the figures and factors that Matilda should consider when deciding whether to accept company car 1.

Question 4 Amas and Amat

a) Amas is an employee earning £42,000 per annum. Which class of National Insurance contributions will he have to pay and how much will he have to pay?

b) Amat is self-employed and made taxable profits of £42,000. Which class or classes of National Insurance contributions will he have to pay and how much will he have to pay?

c) Comment on your findings.

* Question 5 Shula

Shula works for a local newspaper and earns £28,000 per annum. She paid tax on her income of £7,100. She is provided with a petrol driven company car, that has a list price of £17,000 and which emits 100 grams of CO_2/km. Her employer pays for all the fuel used.

During the year, Shula made taxable profits of £11,000 from a self-employed business and she received dividends of £700.

Required:
a) Carry out a tax computation for Shula to determine her total income tax liability for the year and any remaining tax that she owes or is owed.

b) Calculate the total amount of National Insurance contributions that Shula has to make, detailing the various classes of National Insurance that she has to pay.

c) Explain how all of Shula's income tax liability is settled and how her liability for National Insurance contributions will be paid.

Question 6 Rex

Rex owns a hairdressing salon that has been in business for some years. The salon made a profit of £46,400 for the current tax year. Rex also received dividends of £6,200 during the year and he earned interest totalling £1,850, of which £850 was earned in an ISA.

Required:

a) Carry out a tax computation for Rex to determine his total income tax liability for the year.

b) Calculate the total amount of National Insurance contributions that Rex has to make, detailing the various classes of National Insurance that he has to pay.

c) Rex is planning to move the shares that he owns into his wife's name, so that she will receive the dividends in future years. What impact will this have on his income tax liability next year and on his wife's tax liability assuming that she is a basic rate taxpayer and she currently has no dividend income.

* Question 7 Georgia

Georgia is employed as an assistant sales manager on a salary of £26,000 per annum. She received a bonus of £3,000 during the tax year and paid tax on her earnings of £3,700. She has a company car that is fully electric and hence has zero emissions. The car has a list price of £22,000. She is allowed to use the car for personal as well as business use. Georgia inherited a large sum a year ago and as a result has received interest of £1,700 in the last year and dividends of £290.

Required:

a) Carry out a tax computation for Georgia to determine her total income tax liability for the year and any tax due to be paid by her or refunded to her.

b) What advice would you give Georgia about her choice of savings account, in order for her to minimize the tax consequences of the interest she receives.

 Visit the Online Resource Centre that accompanies this book for additional material: www.oxfordtextbooks.co.uk/orc/king_carey2e/

6

Building your savings

 Learning Objectives

After studying this chapter, you should understand:

- Reasons why it is important to have savings
- Risks associated with saving
- The benefits of compound interest for savers
- Different types of savings accounts

Introduction

Some individuals spend more than they earn and have difficulty making ends meet from month to month; others have developed the savings habit and each month manage to put something away for the future. In effect, saving means being prepared to sacrifice current consumption in favour of future benefits. This can be difficult for young people when they are just starting out in adult life or for families with children who may find it a struggle to meet all of their financial commitments. Building up savings helps to provide financial independence and security later on in life, which is a goal worth aiming for.

 Indicative rates

This chapter uses indicative rates that give an indication of the size of certain rates and allowances. Reference should always be made to any suggested websites in order to ascertain the current figures that apply.

Background

Saving involves people placing spare funds in a savings account, in an investment, or in a pension fund. Investments and pensions are dealt with in separate chapters. This chapter concentrates on savings accounts where the amount deposited, known as capital, should not be at risk of loss. There are other types of risk associated with saving accounts, but loss of capital should not generally be one of them.

Reasons for saving

 Ponder point

Can you think of several different reasons for saving?

The reasons for saving can be summarized into three different motives: these are known as the 'transactions motive' which prompts saving for specific spending such as a holiday or retirement, the 'precautionary motive' which provides savings for emergencies, and the 'speculative motive' which provides savings to allow good investment opportunities to be taken advantage of, as and when they arise.

Transactions motive

For most people the strongest reasons for saving stem from the transactions motive and a need to provide funds for housing, retirement, holidays, or other expensive items. Savings are required when purchasing a property, because a mortgage will usually only be offered by a bank or building society if the borrower has a deposit to put down against the purchase. A typical deposit might be 20% of the purchase price. This would mean that a first-time buyer purchasing a property costing £200,000 would need to have saved a deposit of £40,000. Some savings are necessary even for those choosing to rent rather than buy, because a significant deposit is usually required before a property can be rented.

It is important to save for retirement to ensure that a reasonable standard of living can be maintained when individuals are no longer working. The issue of making adequate provision for retirement is discussed in Chapter 12.

Savings are useful when seeking to purchase expensive items, such as a holiday, car, or furniture. Although these items can be bought using credit, having savings can allow special offers to be taken advantage of, as the cheapest deals are often only available when purchases can be paid for in full.

Self-employed people need to have some savings to meet their income tax liabilities, because their tax is payable in arrears.

Precautionary motive

In the UK there is a system of state benefits that provides a measure of support during difficult times, but even so most people need savings to protect their standard of living in the event of a period of unemployment or illness. The precautionary motive drives saving to cover living costs during difficult times.

It is important to have savings to meet other unforeseen expenditure, such as maintenance on a house or a repair bill for a car. When buying a property it is not only a matter of paying the mortgage and the bills, it is also necessary to have some funds available for repairs, such as replacing a boiler or repairing a roof or windows. The expression that you might need to have 'savings for a rainy day' refers to the need to have savings to meet unexpected expenditure.

Speculative motive

Many people have a speculative motive to build up savings in order to be able to take advantage of good investment opportunities at the time that they arise. This includes saving in order to start a business.

The motives for saving are all very closely linked to the reasons for budgeting. Part of the reason for budgeting is to allow for the building up of savings. Having savings should help to avoid the need to resort to expensive loans or emergency lenders. A general rule of thumb is that readily available savings should be equal to between three and six months' income.

The UK household saving ratio

The UK household saving ratio looks at how much of an individual's disposable income is saved. The saving ratio is measured as the difference between income received and the amount spent on goods and services, expressed as a percentage of income received. For example, if an individual had a disposable income of £30,000 and spent £27,000 on goods and services, then the saving ratio would be 10% (3,000/30,000).

The saving ratio is important because it is an indication of the level of savings in the economy; the savings are used via financial institutions to fund investment in businesses to enable growth and expansion. If there is too little saving, then the economy can suffer from a lack of funds for investment; if the saving ratio is too high, indicating too much saving, then the economy can suffer from a lack of consumer spending. This is known as the paradox of thrift. Generally speaking, thriftiness—or being careful with money—is a positive attribute, but a lack of consumer demand can have a negative impact on the economy.

In the UK, the saving ratio fluctuates according to a variety of factors including levels of consumer confidence and the state of the economy. If the economy is growing and consumer confidence is high, individuals do not feel the need to save and the saving ratio falls. In contrast, if the economy is in recession and consumer confidence is low, individuals feel the need to save and the saving ratio increases. According to the Office for National Statistics (2015), the UK household saving ratio was 5% in 2015 having been at 11% in 2010. This contrasts with Germany which has a long-term saving ratio of 16%, (OECD, 2016) and China which has maintained a very high ratio of over 40% during recent decades (China People's Daily, 2016).

The UK household saving ratio has fluctuated in recent years. This is illustrated by Figure 6.1 where it can be seen that household saving in the UK fell steadily

per cent

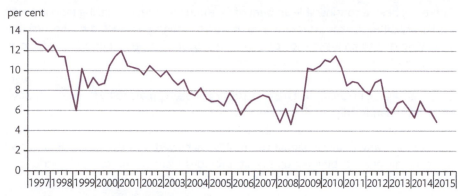

Figure 6.1 The UK household saving ratio
Source: Office for National Statistics, 2015.

from 1997 whilst the British economy was growing, until 2009 when the saving ratio began to climb again as the British economy went into recession. As consumer confidence fell, households increased their saving to meet the precautionary motive. Since 2010 the savings ratio has generally been falling as a result of greater economic stability and higher levels of consumer spending. A Lloyds TSB Bank report indicates that in 2014 one in three households in the UK had no form of saving (Lloyds TSB Bank, 2014).

 Ponder point

Can you envisage any particular problems for an adult in the UK with no savings?

Without savings there is limited financial support to fall back on in times of difficulty, such as unemployment, illness, or unexpected bills. For an individual without any savings, becoming unemployed or ill is likely to cause financial difficulty. Without any savings an individual is unlikely to be able to buy a property or take on a rental lease, and it would only be possible to have a holiday, buy some furniture or a car by getting into debt. In the longer term, without any savings, an individual is unlikely to have a comfortable retirement.

An individual without savings will have no real financial security or independence, no opportunity to help family members, and no safety net.

 Ponder point

Why might the saving ratio be significantly higher in China than in the UK?

There has been a considerable amount of research into the high saving ratio in China and many different reasons for this ratio have been suggested, including the idea that it may be due to an ageing society. China has been through a period of significant growth and economic change, with increasing moves towards capitalism. Many individuals and entrepreneurs are taking advantage of the new opportunities to create personal wealth. In China, welfare has historically been provided by the state, through state-owned industries. With the move away from state ownership and state-funded welfare, there is some uncertainty about future welfare provision. Independence from welfare for many Chinese people can best be achieved through saving. In a period of economic change, building up savings provides security. This can be described as the precautionary motive. In the UK, by way of contrast, the welfare state has been in existence since the late 1940s and in Britain individuals are confident of a certain level of support from the welfare state. Although the level of benefits may change, there is a general reliance on the system. This type of welfare system does not exist to the same extent in China.

It is not only the precautionary motive that contributes to such a high level of saving in China. Some saving is likely to be driven by the transactions motive as it will allow individuals to purchase property and consumer goods and a booming economy provides many opportunities for speculative savings to be invested for growth.

Example 6.1

Two brothers each inherited £100,000. One was a spender and the other was a saver so they used their inheritance in very different ways. The elder brother used his inheritance to pay off his outstanding mortgage of £85,000 and saved the remainder. His younger brother had no mortgage, as he lived in rented accommodation. He wanted his family to share in his good fortune so he gave his three children £15,000 each. He was delighted to have the money to purchase an expensive new sports car, costing £35,000 and he took his family on safari to South Africa, which cost £10,000. The remaining £10,000 was quickly spent on weekend breaks, expensive clothes, and new furniture.

As a result of his careful financial planning, combined with his inheritance, the elder brother has achieved financial security. With no mortgage or rent to pay he has spare income to save or spend on holidays and clothes as he chooses. He has some measure of financial independence, with a fund available for unforeseen expenditure. He is in a position to help his children should they need it and he has savings available towards his retirement.

By way of contrast, his younger brother has not achieved financial security. He is renting a property and has no savings to meet his transactions, precautionary, or speculative needs. He could have chosen to save a significant proportion of his inheritance, perhaps to use it as a substantial deposit towards purchasing a property. He chose instead to give the money away and spend it on consumable items. Hopefully his children will have saved the sums he passed onto them, but he is clearly a spender rather than a saver, and does not choose to sacrifice current consumption for future gain. As a result, he may never achieve the same level of financial security as his brother.

Risks of saving

Selecting whom to entrust your money to is a very important part of controlling risk. In making savings and investments there are two general types of risk, known as adverse selection and moral hazard, which arise as a result of information asymmetry. Information asymmetry describes the situation where not all parties to a transaction have equal access to information. For example, if you are placing some savings with an institution, you will not know as much about that institution and the risks it takes as the people who are running it. They have more information than you do and therefore the available information is asymmetrical or unequal.

As a result of information asymmetry there is always the danger of adverse selection. Adverse selection occurs before any transaction takes place and, in the context of savings, it is the risk of placing savings with a poorly performing institution. It might be performing poorly because the interest rates offered are too low, or it might be because the institution is at risk of failure. An example of adverse selection might be choosing a savings account with an attractive headline rate of interest, but not being made aware that after a certain time the interest rate would drop to a much lower rate.

 Key terms

Information asymmetry in the context of savings refers to the situation where one party to a transaction has access to superior information than the other party.

Adverse selection in the context of savings arises when one party to a transaction has better access to information and the disadvantaged party makes a poor decision.

Moral hazard in the context of savings is the risk that after a transaction has occurred, one of the parties to the deal does not act in good faith.

Adverse selection can be followed by moral hazard. In savings terms, moral hazard can be explained as the risk which occurs after the transaction has taken place (when the savings have been made), and is the risk that the recipient of the funds placed on deposit will not use them wisely, keep them safe, or look after them carefully.

 Key term

The **Financial Services Compensation Scheme (FSCS)** is the UK's compensation fund available to compensate customers of authorized financial services in the event of their failure.

All three risks can be illustrated by the experience of some British savers who, in 2007, opted for the high interest rates offered by a number of Icelandic banks without necessarily understanding the level of risk attached to them. Information asymmetry meant that savers were unaware that the banks were at risk of failure. Adverse selection followed, as savers were attracted to the foreign banks by the high interest rates offered, whilst being unaware of the increased risk. This was followed by moral hazard when the banks failed and were unable to refund savers' deposits. Furthermore, many savers were unaware of the extra risk their savings might be exposed to with a bank that was not covered by the Financial Services Compensation Scheme. At the time, UK bank deposits were covered by the scheme up to £35,000, but this did not extend to foreign banks.

In 2008 the British savers who had placed their savings on deposit with the Icelandic banks were in serious danger of losing their savings when the banks failed. In the end the British government refunded individual investors and then pursued the Icelandic authorities for compensation (House of Commons Treasury Committee, 2009).

A good rule of thumb that can be applied to savings is that if a rate of return relative to the level of risk appears too good to be true, then it probably is. Remembering this rule might help to reduce the chances of adverse selection and moral hazard.

Financial Services Compensation Scheme

 Indicative rate

Amount covered by financial services scheme	£75,000

The most significant risk associated with saving is the risk that the capital invested will fall in value or be lost completely. In the UK, the Financial Services Compensation Scheme means that up to £75,000 of personal savings is guaranteed by the British government should a bank or building society fail. The current limit of the compensation scheme can be checked at http://www.fscs.org.uk. The £75,000 limit is per person and per financial institution; so wealthy savers should consider limiting their savings to £75,000 per institution, thus ensuring that each of their deposits is effectively guaranteed by the British government. The limit for a joint account is doubled, so cover is increased to £150,000 where an account is held in joint names.

It is important to note that the £75,000 limit is per institution and to be aware that in the UK the same institution often owns several different brands and therefore the scheme would only cover up to £75,000 placed with an institution as a whole. It is also important to note that the deposit guarantee scheme does not cover savings held in the Channel Islands or the Isle of Man.

Example 6.2

If an individual placed £100,000 in a deposit account with a high street bank in the UK and the bank failed, then the saver would only be compensated for a loss of £75,000. If instead the saver put £50,000 into two separate deposit accounts with two different institutions in the UK, then the whole amount would be guaranteed under the Financial Services Compensation Scheme.

Inflation risk

Inflation poses a major risk to savers. In order for an amount of capital deposited in a savings account to maintain its value, the return generated by the savings account needs to at least match any changes in the purchasing power of that capital as a result of inflation. If it does not do so for a year or two, this is unlikely to have a significant impact on the capital but if the return generated on a savings product is less than inflation for a few years, the real value of the amount saved will fall. This is a very real risk as it is often the case that savings products offer interest rates that do not match inflation.

Whilst savers may associate risk with losing some or all of their original capital placed with savings institutions, they should also be aware of the risk to capital posed by investing or saving in poorly performing products.

Example 6.3

A saver places £5,000 in an account that pays interest at the rate of 2.5% per annum and leaves the capital and interest earned in the account for five years.

If inflation ran at an average rate of 5% per annum over that five-year period, the saver would need to have £6,381 [£5,000 $\times$ (1.05)^5] in the account at the end of that time in order to have the same purchasing power as she had at the outset.

Given that the account pays 2.5% interest that is added annually, the savings account would grow to £5,657 [£5,000 $\times$ (1.025)^5] over five years. The saver would therefore be £724 worse off at the end of five years because the interest paid had failed to keep pace with inflation.

Hand in hand with the inflation risk goes the danger of not noticing that the interest rate on a savings account has dropped. Banks and building societies rely on attracting new savers with high headline interest rates, which are often only available for a short period of time, perhaps in the form of a bonus percentage. Once a saver has found a good place for their savings, it is important to regularly check the rate of interest being paid on the account and move the savings to a better account if the rate of interest drops. A search of the internet reveals many accounts offering very low interest rates, perhaps as low as 0.1%, with savings languishing there. These savings are not keeping pace with inflation and are falling in value. Banks rely on savers' inertia or lack of focus on their savings, as this helps to generate larger profits for the banks. The money is only costing the bank a very low rate of interest but can be lent out to borrowers at better rates, generating a good return for the banks.

Example 6.4

A non-taxpayer has left savings of £3,500 for two years in an account offering an interest rate of 0.2%. The saver has not noticed that the rate of interest on the account has fallen from its original level of 5%. The same bank has an alternative account available for two years at 4%.

(continued...)

Table 6.1 illustrates the cost to the saver over two years of leaving the savings in the poorly paying account.

Table 6.1 Interest comparison

Savings account	Interest year 1	Interest year 2	Total interest earned over two years
£3,500 @ 0.2%	£7	£3,507 @ 0.2% = £7	£14
Alternative account			
£3,500 @ 4%	£140	£3,640 @ 4% = £146	£286

By leaving the savings in a poorly paying account, it has cost the saver £272 (£286 − £14) in lost interest over the two-year period. Furthermore the savings almost certainly will not be keeping pace with inflation and will be falling in value in real terms.

Savings products generally carry a low risk of loss of capital, except for inflation risk, and as a consequence the rate of return that can be expected is also low. The level of return, the interest rate, will be linked in broad terms to the rate of inflation and to the base rate of interest set by the Bank of England. If the base rate is low, say 2%, then the rates of interest offered by banks and building societies will also be low. Conversely when the base rate is set at a much higher level, say 10%, it would be expected that rates of interest offered on savings accounts would be similar.

 Key term

Base rate is the official rate of interest set by the Bank of England Monetary Policy Committee that is the starting point for all other interest rates in the UK. This is the rate of interest at which the Bank of England will lend to other financial institutions.

Compound interest

Compound interest is very important for savers because it increases the return generated from savings. Each year the amount of interest received increases because, as long as the saver has not withdrawn that interest, it is compounded with interest received in previous years. If interest is withdrawn each year, perhaps to fund spending, then the benefit of compound interest is lost and the return generated by the savings will be considerably smaller. Wherever possible savings should be allowed to accumulate and grow with the benefit of compound interest.

 Key term

Compound interest is interest that is paid on both the original deposit and also any accumulated interest from past years.

Example 6.5

If £2,000 was placed in a deposit account earning 10% interest, this would generate £200 interest in year 1. In year 2 the interest would be calculated on £2,200 at 10% and so the interest earned would have grown to £220.

This is in contrast to simple interest; if the interest is withdrawn each year, then it would not be compounded in this way but would remain the same at £200 each year, and as the interest is being withdrawn each year, the deposit will remain at £2,000 year after year.

The formula to work out the total amount that a savings deposit will grow to is:

$$M = P(1 + i)^n$$

where

M is the future value of the deposit
P is the original capital or deposit
i is the rate of interest
n is the number of years the sum has been on deposit

Example 6.6

A woman deposited £10,000 into a savings account that earned a 5% rate of interest. If no interest or capital was withdrawn, at the end of ten years the deposit would have grown to £16,290.

$$M = 10,000(1 + 0.05)^{10}$$
$$M = 10,000(1.629)$$
$$M = £16,290$$

If the interest was withdrawn each year, there would be no compounding and the interest received would be £5,000 (£10,000 × 5% × 10) in total, instead of £6,290 when the interest is left in the account.

After twenty years, if the interest was reinvested the total balance in the account would be £26,533. If the interest were withdrawn each year, the balance in the account would still be £10,000 after twenty years and the total interest earned on the account would have been £10,000, which is £6,533 less than when the interest was reinvested.

There are two rules of thumb relating to compound interest that can be useful when estimating future sums for savers (and incidentally also for borrowers):

- At a 7% rate of interest, savings (or borrowing) should have doubled after ten years
- At a 10% rate of interest savings (or borrowing) should have doubled after seven years

Example 6.7

A young man, who is not a taxpayer, inherits £10,000 and cannot decide whether to buy a car or to save the money. He finds a fixed term deposit account offering 7% interest, for ten years. He decides to see what the deposit would be worth in ten years' time, assuming that he will not withdraw any interest. Using the formula:

$$M = P(1 + i)^n$$
$$M = £10,000(1 + 0.07)^{10}$$
$$M = £19,672$$

He is surprised to observe that at a 7% rate of compound interest, the deposit would almost double in ten years. His choice is between spending £10,000 on a car immediately or having almost £20,000 in ten years' time. Although he is aware that inflation will reduce the real value or purchasing power of the future sum, he makes the decision to save his inheritance and harness the power of compound interest.

Annual equivalent rate (AER)

All savings accounts must indicate the annual equivalent rate of interest (AER) that the account will generate. The AER is used to standardize the description of the rate of interest on a savings account, based on the number of times that the interest is compounded throughout the year. The AER is based on the assumption that interest is accumulated in the account and is not withdrawn. For example, interest can be paid monthly or annually. An interest rate of 3.93% paid and compounded monthly, assuming no withdrawals are made, is the same as an interest rate of 4% paid annually and compounded just once a year. The account provider must show the AER so that a valid comparison between accounts can be made.

 Key term

Annual equivalent rate (AER) is an interest rate that reflects what the interest rate would be if the interest is paid and compounded every year.

 Ponder point

Consider three accounts, all with an interest rate of 4%. The first has interest paid monthly, the second quarterly, and the third account has interest paid annually. Which account would have the highest AER?

The first account having interest paid monthly will be compounded most frequently and therefore will have the highest AER. The quarterly interest account will have the next highest AER followed by the account that only pays interest once a year.

Monthly interest would be important to a saver who was relying on their savings to provide a regular income; otherwise annual interest is usually acceptable.

 Ponder point

If a couple has a significant amount owing on their mortgage, do you consider that it is appropriate for them to have savings, or should all spare cash be used to reduce the amount of a mortgage?

The rate of interest that a borrower has to pay on a mortgage is usually, although not always, higher than any rate of interest that can be earned on savings. If this is the case it would be cost-effective for any savings to be used to reduce a mortgage, reducing interest on the amount of the borrowing, rather than using those savings to earn a somewhat lower return.

However, as we have seen earlier, it is important to have savings to meet the transactions and precautionary motives and these needs still exist, whether or not there is a mortgage. A couple with a significant amount of borrowing may still have consumer wants and needs that require savings and it is important for all individuals to have savings for the precautionary motive, even more so where there is a significant mortgage.

If there were a substantial amount of savings it would be appropriate to use some of the savings to reduce the mortgage, as long as a reasonable amount of savings was retained.

Tax treatment of savings

Savings deposited in an account with a bank or building society should generate interest. In the UK, basic rate taxpayers have a Personal Savings Allowance which enables individuals to receive interest of up to £1,000 pa, tax-free. Higher rate taxpayers, can receive up to £500 pa of interest, tax-free. Additional rate taxpayers will pay tax at 45% on all of their interest. As interest rates are at a historically low level, quite large amounts of savings would be required to generate such amounts of interest. The majority of savers should find that their interest can be received free from any tax.

National Savings and Investments offer some different tax-free saving opportunities and these are discussed later in the chapter.

An additional way to avoid suffering income tax on interest is to put savings into an ISA. Each year savers can deposit up to a specified amount in a cash ISA and any interest which arises on the account is tax-free.

ISAs

Each tax year, every individual who is a UK resident and over the age of sixteen can invest a certain amount in an individual savings account (ISA). There are two main types of ISA:

- a cash ISA which is a savings account, usually held with a bank or building society
- a stocks and shares ISA which can hold investments in a range of shares and bonds.

Each tax year, an individual can open one cash ISA and one shares ISA. The limits on ISA investment tend to increase with each new tax year and you will find the current year's allowances on the Gov.uk website (http://www.gov.uk).

> ### 🔒 Key term
>
> ISA is an **Individual savings account** that allows income earned on savings and investments to be protected from income tax. There are annual limits to the amounts that can be placed in an ISA.

Table 6.2 Indicative ISA allowances per annum

Individual aged 16 to 18 years	Cash ISA only—limit of £20,000 pa
Individual aged over 18 years	Cash and/or shares ISA—limit of £20,000 pa
Individual aged 18 to 40 years	Lifetime ISA £4,000 (subject to overall ISA limit of £20,000 pa)
Individual aged over 16 years	Help to Buy ISA £2,400 (subject to overall limit of £20,000 pa)

Using the indicative allowances in Table 6.2, the overall maximum that can be invested in ISAs in one tax year would be £20,000 in a cash ISA or £20,000 in a shares ISA or any split between a combination of the two.

There are two specialist cash ISAs available, the Lifetime ISA and the Help to Buy ISA, that are specifically designed to encourage people saving for a deposit on a first home or for retirement. These have far less generous annual allowances than standard ISAs but they do offer savers the opportunity to benefit from government bonuses. The government may also introduce other types of ISA from time to time.

The Lifetime ISA is available to savers between the ages of eighteen and forty. A Lifetime ISA can be used to save for a first home or provide for retirement, from the age of sixty onwards. The government will add 25% each year to the amount saved, so if £4,000 has been saved in a year the government will add £1,000. The account must be used either to purchase a first home or to provide for retirement. If the money is withdrawn before the age of sixty for any other purpose, the government bonus would be lost.

The Help to Buy ISA is targeted at first-time buyers purchasing UK properties. Savers can deposit up to £200 per month and the government will provide a bonus of 25%

when the account is used to purchase a first property. The maximum that can be saved is £12,000 and the maximum government bonus is £3,000. You can have both a Help to Buy ISA and a Lifetime ISA but you can only use the bonus from one of them towards buying a house.

Even though the Personal Savings Allowance means that interest will be received tax-free for most taxpayers, it is still important to consider using ISAs. Every taxpayer can use their ISA allowance each tax year, but once the tax year is over that allowance is no longer available. If savings grow over time it may be that the Personal Savings Allowance is no longer sufficient to cover all interest received and interest will become taxable. At such a point it is not possible to utilize the lost ISA allowances from previous years. Furthermore, once money is placed within an ISA any income is received tax-free, whereas the Personal Savings Allowance may be reduced in line with taxation policy or disappear altogether. Higher rate taxpayers have a smaller Personal Savings Allowance and additional rate taxpayers have no Personal Savings Allowance so ISAs remain especially important to such taxpayers. The Lifetime ISA and Help to Buy ISA provide first-time buyers and pension savers with significant government help towards their goals in the form of the 25% bonuses, which makes such accounts very attractive to these savers.

Example 6.8

A UK resident wants to make maximum use of her cash ISA and opens a cash ISA in a tax year. She puts £12,000 on deposit in that ISA. Using the indicative allowances in Table 6.2, she would be able to put up to a further £8,000 into the account during the tax year.

If an amount is withdrawn from an ISA during a tax year, the saver can still top up their ISA to the limit as long as they do so before the end of the tax year.

Example 6.9

An individual pays £13,000 into a cash ISA in June and withdraws £10,000 from the ISA in September. The maximum amount that person could further invest in his cash ISA would be £17,000 in the current tax year. Using the indicative allowances, £20,000 in total could be put into a cash ISA in a given tax year. That amount can be withdrawn and deposited again within the same tax year, assuming that the ISA rules allow this.

An ISA is frequently described as a 'wrapper'. If savings are held in an ISA, then the savings will earn interest that as a result of being wrapped, are protected from incurring any income tax on the interest earned. At the end of each tax year, any unused ISA allowances from that year, are lost. The saver would then have access to the subsequent year's ISA allowances.

Ponder point

The transactions motive prompts an individual to save for their retirement. In what ways do most people save for their retirement?

An individual saving for their retirement would be most likely to make use of pension funds. The different types of pension funds and other pension arrangements are discussed in detail in Chapter 12, but in the context of savings it is important to realize that saving for retirement constitutes a major part of savings as a whole. A cash ISA and/or a Lifetime ISA would be a useful addition in retirement, providing a flexible supplement to income from a pension scheme. An ISA has the major benefit of providing the saver with control over both access and use of the funds. Access to funds held within a pension scheme is restricted, whereas funds held within an ISA remain in the individual's control. If the maximum permitted amount is deposited in ISAs each year, a significant tax-free fund can accumulate, providing a useful source of income and capital in retirement.

Types of savings accounts

Bank or building society accounts

Savings accounts can be structured in a variety of different ways and banks and building societies are constantly devising new products. Three of the most common types of account are:

- Instant access accounts
- Regular savings accounts
- Fixed rate bonds and fixed term accounts

It is possible to find each of the above type of account available as an ISA.

Instant access accounts

Most people will be familiar with the type of savings account offered by banks or building societies that allows instant access to savings, where the funds can be withdrawn without penalty. The accounts available differ in terms of interest rate offered and whether that interest is paid monthly or annually. Instant access accounts have the benefit that it is possible to access funds easily, but the drawback is that the funds are not beyond temptation and interest rates are usually lower than other options. The accounts also differ in the practicalities of operation, whether this is by post, telephone, internet, or some combination of the three methods.

Regular savings accounts

This type of account allows regular monthly payments to be set up and is very useful to encourage a regular savings habit. However it is not a useful account if an individual is looking to deposit a lump sum, because it is for regular saving rather than one-off deposits. Although the rate of interest for the first year may look high, the small print often reveals that the headline rate of interest only lasts for twelve months and that the return will drop off significantly after that period. The high rate of interest will only actually apply to the amount saved in the first month. The amount saved in the second month will only receive eleven months at the headline rate of interest and so on. Payments must be made into the regular savings account every month and usually there are strict limits on the amounts which can be paid in. A possible drawback of these accounts is their inflexibility, because withdrawals are not usually permitted.

Fixed rate bonds and fixed term accounts

These accounts usually offer better rates of interest than other savings accounts because the funds are tied up for a period of time, typically between six months and five years. Although it is possible to withdraw funds before the end of the term, the penalties applied are likely to be high. This type of account is useful where the funds are not needed for a period of time and where the saver has already built up an amount of savings which can be deposited into the account in the form of a lump sum.

Example 6.10

A basic rate taxpayer with £3,000 to deposit is looking for a savings account. He uses the internet to search for the best available rates of interest. His interest income is significantly below the Personal Savings Allowance.

The search reveals that the savings accounts in Table 6.3 are amongst the 'best buys' for various types of account.

Table 6.3 'Best buy' savings accounts

Type	AER	Min/max investment	Interest paid	Access
Easy access	3.06%	£1,000/£5,000,000	monthly at 3.02%	instant
Easy access	3.06%	£1,000/£5,000,000	annually	instant
Three-year bond	3.8%	£1,000/£250,000	annually	after three years
Easy access cash ISA	3.4%	£1	annually	instant

A comparison of the accounts shows that the two easy access accounts carry identical rates of interest as 3.02% per month compounds to 3.06% per annum. The interest on both of these accounts would only be taxable if it was above the Personal Savings Allowance or if it was earned by an additional rate taxpayer.

(continued...)

The three-year bond has the advantage of attracting a higher interest rate, but the drawback is that the savings will not be accessible for three years. For the basic rate taxpayer, with no other savings income, the gross rate of interest is 3.8% and no tax will be payable. This is a better rate of interest than the tax-free ISA on offer and therefore this account might be suitable for the £3,000, if the amount will not be needed within three years. However, the ISA offers flexibility, the option to add to the savings over time and assurance that the interest will remain tax-free in the future, so it should be given serious consideration.

If the saver is able to commit his savings for a three-year period, then the bond offers the best rate of return, otherwise the easy access cash ISA is a good alternative.

A systematic approach to becoming a saver

Many people find it very difficult to save because they would rather enjoy their money now than in the future. The old expression 'money burns a hole in the pocket' can be true for some people. However, there are plenty of people who have control over their personal finances and have developed the discipline to save regularly. A systematic approach to becoming a saver involves the following steps:

Set objectives

A starting point to building up some savings is to work out what the financial goals or objectives may be. This can help to provide the motivation for saving. For example, the objectives may be to establish an emergency fund equivalent to three months' income and/or to save enough for a special holiday. With a specific goal in mind it should be easier to maintain the discipline required to sacrifice current consumption for future benefit.

Measure financial position

Once the objectives have been established, then preparation of a cash budget helps to clarify how the objectives can be achieved and how much can be regularly saved. A monthly cash budget is a very useful tool in personal finance that can provide a clear financial picture; it sets out income and expenditure and allows the user to make informed decisions about how much can realistically be saved. It encourages the user to engage with their personal finances and make reasonable decisions about savings, based on figures rather than guesswork.

Research suitable accounts

The next step is to research the savings accounts available and assess the interest rates offered together with the terms and conditions attaching to the accounts, remembering to take into account any tax that might be payable on the interest.

Act

Once a suitable account has been identified, an account should be opened and a monthly standing order into the account set up. This is usually the best way to ensure the savings are made as planned and to build up a reasonable sum over time. For some people it is important to put the savings beyond reach, so that the fund cannot easily be accessed, otherwise the temptation to withdraw funds from the savings can be strong.

Review regularly

Once the standing order has been set up and savings begin to accumulate, it is important to regularly check that the rate of interest received on the account is competitive and that progress is being made towards achieving the original objectives. If the interest rate drops or better rates are offered elsewhere, then moving the savings should be considered. It is also important to monitor progress towards the objective and if it appears that the objective will not be met, then further action might be required to get back on track.

Take control

Good savings habits are often established early on in life, with responsible adults encouraging children to save. However, even without that encouragement or without having learned good savings habits early on in life, it is still possible to make the decision to take control and become a good saver. It requires self-discipline and the knowledge that to achieve the long-term goals of financial security and independence it is necessary to sacrifice a certain amount of current consumption for future gains.

Case study—Rachel and her partner

Rachel has not always been a good saver. Although she now works for a large retailer and is in the process of applying for a mortgage and buying a house with her partner, when she was younger she used to spend everything she earned. She has always worked hard but when she was at university she had an expensive lifestyle. She enjoyed spending money on clothes, nights out, running a car, and taking holidays. After graduating from university she settled down with her partner and they reached the decision that they wanted to buy a house together. They needed a minimum deposit of £30,000 and managed to save this sum over three years.

Required:

a) Consider what made Rachel and her partner make the required changes in their lifestyle to become savers?

b) What systematic steps might Rachel and her partner have taken to build up the deposit for their house?

National Savings and Investments

National Savings and Investments is one of the largest savings institutions in the UK and is backed by the British government. Any savings deposited with National Savings are considered to be secure. National Savings and Investments offer a range of savings accounts and premium bonds. At any one time their website can be checked to see what is on offer. Premium bonds are discussed below, but the National Savings offering generally includes savings accounts, ISAs, income bonds, and tax-free index-linked or fixed rate savings certificates. These popular certificates are only issued from time to time and once the whole issue has been sold, the offer is withdrawn. Some issues of tax-free index-linked savings certificates sell out very quickly to individuals seeking to beat inflation and receive a tax-free return.

Premium bonds

Premium bonds are not bonds in the way that corporate and government bonds are described in Chapter 8. Premium bonds are a very popular form of savings in the UK. They are sold by the UK government to raise funds. Instead of paying a fixed amount of interest on sums invested, the interest is paid out as prizes. Each month there is a draw where the holders of bond numbers drawn are paid prizes. The highest prize stands at present at £1 million.

If you have savings invested in premium bonds, there is no guarantee that you will receive prizes but if you hold a reasonable amount of bonds, the probability is that you should receive some return on them, which may be above or below average depending on how lucky you are. The prizes are tax-free which can make them attractive to additional rate taxpayers or savers who earn interest in excess of their Personal Savings Allowance. The capital invested is fully refundable when the investor chooses to redeem them. The maximum amount which can be invested in Premium Bonds per person is £30,000.

 Ponder point

If you had a choice between receiving £200 of lottery tickets or £200 of premium bonds, which would you choose?

The wise choice would be the premium bonds because the money is not lost as soon as the draw is made. The bond numbers would be entered in the monthly prize draw and if you did need the capital, the bonds could be redeemed at any point. Admittedly, lottery prizes are far greater than premium bond prizes, but the odds of winning such a prize are very low.

Credit unions

Credit unions are not-for-profit organizations, run by the members for the members. They are a form of financial cooperative organization and it is estimated that there are around 400 credit unions in the UK (FCA, 2013). They collect savings from members and then use those savings to lend to members; the members usually have something in common, such as belonging to a trade union or a church. Savings accounts with credit union organizations usually pay out a dividend rather than interest; there can be no dividend paid at all if the credit union is not generating a return.

Peer-to-peer lending

Peer-to-peer lending allows savers to lend money to individuals or businesses that need loans, but do not have access to funds from other sources. This form of lending is growing in popularity. Savers are able to benefit through receiving a higher rate of return than is possible with normal savings products, but they are accepting a much greater level of risk in order to generate such a return. Peer-to-peer lending is usually arranged through websites, harnessing the power of the internet to match up savers and borrowers.

Peer-to-peer lending sites allow borrowers to have some say on the riskiness of the loans that they wish to make and many sites will divide up any deposit made by a saver, between a large number of borrowers. This is in order to spread the risk of the loans and to ensure that should any debts turn bad, they are only likely to have a very small impact on any one saver. However, the possibility of some bad debts arising needs to be taken into account in assessing advertised interest rates.

Peer-to-peer lending firms are not regulated or covered by the Financial Services Compensation Scheme so the level of risk is higher than a savings account. They are a good illustration of the principle that risk and return are inextricably linked and that a higher level of return almost always comes at the price of a greater level of risk.

Case study—Imran

Imran has a well-paid job as a commercial lawyer based in London. He enjoys spending his monthly salary on eating out, entertainment, and holidays in addition to the essential living costs he has to meet. Although he has made a small amount of saving in previous years, he feels that the time has come to start saving more. After reviewing his budget he decides that he should be able to save £100 per month by cutting down on entertainment and leisure spending, through having a weekly limit for this type of expenditure. His aim is to build up a fund for emergencies equivalent to six months' salary. Imran is a higher rate taxpayer. He believes that the interest he is likely to earn will not exceed the Personal Savings Allowance available to him as a higher rate taxpayer. He has found the options set out in Table 6.4 for his savings:

(continued...)

Table 6.4 Imran: savings account options

Savings account	AER
Cash ISA	2.5% pa
Two-year fixed rate bond with Southern Building Society	3.0% pa
Regular savings account	2.8% pa for 12 months, then 1.5%
Premium bonds	Entered in prize draw, prizes variable, but equivalent to 1.25%
National Savings index-linked savings certificate	Guaranteed to be above inflation as measured by the retail prices index
Peer-to-peer lending website	Possibly 10%

Imran knows a small amount about saving but cannot decide which would be the best option for his regular savings plan.

Required:

Review and comment on Imran's savings options.

Case study—Oliver

Oliver works in London as an actor. Sometimes his earnings are high and at other times, when he is between jobs, his earnings are quite variable. He has just successfully auditioned for a role and is about to go on tour for six months. Whilst he is on tour he will earn £15,000 for the six months, before tax. As he is self-employed he pays tax in arrears under the system of self assessment, so he receives his income gross (ie before deduction of any tax).

Required:

a) What are the reasons for Oliver to save?

b) What are the systematic steps that Oliver should take to ensure that he returns from his tour with a reasonable amount of savings?

Conclusion

It would be difficult to argue against the idea that having some savings is a desirable situation to be in. We have seen that savings help to provide financial security and independence and are particularly important in retirement. They provide a financial cushion during difficult times and may be needed to meet unexpected expenditure. There are some risks associated with saving, of which the greatest is the risk of erosion of value caused by inflation. In a low interest environment it is difficult to find a rate of interest that keeps pace with inflation.

The risk of loss of capital in the UK has been reduced, following the introduction of the Financial Services Compensation Scheme, which effectively guarantees deposits of up to £75,000 per person with each institution.

Taxation can reduce the returns made by savers but the Personal Savings Allowance allows a significant amount of interest to be earned tax-free. Full use can also be made of ISAs and other tax-free savings opportunities, such as National Savings and Investments.

Becoming a saver requires self-discipline and the knowledge that the potential gains outweigh the short-term pain. There are many different options for savings accounts where the capital is not at risk, offering different rates of interest, different terms, and different means to access those savings. An understanding of compound interest and AER allows for informed comparisons between accounts to be made.

 ## Useful websites

Information on current rates and allowances can be found at:
http://www.gov.uk
Information on the Financial Services Compensation Scheme can be found at:
http://www.fscs.org.uk
National Savings and Investments have a useful website, listing all their products at:
http://www.nsandi.com
There is a clear comparison between the Lifetime ISA and the Help to Buy ISA at:
http:/www.blog.moneysavingsexpert.com
There are many sites that offer comparisons of different savings accounts, including:
https://www.savingschampion.co.uk or **http://www.moneysupermarket.com** or
http://www.comparethemarket.com

 ## References

China People's Daily (2016) *Concerns of China Nearing Debt Crisis Overblown.* Available at: http://en.people.cn/n3/2016/0421/c90000-9047960.html (accessed 20.7.2016)

FCA (Financial Conduct Authority) (2013) *Consultation Paper CP13/7: High-Level Proposals for an FCA Regime for Consumer Credit, page 126.* Available at: http://www.fca.org.uk/static/fca/documents/consultation-papers/fsa-cp13-07.pdf (accessed 27.5.2013)

House of Commons Treasury Committee (2009) *Banking Crisis: The Impact of the Failure of the Icelandic Banks.* Available at: http://www.publications.parliament.uk/pa/cm200809/cmselect/cmtreasy/402/402.pdf (accessed 15.5.2013)

Lloyds TSB Bank (2014) *UK Household Savings Report.* Available at: http://www. lloydsbankinggroup.com/globalassets/documents/media/press-releases/lloyds-bank/2014/140821-value-of-household-savings-final2.pdf (accessed 21.7.2016)

OECD (Organisation for Economic Co-operation and Development) (2016) *OECD Insights.* Available at: http://oecdinsights.org/2016/02/11/a-dash-of-data-spotlight-on-german-households/ (accessed 20.7.2016)

Office for National Statistics (2015) *The Saving Ratio: How is it Affected by Households' and Non Profit Institutions Serving Households' Income and Expenditure?* Available at: http://www.ons.gov.uk/ons/dcp171776_408856.pdf (accessed 21.2.2016)

Practice Questions

Question 1 Quick Questions TRUE OR FALSE?

6.1   The only useful purpose of having savings is to provide for a 'rainy day'.

6.2   It is generally accepted that readily available savings of between three and six months' income are needed to provide a financial cushion.

6.3   Compound interest is interest that is paid on both the original deposit and also any accumulated interest from past years.

6.4   At an interest rate of 7% with interest compounded and no withdrawals, the amount held in a savings account will almost double in ten years.

6.5   AER stands for the annual equivalent rate and is a useful measure for comparing the rate of return on savings accounts.

6.6   If inflation is running at 10% and savings are kept under the mattress, the real value of the savings will halve in seven years.

6.7   The FSCS is a government-backed scheme in the UK that guarantees regulated bank and building society accounts up to £30,000.

6.8   As a result of the FSCS, there are no risks associated with keeping savings in a deposit account with a regulated bank.

6.9   Premium bond prizes are subject to income tax.

6.10   An account that has an interest rate of 5%, with interest paid monthly, will have the same AER as an account with an interest rate of 5%, paid annually.

Question 2 Savings Account Risks

What are the risks associated with keeping savings in a bank savings account, and how might those risks be reduced?

Question 3 Olga

Olga estimates that she will need £30,000 in ten years' time to pay for a special expedition that she is planning. She has just inherited £12,000 and she is hoping this will fund her trip. She has placed her inheritance in a savings bond, earning a gross rate of interest of 7%. She is a basic rate taxpayer but her interest will not exceed the Personal Savings Allowance for the foreseeable future.

Required:

Assuming she does not withdraw any interest and that interest rates remain the same, advise Olga as to the amount that will be in her account in ten years' time, so that she can establish whether she will have enough to fund her expedition.

Question 4 Callum and his partner

Callum and his partner work for the same company and operate their finances jointly. They have always wanted to take a gap year and go travelling, but they have never had enough savings to make this possible. At the age of twenty-four they make up their minds to go travelling for six months in the following year. They are both very sociable people and love going out after work and going to music festivals. They are occasionally offered overtime by their employer but they usually decline the opportunity, preferring to make the most of their leisure time together.

Required

Identify the practical steps that Callum and his partner should take to ensure that they are able to go travelling next year.

* Question 5 General Risks of Saving

Explain what is meant by information asymmetry, adverse selection, and moral hazard and consider how those risks can be reduced, in the context of saving.

* Question 6 Majid

Majid is a basic rate taxpayer who has saved a total of £6,000 in an ISA in previous tax years. This ISA is now paying a very poor rate of interest, at 0.5%. Majid is hoping to purchase a house in three years' time, but meanwhile he is looking for the best place to keep his savings until that time. He carries out some research and is interested in the options set out in Table 6.5:

Table 6.5 Majid: savings account options

Type	Gross interest	Min/max investment	Interest paid	Access
Premium bonds	Equivalent to 1.25%	£1/£30,000	monthly prizes	instant
Easy access	2%	£1,000/£5,000,000	annually	instant
Three-year bond	5%	£1,000/£250,000	annually	after three years
Fixed rate three-year cash ISA	4.85%	£1	annually	six months loss of interest
Regular savings account	4.8%	£10/£600 per month	annually	after 12 months

Required:

Discuss which account would be most suitable for Majid, assuming that his interest income will not exceed the Personal Savings Allowance.

 Visit the Online Resource Centre that accompanies this book for additional material: www.oxfordtextbooks.co.uk/orc/king_carey2e/

7

Understanding capital gains tax and inheritance tax

Learning Objectives

After studying this chapter, you should understand:

- The basic principles of how capital gains tax is calculated
- Some simple tax planning steps to reduce capital gains tax
- How to calculate the liability of an estate to inheritance tax
- Some simple tax planning steps to reduce inheritance tax

Introduction

Capital gains tax and inheritance tax are both forms of direct taxation, closely linked to the ability of an individual to pay. They are also known as wealth taxes or capital taxes. It can be argued that capital gains tax is necessary to ensure fairness within a tax system, otherwise income would be taxed whilst capital gains would be excluded from the tax regime. It was this argument that led to the introduction of capital gains tax in the UK in 1965. Approximately 190,000 people pay capital gains tax each year (HMRC, 2015) and although it raises relatively little revenue, it is felt to provide a level playing field to ensure that both gains and income are taxed fairly.

This chapter provides an introduction to capital gains tax (CGT) and inheritance tax because it is important to understand the principles of both taxes for personal financial planning purposes. However, in view of the complexity of some of the legislation, a broad-brush approach is taken. For more detailed rules on capital gains tax and inheritance tax, Her Majesty's Revenue and Customs (HMRC) website should be referred to at http://www.gov.uk

 Indicative rates

This chapter uses indicative rates that give an indication of the size of certain rates and allowances. When carrying out a real-life computation, it will be necessary to refer to

the HMRC website (http://www.gov.uk) for details of current tax rates and allowances. The indicative rates are set out in Table 7.1

Table 7.1 Capital gains tax: exemptions and bands

Annual exemption amount	£12,000
Personal possessions exemption	£6,000
Taxable income band	**Capital gains tax rate**
Up to £32,000 (standard rate)	10%
Standard rate residential property	18%
£32,000 upwards (higher rate)	20%
Higher rate residential property	28%
Entrepreneurs' relief lifetime limit	**Capital gains tax rate**
Up to £10,000,000	10%
£10,000,000+	18% or 28% as appropriate

Capital gains tax (CGT)

If you sell an asset in the UK and make a gain on that sale, a 'capital gain', then you may be liable to capital gains tax (CGT) on that gain. This will only happen with assets that usually increase in value. It should be noted that capital gains tax does not apply on death, although there may be a liability for inheritance tax instead.

> **? Ponder point**
>
> Can you think of a number of different assets that might increase in value?

Some assets may increase in value, for example property and land, antiques, jewellery, and shares. It is these types of asset that may be subject to capital gains tax. Many assets, cars in particular, actually decrease in value over time and with use.

Exemptions from capital gains tax

Certain assets are specifically exempt from CGT and these include a 'principal private residence' or main home, providing that it is where the individual concerned has been living. A taxpayer with two or more homes, which they occupy, may elect which property is to be their principal private residence for tax purposes. Married couples or civil partners can have one principal private residence between them. Second homes, holiday homes, or buy-to-let properties are not exempt from CGT. Cars however are specifically exempt from CGT, including vintage cars even though they may increase in value. Gilts, which are government bonds, and qualifying corporate bonds are specifically exempt from CGT.

 Ponder point

What effect do you think the principal private residence exemption from CGT is likely to have had on property prices in the UK?

Many people would argue that the principal private residence exemption in the UK has the effect of inflating house prices, when compared to other assets. The fact that there is no tax to pay on any gain that may be made on selling a home could encourage taxpayers to invest in their home, rather than other assets.

Another important exemption is the exemption for chattels when they are sold for less than £6,000. The term 'chattels' is defined as tangible movable property, meaning that the asset can be physically touched and that it is capable of being moved. In effect the term chattels is really referring to personal possessions. This personal possessions exemption removes many small disposals of assets from the CGT regime, thus simplifying CGT computations.

 Ponder point

Which of the assets you thought could increase in value would be classified as personal possessions?

Assets likely to increase in value that would be classified as personal possessions include jewellery, paintings, antiques, stamps, and fine wines, amongst others. If the item is sold for £6,000 or less it will be exempt from capital gains tax. Land and buildings are the main examples of assets that might increase in value but would not be classed as personal possessions. Shares are not classified as personal possessions either.

The CGT annual exemption

Each year a taxpayer can make a certain amount of capital gains without paying any CGT. This allowance is similar to the personal allowance for income tax purposes and this text assumes an indicative annual exemption of £12,000 when preparing a CGT computation.

The CGT computation

A gain for CGT purposes is worked out in the same way that a taxpayer would work out a gain if she wanted to know how much of a 'profit' she had made on selling an asset. It begins with the disposal value, which is usually the proceeds from selling the asset or how much was received from the sale. Then the cost of the asset is deducted from the proceeds to work out the gain. Any costs incurred when selling the asset, such as auctioneer's fees, should be deducted from the proceeds. Similarly any costs incurred when buying the asset, such as legal fees, should be added on to the cost. Any costs arising from improving the asset, but not the costs of maintaining it, can be deducted. If an asset is given away or sold at a price below the market price then the actual sales proceeds would be replaced by the market value of the asset on the date of disposal.

An example of a CGT computation is shown in Table 7.2.

Table 7.2 Example of a capital gains tax computation (Figures are for illustration only)

	£	£
Proceeds from selling a painting		100,000
Less: auctioneer's fee		10,000
Net proceeds		90,000
Cost	27,000	
Restoration fees	2,000	
Less: total cost		29,000
Capital gain		61,000
Less: annual exemption		12,000
Taxable capital gain		49,000

This computation follows a standard structure, beginning with the proceeds from disposing of the asset, deducting any costs of disposal, and comparing this to the cost of the asset itself together with any improvement costs. This allows the capital gain or loss to be calculated. Then the annual exemption is deducted to arrive at the amount of the taxable capital gain.

Indicative rates of capital gains tax

The rate at which a taxpayer pays capital gains tax depends on their other taxable income. If they are a basic rate taxpayer then the standard rate of CGT is 10% up to the limit of the remaining basic rate band and 20% on any gains falling above that limit. These rates are lower than the equivalent income tax rates. This text assumes that the limit of the basic rate band for income tax is £32,000.

Example 7.1

Capital gains tax computation

Taking the taxable capital gains figure of £49,000 from Table 7.2 and assuming the taxpayer has no other income or capital gains during the year, capital gains tax would be due as follows:

Amount of gain £	Tax rate	Capital gains tax due £
32,000	10%	3,200
49,000–32,000 = 17,000	20%	3,400
	Total capital gains tax due	6,600

 Key term

Probate value means the value of an asset at the date of inheritance and is equivalent to cost for an inherited asset in the CGT computation.

Case study—Tian (1)

Tian inherited a very unusual expanding octagonal antique table from her grandmother. The probate value was registered as £23,000. Tian used the table on special occasions for twenty years. At one point she spent £1,000 having the table French polished to enhance its value and she also spent £750 having a broken table leg repaired. She decided to sell the table when updating her home to achieve a more modern look. The table was auctioned in London and was bought by a specialist collector for £87,200. Tian had to pay an auctioneer's fee of 20% of the price.

Required:

Assuming Tian made no other gains in the year, calculate how much capital gains tax she would have to pay, assuming she is a higher rate taxpayer.

Shares and CGT

Special rules are needed for calculating the capital gain on the sale of shares, because a taxpayer may have been trading in those shares for several years and it can be difficult to establish the exact cost of the shares sold. For most disposals a weighted average cost can be taken, as illustrated in Example 7.2. The weighted average cost of the shares is calculated by dividing the total cost of all the shares purchased by the total number of shares purchased, to arrive at an average cost per share, to be used in the capital gains tax calculation.

Example 7.2

A taxpayer has been buying shares in a retail firm, Owen plc. She bought shares over several years and the purchases are set out in Table 7.3:

Table 7.3 Shares purchased in Owen plc

Timing of purchase	Number of shares	Price per share £	Cost £
Five years ago	200	3	600
Three years ago	1,000	2.50	2,500
Last year	2,000	3.25	6,500
Total	3,200		9,600

She is thinking of selling half of the shares because the price has risen to £4 per share and the money is needed for a new venture. The capital gain that she would make from the disposal, ignoring any dealing costs, can be computed.

		£
Proceeds	(1,600 × £4 per share)	6,400
Less: weighted average cost of the shares	1,600 shares × (9,600/3,200) = 1,600 × £3 per share	4,800
Capital gain		1,600

Example 7.2 demonstrates that as shares are bought over the years, the number of shares and the value of the shares are pooled. When the taxpayer decides to sell some shares, it is not necessary to match up the purchase and sale of shares exactly. Instead, a weighted average cost of the accumulated share pool is taken, to work out the cost of the shares sold.

For more complex buying and selling deals, particularly where the shares are bought and sold within short periods of time, more complex rules apply.

ISAs (individual savings accounts)

Gains arising on investments held in an ISA are free from capital gains tax. Each tax year every individual who is UK resident and over the age of sixteen can invest a certain amount in ISAs, as discussed in more detail in Chapter 6.

The limits on ISA investment tend to increase with each new tax year and you will find the current year's allowances on the government website; indicative amounts are in Table 7.4.

Table 7.4 Indicative annual ISA allowances

Individual aged 16 to 18 years of age	Cash ISA only Limit of £20,000
Individual aged over 18 years	Cash and/or shares ISA—limit of £20,000

Using these indicative allowances, the overall maximum that can be invested in ISAs in a tax year would be £20,000. Individuals can choose to put the whole £20,000 into a shares ISA or the whole 20,000 into a cash ISA or to split £20,000 between a cash ISA and a shares ISA as they choose.

This allows taxpayers to shelter dividend income and capital gains within an ISA, up to the specified investment limits. Many taxpayers do not have to pay CGT, due to the significant annual exemption, but nevertheless the availability of an ISA to shelter further potential capital gains can be useful, particularly for higher rate taxpayers who are also able to avoid any higher rate tax on dividend income. If shares are held within an ISA it does, however, mean that any capital losses are not available to be set against capital gains.

CGT gains and losses

In any one year a taxpayer with an assortment of gains and losses on the disposal of assets would calculate the gain or loss on each individual asset disposal. Having done that, the gains and losses are added together to give the overall position for the year. If losses exceed the total gains, then the net loss is carried forward to offset against future gains. If there are net gains for the year, the annual exemption is deducted from the net gains to give the taxable gains and the CGT liability is calculated on the taxable gains.

Example 7.3

During one tax year a basic rate taxpayer makes two capital gains of £15,000 and £11,000 and a capital loss of £3,000. If his taxable income is £14,000, the capital gains tax liability would be calculated as shown in Table 7.5:

Table 7.5 Capital gains tax computation

	Total gains/losses £
Capital gain	15,000
Capital gain	11,000
Capital loss	(3,000)
Net capital gains	23,000

Less: annual exemption	12,000
Taxable gains	11,000
Capital gains tax @ 10%	1,100

Table 7.5 shows how all the gains and losses that have occurred during the year are added to-gether, the annual exemption is deducted, and the CGT payable is worked out at the appropri-ate rate. This taxpayer had more than £11,000 remaining in his basic rate band and hence the gains are taxed at 10%.

Case study—Tian (2)

The year after Tian sold her antique table she decided to dispose of several other assets in order to raise more capital to invest in the family business. She was pessimistic about the prospects for the stock market, so she sold some shares that she had bought five years earlier. The shares had originally cost £1,500 and she had paid a dealing fee of £12 on acquisition of the shares. She sold the shares for £750 and paid a £10 dealing fee.

Tian sold some fine wines, which she had bought as an Investment some years ago. She had invested £3,000 in the wine and she sold it for £5,000. She also sold an antique emerald necklace for £20,000, which had originally cost her £11,000. Finally, Tian sold all the units that she held in a unit trust fund for £37,000, having invested £10,000 in the fund originally.

Required:

a) Calculate the gain or loss on each asset disposal that is chargeable to CGT.

b) Add together all the taxable gains and losses for the year and work out how much capital gains tax Tian has to pay, assuming that she has £10,000 remaining in her basic rate band.

Tax planning for capital gains tax

There is scope for a reasonable amount of straightforward tax planning in order to minimize an individual's liability for CGT, because a person usually has control over the timing of any disposals of assets and every year a taxpayer is entitled to make tax-free gains up to the amount of the annual exemption. Furthermore, transfers of assets between a married couple or civil partners can be made between the couple without incurring any gains. The value at which an asset is transferred between spouses is de-scribed as 'no gain/no loss' and is often equivalent to the cost of the asset. ISAs provide a tax-free wrapper for shareholdings, up to the specified limits.

> **? Ponder point**
>
> Can you think of any steps a husband and wife could take to minimize their CGT liability?

There are four straightforward steps that a couple can take to minimize any CGT liabilities:

- The disposal of assets standing at a profit can be carefully timed so that they fall into different tax years in order to make full use of each year's annual exemption.
- Where an asset is likely to make a loss then careful timing of any disposal can ensure that such a loss reduces the taxable amount of any gains, because losses can be deducted from gains.
- Transfers between husband and wife or civil partners take place at a no gain/no loss valuation, so assets can be transferred between a couple, prior to a subsequent disposal, to ensure that both tax-free annual exemptions can be utilized.
- Shareholdings can be held within an ISA so that no CGT liability will arise from any capital gain on disposal, although this has the drawback that any capital losses are not available to be set against capital gains.

Example 7.4

A couple in a civil partnership have jointly owned a holiday home for ten years that they are about to sell. The property sale will make a gain of £20,000 for each partner. One of the partners has some shares that he is considering selling that are likely to make a loss on disposal of £15,000. He also has an antique chair that he would like to put into an upcoming auction. The chair is likely to make a gain of £13,000. In addition, he has a painting that he would like to dispose of quickly that may make a gain of £10,000.

The couple could minimize their CGT liability by disposing of the property in the same year that the shares are sold at a loss. The loss could be set against the capital gain on the holiday home, reducing or extinguishing the CGT liability for one partner. The benefit of not holding the shares in an ISA is that the loss on disposal can be offset against the gains. This is not possible where shares are held within an ISA.

If possible, the couple should wait until the following tax year to dispose of the other two assets. One asset should be transferred between the partners, so that on disposal of the assets both annual exemptions can be utilized. In this way only a very small amount of CGT would be payable.

Case study—Tian (3)

Required:

Tian is married to Brian. Identify any simple tax planning steps that Tian could have taken to reduce the capital gains tax liability on her disposals in case study Tian (2).

Reliefs from CGT

There are several important reliefs from CGT available to taxpayers who are in business, such as rollover relief. This allows a business to sell an asset and reinvest the proceeds into a new asset without incurring a CGT liability at that time. The tax is rolled over until such time as there is a subsequent disposal without reinvestment. Without this relief it would be difficult for businesses to reinvest and grow. Similarly, gift relief allows assets to be passed from one generation to the next. The most common example of gift relief would apply to passing on shares in a family business. Both parties to the transaction have to agree to defer the CGT. The very important entrepreneurs' relief reduces the CGT liability of a business owner who sells all or part of his business. For these taxpayers selling a business there is a special rate of 10% on gains, up to a lifetime limit of £10m of taxable capital gains.

Example 7.5

A successful entrepreneur, who is a higher rate taxpayer, sells some of the shares in his company and makes a very large capital gain of £7.5m. He has already used his annual exemption on selling some antiques. The CGT due on the sale of these shares would be £750,000 (10% of £7.5m).

The following year he sells some more shares in his company and makes a gain of £10m. His CGT in this year, assuming he has already used his annual exemption, is:

£2.5m at 10%	£250,000 (using up the rest of the lifetime limit)
£7.5m at 20%	£1,500,000 (as he is a higher rate taxpayer)
CGT payable on second disposal of shares	£1,750,000

Entrepreneurs' relief reduces the rate of CGT on disposal of a business to 10%, for gains of up to £10m. Once gains of £10m have been made, the rate of CGT reverts to 20% for higher rate taxpayers.

Administration of CGT

Taxpayers should report gains to HMRC using the income tax self-assessment form, but there is no need to report disposals of assets to HMRC providing that the total value of disposals in the year is less than four times the annual exemption and that the total of any gains made is less than the annual exemption. If a taxpayer wants to record a capital loss in order that it can be offset against future capital gains, then HMRC must be notified of this. If CGT is payable, it must usually be paid by 31 January following the end of the tax year in which the gain is made.

Inheritance tax

 Key term

Estate means the total value of an individual's goods and possessions when they die. It includes all property, investments, and anything of value after deducting any liabilities.

Residence for tax purposes means the country where a person lives which is generally recognized when they are physically present in a country for more than six months in a tax year.

Domicile is generally accepted to be the country you consider to be home, which is often, but not always, your country of birth.

Descendants refers to children or grandchildren of the deceased, including step, adopted, and foster children. The term 'direct line' is also used for direct descendants.

Main residence means the family home, not a holiday home or second home.

Inheritance tax is a tax that usually becomes payable on death. The name suggests that the tax might be paid by a person receiving an inheritance from an estate but actually, in most cases, the tax is paid out of the deceased's estate, before any distributions can be made. There have been taxes on death in the UK for many years, often described as death or estate duties.

Inheritance tax applies to the worldwide assets of an individual who is domiciled in the UK. This applies even if the person is not resident in the UK for income tax purposes. If the individual is not domiciled in the UK, then inheritance tax is only charged on assets which are located in the UK.

It is possible to have moved away from the UK, to Spain for example, but still be domiciled in the UK for tax purposes. Keeping a home and family in the UK, or just keeping links with the UK, would imply a UK domicile for tax purposes. Equally it is possible to be resident in the UK for tax purposes, yet not domiciled here. These individuals are often referred to as 'non-doms'.

There is an exemption for inheritance tax purposes known as the nil rate band. When an individual who is domiciled in the UK dies, the value of their worldwide goods and possessions must be established. If this comes to more than the nil rate band then inheritance tax has to be paid at 40% on the value of the estate in excess of the nil rate band. Many houses, particularly in London, are now worth more than the nil rate band and this has prompted the government to introduce an extension known as the main residence nil rate band, which will be fully in place by 2020/21.

Table 7.6 Indicative rates for inheritance tax

	Band	Inheritance tax rate %
Nil rate	0 to £325,000	0
Main residence nil rate band	Next £175,000	0
	Remainder of estate	40

With a married couple or civil partnership, if everything is left to the husband, wife, or partner then no inheritance tax is due on the first death, because any transfers between spouses or civil partners are exempt from inheritance tax. On the second death, both nil rate bands can be added together to allow £650,000 to be passed on tax-free to the next generation, or whoever benefits under the will.

When the estate includes a main residence or family home that is passed on to direct descendants, then the nil rate band will be expanded by a further £175,000. In effect, most couples who pass on a home to their descendants will be able to leave an estate of £1 million, 2 × (£325,000 + 175,000) without suffering inheritance tax. However, the legislation is rather complex in order to prevent abuse of the main residence nil rate band. There is a tapered reduction of the main residence band where an estate (before deducting any reliefs or exemptions) exceeds £2 million, and there can be no main residence nil rate band for estates worth more than £2.35 million. Thus, unlike the nil rate band, not all estates will be able to benefit from the main residence extension band.

Example 7.6

If a single person with no descendants died leaving an estate worth £500,000, the inheritance tax computation would be as set out in Table 7.7:

Table 7.7 Inheritance tax computation

	£
Value of estate	**500,000**
Less: nil rate band	325,000
Taxable estate	175,000
Inheritance tax due on estate at 40%	70,000

The nil rate band is deducted from the value of the estate and the taxable portion that remains is subject to inheritance tax at 40%. There can be no main residence nil rate band because the deceased had no descendants. Example 7.7 illustrates how an unused nil rate band and an unused main residence nil rate band can be added to that of a spouse or civil partner.

Example 7.7

A widower died leaving a house worth £700,000 and other assets amounting to £400,000. His wife had died two years previously, leaving everything to her husband. The widower made a will leaving the entire estate to be shared equally between his two children. The inheritance tax computation would be as set out in Table 7.8:

(continued...)

Table 7.8 Inheritance tax computation

	£
Value of estate (700,000 + 400,000)	1,100,000
Less: two nil rate bands	650,000
Less: two main residence nil rate bands	350,000
Taxable estate	100,000
Inheritance tax due on estate at 40%	40,000

Exemptions from inheritance tax

Table 7.9 Inheritance tax: exemptions

Amount	Exemption
£250 per person	Small gifts
£5,000 on marriage	Gift from parents
£3,000	Annual exemption amount

The potential liability of an estate to inheritance tax might encourage taxpayers to give away large amounts of their possessions or money towards the end of their life, in order to prevent significant amounts of inheritance tax being paid on the value of their estate, by reducing the value of the estate to the amount of the available nil rate band. However, a general principle of inheritance tax is that any gifts made by the taxpayer before death are deemed to reduce the nil rate band.

There is a major exemption to this principle, which is that gifts and transfers amounting to normal expenditure out of income, providing they do not cause the donor's standard of living to fall, are exempt transfers and do not need to be deducted from the nil rate band. There are also some specific exemptions, including small gifts of up to £250 to individuals, which qualify as exempt transfers. The legislation also allows for reasonable gifts in relation to marriage or civil partnership. For example, parents of the bride or groom can give £5,000 each. Furthermore, transfers of up to £3,000 per year for any reason are also exempt. These exemptions are set against any gifts made during the year, in chronological order. If the annual exemption is not used in any particular year then it can be carried forward for one year, but no further than that. Political donations and gifts to charities are exempt transfers for inheritance tax purposes.

Example 7.8

A taxpayer made the following gifts during the year (listed chronologically below), having made no gifts during the previous year. None of the gifts could be considered to be normal expenditure out of income. Which of the gifts would be exempt from inheritance tax?

i.	Gift to friend	£200
ii.	Wedding gift to son	£7,000
iii.	Birthday gift to civil partner	£10,000
iv.	Donation to political party	£10,000
v.	Gift to daughter	£30,000

Solution

	Gift		Exempt amount
i	Gift to friend	Exempt, small gift	£200
ii	Wedding gift to son	£5,000 exempt, £2,000 covered by annual exemption	£7,000
iii	Birthday gift to civil partner	Exempt altogether, transfer between partners	£10,000
iv	Donation to political party	Exempt altogether, political donation	£10,000
v	Gift to daughter	£1,000 from current annual exemption, £3,000 from previous annual exemption, leaving £26,000 potentially liable to inheritance tax	£4,000

Potentially exempt transfers (PETs)

As previously mentioned, a general principle of inheritance tax is that any recent gifts made by a taxpayer before death reduce the amount of the nil rate band and are not tax effective.

The inheritance tax legislation includes some special rules on gifts made within seven years of death, which allows a limited tax deduction for such gifts. Any such gifts are known as potentially exempt transfers or PETs and when a taxpayer dies any PETs made within seven years of death should be deducted from the nil rate band, effectively using up a proportion of the nil rate band. These gifts are subject to tax on a sliding scale, depending on how long ago the gifts were made. Gifts made more than seven years before death do not reduce the amount of the nil rate band.

 Ponder point

If you were a wealthy taxpayer do you think you might be inclined to give away your money and possessions as the end of your life became near?

Attitudes to passing on wealth vary enormously. Some people choose to give away large amounts of their estate to prevent more than necessary going to 'the taxman'. Others choose to hold onto their wealth in case of need and do not worry about the tax consequences.

When a taxpayer dies, the nil rate band is first applied to any gifts made during the last seven years. Where inheritance tax is due on such gifts on the death of a donor, it is payable by the recipient. If the gifts were made during the last three years before death, then there is no reduction in the inheritance tax due. If the gifts were made more than three years before death there is a reduction in the tax payable by the recipient, known as taper relief, as set out in Table 7.10:

Table 7.10 Inheritance tax: taper relief (tax reduction) on PETs

Period between transfer and death	Tax reduction
3–4 years	20% reduction in tax due on gift
4–5 years	40% reduction in tax due on gift
5–6 years	60% reduction in tax due on gift
6–7 years	80% reduction in tax due on gift
More than 7 years	100% reduction in tax due (in other words no tax is payable at all on a gift if the gift was made more than 7 years earlier)

Example 7.9

If a UK taxpayer died leaving an estate worth £400,000 consisting of investments and cash, how much inheritance tax would be due, assuming that he had given away £100,000 to his son, 5.5 years before he died? (He regularly used his annual exemption of £3,000 on other gifts.)

The simplified inheritance tax computation would be as set out in Table 7.11:

Table 7.11 Inheritance tax computation

	£
Nil rate band	325,000
Less: PET made 5.5 years previously	100,000
Remaining nil rate band	225,000
Value of estate	400,000
Less: nil rate band	225,000
Taxable estate	175,000
Inheritance tax on estate at 40%	70,000
Less: taper relief on PET	
100,000 @ 40% × 60% taper relief	24,000
Inheritance tax due	46,000
(£16,000 payable by the son on the gift and £30,000 payable by the estate)	

First of all it is necessary to reduce the nil rate band by the amount of any transfers that do not qualify for exemption. Tax is then calculated at 40% on the taxable value of the estate, but taper relief is available at an increasing rate depending on how long ago any gifts were made. In this example, because the gift was made 5.5 years ago, the inheritance tax on that particular gift is reduced by 60%. Without the taper relief the tax due on the gift would be £40,000 (£100,000 × 40%). The taper relief reduces the tax by £24,000 (£40,000 × 60%) so the inheritance tax due on the gift following the death of the donor is £16,000. If the gift was made more than seven years before death it would not reduce the nil rate band and there would be no tax to pay.

Case study—Tian (4)

Tian's unmarried uncle died and left an estate comprising a house worth £400,000, bank deposits of £240,000, and a small share portfolio held in an ISA account valued at £30,000. The will distributed the estate amongst the family and Tian is due to inherit £20,000. Eight years previously the uncle had given away £80,000, distributed equally amongst his family and then 3.5 years ago he had given them a further £90,000. He regularly used his £3,000 annual exemption on other gifts. He had no children.

Required:
What is the inheritance tax due on the estate of Tian's uncle?

? Ponder point

Can you foresee any difficulties where taxpayers focus on avoiding inheritance tax and decide to reduce their assets to close to the amount of the nil rate band at least seven years before they die?

Because most of us are unable to predict how long we will live or exactly what our income needs will be, it is difficult for most taxpayers to make significant gifts seven years or more before our deaths. If we give away too much we may end up without enough to live on and if we give away too little then our estate will still be liable to inheritance tax.

Example 7.10

A UK taxpayer aged seventy is thinking about inheritance tax planning. The taxpayer has a house worth £500,000 that she plans to leave to her daughter and other more liquid assets including a share portfolio and bonds worth £500,000. Each year she spends most of her pension and investment income and does not anticipate that she will need to spend any capital within the next few years. She works out that if she lives for a further ten years and takes no action with regard to inheritance tax, then the inheritance tax bill for the estate on her death will be £500,000 @ 40%, which amounts to £200,000. She decides to take the following action:

- Immediate gifts to two grandchildren of £50,000 each, which could be PETs
- Further gift to one grandson on his marriage of £2,500 which would be exempt
- Annual gifts of £3,000 in cash to her daughter for ten years which would be exempt

These gifts could be made from her bonds and would reduce the value of her estate by the total amount of the gifts of £132,500. If she lived for ten years after the immediate gifts, and the value of her remaining assets remained unchanged, the inheritance tax computation would be as set out in Table 7.12:

Table 7.12 Inheritance tax computation

	£
Value of estate on death (£1,000,000 less gifts as above of £132,500)	867,500
Less: nil rate band	325,000
Less: main residence nil rate band	175,000
Taxable estate	367,500
Inheritance tax due on estate at 40%	147,000

How much inheritance tax has been saved as a result of the gifts made?
The tax saved by making the gifts is the difference between her original estimate of inheritance tax of £200,000 and the eventual inheritance tax bill of £147,000. By making gifts some time before death and using up her annual exemption she has reduced the inheritance tax liability by £53,000.

Example 7.10 illustrates how inheritance tax can be reduced through a combination of gifts made more than seven years before death and use of the annual exemption of £3,000.

Gifts with reservation

A taxpayer interested in reducing any inheritance tax due on their estate might consider giving away a significant asset or part of an estate whilst retaining the right to use that asset. For example, a retired couple might decide to pass ownership of their house to their children, but continue to live in the property, without paying any rent to the new owners. In theory this might satisfy the seven-year PET rule, assuming the couple live for many years, whilst allowing them to continue to use the asset. In practice anti-avoidance legislation has been introduced, dealing with 'pre-owned assets' which means that this type of transfer is not effective for inheritance tax purposes, unless a commercial rent is paid to the new owner. If this does not happen, it is as if the gift has not taken place and the whole value of the house must be added back to the estate on death.

 Ponder point

Do you think individuals should worry about inheritance tax, as by definition, if inheritance tax is due, then the taxpayer is no longer around to worry about it?

Inheritance tax or estate planning is big business for accountants, lawyers, and financial planners. It may be that it is difficult for taxpayers to accept that a significant proportion of their hard-earned wealth, most of which has already been taxed at least once, may go into tax revenues after their death. Other taxpayers are more pragmatic and take the view that inheritance tax is not something to worry over and that, anyway, the government needs the income raised from taxes in order to fund its expenditure.

Conclusion

Capital gains tax (CGT) is generally due when assets are disposed of for more than they cost. It was introduced in the UK many years ago to bring a perceived element of fairness into the tax system. Without some form of CGT, there would be no taxation of capital gains but significant taxation of income, which many people would consider to be unfair. ISAs, the annual exemption, the chattels exemption, and the principal private residence exemption are all important in reducing the liability for CGT for the majority of the population.

The principal private residence exemption means that there is no tax to pay if a gain is made on disposing of your home. The annual exemption means that for most taxpayers capital gains tax can easily be reduced or even avoided altogether through careful timing of the disposal of assets.

Inheritance tax is mainly payable on an estate following the death of an individual. There is a significant nil rate band that will be extended by the main residence nil rate band. Given the increasing value of property within regions of the UK there will still be families who incur an inheritance tax liability on the death of a homeowner. The liability for inheritance tax can be reduced or avoided altogether by distributing assets more than seven years before death occurs. Most people are unable to predict their demise quite so accurately and many people choose to hold on to their assets as long as they live, often for very valid reasons. There are other important reliefs within the inheritance tax legislation, including the annual exemption of £3,000, gifts on marriage, gifts on other occasions, and regular gifts out of income.

 ## Useful websites

Details of the current tax rates and allowances:
http://www.gov.uk
Details of the main residence nil rate band can be found at:
https://www.gov.uk/government/publications/inheritance-tax-main-residence-nil-rate-band-and-the-existing-nil-rate-band/inheritance-tax-main-residence-nil-rate-band-and-the-existing-nil-rate-band

 ## References

HMRC (Her Majesty's Revenue and Customs) (2015) *Statistics*. Available at: https://www.gov.uk/government/uploads/system/uploads/attachment_data/file/493165/CGT_National_Statistics_2015.pdf (accessed 9.2.2016)

 ## Practice Questions

Question 1 Quick Questions TRUE OR FALSE?

7.1   All disposals of assets are subject to capital gains tax.

7.2   Shares sold for less than £6,000 would be covered by the personal possessions exemption.

7.3   Transfers of assets between husband and wife are made at 'market price'.

7.4   The rate at which CGT becomes payable is dependent upon the individual's taxable income for income tax purposes.

7.5   Costs incurred in improving an asset can be deducted in a CGT computation.

7.6   The nil rate band together with the main residence exemption will always allow a couple to pass on a property worth up to £1million to their descendants, free of inheritance tax.

7.7   Inheritance tax can be avoided by giving away your assets two years before death.

7.8   If a taxpayer does not use up all of their nil rate band, through distributing assets on death, the unused portion of the nil rate band can be passed on to a spouse or civil partner.

7.9   Gifts of up to £10,000 each year are exempt from inheritance tax.

7.10   Potentially exempt transfers made up to seven years before death reduce the amount of the taxpayer's nil rate band for inheritance tax.

Question 2 Fred

Fred, a higher rate taxpayer, is considering selling some assets as follows:

a) A valuable stamp collection jointly owned with his wife. The collection cost £150,000 ten years ago and buying costs were £2,000. The selling price is estimated at £295,000 and selling costs would be £5,000. Three years ago they spent £10,000 adding a small first day covers section to the collection. (Note: gains on jointly held assets should be shared between taxpayers, equally in this case.)

b) An antique chair which cost £2,500 two years ago and is now worth £4,000. Auctioneer's fee on sale would be 20%.

c) 20,000 shares in Simeone plc which had been bought five years ago for £30,000. Fees for the purchase were £250. The selling price is estimated to be £50,000 with fees of £1,500.

d) A painting for which he paid £20,000 seven years ago. The artist has fallen out of fashion and the estimated guide price for sale is £10,000, with auctioneer's fee of 20%.

Required:

a) **Estimate Fred's CGT liability, assuming he is a higher rate taxpayer.**

b) **Advise him of some tax planning steps that would reduce his liability.**

Question 3 Maurice

Maurice died, having made the following lifetime gifts:

A gift to his daughter, ten years earlier of £40,000, and a gift to his son, 3.5 years previously, on his son's marriage, of £50,000. The value of the estate on death was £575,000, which was all left to his two children. The estate consisted of a main residence worth £300,000 and other assets of £275,000. He had made no other significant gifts during his lifetime.

Required:

Calculate the inheritance tax due on Maurice's estate.

*Question 4 Jack and Francesca

Jack and Francesca, a married couple, have jointly owned a holiday home in Cornwall for five years. The property cost them £140,000 and is now valued at £200,000. Over the years they have spent £8,000 putting in central heating, as there was no central heating installed when they bought the property. They had to pay solicitor's fees of £1,200 when the property was bought. They have spent £2,000 on having the roof repaired. Selling costs are estimated to be £6,000. (Note: gains on jointly held assets should be shared between taxpayers, equally in this case.)

Jack has taxable income of £7,000 for the year and Francesca has taxable income of £40,000.

Required:

Calculate the CGT due for Francesca and Jack.

* Question 5 Cecilia and Simon

Cecilia was married to Simon and they lived together in the jointly owned family home. Cecilia died leaving the rest of her estate, consisting of cash and investments valued at £350,000, to her three sons. Simon regularly used his annual exemption of £3,000 on gifts to their family. One year after his wife's death, Simon gave £100,000 to each of their three sons. He died 5.5 years after making the gifts, leaving the family home worth £600,000 and assets of £200,000, to be shared equally between their three sons.

Required:

Calculate the inheritance tax due on Simon's estate.

Visit the Online Resource Centre that accompanies this book for additional material:
www.oxfordtextbooks.co.uk/orc/king_carey2e/

8   Investing for the future

⊙ Learning Objectives

After studying this chapter, you should understand:

- The range of investment classes available
- The relationship between risk and return
- How to measure the return earned on shares
- The benefits of collective investments
- The main types of collective investment available
- Tax effective ways of investing

Introduction

Many individuals choose to make investments in shares and bonds and many more will be investors without necessarily being aware that they are. Pension funds and insurance companies, known as institutional investors, are major holders of investments in the UK. They typically hold a range of investments including shares, bonds, gilts, and commercial property. Many people will have an interest in investments that are either directly held by them or indirectly held on their behalf by these institutional investors. This chapter will focus on investments held in shares, bonds, and gilts either individually or as part of a collective investment.

There are some employers who run schemes that encourage employees to become shareholders in their company and employees taking advantage of the scheme may become shareholders.

Looking back over the last fifty years in the UK, the Barclays *Equity Gilt Study*, as quoted by the This is Money website, shows that the returns earned from investing in shares have significantly outperformed the returns earned by savers using bank deposits. The financial crisis of 2007 and continuing uncertainty in European and world economies has led to volatile returns from equities over the decade to 2015. This serves to highlight the potential risk of investing which has always been a fundamental consideration in deciding on whether to invest, where to invest, how much to invest, and how long to hold investments for.

There is an abundance of terminology connected to investing and understanding some of the key terms is essential to being able to ask the right questions. Recognizing the risks and potential returns of different types of investment empowers individuals to understand what to look out for in making investments and ultimately to make informed decisions.

Background

Investing and saving are similar activities in that both involve people putting spare funds in a savings account or in an investment, in the hope of receiving a return on those funds. Where money is put into savings, often in a bank or building society account, the amount deposited, known as the capital, is rarely at risk of being depleted or lost, except as a result of the effects of inflation. (Example 8.2 demonstrates this risk to capital.) Where money is put into investments, the capital will be at risk of falling in value, or being lost completely. The nature of the investment will determine its riskiness, with some investments having very low risk, some being extremely risky, and there is a whole range of investments carrying risks in between those two extremes.

Risk and return

The general principle that can be applied to investing is that the greater the risk attached to a product, the greater the potential return investors in that product expect to receive. Investors in products that carry a low risk will expect to receive relatively low rates of return. Investors in high risk products will demand much higher rates of return to compensate them for accepting that the actual rate of return is less predictable and the capital they have invested is more likely to fall in value when placed in that investment. Figure 8.1 shows a graph of the relationship between risk and expected return.

There are many risks associated with investing but the most significant one is the risk that the capital invested will fall in value or be lost completely.

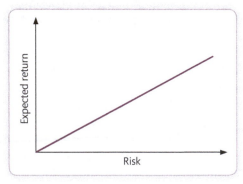

Figure 8.1 Graph of risk vs expected return

> ## Example 8.1
>
> If an individual invests in a high risk investment, he will expect to be rewarded with a higher rate of return and, in doing so, will accept that he is relatively more likely to suffer a loss of the capital he invested.

Whilst investors and savers tend to associate risk with losing some or all of their original capital invested, they should also be aware of the risk to capital posed by investing or saving in poorly performing products. For the capital invested to maintain its real value, the return generated needs to at least match any change in the purchasing power of that capital as a result of inflation. If it does not do so for a year or two, it may not have a significant impact on the capital, but if the return generated on a savings or investment product is less than inflation for a few years, the real value of the capital invested will fall. The risk of returns not keeping pace with inflation applies equally to savings or investments.

> ## Example 8.2
>
> A person places £10,000 in an investment that pays interest at the rate of 2.5% per annum, and he leaves the capital and interest earned in the account for ten years. If inflation ran at an average rate of 4% per annum over that ten-year period, the investor would need to have £14,800 (£10,000 $\times 1.04^{10}$) in the account at the end of that time in order to have the same purchasing power as he had at the outset. Given that the return is 2.5% per annum and it is always reinvested, the investment would grow to £12,800 (£10,000 $\times 1.025^{10}$) over ten years. The investor would therefore be £2,000 worse off at the end of ten years because the return on the investment would have failed to keep pace with inflation.

Attitudes to risk

Different investors will have different attitudes to risk. Some individuals are prepared to accept much higher levels of risk than others, perhaps due to personal circumstances, personality, or age. As people get older, they tend to become more risk averse as they have more financial responsibilities to consider and are aware of the need to protect their capital for retirement. Some people will be happier to accept higher levels of risk knowing that their returns will be less certain but the range of possible returns is much greater.

Before any potential investor makes investment choices, they should consider their personal attitude to risk and the extent to which they are prepared to accept risk in order to seek out higher returns.

Investments can be categorized into asset classes according to the characteristics that they exhibit and this chapter considers two fundamental types of asset classes:

- Shares, also known as equities
- Bonds

Cash and deposits are discussed in Chapter 6.

Shares

 Key terms

An **asset class** describes a group of investments that exhibit similar characteristics.
Shares give their holders a share of the ownership of the company in which they are held.
Shares are often referred to as equities.

When you own shares in a company, you effectively own a part of the company. As one of the owners of the company you will, in theory at least, share in its success or failure. Shareholders are entitled to attend and vote at the company's annual general meeting, and hence have a means of letting their opinions be known. The most common type of share is an ordinary share and this will be the type of share this chapter focuses on.

Shareholders hope to be rewarded for making their investment in shares by:

- receipt of a dividend, and/or
- an increase in the value of their shares.

 Key term

Dividends may be paid to shareholders in a company. They are paid from company profits to reward shareholders for investing in the company.

A dividend is an amount paid by a company to its shareholders based on the profits the company has made. Companies do not have to pay dividends and, conversely, they can choose to pay a dividend in a year when a loss has been made assuming they have reserves available. Many large companies aim to pay a regular dividend that increases year on year.

Listed and unlisted companies

 Key term

A **stock exchange** is a market where investments, principally company shares, can be bought and sold.

When companies are first formed, the original shareholders are often drawn from the business founders and their friends and family. Once companies reach a certain size, they may wish to raise more external finance. Ultimately, at a certain size, they may decide to seek a listing on a stock exchange in order to enable them to access a much wider pool of potential investors. These companies are described as listed and all other companies are unlisted.

 Key term

Listed shares are shares in companies that are traded on a stock exchange. The price of the shares will be publicly available on websites and in newspapers.

Once shares are listed, this means that investors and potential investors can buy and sell their shares relatively easily. They can find the share price in daily newspapers and online. The share price represents the current value of each share; that is, the amount at which it can be bought or sold.

It is usually only larger companies that obtain a stock exchange listing as it is expensive to do so and greatly increases the pressure on management caused by the extra regulation that goes with a listing. The vast majority of companies in the UK are unlisted but it is very unlikely, unless you become personally involved in a company, that you would consider investing in anything other than listed investments. This chapter will focus on listed investments.

Share prices

When a company is listed, its share price is publicly available. Share prices, in theory, reflect the future profitability of the company as far as those trading in the shares can ascertain. That is why when companies announce unexpectedly good or poor results or significant news, the company's share price often shows a significant increase or decrease.

There are, however, many other factors that impact on share prices that are outside the control of the business. General share price movements occur when economic circumstances change, whether the change is specific to a particular sector, the economy as a whole, or as a result of international trends. Market optimism or pessimism can change quickly and it is extremely difficult to predict when share price increases or decreases will occur.

Investing in the shares of one or a few companies is very risky. In order to reduce risk, individuals wishing to invest in shares are advised to invest in a wide range of companies so that if one or two investments prove to be poor choices, this is likely to be balanced by some investments in the portfolio performing better. This strategy is known as diversification. Choosing a diversified portfolio of investments would be very time-consuming and only possible for investors with very significant sums to invest. A common way of arriving at an instant portfolio is for individuals to invest in a collective investment and, in so doing, achieve a portfolio which often includes shares in many companies and other investment classes.

 Key terms

Diversification is achieved by investing in a wide range of investments in order to reduce the risk posed by making a small number of investments that then perform poorly.
A **portfolio** is a variety of investments held together.

Measuring return on shares

Shareholders and potential shareholders will be interested in how company shares are performing and certain key information is available in the financial pages of most newspapers and on a range of websites; these measures are commonly discussed when company results are announced.

Dividend per share

Dividend per share represents the amount of dividend that a company pays each year to its shareholders and it is quoted in pence per share. This measures the income that shareholders would actually receive during a year but takes no account of any increase in the value of their shares.

Dividend yield

 Key term

Dividend yield measures the rate of return earned from dividends received by shareholders, by comparing the annual dividends received per share with the market price of that share.

$$\text{Dividend yield}\,(\%) = \frac{\text{Annual dividends received per share} \times 100}{\text{Market price per share}}$$

Dividend yield measures the rate of return that shareholders are receiving by way of a dividend, based not on the amount the shareholder paid for their shares when they bought them, but based on their current market value. This is a useful measure as clearly the shareholder has the choice to sell or keep their shares and, if they sell them, they will receive their current value. As the share price fluctuates, so too will the dividend yield. Comparing dividend yields between companies is a useful means of comparing the relative return from dividends paid.

Example 8.3

A shareholder has owned shares in two companies, X plc and Y plc, for one year and Table 8.1 provides information on these two investments.

Table 8.1 Share price and dividends paid: X plc and Y plc

Company	Shares purchased	Share price at end of year	Dividends paid in year
X plc	200 shares at £3.40 per share	£3.60	4 pence per share
Y plc	320 shares at £1.15 per share	£1.00	4 pence per share

Although both X plc and Y plc paid the same dividends per share, the dividend yields are very different:

Dividend yield for X plc = 4/360 × 100 = 1.1%
Dividend yield for Y plc = 4/100 × 100 = 4.0%

The actual dividends paid per share does not reflect the true return that shareholders are earning, whereas the dividend yield clearly shows that the return, by way of dividend, earned on the shares is much greater for Y plc than for X plc.

Dividends are one of the ways in which shareholders are rewarded for investing in a company but dividends and dividend yield take no account of any benefit the investor may have had as a result of an increase in the share price, or any loss they may have suffered as a result of the share price falling. This overall return is best measured using total shareholder return.

Total shareholder return

 Key term

Total shareholder return measures the total return received by shareholders by combining the dividends received with any capital gain or loss made, expressed as a percentage of the share price at the beginning of the year.

$$\text{Total shareholder return for year (\%)} = \frac{\text{Dividend per share} + \text{increase in share price}}{\text{Share price at start of year}} \times 100$$

When total shareholder return is measured for a year, then the total dividends received during the year are included plus the total increase in the share price over the course of the year. Any decrease in the share price would be deducted.

Example 8.4

Consider the details of the shareholder from Example 8.3: he has owned shares in two companies, X plc and Y plc, for one year and Table 8.2 provides information regarding these two investments.

Table 8.2 Share price, dividends paid, and dividend yield: X plc and Y plc

Company	Shares purchased	Share price at end of year	Dividends paid in year	Dividend yield
X plc	200 shares at £3.40 per share	£3.60	4p per share	1.1%
Y plc	320 shares at £1.15 per share	£1.00	4p per share	4.0%

$$\text{Total shareholder return (X plc)} = \frac{(4+20)}{340} \times 100 = 7.1\%$$

$$\text{Total shareholder return (Y plc)} = \frac{(4-15)}{115} \times 100 = -9.6\%$$

Now that the share price movement is taken into account, the fall in Y plc's share price has led to the total shareholder return showing a negative return of 9.6%. The investment in X plc however returned a healthy positive 7.1% return to the shareholder as a result of the increase in the share price and the dividend paid.

 Ponder point

If two companies have identical total shareholder returns of 10%, do you think it is likely to matter to a shareholder that one of the companies pays high dividends and the other pays no dividend?

In order to answer this point, one would need to know more about the shareholder. If the shareholder is reliant on receiving a regular income from investments held, then that shareholder would be unhappy at receiving no dividends from one of their investments. Even though that share has increased in value by 10% over the course of the year, the shareholder would have received no income from it.

On the other hand, if the shareholder is unconcerned about receiving income from shares during the year, then that shareholder should be equally happy with the return generated by both companies. (These remarks assume that the tax treatment of income and gains is identical.)

Earnings per share (eps)

 Key term

Earnings per share (eps) is a measure of the profit after tax generated by each share the company has in issue.

Earnings per share is a useful measure that shows how well a company is generating profits for its shareholders. It is a measure of the profit per share, regardless of the amount actually paid out as a dividend. Looking at the way that a company's earnings per share changes over time will indicate immediately whether the company is trading more or less profitably year by year. It is not meaningful to compare one company's earnings per share to that of another because shares in different companies can have very different market values.

A company's earnings per share figure is shown in their financial statements. It can be computed in various ways and the first figure quoted will usually be the basic eps. This measure is computed in the same way by all companies and is a good starting point for looking at the movement in a company's profits per share over a few years.

The reason that investors own shares is to gain a return on those shares and the share price is acknowledged as being closely tied to the company's expected future profitability. Hence shareholders and analysts closely review the eps measure as it forms the starting point for future forecasts.

The P/E ratio

 Key term

The **P/E ratio** measures market expectations for a company's future profitability. It is calculated by dividing the share price by the earnings per share.

The price/earnings ratio is usually known as the P/E ratio and it measures the relationship between the share price and the earnings per share.

$$P/E \ ratio = \frac{Price \ per \ share}{Earnings \ per \ share}$$

The resulting figure is known as the multiple.

The higher the P/E ratio the greater the market's expectations are for the earnings (profits) of that company to increase. Where there are two companies earning stable profits and operating in the same market sector with similar prospects, you would usually expect them to have similar P/E ratios.

Example 8.5

A listed company had earnings per share of 20 pence and the share price was £2.00 giving a P/E ratio of 200/20 = 10.

When economic indicators for the sector in which the company operated suddenly took a downturn, investors reacted in such a way that the share price fell to £1.60 causing the P/E to fall to 8 (160/20). There would have been no immediate effect on the company's declared profits, the fall in the P/E being caused by the market's reduced expectations for profit growth in the future.

Example 8.6

Two companies, A plc and B plc, both operate within the same sector and are of a similar size. Table 8.3 shows the data for both companies as at their last year end:

Table 8.3 Data on shares: A plc and B plc

	A plc	B plc
Earnings per share	30 pence	32 pence
Dividend per share	5 pence	15 pence
Share price	£2.10	£1.70

The P/E ratio and the dividend yield can be calculated and used to reveal more about the companies.

P/E ratio

$$P/E \ ratio(A \ plc) = \frac{210}{30} = 7$$
$$P/E \ ratio(B \ plc) = \frac{170}{32} = 5.3$$

The higher P/E ratio for A plc shows that the market expects stronger growth in profits for A plc than for B plc.

Dividend yield

$$\text{Dividend yield} = \frac{\text{Annual dividends received per share}}{\text{Market price per share}} \times 100$$

$$\text{Dividend yield (A plc)} = \frac{5}{210} \times 100 = 2.4\%$$

$$\text{Dividend yield (B plc)} = \frac{15}{170} \times 100 = 8.8\%$$

The dividend per share figure is much greater for B plc than A plc and this is reflected in the much higher dividend yield figure for B plc. Shareholders in B plc will have earned a much greater return on their shares by way of dividend during the last year.

 Ponder point

As a potential shareholder, would you choose to buy shares in A plc or B plc?

Before answering this Ponder point, you would want to receive more information about both companies. For example, what has happened to the share prices of both companies over the last year? Despite a large dividend yield, it is possible that total shareholder return may not be so attractive for B plc as for A plc. Potential shareholders should be very interested in all the figures and ratios but should be even more interested in the company management team, its products or services, the prospects for the sector in which it operates, and the economic conditions where the business trades. For an individual to carry out the level of research necessary would be very time-consuming and most people would not have the skills necessary to do it. As we will discover later in the chapter, it is possible to invest in managed collective investments where you effectively employ specialist investment managers to carry out that research and choose which investments to buy and sell.

Case study—Tian and Brian

Tian and her husband Brian, a couple both in their fifties, have purchased small shareholdings in three companies, over the last few years. They have been too busy running their own business to review the performance of these shares in recent years. Table 8.4 provides details for the shares they own.

(continued...)

Table 8.4 Tian and Brian: data for shares owned

Company	Share price–current	Share price–one year ago	Earnings per share	Dividends per share
Beech plc	£4.00	£3.90	24.7 pence	7 pence
Oak plc	£1.51	£1.60	19.8 pence	9 pence
Elm plc	£1.36	£1.28	11.0 pence	None

Required:

Prepare answers to the following issues that Tian and Brian would like to understand:

a) How each of the shares has performed over the last year by considering the dividend yields and total shareholder returns. Brian has read that 'average total shareholder return' is currently at 4.0% on listed shares and would like to see how the performance of their investments compares to this.

b) What the current P/E ratios reveals about the market's view of the future prospects for each company.

c) Whether they should sell those shares which have the lowest P/E ratio.

The financial pages

Information on listed shares is available from a range of websites and the financial pages of many newspapers. When using ratios provided by these sources, it is advisable to check the basis of the calculations. An example of typical information that might be available for listed shares is shown in Table 8.5.

Table 8.5 Typical listed share information

Company	Previous close	Day's range	52 week High	52 week Low	P/E
Groceries (retailer)	244.2	244–245	255.1	229.0	11.5
Yogajim (leisure)	67.0	66–67	69.6	15.3	28.1
Gelectric (utility)	342.7	340–343	357.7	273.1	8.1

KEY to headings

Previous close	The share price at the end of the previous day
Day's range	The movement in the share price over the previous day
52 week–High	The highest share price recorded over the last year
52 week–Low	The lowest share price recorded over the last year
P/E	The price/earnings ratio

The figures shown in Table 8.5 reveal information about the market's view of each of the companies.

All of the share prices have shown movement over the last year but Yogajim's share price has been the most variable as the market had clearly been concerned about its future prospects. The share price is currently near the top of its 52-week range and the P/E for Yogajim at 28.1 indicates that the market is expecting profit growth in future years from current levels. The high P/E may have arisen because Yogajim, having re-ported very low profits, is expected to show a recovery in its profitability in the future.

Groceries' share price has remained relatively stable over the last year indicating that it is probably a stable company generating reliable profits. Its moderate P/E would be further evidence of this stability.

Gelectric has a P/E ratio of 8.1 which is lower than for the other companies in the table. This may indicate that the market is expecting less growth in profits for this com-pany. A low P/E can arise because a company has reported particularly good profits and the market does not expect those profits to increase at a fast rate in future years. If Gelectric plc's profits have been stable, this may explain why the opportunity for the company to grow its profits in the future is seen as more limited than for companies that have made losses or low profits in recent years.

In addition to considering share prices and P/E ratios, most potential investors would also look closely at the level of dividends that the company has paid and the dividend yield.

Bonds

 Key term

Bonds are long-term loan contracts that can be issued by companies or by the government.

Bonds are long-term loan contracts issued by companies, and other institutions, that usually pay a fixed rate of interest on the amount borrowed. The interest paid on bonds is often known as the coupon. There are many investments that describe themselves as bonds that are not bonds in this sense: for example, premium bonds, insurance bonds, investment bonds. Corporate bonds are bonds issued by companies and government bonds, known as gilts, are bonds issued by the UK government.

Bonds have a nominal value, also known as the face value, which is the base value on which the interest is calculated. When a bond has to be repaid, on its maturity date, the nominal value is repaid. Throughout the bond's life the interest is usually paid half-yearly.

 Key term

Nominal value, also known as face value, is the base value of an investment and it remains fixed whilst the market value of the investment is likely to vary over time. When investments are first issued, they are often issued at nominal value.

Example 8.7

A company issues a ten-year bond that pays interest at 7% per annum, payable half-yearly. Any bondholder buying £100 nominal value of the bonds, would receive £7 interest each year, in two payments of £3.50 each. If the investor keeps the bonds for ten years, he will receive the initial capital of £100 back at that time.

Bonds are considered to be lower risk investments than shares because the return on bonds is usually more predictable and is more likely to be paid. The interest payable on bonds has to be paid to bondholders. This contrasts with dividends that do not have to be paid to shareholders. Before any dividends can be paid, the company must pay all bond interest due. Bondholders are lenders to the company, whereas shareholders are the owners. Many bonds are issued as debentures, where the debt holders have power to take control over some or all of the assets of the company if interest and/or capital repayments are not made when due.

 Key term

Debentures are long-term company debt where security on some or all of the company's assets is usually provided to the debenture holders.

The vast majority of bonds have a redemption date, when the nominal amount of the debt is repayable by the company. Again, this contrasts with money invested in shares that is not repayable, except in rare circumstances.

 Ponder point

Bonds are considered lower risk investments than investing in shares. Can you think of any advantages of investing in shares rather than bonds?

There are several advantages of investing in shares rather than bonds. One of the major advantages of investing in shares is that shareholders should benefit if the company experiences long-term growth, by receiving increasing dividends and a rising share price. The disadvantage for bondholders in such a company is that they are tied to a fixed rate of return and will not benefit to any greater extent if the company performs well.

Another advantage of holding shares is that shareholders can attend and vote at the company's annual general meeting. Bondholders have no way of voicing their opinions, as they are not entitled to attend the AGM.

Bonds are long-term loans and although many holders may keep them to maturity, it is possible to buy and sell bonds during their term. The price at which they are sold, the market price, will be affected by current interest rates.

Interest yield

 Key term

Interest yield measures the return on a bond by comparing the interest received with the market price of the bond.

The interest yield on bonds, or any interest bearing investment, is measured by comparing the interest received with the market price of the bond.

$$\text{Interest yield (\%)} = \frac{\text{Interest received}}{\text{Market price of bond}} \times 100$$

This measures the rate of return that a bondholder is receiving and an investor would expect bonds carrying similar levels of risk, to have similar interest yields.

When the market price of a bond differs from the nominal value, then anyone buying a bond should be aware that the nominal price will be repaid at redemption.

Example 8.8

Some years ago, an investor bought £1,000 of thirty-year bonds, at nominal value, that pay interest at the rate of 6% per annum. The bondholder would have received £60 interest each year.

After holding the bonds for six years, the investor sold them for £800.

The new investor yield is:

$$\frac{\text{Interest received}}{\text{Market price of bond}} \times 100 = \frac{60}{800} \times 100 = 7.5\%$$

The new investor is receiving a better interest yield because the bonds were acquired below their nominal value. If the new investor holds on to the bonds for the next twenty-four years, then he will be repaid £1,000 by the company at the redemption date.

As he paid £800 for the bonds, he would also make a gain from this increase in the capital value. The yield can be recalculated to take this into account and if this is done, the yield is known as the yield to redemption.

 Ponder point

What factors might cause the bond prices to change over time, given that the interest rate on the bond is fixed?

Factors that will affect the bond price will be interest rates generally, returns that can be received on similar bonds, the economic conditions, including inflation rates both at the time of the sale and expected in the future, and how safe the bond is considered to be, measured by its credit rating.

If potential investors are looking to buy a bond and expect an interest yield higher than the declared rate of interest on the bond, they will only be prepared to pay a price below nominal value. Conversely, if potential investors are looking to buy a bond and expect an interest yield lower than the declared rate of interest, they should be prepared to pay a price above nominal value.

Example 8.9

Company A issues bonds, at nominal value, that pay interest at the rate of 5% per annum:
   Nominal value of bonds held and price paid = £100
   Interest on £100 (nominal value) of bonds = £5

$$\text{Interest yield} = \frac{5}{100} \times 100 = 5\%$$

Some while later, interest rates generally have risen and equivalent bonds issued at that time carry interest at the rate of 7%. To allow for this increase in interest rates, the market value of Company A bonds would fall to £71, so that new investors would earn an effective rate of 7% interest per annum.
Market price of £100 (nominal value) of bonds in company A = £71
Interest on £100 (nominal value) of bonds = £5

$$\text{Interest yield} = \frac{5}{71} \times 100 = 7\%$$

If the market price did not fall in this way, no holder of the Company A bonds would be able to sell their holding as no logical investor would buy them at £100 and accept a 5% yield.

Credit rating

 Key term

A **credit rating** attempts to measure the riskiness of a specific organization's or a specific country's debt. The better the credit rating, the more likely it is that interest payments and capital repayments will be made when due.

Credit ratings attempt to measure the riskiness of a particular organization's debt so that potential investors can make an informed decision on which ones they are prepared to lend to. Three of the main credit rating agencies are Moody's, Standard and Poor's, and Fitch and companies pay these agencies to have their bonds credit rated.

The highest rating is AAA and bonds rated AAA would be considered extremely low risk. It is considered very unlikely that interest and capital payments would not be met where bonds are AAA rated. The ratings then gradually decline as follows: AAA, AA, A, BBB, BB, B, CCC, CC, C, and D, where the letters can be slightly modified by the addition of a plus (+) or a minus (−) sign. Table 8.6 shows extracts from Standard and Poor's rating descriptions:

Table 8.6 Extracts from Standard and Poor's rating descriptions

Rating	Likely capacity to make interest and capital repayments
AAA	Extremely strong capacity
A	Strong capacity but somewhat susceptible to adverse economic conditions
BBB	Adequate capacity to meet financial commitments but more subject to adverse economic conditions than A grade debt
CCC	Currently vulnerable and dependent on favourable business, financial, and economic conditions to meet financial commitments
D	Company is in default (due payments have not been made)

 Ponder point

If you were investing in bonds, what would be the lowest credit rating that you would be prepared to accept?

This is a very personal question and one that is directly linked to each individual's risk profile. Some people are more risk averse than others. The lower the credit rating, the riskier the bond, but to compensate for this, bondholders will usually expect a higher rate of return. Hence there is a balance that needs to be found.

Another factor that an investor would be influenced by is the extent to which the amount to be invested in a bond is a sum that the investor can afford to lose. For example, if the potential sum to be invested represented 3% of your life savings, you might be prepared to accept bonds with a lower credit rating than if it represented 30% of your life savings.

Government bonds (gilts)

 Key term

Gilts are UK government bonds issued at a declared rate of interest in order to raise money for government spending.

The UK government issues debt, known as government bonds or gilts, in order to finance the difference between its income and expenditure. Investing in UK gilts is considered extremely safe as the likelihood of the government defaulting on its interest and capital obligations is considered extremely remote.

Gilts are issued for a fixed term and they carry a predetermined rate of interest that may be stated in absolute terms or as a figure linked to the retail prices index.

Example 8.10

'3.75% Treasury 2025' would describe gilts that paid £3.75 for every £100 nominal value of stock held. The gilts would be redeemable on a specified date in 2025.

If the market value of the gilts was £1.15½, then their yield would be:

$$\text{Interest yield} = \frac{\text{Interest received}}{\text{Market price of bond}} \times 100 = \frac{3.75}{115.5} \times 100 = 3.25\%$$

The yield to redemption would be significantly lower than the interest yield above, as the yield to redemption takes account not only of the interest payable but also of the fact that the investor will only be paid £100 for gilts which are currently valued at £1.15½.

Gilts are rated one notch down from AA and are considered one of the safest investments to hold because the British government has never yet defaulted on a payment.

Investment performance

It is very difficult to forecast what will happen in the future to share prices, bond prices, and gilt prices. It will depend on company performance as well as economic conditions nationally and internationally and general levels of optimism or pessimism. Looking back at historical returns can give some perspective on returns earned over the years.

Barclays Capital carries out an annual 'Equity Gilt' study into investment performance both in the short and in the longer term. Figures from a study, summarized in Figure 8.2, show the real investment returns by asset class, where the real rate of return takes account of any loss in spending power caused by inflation. Corporate bond figures are available from 1999 onwards.

From Figure 8.2, you can see that over the time frame of ten years, twenty years, and fifty years to the end of 2013, equities have brought the best returns to investors. There is a general belief that equities will outperform certain other classes of investment if held for long enough. In the twenty-year period, equity prices have at times fallen sharply, caused by the financial crash in 2007, the dot-com crash, and many other national and international events. Despite these sharp falls, equities have still proved to be the best performing asset class over the twenty-year period. Cash has provided the poorest rate of return over all the time frames.

Figure 8.2 Real investment returns

Source: Barclays *Equity Gilt Study* (2014) (as quoted in This is Money http://www.thisismoney.co.uk/money/diyinvesting/article-2563014/Shares-outdo-savings-bonds-gilts-50-years-finds-Barclays-Equity-Gilt-Study.html).

 Key term

Equities is the term used for shares owned and is often used when referring to multiple shareholdings. Equity holders are the shareholders (owners) of a company.

The Barclays *Equity Gilt Study* (2014), as quoted on the This is Money website, gives examples of the 2013 value of £100 invested in 1899, in equities and in cash. The real value of those investments in 2013 has been computed, assuming first that all income earned was withdrawn and not reinvested and, secondly, that all income earned was reinvested. The results are shown in Table 8.7.

Table 8.7 Table showing the 2013 value of £100 invested in 1899

Type of investment	Amount invested in 1899	Real value in 2013	
		If income not reinvested	If income reinvested
Equities	£100	£191	£28,386
Cash	£100	Figure not available	£261

Source: Barclays *Equity Gilt Study* (2014) (as quoted in This is Money http://www.thisismoney.co.uk/money/diyinvesting/article-2563014/Shares-outdo-savings-bonds-gilts-50-years-finds-Barclays-Equity-Gilt-Study.html).

The importance of reinvesting income to ensure the long-term growth of a portfolio is clearly demonstrated by the enormous difference between the real value of the equity portfolio if income has been reinvested, £28,386, compared to its value at £191 if the income has not been reinvested.

The difference between the real value of an equity portfolio held for 114 years to 2013, compared to cash savings shows why equities are considered to offer the best long-term returns for investors.

 Key term

Real value measures the value of an investment after taking the effect of inflation into account.

Data such as that shown in Figure 8.2 and Table 8.7 demonstrates why equities are often put forward as the preferred choice in order to achieve better long-term returns on investment. The last ten years have challenged this view and as share prices can be volatile, equities should always be considered a long-term investment.

Diversification

If an investor is lucky enough to invest in a company's shares that pay good dividends and show a healthy increase in their share price, that investor will be a happy one. If, however, the shares chosen result in no dividends and a fall in share price, that investor will be disappointed to have chosen a poor investment.

Investing in one or a small number of investments is the equivalent of 'putting all your eggs in one basket'. If that basket drops, most, if not all, of the eggs will be broken. This metaphor corresponds well to the situation where an investor puts all their money in one company that goes on to perform badly, and a large part of the sums invested are lost. Ideally investors should aim to spread their risk by diversifying. This would involve investing in a range of investment classes: equities, bonds, gilts, and cash. Within investment classes, particularly for equities and bonds, the amount invested should be further spread between a range of companies across sectors and possibly across a range of geographical areas.

Collective investments

 Key term

Collective investments use funds provided by a large number of investors to invest in a wide range of investments that may be spread across asset classes including: equities, bonds, gilts, and deposits.

Collective or pooled investments represent the most efficient way that investors, without very large sums to invest and time to spend researching investment choices, can invest in a diverse range of investments.

A collective investment is a fund that uses money provided by investors to invest in a collection of shares, bonds, gilts, cash, and sometimes other investment products. There are significant advantages of using collective investments rather than attempting to build an individual portfolio.

One advantage of collective investments is that even investors with small sums to invest can benefit from a diverse portfolio of investments. Putting together an individual diversified portfolio is only possible where an investor has significant sums to invest. Creating one would involve investing in multiple investments. A second advantage is that the composition of the fund may be actively managed by investment managers who will have the time and expertise that an individual investor is unlikely to have. Some funds though are controlled by a computer.

There are some disadvantages, the main one being the costs involved as fund charges can significantly reduce the long-term returns earned.

Unit trusts, OEICs (open-ended investment companies), or investment trusts are all examples of collective investments explained later in the chapter. High street banks, investment banks, and other institutions offer these funds. Two of the most popular types of fund are:

- Actively managed funds
- Tracker funds

Actively managed funds

 Key term

An **actively managed fund** is a collective investment where a fund manager makes the investment choices.

An actively managed fund is one that has a fund manager and investment team who research and choose the investments in the portfolio. Individual funds will have specific objectives that may be stated in terms of the geographic area they plan to invest in, the sector or sectors they plan to invest in, the relative size of the businesses they plan to invest in, whether they are aiming for high income or long-term growth, etc.

Example 8.11

Two examples of fund objectives are as follows:

- *Fund One's investment objective* is to achieve long-term capital growth from a portfolio primarily made up of the shares of UK companies. The fund will have a blend of investments in smaller and medium-sized companies.

(continued...)

- *Fund Two's investment objective* is to primarily focus on China through investment in Chinese securities listed in China and Hong Kong, as well as securities in non-Chinese companies which derive a significant portion of their earnings from China.

Tracker funds

Tracker funds are funds whose composition is dictated by the index they seek to track. A FTSE 100 tracker would invest in all the shares that comprise the FTSE 100 at any point in time and in direct proportion to the relative size of the companies that comprise that index.

 Key term

The **FTSE 100 share index** is an index based on the UK's largest 100 listed companies where the size is measured by each company's market value.

The companies which constitute the index change from time to time and any change will trigger the fund to buy and sell investments so that the portfolio held by the tracker matches the composition of the revised index. This type of fund does not need a manager to make investment decisions and can be computer controlled. As a result, its charges are usually relatively low.

 Ponder point

If an investor chooses to invest in a tracker fund, will their return be guaranteed to match the return earned by the index?

The return earned on an index tracker will underperform that achieved by the asset class, because of the charges made by the fund.

 Ponder point

Collective investments are a popular choice for many individual investors because they allow them to hold a wide range of investments. Can you think of any reasons why an individual investor might choose not to invest in a collective investment?

There will be some investors who prefer to make their own investment choices rather than relying on a fund manager to make choices for them. They might not consider tracker funds because they do not want exposure to companies just because they happen to form part of an index. There will be people who want to do their own research, make their own investment choices, and hence feel more directly responsible for how those investments perform. In addition, investors may prefer not to pay the costs charged by certain funds.

Fund charges

Fund charges can vary hugely and should form a key part of any decision to invest in a particular fund. Charges levied can include:

- the initial charge for investing in the fund
- the ongoing charges figure (OCF) for managing the fund.

These charges can have a significant impact on the returns to investors.

 Key term

The **ongoing charges figure (OCF)** measures the total annual charge made to cover the costs of managing a fund. It does not include all the costs that the fund may incur, for example trading costs.

Initial charges and ongoing charges may not, at first glance, seem to be high but they can have a real impact on the actual return received by investors. The ongoing charges figure for actively managed funds will be higher than for tracker funds.

Example 8.12

An actively managed fund has an ongoing charges figure of 2% and a tracker fund has an ongoing charges figure of 0.3%. If both funds generate a return of 5% during the year, the investors in the tracker fund will benefit to a far greater extent than the investors in the managed funds. Ignoring any trading costs:

Net return after costs, to investors in managed fund 5% – 2% = 3%

Net return after costs, to investors in tracker fund 5% – 0.3% = 4.7%

The impact of fund charges, even if the percentages appear small, can be very significant on the returns that investors earn in the long run.

Example 8.13

An investor with £20,000 to invest is considering two possible options:

1. To choose and make investments for himself, and incur £100 in fees.
2. To invest in an OEIC that makes an initial charge of 2% and has an OCF of 1%.

(continued...)

Assuming that under both options the investments earn a return of 4% per annum, and that any fees charged are based on the size of the fund at the year end, Tables 8.8 and 8.9 summarize the value of each portfolio over a ten-year period.

Table 8.8 Value of portfolio of investments over ten years where £20,000 is self-invested

	Value of portfolio at start of year £	Return (4% pa) £	Fees £	Value of portfolio at end of year £
At beginning	20,000		100	19,900
Year 1	19,900	796	–	20,696
Year 2	20,696	828	–	21,524
Year 3	21,524	861	–	22,385
Year 5	23,280	931	–	24,211
Year 10	**28,324**	**1,133**	**–**	**29,457**

Table 8.9 Value of portfolio of investments over ten years where £20,000 is invested in an OEIC

	Value of portfolio at start of year £	Return (4% pa) £	Fees £	Value of portfolio at end of year £
At beginning	20,000		400 (2% initial cost)	19,600
Year 1	19,600	784	204 (OCF 1%)	20,180
Year 2	20,180	807	210	20,777
Year 3	20,777	831	216	21,392
Year 5	22,026	881	229	22,678
Year 10	**25,485**	**1,019**	**265**	**26,239**

Tables 8.8 and 8.9 demonstrate that the fund charges made by the OEIC have a marked difference on the value of the investments over five years and, even more so, after ten years. After five years, the self-invested portfolio would be worth £1,533 more than the same funds invested in an OEIC and the difference rises to £3,218 (£29,457 – 26,239) after ten years. (This does assume that the self-invested portfolio generates the same return as the OEIC.)

Example 8.13 highlights the impact over time of relatively low levels of fees on the value of a portfolio held in a fund. Even modest levels of fees have a significant impact on the returns to investors. However, this needs to be balanced against the benefits of using collective investments for most individuals as they enable investors to benefit from a wide portfolio and they do not have to manage their investments.

The impact of fees means that fund managers have to achieve above average returns in order to provide a return to investors that is comparable to a tracker fund with lower fees. Even modest levels of fees make a significant difference to the growth of the fund over time, and hence care needs to be given to fund selection.

Choosing a fund

There are many different factors to consider when choosing a fund to invest in. First, the nature and hence the riskiness of the fund should be considered. For example, equity funds are considered to carry a higher risk than bond funds. Funds with international exposure are usually considered higher risk than UK-based funds. Secondly, the past performance of the fund can be reviewed. It does not follow that a fund that has been performing well will necessarily continue to do so. However, a management team that has generated better than average returns over a number of years is likely to give potential investors some confidence. Experienced investors may well follow the careers of certain fund managers and move their funds when the fund manager moves. Thirdly, consideration should be given to the ongoing charges as funds that have high levels of expenses will absorb more of the returns earned on those funds.

Ethical funds

For investors who are concerned about putting money into companies whose activities they may not want to support, there exists a range of ethical funds that only invest in carefully selected companies who meet their investment criteria.

 Ponder point

What sort of company activities might be considered by some investors to be unethical or unacceptable?

The list of activities that some people may consider unacceptable is long. Ethical investors may wish to avoid companies that engage in animal testing or are in any way connected to trading in armaments, gambling, or tobacco. They may want to be certain that companies they invest in do not exploit their workforce or that they are businesses that proactively seek to minimize their environmental impact.

The range of ethical funds available allows investors to choose funds that match their personal investment objectives as closely as possible.

Fund structures

There are three common ways in which collective investments can be structured: unit trusts, OEICs (open-ended investment companies), and investment trusts. From the perspective of a small investor, it is interesting to note the differences between how they are structured but is unlikely to influence their choice of fund. The key characteristics of unit trusts, OEICs, and investment trusts are summarized in Table 8.10.

 Key terms

A **unit trust** is a collective investment in which the investor buys units. The price of each unit depends on the valuation of the underlying portfolio of investments.

An **open-ended investment company (OEIC)** is a collective investment in which the investor buys shares. The price of the shares depends on the valuation of the underlying portfolio as the shares in the OEIC itself are not traded on a stock exchange.

An **investment trust** is a collective investment in which the investor buys shares that are listed on the stock exchange and the price of the shares is determined by supply and demand.

An **open-ended fund** is one that can increase or decrease in size according to demand.

Table 8.10 Characteristics of unit trusts, OEICS, and investment trusts

Structure	Units or shares?	Open-ended?	Pricing
Unit trust	Investor buys 'units'	Open-ended	Unit price is linked to value of the investments held in unit trust
OEIC	Investor buys shares in OEIC	Open-ended	Share price is linked to value of the investments held in OEIC
Investment trust	Investor would buy shares in investment trust, actually a company	Not open-ended	Shares are traded on stock exchange and the price quoted will be determined by supply and demand

Investing in collective funds will allow investors to benefit from holding a portfolio of investments and hence to spread their risk, even when relatively small sums are involved. Many investors would be best advised to hold as much as they can of their investments in an ISA, an individual savings account, that will allow them to benefit from the dividends and capital gains arising on their investments, with the minimum tax payable.

ISAs (individual savings accounts)

ISAs offer taxpayers a tax effective means of saving and investing. There are two types of ISA: a cash ISA (basically a savings account) and a stocks and shares ISA which can hold investments in a range of shares and bonds. Each tax year every individual can open one cash ISA and one shares ISA. The limits on ISA investment tend to increase with each new tax year and you will find the current year's allowances on the Gov.uk website. Table 8.11 shows indicative ISA allowances.

Table 8.11 Indicative ISA allowances

Individual aged 16 to 18 years of age	Cash ISA only Annual limit of £20,000
Individual aged over 18 years	Cash ISA and/or shares ISA Annual limit of £20,000

Using these indicative allowances, the overall maximum that can be invested in ISAs in a tax year is £20,000. Individuals can choose to put the whole £20,000 into a shares ISA or £20,000 into a cash ISA or some split between the two.

Example 8.14

An individual aged twenty-five opens a cash ISA account in a tax year and puts £4,000 on deposit in that ISA. Some of the options available to that person to make further ISA investments in that tax year are as follows:

- An additional £16,000 could be deposited in the cash ISA
- £16,000 could be invested in a shares ISA
- £16,000 could be invested in ISAs, split between the cash ISA and a shares ISA

All three of the above options would enable the individual to use their annual ISA allowance in full.

If an amount is withdrawn from an ISA during a tax year, the saver can still top up their ISA to the limit as long as they do so before the end of the tax year.

Example 8.15

An individual pays £5,000 into a cash ISA and £5,000 into a shares ISA in June. In October, investments that had cost £2,500 are sold from the shares ISA. If this person wishes to top up both ISAs before the end of the tax year, then a total of £12,500 could be deposited in the ISAs before the end of the tax year. (This brings the total amount invested during the year to £20k: £5k + £5k–£2.5k + £12.5k = £20k)

ISA as a tax wrapper

An ISA is frequently described as a 'wrapper'. If savings are held in an ISA, then the savings are wrapped and the saver will not have to pay any income tax on interest earned in the ISA. Savings held in a savings account which is not an ISA account, may incur interest that is taxed if the account holder earns interest in excess of their Personal Savings Allowance.

When investments are held in an ISA, then the investments are protected by the wrapper from incurring any capital gains tax. Dividends arising in the ISA are tax-free.

ISAs and tax-free allowances

ISAs are an option that allows savers and investors to protect dividends and interest earned from income tax and any gains arising are protected from capital gains tax.

In recent years, the government has introduced tax allowances that reduce the income tax payable on interest and dividends, particularly by basic rate taxpayers.

The Personal Savings Allowance (PSA) allows basic rate taxpayers to receive £1,000 of interest each year, tax-free. The Dividend Allowance (DA) allows shareholders to receive £5,000 of dividends tax-free each year.

As a result of these allowances, there could be a temptation to think that ISAs are no longer relevant. However, there are good reasons why ISAs should be utilized where possible:

- The interest rates on cash ISAs are often good. To earn the highest interest rates on non-ISA savings accounts, you often have to commit to not withdrawing any of your savings for a number of years.

- Every taxpayer can use their ISA allowance each tax year but once the tax year is over that allowance is no longer available. Over time, many people's savings and investments will rise and in the future, the Personal Savings Allowance and Dividend Allowance may not be adequate to protect the amount earned from income tax. (The allowances may not even exist at all as government tax policies are subject to change.) If in the future, the DA and the PSA are not adequate to protect savings and investment income, then the lost ISA allowances from previous tax years cannot be used and interest and dividends would be taxed.

- The PSA and the DA may be reduced in size at any point as taxation policy is constantly being revised. The same can be said of ISA allowances but once money has been placed in an ISA, it is protected.

- Some basic rate taxpayers may over time become higher rate taxpayers and start to lose the PSA.

- The only way to protect investments from a capital gains tax liability is to hold them in an ISA.

Example 8.16

Investor A holds £50,000 in cash ISAs and £160,000 in share ISAs, having invested in cash ISAs and share ISAs over a number of years. Investor B holds £50,000 in a bank deposit account and £160,000 of investments in shares and bonds without taking advantage of ISAs. Table 8.12 shows how any income and gains arising from the investments would be taxed if both investors are basic rate taxpayers.

Table 8.12 Investors A and B are basic rate taxpayers

	Investor A (ISA investor)	Investor B (Non-ISA investor)
Interest on savings account	No income tax	20% income tax on any interest in excess of the saver's Personal Savings Allowance
Dividends on shares	No income tax	7.5% income tax on any dividends in excess of the investor's Dividend Allowance
Capital gain on shares	None	10% capital gains tax on gains in excess of the annual exemption

Transferring ISAs

It is possible for an individual to transfer their ISAs between providers with no loss of tax relief. This transfer needs to be done as an ISA transfer. If an individual had an ISA account that they closed, intending to reinvest the sums elsewhere, then the ISA wrapper (and tax exempt status) that surrounded those funds would have been lost when the account was closed. In order to transfer an ISA, the new provider needs to be informed of the intention to move the ISA funds and the new provider then arranges the transfer from the old provider.

Junior ISAs (JISAs)

Junior ISAs are available to those under eighteen who live in the UK and who meet certain criteria. The allowances are much lower than for adult ISAs. The only person permitted to make withdrawals is the child once they have reached the age of eighteen. Parents, grandparents, and family friends can invest into a child's Junior ISA and the account is managed on the child's behalf by a 'registered contact', usually a parent.

All sixteen and seventeen year olds will be able to take advantage of both the Junior ISA allowances as well as the adult ISA allowances, should they have available funds to invest.

> **? Ponder point**
>
> Junior ISAs are designed to encourage families to save for their children. What concerns might parents have about building up a significant fund on their child's behalf?

Parents making savings on their children's behalf are likely to be doing so in order to build up a fund to help their child cover university costs, buy a first car, or have a deposit for their first home. As the child can withdraw the funds when they reach eighteen, parents are likely to be concerned that their children could spend the funds unwisely.

Case study—Imran

Imran has a well-paid job as a commercial lawyer based in London. He enjoys spending his monthly salary on eating out, entertainment, and holidays, in addition to the essential living costs he has to meet. He has made a point over the last couple of years of using his annual bonus to buy investments, so that he can start to build up a fund of savings and investments. He also owns some shares he inherited and some shares in a company, Rosier plc, that his instincts and research had led him to believe would do well.

The investments Imran owns are shown in Table 8.13.

Table 8.13 Imran: schedule of investments owned

Investment	Held in an ISA	Cost	Current value
300 shares in MOG plc (inherited 5 years ago)	No	£1,600	£1,400
120 shares in Thyme plc (inherited 5 years ago)	No	£7,030	£11,890
50 shares in Rosier plc	No	£900	£900
FTSE 100 UK tracker fund	Yes—opened last year	£8,000	£8,500
Bonds and gilts fund	Yes—opened this year	£5,500	£5,600

Imran knows a certain amount about investing but has a few queries and is seeking some advice on his portfolio. Imran tells you the following about his approach to investing:

- He considers that he is prepared to accept riskier investments if that means gaining better returns. He is also keen to build up his fund so that he is in a position to put down a deposit on a property in the next couple of years.
- Thyme plc shares have recently surged in value and this boost to Imran's fund has led him to believe that he will very soon have enough funds tied up in savings and investments to enable him to put down a deposit on his first flat.
- Imran has savings in a deposit account that amount to £3,000 on which he is earning very little interest. As bonds and gilts are usually considered a low risk investment, he is considering withdrawing his savings from a deposit account and using the funds to invest in the bond and gilts fund.

Venture capital trusts

Venture capital trusts are a form of investing that attracts generous tax relief. The investments are riskier than those that would be held in an ISA and, to benefit from the tax savings, the shares have to be held for a long time. Venture capital trusts are required to invest in unlisted companies; these companies are usually at an early stage of their development and growing fast. Venture capital provides funds for these young, growing businesses to expand.

Investors buying shares in venture capital trusts can reduce the income tax liability on their earnings and other income, and avoid capital gains tax on any long-term increase in the value of shares held in the fund. The investments in a venture capital trust are higher risk than investing in established, listed companies. Hence, they will not be suitable for many individuals who do not want to enter into higher risk investments.

Buying and selling investments

Equities and collective investments can be bought and sold online or over the phone and these are probably the quickest and easiest methods to use.

Execution-only brokers, where an investor does not receive any advice on the investments they make, charge the lowest fees and brokers who do provide investment advice charge higher fees. This advice can be heeded or ignored. Individual shares can be bought and sold, with the scale of fees payable varying from broker to broker. Any potential investor should consider how many transactions they anticipate making in any one year, as this is likely to determine which broker would be the cheapest to use.

Investing in equities entitles shareholders to receive annual financial statements, to attend and vote at company annual general meetings, and, in a few cases, certain shares carry shareholder discounts or perks. If the shares are bought via a broker, then technically a nominee service owns the shares, the investor has 'beneficial rights' to the shares but is not necessarily entitled to any shareholder perks. This arrangement does have a benefit for shareholders as it means the buying and selling of shares is much simpler than it would otherwise be.

It is less common for individuals to invest in corporate bonds or gilts directly. Most people who have bonds and gilts hold them indirectly, by investing in collective funds.

There are online fund supermarkets or platforms where a wide range of collective investments can be bought and sold, whether inside an ISA or not.

Share scams

There are many ways in which people have been tricked into losing a great deal of money as a result of investing in worthless shares. Share scams frequently start with an unsolicited phone call where the recipient of the call is offered the opportunity to buy shares in a company. The fraudsters rely on using high pressure selling techniques and the offer of high returns that seem almost risk-free, to tempt would-be investors to part with their cash. Investors are told that quick action is required and the individual may be guided to look at a website or glossy brochure that has been produced for the purpose. Once investors have parted with their cash, the shares turn out to be non-existent or worthless and the trader disappears.

'If it sounds too good to be true, it probably is' is a proverb that certainly applies to investment. The manner in which fraudsters operate is likely to keep changing as their schemes are drawn to the public's attention. It is always advisable to be highly suspicious of cold callers and to ensure that any firm you plan to use is regulated by the Financial Conduct Authority. Their website has an up-to-date list of authorized firms.

Relative risk

This chapter has introduced many different types of investment and the importance of recognizing the relative riskiness of each type of investment has been discussed. Investing means putting money into a product where the returns will be uncertain and although higher risk investments should carry higher rates of return, there will be greater risk that the returns will not be made or worse still, capital lost. Ranking investments according to risk is not an exact process, but a guideline to the relative riskiness of some of the asset classes discussed in this chapter is shown in Figure 8.3.

Lower risk	Bank deposits
	Gilts
	Corporate bonds
	A collective investment—invested in equities and bonds
	A collective investment—primarily invested in equities
	Individual company shares
Higher risk	Venture capital trust

Figure 8.3 Relative risk of asset classes

Ponder point

How would an ISA wrapper affect the riskiness of an equity investment?

An equity investment will be equally risky whether it is held in an ISA or outside an ISA.

Conclusion

Having some understanding of investment products is essential for anyone making investments for themselves and a useful life skill for anyone wishing to understand the way that pension and insurance companies manage their funds. Increasingly individuals are given choices over how their pension savings are invested.

Equities are high risk investments that over many decades have given better returns to investors. The decade to 2015 has challenged the notion that in the long run shares will nearly always yield the best returns for investors as markets and prices have been very volatile. Corporate bonds are generally considered a safer option than equities but the capital is never entirely secure as bond prices can fall in value and companies can fail. UK gilts are a safer option, where the funds are loaned to the UK government.

In order to spread the risk of choosing a few investments and ending up with your returns dependent on the performance of a small number of companies, most investors should consider choosing collective investments. Collective investments allow even a small investor to acquire a stake in a wide range of investments and, depending on their choice of fund, the investments may include some or all of the following: equities, corporate bonds, gilts, and cash deposits. When choosing a fund, attention should be paid to the level of fees charged as these can significantly impact on the growth of the fund over the longer term.

ISAs allow UK investors to minimize the impact of taxation on the returns from their investments and with relatively generous annual allowances, most people should consider holding their investments and savings in an ISA. Although the Personal Savings Allowance and the Dividend Allowance allow interest and dividends to be received tax-free up to their limit, there is no guarantee that these allowances will continue at their present level in the future.

Venture capital trusts attract generous tax reliefs but are only appropriate for investors who can afford to take a greater risk with a part of their portfolio and are prepared to do so.

 Useful websites

Websites for the three main credit rating agencies:
http://www.moodys.com
http://www.standardandpoors.com/ratings/definitions-and-faqs/en/us

http://www.fitchratings.com

Website for information on gilts:

http://www.dmo.gov.uk

Website for information on ethical investing:

http://www.the-ethical-partnership.co.uk

Websites for some fund supermarkets—information on a wide range of collective investments and SIPPS:

http://www.fidelity.co.uk

http://www.hl.co.uk

The website for the Financial Conduct Authority, including an up-to-date list of firms that have been authorized by them:

https://www.the-fca.org.uk

 ## References

Discussion of Barclays *Equity Gilt Study* (2014). Available at:

http://www.thisismoney.co.uk/money/diyinvesting/article-2563014/Shares-outdo-savings-bonds-gilts-50-years-finds-Barclays-Equity-Gilt-Study.html (accessed 28.7. 2016)

 ## Practice Questions

Question 1 Quick Questions TRUE OR FALSE?

8.1   The greater the risk of an investment product, the higher the return that can be expected to be received from that product.

8.2   Dividends are payments made by all companies to their shareholders.

8.3   Investing in a diversified portfolio of shares is considered less risky than investing in two or three different companies' shares.

8.4   Earnings per share measures the profit earned per share.

8.5   Total shareholder return takes into account the dividends received as well as any capital gain or loss on the value of the shares.

8.6   Bonds are long-term loan contracts that are not repayable.

8.7   A company with an AAA credit rating is considered to be highly risky.

8.8   '4% Treasury Stock 2020' is a description of government bonds (gilts) that pay interest at 4% on nominal value and are repayable any time before 2020.

8.9   A tracker fund is a collective investment whose composition is determined by the shares that comprise the index being tracked.

8.10   Gilts are considered to be a safer investment than equities.

Question 2 Sandy

Sandy has owned 400 shares in Pepper plc for four years and is concerned that he has received no dividends during that time although he believes that the company is doing well. He has been provided with Table 8.14 containing information for Pepper plc over the last four years:

Table 8.14 Pepper plc: earnings per share and share price

	Year 1	Year 2	Year 3	Year 4
Earnings per share (pence)	4.0	4.5	6.1	7.1
Share price at year end (pence)	36.0	40.5	66.4	65.1

Required:

a) Comment on the company's eps over the last four years.

b) Calculate the P/E ratio at each of the four year ends and interpret your findings.

c) Calculate the TSR (total shareholder return) for the last two years and comment on your findings.

d) Comment on Sandy's disappointment over the lack of dividends during the last four years.

* Question 3 Roger

Roger owns some corporate bonds, gilts, individual company shares, and shares in various collective investments. He inherited all these investments from his uncle four years ago. He has been pleased to receive the interest and dividends but has never understood how these various asset classes work.

Required:

a) Explain the difference between gilts, corporate bonds, and shares.

b) Describe what is meant by collective investments.

c) Rank all the investments according to their relative risk.

d) Explain the difference between the nominal value and the market value of a corporate bond and the factors that may cause the market value of bonds to change.

e) Roger owns £10,000 nominal value of the '4% Treasury Stock 2034'. Over the last year, its value increased from £115 to £130 per £100 nominal value. What does this reveal about likely interest rate movements during the year?

f) Roger's two corporate bond holdings have been credit rated as follows:

Flap plc–credit rated AAA

Collar plc–credit rated BBB

Explain what these credit ratings reveal about the riskiness of the bonds.

g) Information gathered in relation to Roger's two individual shareholdings is shown in Table 8.15.

Table 8.15 Information regarding Roger's shareholdings

	Price (pence)	Dividend yield (%)	P/E
Annie plc	210	4.5	10.1
Pancake plc	405	1.3	18.2

What does the dividend yield and the P/E reveal about the two shareholdings?

* Question 4 Winston and Alfie

Winston and Alfie are civil partners who are both higher rate taxpayers. Over the last few years they have both built up a good level of savings. They are interested in making some investments as they have read that in the long run equities and bonds generally provide better returns than savings accounts.

Guided by a friend who is an active investor, they have been researching various products and have identified the funds shown in Table 8.16 as ones they are considering investing in.

Table 8.16 Winston and Alfie: possible fund choices

Fund	Initial charges	Ongoing charges
Tracker fund FTSE 250	0%	0.5% per annum
Managed UK equity and bonds fund	1.5%	2% per annum
International equities managed fund	2%	3% per annum

Required:

a) Explain the benefits of investing in a collective investment.

b) Explain what is meant by a tracker fund and by an actively managed fund.

c) Assess the three funds based on the following market predictions for the next year, and comment on your findings:

The FTSE 250 is expected to generate a return of 4% per annum.

The Managed UK Fund aims to generate a return of 6% per annum.

The International Fund aims to generate a return of between 4% and 8% per annum.

d) Winston and Alfie have a total of £55,000 that they wish to invest. Should they invest in their chosen funds using an ISA and, if so, how can they get the maximum benefit from their ISA allowances?

Visit the Online Resource Centre that accompanies this book for additional material: **www.oxfordtextbooks.co.uk/orc/king_carey2e/**

9 Buying your own home

Learning Objectives

After studying this chapter, you should understand:

- The historical reasons behind the popularity of home ownership in the UK
- The advantages and disadvantages of renting a home or purchasing a home
- The main types of residential mortgage product available
- The costs involved in buying a property
- The importance of taking individual circumstances into account when considering the suitability of home ownership and different mortgage products

Introduction

This chapter focuses on the decision individuals face concerning whether to buy their own home or whether it might be better to rent a property. The different types of mortgages are discussed together with costs of purchase and other factors affecting the 'rent or buy' decision.

Most people will never have enough savings to buy a property outright and hence a mortgage is taken out to finance the purchase. A mortgage is a loan made by a bank or building society to enable individuals to buy their own home. The lender is given security over the property, which means that if repayments on the mortgage fall into arrears, then the lender can take possession of the property and sell it to recover the loan and any interest owing to them.

Indicative rates

iR

This chapter uses indicative rates that give an indication of the size of certain rates and allowances. When carrying out a real-life computation, it would be necessary to refer to the Gov.uk website (http://www.gov.uk) for details of current tax rates and allowances.

Historical context of home ownership in the UK

In post-war Britain during the 1950s, the bank manager was a powerful figure with significant standing in the community. At that time, in order to obtain a mortgage, you had to be a good customer of the bank, with a secure job, and a solid character. An interview with the bank manager was required to consider whether you were an appropriate person to receive the benefit of a bank mortgage. The banks and building societies were small and cautious and lending was limited.

Things changed gradually with growing affluence. When Margaret Thatcher came to power in the UK in 1979 local authority housing (council housing) was sold to its tenants under the 'right to buy' initiative, designed to increase the proportion of home ownership in Britain. Furthermore tax relief was given on mortgage interest payments until 2000 to encourage home ownership. Since the 1980s, the regulations governing financial institutions, including mortgage lenders, have been significantly relaxed, leading to the availability of a much wider range of mortgage products and lenders competing to make as many mortgage loans as possible.

During the boom years of the early twenty-first century the banks became less and less cautious in their lending and more aggressive in competing for mortgage business. It became possible to borrow up to 125% of the value of a property. The underlying assumption was that house price inflation could be relied upon to increase the value of the property and hence the security of the lender, such that, over time, the property became worth more than the mortgage. The flaw in the argument became obvious when house prices began to fall and many owners realized that they owed more on their mortgage than their property was worth. Where the mortgage on a property exceeds the value of that property, the homebuyer is said to be in a position of negative equity. With hindsight, the riskiness of the banks' lending policies became obvious.

Key term

Negative equity is the term used to describe the situation where the value of a property is lower than the outstanding mortgage on the property.

Ponder point

Would it be possible for a homebuyer to be in a position of negative equity at the start of the homebuying process?

Where loans in excess of 100% are made to homebuyers, this immediately puts them into a position of negative equity.

If homebuyers find themselves in the position of having negative equity, it can make moving home difficult, if not impossible, because the amount owed on the mortgage is greater than the value of the property. This is often described as being trapped by negative equity. Generally the most straightforward course of action is to wait and hope that property prices will rise and reverse the position. If that is not possible then it is worth considering different options for paying off some of the mortgage and reducing it to below the value of the property. If this can be done, it allows the homebuyer to sell the property and move on.

Following the financial upheavals of 2007 and 2008, the banks have reverted to their cautious lending policies and by 2011 it was no longer easy to obtain a mortgage without having an initial deposit to put towards the cost of the property. For younger people it can be difficult to save enough for the initial deposit on a property, although from time to time the government offers certain schemes that provide help to first-time buyers.

 Ponder point

What do you think is the percentage of owner-occupied housing in the UK? How do you think the UK compares with other countries in Europe?

According to Eurostat (2016), the proportion of homes that were owner-occupied in the UK stood at 70% in 2014. This was higher than Germany and Austria but lower than many other European countries, including Romania and Spain. The average figure for European countries was approximately 70%, so the UK is in line with the European average.

In the UK, in common with many other parts of Europe, there seems to be a cultural imperative to own your own property. The main reasons for this include a need for security and the higher perceived social status of homeowners, compared to renters. There is a major benefit to home ownership once retirement is reached, because housing costs are significantly reduced, as the mortgage should have been paid off. A home can also be a substantial repository of wealth and homeowners are able to pass this wealth on to their beneficiaries when they die. Becoming a homeowner will usually have a positive impact on a person's credit rating, as long as mortgage payments are made on time.

 Ponder point

In other parts of the world the rental property market is much larger than it is in the UK. What factors might contribute to this situation?

In many countries it is considered far more acceptable for individuals or families to rent their home for an extended period of time. Often one of the main factors contributing to this is the legal position of tenants and the tenancy agreements that are available. In many countries it is possible to take out a long-term assured tenancy agreement and to live in the same property for many years. In the UK most tenancy agreements do not offer the same long-term security. With a long-term tenancy agreement the landlord may allow the tenant to make changes to the property as if it were his own home. There may be a good supply of quality rental properties at reasonable rents. Overall responsibility for the rented property remains with the landlord and this gives the tenant freedom from responsibility and ties.

Some countries have more stringent mortgage lending requirements with higher deposits required and mortgages less freely available, making it difficult to purchase a property. In countries where property prices are stable there is less of a perceived need to get on the property ladder to take advantage of rising prices. Finally there may simply be a cultural difference and the desire for home ownership with all of its risks and rewards may not be as strong as it is in the UK.

Everyone needs somewhere to live and for most people the decision is between buying a property and renting a property. For some individuals property represents an investment opportunity and in the UK there has been a large expansion in the 'buy-to-let' market. The consideration of property as an investment is discussed in Chapter 10 whilst this chapter concentrates on the implications of owning your own home.

Property prices

Property ownership has usually been seen as a solid investment proposition within the UK, as homeowners who bought a property in previous decades have seen properties increase substantially in value. However, property prices have been quite volatile over time. Following the financial turmoil of 2007–2008, property prices fell quite markedly, particularly in certain parts of the UK, as measured by the Nationwide House Price Index (Nationwide, 2016) and as seen in Figure 9.1.

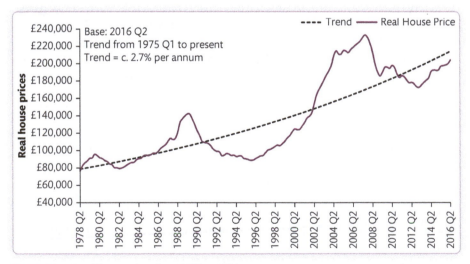

Figure 9.1 UK real house prices from 1978 to 2016
Source: Nationwide Building Society.

Data from the Nationwide House Price Survey reveals how much homeowners have benefited from property price rises in the past, but there is no certainty of any continuation of this in the future. The graph shows what has happened to house prices in 'real terms' after adjusting for inflation between 1978 and 2016.

Rent or buy?

For many people the question of whether to rent or buy is answered by economic necessity. In order to buy a property you need to have a reasonable sum (usually at least 10–20% of the value of the property) to put down as a deposit. You also need a good credit rating, a reasonable level of income, and secure employment or income in order to be offered a mortgage. The greater the level of deposit that can be made, the cheaper the mortgage deal that can be secured.

If you are not in a position to get a mortgage then renting is your only option and this applies very often to younger people. Over time, renting a property will cost more than purchasing one, but in the short term renting can be considerably cheaper. There are individuals who may choose to rent rather than purchase a property, even though they might meet the criteria for obtaining a mortgage.

 Ponder point

Why might some people prefer the option of renting a property, even though they might be in a position to take on a mortgage?

There are many positive aspects to renting, as opposed to buying, a property. The first thing to consider is flexibility. Renting can be a short-term option and allows the tenant to move on, perhaps to a different location. There is only a very short financial commitment when renting. The tenancy agreement might last for between six months and a year, and this is very different to the financial commitment made in taking on a mortgage. A mortgage is a considerable tie and to some people it will feel like a burden. When renting a property, the landlord is usually responsible for all the repairs and maintenance to the property. With home ownership, the costs of the maintenance and repair of the property can be significant and are often overlooked when the decision to take on a mortgage is made. The home will need to be maintained to make it agreeable to live in and, in the long term, to preserve its value.

It is often possible to rent a property more cheaply than the cost of paying for a mortgage on it, particularly at the higher end of the property market. This enables the tenant to live in a more desirable property than would otherwise be the case. If a property is rented rather than bought, then savings are not tied up in a home and that money remains available for potentially profitable investment elsewhere.

The costs involved in signing a rental agreement are minimal, compared to the costs involved when taking on a mortgage. A mortgage is a significant financial commitment and the purchaser needs to be confident that they will be in a position to pay the mortgage for many years to come. If mortgage payments are not met, then the lender can repossess the property. The number of properties repossessed in the UK fluctuates each year, with repossessions usually increasing during periods of economic downturn, especially if interest rates rise. When a property is repossessed, the borrower is forced to leave their home and they may lose all or part of the deposit they originally put towards the purchase of the property. Furthermore, if the forced sale of the property does not realize more than the outstanding mortgage, the lender can seek recovery of the outstanding balance from the borrower. Thus a borrower can find that, even after losing their home and deposit, they remain in debt to the bank or building society. On average, approximately 30,000 homes are repossessed each year (Council of Mortgage Lenders, 2016).

If house prices are falling then individuals are better off renting a property, otherwise their major asset is liable to depreciate. Between 1989 and 1995 house prices fell by 15–25%, which meant that many owner-occupiers found themselves in negative equity, trapped by their mortgage, and unable to move.

 Ponder point

What are the benefits of home ownership compared to renting?

For most people, history has shown that owning a home will prove to be a profitable investment in the long term. The fact that in the UK there is no tax to pay on any gains that you may make on your own home has tended to encourage people to invest in this kind of asset. House prices in general have risen faster than the rate of inflation and they are normally more stable than the price of shares. The rapid price increases in the 1980s were an exception to this and were followed by a price crash in the early 1990s. Increases are usually in line with increases in earnings or spending power, but this is by no means guaranteed.

Home ownership provides security of occupation as long as the mortgage is paid. With a tenancy agreement there is no guarantee that the agreement will be renewed at the end of the term and tenants may find that they are regularly searching for accommodation. In the UK, home ownership is seen to confer a higher social status than renting. Once the mortgage is paid off, homeowners will find themselves with a substantial asset that can be sold to release capital without any tax to pay.

 Ponder point

What factors contribute to rising property prices?

The main factor causing property prices to rise is shortage of supply under the laws of supply and demand. If there is not enough supply relative to demand, which has been the case in the UK for some time, then prices are forced upwards. The number of households in the UK has risen sharply in recent decades and the quantity of available housing has failed to keep up with the increased demand created.

The state of the economy plays an important role in property price movements. Prices are likely to rise in times of economic growth and will usually fall during a recession. When people are confident about their job security and future prospects, consumer confidence increases demand for property and causes prices to rise.

Low rates of interest are another factor that encourages people to buy property, with the effect of pushing up demand. Inflation in the economy as a whole is also likely to cause house prices to rise.

The majority of people need the help of a bank or building society in buying a home, in the form of a mortgage.

Types of mortgage

 Key terms

A **mortgage** is a secured loan made to homebuyers to enable them to buy their property. If the borrower does not keep up repayments on the mortgage, the security would enable the lender to take possession of the property and sell it to recover any amounts owed to them.

The **mortgage term** is the length of time that a mortgage lasts for, usually ranging between five and thirty-five years.

Capital borrowed on a mortgage is the amount borrowed from the lender, under the mortgage agreement, secured against the value of the property.

A mortgage is a type of loan secured against a property. This means that the bank or building society that advances the mortgage has security over the property. If the borrower defaults (stops making mortgage payments), then the lender is able to step in and repossess the property. The lender can then sell the property in order to recoup any amounts outstanding on the loan.

After the initial loan has been made, the borrower usually makes monthly payments to the lender. This continues for the duration of the mortgage, known as the term, which typically might be twenty-five, thirty, or thirty-five years. Banks and building societies offer a whole range of mortgage products with different terms and conditions. The borrower needs to seek out the product that best meets their needs. The term 'capital' is the term often used to describe the amount that has been borrowed.

Repayment mortgage

 Key term

A **repayment mortgage** is one where both the interest and capital are repaid over the term of the mortgage. By the end of the mortgage term, the loan will have been repaid.

A repayment mortgage is one where each monthly payment includes an element of both capital and interest. At the end of the mortgage term the whole of the loan will have been repaid. The monthly payments may seem high relative to other options, and this is because the payments include both elements. At first, the payments comprise mainly interest and a small element of capital. This changes over time until, towards the end of the mortgage term, each payment consists mainly of capital with smaller amounts of interest. For many people, a repayment mortgage is the most appropriate type of mortgage because it ensures that the loan will be completely repaid by the end of the mortgage term.

Example 9.1

A repayment mortgage for £100,000 carrying interest at 5% and with a term of twenty-five years, would cost the homebuyer £585 per month or £7,015 per annum. The way in which this payment is split between interest and capital is shown in Table 9.1. (This assumes the interest rate remains unchanged throughout the mortgage term.)

Table 9.1 Illustration of a repayment mortgage

Year	Total annual payments £	Interest paid in year £	Capital repaid in year £	Capital owing at year end £
1	7,015	4,953	2,062	97,938
10	7,015	3,784	3,231	73,284
20	7,015	1,694	5,321	30,978
25	7,015	186	6,829	Nil

Note that at the end of the mortgage term, the mortgage loan is repaid in full.

Interest-only mortgage

 Key term

An **interest-only mortgage** is one where only the interest is paid on the mortgage loan. No capital repayments are made and at the end of the mortgage term the borrower will still owe the lender the full amount borrowed.

Banks and building societies used to offer interest-only mortgages but these are becoming increasingly rare. They involve no repayments of capital but the borrower should arrange some means of repaying the mortgage at the end of the term. This will be some form of savings product where the borrower can build up sufficient savings over the period of the loan, to enable the capital sum to be repaid at the end of the mortgage term. In the past, endowment policies were sold in this capacity, but they have now become discredited for failing to achieve enough growth to repay the mortgage.

The monthly payments under an interest-only mortgage are less than under a repayment mortgage because only the interest is being paid. However, overall this type of mortgage is more expensive because interest is paid on the full amount of the capital for the whole of the term. This contrasts with a repayment mortgage where the amount of capital owing is constantly reducing and thus the interest charge decreases over time. Interest-only mortgages are often used to purchase buy-to-let properties, covered in Chapter 10. They carry an element of risk as the repayment vehicle used alongside the mortgage may not yield enough to pay off the loan. If the capital is not being repaid, then the borrower is essentially renting the property from the bank. At the end of the mortgage term the mortgage will not be paid off and the bank or building society could repossess the property.

Example 9.2

An interest-only mortgage for £100,000 carrying interest at 5% and with a term of twenty-five years, would cost the homebuyer £417 per month or £5,000 per annum. The way in which this payment is split between interest and capital is shown in Table 9.2. (This assumes the interest rate remains unchanged throughout the mortgage term.)

Table 9.2 Illustration of an interest-only mortgage

Year	Total annual payments £	Interest paid in year £	Capital repaid in year £	Capital owing at year end £
1	5,000	5,000	Nil	100,000
10	5,000	5,000	Nil	100,000
20	5,000	5,000	Nil	100,000
25	5,000	5,000	Nil	100,000

Whilst the interest-only mortgage repayments are significantly smaller than a repayment mortgage, the capital remains unpaid at the end of the mortgage term.

Repayment vehicles

With an interest-only mortgage the borrower should have some form of savings policy that will repay the loan at the end of the term. This could be achieved by using regular ISA savings or regular investments into an investment fund.

Mortgage interest

There are many different ways in which banks and building societies can charge interest on a mortgage: fixed rate, standard variable rate, and tracker mortgages are three of the most common options.

Fixed rate mortgage

 Key term

A **fixed rate mortgage** is one where the interest rate charged on the loan is kept fixed, usually for a certain period of time. At the end of the fixed rate term the rate of interest will change to the follow-on rate, which is often, but not always, the lender's standard variable rate.

A fixed rate mortgage means that the rate of interest which applies to the mortgage is fixed for a certain period of time, which can vary from one year to ten years, or very occasionally they run for even longer. This provides some certainty for borrowers, who are able to budget for their mortgage payments. However, if interest rates fall, it might mean that the borrower is locked into a relatively expensive rate of interest. Conversely if rates rise, then the fixed rate option might become good value. The banks are constantly revising their fixed rate offers in the light of their expectations of what will happen to interest rates. At any one time the range of fixed rates offered is likely to be higher than variable rates, because the lender is taking the risk of any movement in interest rates.

In 1991 mortgage rates increased from 8% to 13% in just six months and reached a peak of 16%. Any borrower on a fixed rate mortgage was in a fortunate position because their mortgage payments remained the same. Any borrower on a variable rate mortgage saw their mortgage payments increase continuously. For some people their mortgage became unaffordable, they stopped making mortgage payments, and the mortgage lender repossessed their home.

A fixed rate mortgage allows borrowers the opportunity to budget for their mortgage payments and provides some certainty within the term of the fix. Fixed rate mortgages usually tie the borrower in with early repayment charges, meaning that if the borrower wants to change the mortgage before the end of the agreement, they will have to pay charges. These could, for example, amount to 1% of the outstanding balance. Longer-term fixed rates, over five years, tend to be more expensive and may have more onerous early repayment charges.

Standard variable rate mortgage

 Key term

A **standard variable rate mortgage (SVR)** is one where the interest rate charged increases and decreases at the lender's discretion.

A standard variable rate mortgage (SVR) is one where the rate of interest is set by the lender, loosely based on the base rate of interest fixed by the Bank of England's Monetary Policy Committee. The lender determines the actual rate of interest and may, or may not, choose to change the rate every time the base rate alters, or to factor in other economic issues in setting their standard variable rate. A borrower with a standard variable rate mortgage may benefit when interest rates are low, but they may find themselves subject to increased mortgage payments if conditions change. A 1% increase in interest rates on a £200,000 mortgage will increase mortgage payments by approximately £167 a month. This amount can make a significant difference to a family budget and the risks of a variable rate mortgage should be balanced against the potential rewards. The standard variable rate is the mortgage rate usually charged when the fixed or discounted period on a mortgage deal ends, known as the follow-on rate.

Tracker mortgage

 Key term

A **tracker mortgage** is one where the interest rate charged on the loan increases and decreases in line with movements in the Bank of England's base rate.

A tracker mortgage has similarities to the standard variable rate mortgage. There is one difference, however, which is that the interest charged on a tracker mortgage will track movements in the Bank of England's base interest rate, whereas a standard variable rate mortgage might or might not track such changes. A tracker mortgage is also known as a variable rate mortgage that is linked directly to the base rate of the Bank of England. As a result, the mortgage interest rate will fluctuate based on the increase or decrease in the Bank's base rate. The tracker rate can apply for a fixed time period or for the entire duration of the mortgage term.

This type of mortgage may be an appropriate choice for borrowers needing lower payments during the initial stages of the loan, because a variable rate is likely to be cheaper than a fixed rate, but it carries the risk that interest payments could go up at any time, depending on movements in the base rate.

Example 9.3

If the Bank of England base rate is 2.25% and the rate for the tracker mortgage that is being offered by the building society is to be 1.5% over the base rate, then the tracker interest rate will be 3.75%. If the base rate rises to 2.50%, the tracker interest rate will become 4.00%.

Offset and current account mortgages

In recent years banks have become more innovative in developing mortgage products and have developed an offset mortgage. This allows interest to be paid on the mortgage loan outstanding, after deducting any savings or current account balances with the bank or building society. If a customer expects their savings or current account balance to be high at various times, they could consider an offset mortgage. It can be quite complicated to work out whether this would be cheaper than a conventional mortgage, but there are internet tools that can carry out the calculation.

Example 9.4

Hugo plans to take out a £220,000 mortgage with his building society. After paying the deposit on the property and meeting the purchase costs, he will have savings of £40,000 in his building society savings account. If he chooses an offset mortgage, interest will only be charged on £180,000 (220,000 − 40,000) rather than the £220,000 that he has borrowed. He will not, of course, receive any interest on his savings, but because mortgage rates for borrowing are usually considerably higher than interest rates on savings, he will benefit.

The deposit

The larger the deposit or the amount of equity in the home, the cheaper the mortgage will be. This is measured by the value of the mortgage loan relative to the value of the property being purchased, known as the loan to value (LTV) ratio.

 Key terms

Equity in a home is the difference between the likely sale price (the property's current valuation) and the mortgage loan outstanding.

Loan to value (LTV) measures the value of the mortgage loan relative to the value of the property being purchased. The bigger the deposit, the lower the LTV ratio.

If the property is worth £100,000 and the borrower is seeking a mortgage of £60,000, then the LTV ratio is 60% (60,000/100,000). This would secure a comparatively cheap mortgage. If, on the other hand, the borrower is seeking a mortgage of £80,000, the LTV ratio would be 80% and the interest rate offered would be higher.

The annual percentage rate (APR)

 Key terms

The **annual percentage rate (APR)** aims to measure the cost of borrowing, taking into account the interest charged and any unavoidable costs that the borrower will have to meet, quoted as an annual rate.

Redemption charges or **early repayment** fees are a form of penalty for paying off a mortgage early or ending a mortgage deal before the end of its term.

Follow-on rate is an indication of the variable rate of interest that will apply to a mortgage once a fixed rate term has been completed. A homebuyer would usually consider remortgaging at this point.

Arrangement fees are the charges made by lenders for setting up or arranging a mortgage and they vary significantly between different mortgages and lenders.

Given the range of mortgage products available with fixed and variable interest rates, variable arrangement fees, and early redemption charges, it has become increasingly complex to identify the true cost of each mortgage loan. The annual percentage rate (APR) provides an indication of how expensive a loan is, as it takes account of the interest that will be charged, plus any unavoidable charges, such as arrangement fees. The APR is quoted as an annual rate and it allows borrowers to compare loans to provide an indication of which loans are more or less expensive. Lenders must quote the APR attaching to a loan but it may not necessarily take into account all the costs of borrowing. The APR is often quoted as a typical APR because the rate charged will vary according to the borrower's credit rating.

Whilst the APR gives an indication of how expensive the interest on the loan is, there may also be other costs included in the loan that are not reflected in the APR. For example, early redemption penalties would not be taken into account, as they are avoidable. Another drawback with the APR is that it is calculated over the full term of the mortgage. Most homebuyers would not keep one mortgage for the whole term; assuming they are in a position to do so, they are likely to take out a new mortgage when a fixed rate mortgage comes to an end, or if a new competitive mortgage becomes available. (However, it might not be possible to remortgage if income had fallen significantly in the meantime, or circumstances had changed making a new loan unlikely.) The APR can provide a useful benchmark by which to compare the main cost, the interest charge, of different loans, providing the measure is understood.

Example 9.5

A potential borrower has found the following five-year fixed rate mortgage products for a twenty-five-year term. He would like to borrow £150,000, but he needs some clarification of the differences between them in order to choose the best mortgage for his circumstances. He has savings for the deposit of £50,000. Each of the mortgages offers a free valuation and there are varying penalties for redeeming the mortgage early, within five years. In all cases the follow-on rate is the lender's standard variable rate (SVR). Table 9.3 compares four five-year fixed rate mortgage products from different lenders.

(continued...)

Table 9.3 Extract from table of rates for five-year fixed term mortgages

Provider	LTV	Interest rate	Indicative follow-on rate (SVR)	Arrangement fee	APR	25-year total cost
Homely	65%	2.89%	3.69%	£1,999	3.6%	£226,324
1st Positive	75%	3.69%	3.69%	£499	3.8%	£230,392
Coalition	75%	3.39%	4.74%	£0	4.3%	£240,083
Espanol	75%	3.59%	4.74%	£995	4.5%	£251,521

The first mortgage offered by Homely Bank is not available to the borrower as he has a deposit of 25% (50,000/200,000) rather than the 35% required for a 65% LTV offer. The other three all require a 25% deposit, so he would be able to apply for any of these. The APR is helpful for an overall comparison, but he may choose to remortgage at the end of his fixed rate term, once there are no longer penalties for remortgaging. The Coalition mortgage is likely to offer the best value, with the cheapest fixed interest rate and no arrangement fee. Although the APR is higher than that for the 1st Positive mortgage, the APR is calculated over the life of the mortgage and he is unlikely to keep the mortgage for the whole twenty-five-year term, hence he will not pay the follow-on rate. Assuming that he keeps the mortgage for five years and then seeks a competitive alternative at that time, Coalition provides the best option.

Other costs of buying a property

Indicative rates

The rates given for Stamp Duty Land Tax (SDLT) are indicative, giving an indication of the rates and tax-free amounts. When carrying out a real-life computation, it would be necessary to refer to the Gov.uk website for details of current tax rates and allowances.
    Other costs involved in purchasing a home include:

- the legal fees incurred in engaging a solicitor or conveyancer to carry out the transfer of the legal ownership of the property
- Stamp Duty Land Tax (SDLT) payable on properties worth more than £125,000. The rate of tax varies from nil for properties costing less than £125,000 up to 12% for properties costing over £1.5m purchased by individuals
- survey fees paid to a surveyor who inspects the property to check that it is structurally sound and that the agreed purchase price represents a reasonable valuation
- life assurance should be taken out by borrowers with dependants, to ensure that the mortgage would be paid off in the event of the death of one of the borrowers.

In addition to the costs involved in buying a property, a new property owner will need to budget for the cost of any repairs needed, property insurance, furnishings, utility costs, and so on.

How much to borrow?

The question of how much it is advisable to borrow is one to which careful consideration should be given. Just because a lender is happy to loan a particular amount, does not indicate that it is wise to borrow that amount. In the recent economic climate of reserved lending by banks and building societies, they do not tend to lend unwisely but there have been times when they have been prepared to make loans that were ill-advised from the borrower's perspective.

Historically banks would lend money for a mortgage based on multiples of salary, which might, for example, have been three times the main earner's annual salary plus the annual income of a spouse or partner. In the early 2000s, loans of up to six times salary or higher were made and often these loans consumed an unreasonable proportion of a borrower's after-tax income, leaving them with inadequate funds to cover day-to-day living costs and certainly with no reserves if anything unexpected occurred.

With the advent of increased fees for higher education, many graduates will have accumulated significant levels of student debt. In order to take this into account, many banks now decide on the amount they are willing to lend based on the borrower's credit rating, their level of after-tax income, and any student debt repayments that will have to be made.

Many commentators advise that you should not commit more than one-third of income after tax, National Insurance, and student loan repayments in mortgage payments. This can be a useful rule of thumb to apply. There are any number of useful online mortgage payment calculators that allow a potential borrower to establish the monthly repayments on any amount of borrowing, over any term, at any rate of interest. These tools are helpful in working out what level of mortgage can be afforded.

Case study—Rachel and her partner

Rachel is twenty-five years old and in a long-term relationship. She is a graduate trainee with a large retail company and has risen to the position of manager of the food hall in a large store, earning £45,000 per annum. Her remuneration package also includes life assurance of three times salary. She and her partner are considering buying a four-bedroom town house, having rented an apartment for several years. They are wondering how much they can afford to borrow on a mortgage. Rachel has a significant amount of student debt of £28,000 outstanding from her degree, but no other debts. She is the main earner as her partner earns £25,000 per annum.

Rachel and her partner have saved up a deposit of £30,000 towards the property, which is on the market for £240,000. They are considering taking out a mortgage for £210,000 and have worked out (from the mortgage payment calculator) that, at a 4% rate of interest, the monthly payments on a twenty-five-year repayment mortgage would be £1,120.

Required:

a) **What are the issues that Rachel and her partner should consider before choosing the type and amount of mortgage?**

(continued...)

b) What type of mortgage would you suggest the couple chooses?

c) What will the LTV ratio be?

d) If mortgage interest rates are 4% and they take out an interest-only mortgage, how much interest would they have to pay over a twenty-five-year term, assuming interest rates do not change?

e) Using the same assumptions, and the monthly mortgage payments given earlier, what would be the total interest payable under the repayment option and why is this less than under the interest-only option?

(Hint: work out the total of the monthly payments for twenty-five years and then deduct the amount borrowed, to arrive at the amount of interest charged.)

f) The couple's income after tax, National Insurance, pension contributions, and student loan repayments comes to approximately £42,000 per annum. Using the rule of thumb that you should not commit more than one-third of available income (after tax and other commitments) to covering mortgage payments, how much can they afford to commit in monthly mortgage payments if they follow this advice?

g) Identify the one-off costs that they will have to pay in buying their own home.

h) If inflation is running at 5% what effect will this have on the value of their mortgage (note, not the house but just the mortgage) and what effect might it have on interest rates?

i) Rachel and her partner have been offered a tracker mortgage for £210,000, currently at 3.39%, or a five-year fixed rate mortgage at 4.99%. There is no fee for the tracker, but the fixed rate mortgage has a £995 fee. There is also a sliding scale of early repayment fees. Assuming the tracker mortgage rate does not change for one year, work out the difference in interest and fees payable under the two options for the first year of the mortgage (ignoring repayments) and consider which mortgage they should take out.

j) Would your advice to the couple be any different if Rachel said she was not enjoying her job and was thinking of retraining as a teacher?

Shared ownership

 Key term

Shared ownership schemes allow buyers who cannot raise adequate funds to buy their own home, to buy a share of a property and rent the remainder. Over time, they can increase the proportion of the property that they are buying.

Shared ownership is an alternative route into home ownership and can be an affordable way to get into the housing market. If a purchaser cannot raise adequate funds to buy a property, they can buy part of their home and rent the remaining part.

The homeowner might buy a 25%, 50%, or 75% share in the home and pay rent on the share that is not being purchased, normally set at an 'affordable' rate. The bigger the share that is purchased, the less rent there is to pay. When the purchaser can afford to do so, they can buy more shares until they own the home outright in a process known as 'staircasing'.

The other share in a shared ownership property is usually owned by a housing association. Alternatively, some shared ownership homes are provided by house builders directly via shared equity schemes. The majority of shared ownership homes are found in major cities and the biggest concentration of shared ownership flats to buy is in London. There are also rural schemes available in some areas.

Rent-a-room relief

Renting out a room in a house can be a good way of making extra money, tax-free. If a homeowner is struggling to pay a mortgage, this can be a useful way of obtaining a contribution to help with the mortgage payments. Rent-a-room relief is a scheme that allows a homeowner to receive up to £7,500 gross income each year from a lodger, free of income tax. To qualify for the tax relief, furnished residential accommodation must be let out in the person's main home. The relief does not apply to rooms let as an office or for other business purposes. Anything charged to tenants for meals, cleaning, laundry, and so on must be added to the rent received when calculating gross rents and no expenses can be deducted. If the rent is more than £7,500 then the whole amount is taxable.

Remortgaging

 Key term

Remortgaging is the process of replacing an existing mortgage with a new mortgage product when the borrower is not moving home. The reason for doing this is usually to secure a lower and/or a fixed interest rate or to borrow a larger amount of capital.

Remortgaging is the process of replacing an existing mortgage with a new mortgage product when the borrower is not moving home. This is commonly done when a fixed rate mortgage deal comes to an end but it can be done at other times where it becomes clear to the borrower that better deals are available to them than their current mortgage offer.

In the past, it became common practice for individuals to remortgage to enable them to borrow a larger amount so that they could pay off more expensive debts they had accumulated (for example, overdrafts and credit cards) with the additional loan received. Homebuyers were able to do this where they had built up equity in their properties as a result of property price rises. The increased value of the property meant that increased security was available to the banks and building societies. When house prices are stable or falling, and remortgage deals demand lower LTV ratios, this option may be less available.

Remortgaging will usually incur costs for the homebuyer, including valuation fees, legal fees, and sometimes fees charged by the new lender.

Equity release schemes

 Key term

Equity release schemes enable older homeowners to release some of the capital tied up in their homes, whilst continuing to live in them.

For many individuals, the investment that they have in their own home will turn out to be their major asset as they approach retirement, when hopefully their mortgages are fully paid off. One way of releasing part of the value of their property is to downsize to a cheaper home. This will release funds that can be invested in savings accounts, pension funds, or however the individual chooses. If the homeowner wants to release part of the capital or equity from their homes without having to move, then equity release schemes are a possibility.

Equity release schemes allow homeowners, usually retired homeowners, to unlock some of the capital tied up in their property in order to provide an income or a lump sum amount. There are two main types of equity release plans available: lifetime mortgages and home reversion plans.

Lifetime mortgage

A rolled-up interest lifetime mortgage is a product where the lender loans a lump sum to an older homeowner or owners, in exchange for a charge against the value of the home. No interest is paid until either the last borrower dies or the property is sold and the loan repaid. Over the course of the loan, the interest is 'rolled up' which means that it is added to the loan either monthly or annually which can significantly increase the amount to be repaid. It is possible that the effect of this increasing loan might be partially offset by any future rises in property prices.

The amount that can be borrowed depends on the value of the property and the age of the homeowners. The older the owners are, the higher the percentage of the value of the property which the lender will be prepared to lend. These mortgages may carry fixed or variable rates of interest. A lifetime mortgage is designed to be a long-term commitment and would require very serious exploration of all the costs before such an arrangement was entered into. If repaid early, it may result in early repayment charges being applied.

It can be useful to consider that at an annual interest rate of 7%, the amount of any borrowing will double in ten years. So £50,000 borrowed under such a lifetime mortgage would become £100,000 in ten years' time, which is a significant change to the amount borrowed in a relatively short space of time.

Home reversion plan

With a home reversion plan, all or a part share of the property is sold to an investment company, which allows the owner or owners to continue living in the property for the rest of their lives. The agreed price paid for the property is usually between 20% and 50% of its value, depending on the homeowner's age and health and that of any spouse or partner. In return, the home reversion company provides a lump sum and a guarantee that the owner can remain in the property completely rent-free for as long as they live, or until the property is sold. If all of the property has been sold under the scheme, the home will belong to the investment company on the death of the owner.

Example 9.6

Assume a homeowner takes out a home reversion plan with the following agreed terms:

- The property is valued at £180,000
- The investment company will buy half of the property and pay the owner £36,000 based on 40% of half of the property's value (£90,000 × 40%)

When the owner dies a few years later, the property is sold for £240,000. At this point the investment company will receive their half share, amounting to £120,000, and the estate of the owner will receive the remaining £120,000. In this example the home reversion plan has proved to be an expensive option for the borrower and his heirs.

 Ponder point

What are the possible disadvantages attaching to lifetime mortgages and home reversion plans?

Both of these schemes carry risk and are expensive. The interest that accumulates on a lifetime mortgage can be substantial. The existence of such a mortgage may limit the possibilities for the older person to move in their later years when they may wish to change the type or location of their property.

Under a home reversion plan the older homeowner, or rather their heirs, could lose out substantially if they do not live for long after the plan is taken out.

With both of these equity release schemes, the value of the estate left to their heirs will be substantially reduced.

Case study—Oliver

Oliver is an actor and his income fluctuates depending on his work, between £10,000 and £30,000 per annum. In a typical year he expects to earn £20,000. He has £30,000 of student debt outstanding from his drama studies degree and he is at the limit of his overdraft arrangement with the bank. He lives in London, renting a shared flat. He has a long-term girlfriend, also renting a flat in London, who has a steady job earning approximately £24,000, and no student debt. If Oliver gets an acting job, it might not be in London and may involve going on tour. Oliver has been thinking about asking his parents whether they would consider lending him the money for a deposit on a flat in London, because he and his girlfriend are frustrated with paying rent and feel that a mortgage would be a better option.

Required:

Advise Oliver and his girlfriend whether, in their current position, they should seriously consider buying a flat in London with the help of a deposit loaned by Oliver's parents and a mortgage from the building society.

Case study—Theo and Kate

Theo and Kate are married and have three small children. Theo earns £29,000 in a public sector job, employed by the National Health Service. Kate runs her own business from home from which she generates an income of £500 per month.

They live in a detached house worth £220,000, which they are buying with the help of a £150,000 repayment mortgage, with a twenty-five-year term. They have a fixed rate mortgage that costs £780 per month. The couple have no savings.

Theo and Kate have three credit cards between them, each with a credit limit of £3,000 that has been reached. The interest on their credit card debts is running at £1,800 per annum and the couple make the minimum payments to the three credit card companies totalling £225 per month. Each month their overdraft with the bank reaches its authorized maximum of £4,000 and interest on this is £600 annually. Their outgoings include £700 per month for living costs and utility bills, the cost of running the car amounts to £100 per month, and food costs amount to £600 per month for the family.

Theo pays income tax of approximately £3,300 per annum and makes National Insurance contributions of £2,280 each year. He is also a member of his employer's pension scheme and makes contributions amounting to 8% of his salary. Assume that Kate has no income tax to pay on her income and expects to pay only a very small amount of National Insurance contributions that can be ignored.

Because of earlier difficulties in Theo and Kate's credit history they are unable to remortgage their house, as the bank is unwilling to increase the size of the mortgage. Theo has been taking the family away each year for a holiday, but because of his overdraft and credit card position he thinks he will be unable to do so this year. The car has a major service coming up and needs new brakes, but is worth very little.

Required:

a) **Using the figures provided, calculate Theo and Kate's joint monthly income after pension contributions, tax, and National Insurance.**

b) Make a list of Theo and Kate's major assets and liabilities.

c) Assess the size of the couple's mortgage relative to their income, after tax and other commitments. Compare their available monthly income to their expenditure. Discuss whether you consider that they have taken on too large a mortgage and assess the riskiness of their position.

d) Can you advise on any steps they could consider taking in order to improve their situation?

Conclusion

Housing is a long-term investment and a mortgage should not be entered into lightly. It is a major financial commitment and borrowers should ensure that they will be able to maintain the payments on their mortgage. If they fail to keep up the payments, their home will be at risk and it may cost them a substantial amount of money.

There are both costs and benefits to home ownership and both sides of the coin should be considered before the decision to purchase is made. The benefits are well known and include the satisfaction and confidence of knowing your home is your own. Home ownership is perceived as leading to increased social status; it will reduce housing costs in retirement and establish an asset that can be passed on to the next generation.

The risks and costs are less frequently discussed and include the risks of falling prices, rising interest rates, substantial maintenance costs, and the inflexibility of property compared to other assets. However, for many people the benefits outweigh the costs and the desire to own property is strong. Having saved for a deposit, budgeted carefully, and found a suitable mortgage product, it is possible that buying a property may prove to be a good long-term investment proposition. The future movement of house prices is always uncertain, but historically house price movements have proved less volatile than stock markets.

 ## Useful websites

The BBC Homes page has a simple mortgage payment calculator that will calculate the monthly payments on any mortgage:
http://bbc.co.uk/homes
Money saving expert has a useful free guide to buying a property and obtaining advice about mortgages:
http://moneysavingexpert.com

 ## References

Council of Mortgage Lenders (2016) *Press releases*. Available at: https://www.cml.org.uk/news/press-releases/3731/ (accessed 4.7.2016)

Eurostat (2016) *Distribution of Population by Tenure Status*. Available at http://ec.europa.eu/eurostat/statisticsexplained/index.php/ (accessed 4.7.2016)

Nationwide (2016) *UK House Prices Adjusted for Inflation*. Available at: http://www.nationwide.co.uk/about/house-price-index/download-data#xtab:uk-series (accessed 5.7.2016)

Practice Questions

Question 1 Quick Questions TRUE OR FALSE?

9.1   A useful rule of thumb is not to commit more than 50% of after-tax income to mortgage payments.

9.2   The mortgage term is the period over which a mortgage loan is borrowed.

9.3   If a borrower defaults on their mortgage payments, the lender can repossess the property.

9.4   An interest-only mortgage means that at the end of the mortgage term only part of the capital will have been repaid.

9.5   A repayment mortgage will require lower monthly payments than an interest-only mortgage at the same rate of interest.

9.6   It is important to get onto the property ladder as soon as possible, because of rising property prices, whether or not your circumstances are settled.

9.7   The interest rate on a tracker mortgage is always directly linked to the base rate set by the Bank of England.

9.8   A mortgage product offered on a 65% LTV requires a deposit of 35% of the value of the property.

9.9   The APR is the only thing to consider when comparing different mortgages.

9.10   Use of an equity release scheme would require very careful consideration.

Question 2 Elliott

Elliott, who has a secure job in engineering, is purchasing a flat in Birmingham for £215,000 and he has saved a deposit of £40,000. He is considering two potential mortgage deals: both are twenty-five-year repayment mortgages and their details are set out below. Assume that the Bank of England base rate is set at 2% and inflation is running at 3%. The economy is in a period of growth:

- A variable tracker mortgage with the Image Building Society at 4.47% for two years, then moving to SVR. The arrangement fee is £999 and the building society valuation fee is £325. Early repayment fees, payable during the first two years, are 1% of the outstanding balance. The APR is 4.4%.

- A fixed rate mortgage with Farleys Bank, at 5.8% for five years, then moving to SVR. The arrangement fee is £550 and the bank valuation fee is £145. Early repayment fees are 3% of the outstanding balance for the first two years, 2% for the next two years, and then 1% for the fifth year. The APR is 5.1%.

Required:

a) Carry out some basic calculations to give an overall guide to the costs of the two mortgages for the first two years.

b) List the questions that Elliott would need to consider before making his choice of mortgage.

c) In what circumstances would Elliott be best advised to take out the tracker mortgage?

Question 3   Ashma

Ashma is looking to purchase a property and Table 9.4 details some three-year fixed rate mortgage products for a twenty-five-year term that she has identified. She would like to borrow £120,000. She has savings for a deposit of £14,000. Each of the mortgages offers a free valuation and there are varying penalties for redeeming the mortgage early, within five years.

Table 9.4 Extract from best-buy mortgage tables

Provider	LTV	Interest rate	Follow-on rate	Arrangement fee	APR
Hampton	85%	2.59%	5.79%	£1,695	5.1%
Eastern	90%	2.69%	3.69%	£1,999	3.5%
Northern	90%	2.44%	5.49%	£995	5.3%

Required:

Consider which mortgage would represent the best value for Ashma, assuming that she will choose to remortgage in five years' time.

* Question 4   Ted

Ted is twenty-seven and would like to buy a property in the Midlands. He is an IT manager, earning £38,004. He has been living in shared accommodation for some time, but he has reached the point where he would like to live on his own. He has recently had a performance review with the company directors and they have indicated that they think he has good prospects with their firm.

Ted has just received an inheritance of £37,000 and he would like to use that as a deposit on a property. He has £17,000 of student debt outstanding. He has seen a city centre two-bedroom apartment for £190,000 and a quick telephone call with the bank has established that they have a variable rate repayment mortgage, with a twenty-five-year term, currently at 5%, that they would be prepared to offer him. They would be prepared to lend up to £151,000. Ted checks the mortgage payment calculator and sees that this would require monthly payments of £893. He notices that an interest-only mortgage would be £629 and that option sounds attractive to him. He is surprised to notice that the calculator warns him that the repayments would rise to £1,601 per month if interest rates were 12% and decides to ignore that information in making his decision.

Required:

a) Calculate Ted's annual income, after tax, National Insurance, and student loan repayments and consider how much he can afford in mortgage repayments.

b) Prepare a list of key points for Ted to consider before proceeding with this purchase.

c) Ted realizes that he could afford an interest-only mortgage. Advise Ted on whether the interest-only mortgage would be a good option.

d) Consider whether Ted should go ahead with this property purchase.

* Question 5 Fred and Jo

Fred and Jo would like to buy a country cottage and they estimate that they need £300,000 for their dream property in the South West. They already own a buy-to-let property in Leeds, which has no mortgage outstanding, that they bought in joint names for £70,000 many years ago. It is now worth £200,000. Their original costs of purchase were £1,000 and they antici-pate selling costs of £3,000. Jo has another investment property that she is selling for £55,000 that will realize a capital gain of £27,000, after accounting for all costs. They have no other savings. Both Fred and Jo are higher rate taxpayers.

Required:

a) How much will Fred and Jo realize after capital gains tax, if they sell both investments in the current tax year?

b) If they take a mortgage on their dream home, what will the LTV be and what impact will this have on their mortgage rate?

c) Would you advise Fred and Jo to put all of their savings into buying the country cottage?

Visit the Online Resource Centre that accompanies this book for additional material:
www.oxfordtextbooks.co.uk/orc/king_carey2e/

Investing in buy-to-let property

 Learning Objectives

After studying this chapter, you should understand:

- The reasons behind the growth in popularity of buy-to-let property investment
- Appropriate means of financing the purchase of buy-to-let properties
- How to assess the viability of a buy-to-let proposal
- The tax implications of owning property as an investment

Introduction

It has become increasingly popular for individuals to become owners of more than one property. Sometimes as a result of owning their own homes, potential investors understand and appreciate the tangible nature of property and the benefits it can bring. Many have identified property as an investment opportunity and, in increasing numbers, have bought a second property as a buy-to-let investment. In some instances buy-to-let investors own multiple properties. The property is rented out with the owner expecting to benefit from the net rental income and, in the long term, from any increase in the property's value.

Some people own second homes as holiday properties, both within the UK and overseas, and often these properties are rented out for part of the year. This chapter focuses on buy-to-let properties and the issues surrounding holiday properties are not considered.

> **Key terms**
>
> A **buy-to-let investment** is a property purchased for the purpose of renting it to tenants. The aim of the investor is to generate a return from rents received and possibly a gain from any increase in the property's value.
>
> A **landlord** is the person owning a buy-to-let property and, as a landlord, that person will have responsibilities to ensure that the property is safe for tenants to live in, is adequately maintained, and meets all the legal requirements of a rented property.

Background

Over the last ten to fifteen years, there has been increased interest from individuals in owning properties as buy-to-let investments. The increased popularity has come about as a result of a number of factors. Volatile and unpredictable stock market movements have led to disenchantment with shares and disappointing pension fund returns have prompted investors to consider property as an alternative investment. Investing in a fund made up of shares and bonds gives individuals little control over the investment choices made on their behalf whilst their savings are subjected to risks that they may or may not wish to take.

In contrast to choosing investment funds, an individual opting to invest in a buy-to-let property can see the actual asset and can make an individual choice as to which property to buy. Being able to physically inspect an asset is appealing to many people as they can assess the property and its location before they buy it. Once purchased, they can manage and monitor the asset, enabling them to exercise their personal judgement as to whether to continue the investment or sell the property. The potential landlord can assess the possible risks and returns of the property and make their own decisions.

In the past the UK tax system made buy-to-let investments attractive but changes introduced in 2016 mean that the taxes payable by landlords have increased.

Demand for rental housing

Demand for rental housing has been increasingly buoyant for a number of reasons, including the growth in the number of households requiring homes and the difficulty, particularly for first-time buyers, of affording mortgage payments.

According to the Office for National Statistics (ONS) (2010), the number of households is projected to rise at least into the 2030s. Figure 10.1 shows the projected growth by household type.

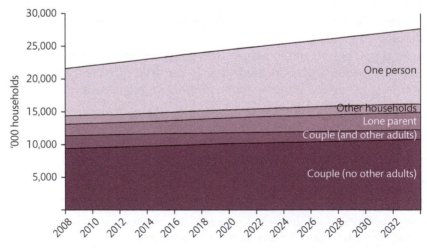

Figure 10.1 Projected number of households by household type in England

Source: Office for National Statistics, 2010.

The ONS (2010) reports that the principal cause of the anticipated growth in the number of households is due to the combined impact of fertility, life expectancy, and net migration. Divorce and family breakdown, leading to more and smaller family groups, will further increase the number of expected households. Each household requires somewhere to live.

Job security has been falling and increasing numbers of people are working on temporary contracts. This has led to individuals and families not wishing or able to take on mortgages and hence deciding to rent. Where there is a desire to join the property ladder, many first-time buyers cannot afford to do so and those that do so eventually have to rent for extended periods whilst they can save for the deposit needed.

Figure 10.2 shows a graph based on data produced by the Nationwide Building Society (2015a) that aims to measure how affordable housing is. The first-time buyer affordability percentage is found by comparing average mortgage payments, on new loans made, with average take home pay. From Figure 10.2, it can be seen that from 1995 up to 2007 the trend was for mortgage payments to absorb an increasing percentage of average take home pay for first-time buyers. Following the 2007 financial crisis, mortgage payments became more affordable, although by 2015 the index remains above 30%, significantly higher than the 20% figures seen in the 1990s. The inability to afford mortgage payments is one of the key factors causing many more people to rent rather than buy their own home.

Another factor causing more potential first-time buyers to rent rather than buy is that, since the financial crisis, mortgage lenders have been demanding bigger deposits from homebuyers. Unaffordable housing and the need for large deposits has led to more people wanting to rent accommodation. With little publicly funded housing available, buy-to-let landlords fulfil a vital role in providing accommodation.

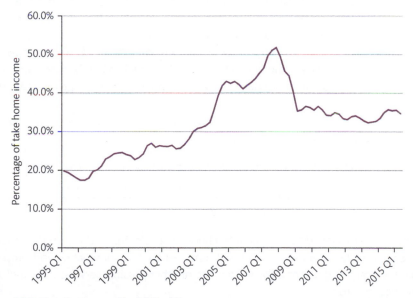

Figure 10.2 First-time buyer affordability (%)

Source: Nationwide Building Society, 2015a.

Benefits of investing in a buy-to-let property

There are many potential benefits of investing in buy-to-let properties which help to explain the popularity of property as an investment. An important factor influencing many buy-to-let landlords is that they have control over their choice of property. They can carefully examine and check over any potential property before considering a purchase. Once purchased, they will own a tangible asset that they can visit, understand, and manage in a way that many other forms of investment, for example shares and bonds, do not allow.

The landlord can set the rent required (having done some market research), determine the terms of the rental, be involved in choosing the tenants, and will be the one to decide when to put the property up for sale. These decisions must comply with any legal requirements placed on landlords.

Buy-to-let landlords can expect to receive a regular income from the rent and they would usually expect the rental income to provide a reasonable return on any sums invested.

Demand for rental properties in many areas is high and this is unlikely to change in the foreseeable future. This should ensure that tenants can be found fairly easily if the rent required is set at an appropriate level. Demand is not consistent throughout all areas of the country and can even vary within towns and cities, hence choice of location is very important.

Another potential benefit of investing in property is that, over time, the property may increase in value, known as a capital gain, although any gain would be liable to capital gains tax. (Capital gains tax is covered in Chapter 7.) Property price movements are discussed in some detail in Chapter 9, and it is certainly the case that property prices can show significant rises but also significant falls.

Owning and renting out a buy-to-let property is something that most people can do alongside their regular employment or work. Nonetheless it is likely to consume a significant amount of time, especially if an agent is not used to manage the property.

 Ponder point

Can you think of typical tasks that an agent can be engaged to carry out on behalf of the landlord?

Agents can be engaged to find tenants, check their references, draw up the tenancy agreement, collect the deposit and rent, ensure that all maintenance and property repairs are carried out promptly, and a range of other possible services that landlords may choose to use.

Disadvantages of investing in a buy-to-let property

There are many possible disadvantages of investing in buy-to-let properties that any potential investor should reflect upon. Once an investor owns a buy-to-let property, he takes on all the responsibilities of being a landlord, responsible for maintaining the property, ensuring that it is safe, and that all legal requirements are met. The extent to which the landlord decides to manage the property on his own will determine the time commitment needed. This can be considerable and the timing can be unpredictable as problems may arise at any time. It is possible to use an agent to find suitable tenants and to manage the property for you. However, this will reduce the return as the agents will require a monthly fee for doing so.

The property market is unpredictable and there is no guarantee that property prices will rise. There have been occasions when prices have remained stagnant and times when prices have fallen markedly; the Nationwide Building Society (2015b) survey of average UK house prices shows that prices fell by an average of 19% from 1989 to 1995. Investors should consider a buy-to-let property as a long-term investment and not expect to make a quick return on their investment.

There will be occasions when the property is unoccupied either because tenants cannot be found or because maintenance or repair work needs to be carried out between tenancies. This possibility should always be factored into any property appraisals as the mortgage and certain other costs will need to be paid regardless of whether or not the property is occupied.

One significant disadvantage of property investment is that it is rather inflexible; if the owner wishes to release some capital, then part of the property cannot be sold. The entire property has to be sold. When properties are bought and sold, it is a time-consuming and expensive process and finding a buyer for a property can be an unpredictable process.

Choosing a buy-to-let property

The type of property chosen should take into consideration a number of overlapping factors. The size and location of the property will be restricted by the amount of finance that the investor wishes to invest, which in turn will be limited by the amount of funds that can be raised.

Careful research needs to be carried out into the neighbourhood in which any chosen property is located. For example, if the property is likely to suit young professionals, they will expect good communication links. If it is likely to suit a family, then good local schools will make a property more attractive to them. Having identified the type and location of a property, the landlord needs to find out about the rent charged on similar properties in the area and the ease with which tenants have been found.

The location of the buy-to-let property will need to be within easy reach of where the landlord lives if he plans to manage it without the use of an agent. The condition of the property also needs to be taken into account. If it needs significant repairs and refurbishment, then funds will need to be set aside for this purpose and the costs taken into account in computing the net rental income.

Any potential investor in property needs to ensure that they can afford to cover all of the costs that will have to be met in buying the property and getting it ready to rent. When property is purchased as a buy-to-let investment, then there is stamp duty payable at higher rates than when a homebuyer buys a property to live in. Table 10.1 shows the stamp duty rates on properties costing up to £925,000.

Table 10.1 Stamp Duty Land Tax payable on buy-to-let properties

Property price	Rate paid on portion of price within each band
Up to £125,000	3%
Over £125,000 and up to £250,000	5%
Over £250,000 and up to £925,000	8%

Overall, the landlord needs to consider how much he can afford to invest in a property, the likely rental income that can be achieved, the needs of potential tenants, and the likely prospects for the area. If the property is attractive to potential tenants and there are good prospects for the local area, these factors should help to ensure fewer vacant periods and reasonable capital growth, if property prices in general remain buoyant. One potential pitfall to avoid is the danger of focusing on choosing somewhere that the landlord would like to live, rather than one that has good rental potential.

Financing buy-to-let investments

 Key term

A **buy-to-let mortgage** is a mortgage made by a bank or building society to purchasers of properties that are to be rented out and it is usually an interest-only mortgage.

Investors in buy-to-let properties are not eligible to borrow using a homebuyer mortgage; they are required to take out a buy-to-let mortgage, which is usually interest-only. The interest rates charged on these mortgages are higher than for homebuyer mortgages and the deposit required is usually greater. As with homebuyer mortgages, the higher the deposit, the lower the loan to value (LTV) ratio and the better the interest rate offered. Typically deposits of between 30% and 40% are required. This amount is likely to represent a significant sum of money.

Ponder point

Can you think of ways in which potential buy-to-let investors might raise a significant deposit?

Investors may be able to finance the deposit from savings they have accumulated or sometimes by remortgaging their own home in order to release some of the gain built up as a result of its increase in value.

Buy-to-let mortgages can be fixed rate or variable rate in the same way as for home-buyer mortgages and similar considerations will apply when deciding which to choose. If interest rates are expected to rise, then it will be worthwhile considering a fixed rate mortgage, whereas if interest rates are expected to fall, a variable rate mortgage may prove more advantageous. In order to increase the predictability of the investment, many investors opt for a fixed rate mortgage.

When a new mortgage is taken out or when a mortgage is rearranged, the lender may charge an arrangement fee. This fee may be quoted as a percentage of the property price or as a fixed amount and it needs to be taken into account when choosing which lender to use.

Appraising a buy-to-let investment

Once a property has been found and a suitable mortgage product identified, the investor will need to identify and estimate all of the relevant costs associated with the property.

 Ponder point

When purchasing a buy-to-let property, what initial costs, in addition to the purchase price, might the would-be landlord expect to incur?

There are many costs associated with the purchase of a property in the UK. These are likely to include:

- Stamp Duty Land Tax payable at rates dependent on the property's price
- fees payable for the conveyancing work needed to secure the legal transfer of the property's ownership
- fees payable to a surveyor who reports on whether the property is structurally sound and whether the price agreed represents a reasonable valuation of the property
- mortgage arrangement fees.

Once acquired, the property may need some improvements or repairs to be carried out. There is legislation that all landlords must comply with and this will involve costs for inspections such as carrying out electrical and gas safety checks and arranging for energy efficiency certificates to be issued. Furniture, floorings, and fittings (kitchen or bathroom) may need to be purchased. Properties can be rented out furnished or unfurnished.

To arrive at the overall cost of a property, all of the costs associated with buying the property and getting it ready for rental will need to be taken into account, including Stamp Duty Land Tax, surveyor's fees, and conveyancing fees.

 Ponder point

Once the property has been purchased, what costs is the landlord likely to incur in running the property?

There is a long list of possible costs that may be incurred: mortgage interest (usually the major cost), agent's fees, property insurance, maintenance, repairs, and service charges. Some of these costs will be higher than if the equivalent property were owner-occupied as, in general, tenants tend not to be as careful as owner-occupiers. Tenants will usually be responsible for paying council tax and for meeting the cost of utility bills: electricity, gas, water, broadband, and telephone.

Example 10.1

A landlord rents out a property for an average of eleven months each year, for a rent of £1,050 per month. Agent's fees of 10% are payable, insurance costs are £475 per annum, repairs cost £280 per annum, and other costs of running the property amount to £110 per annum. The interest-only buy-to-let mortgage on the property is for a loan of £125,000 with an interest rate of 5%.
Table 10.2 shows the computation of net rental income.

Table 10.2 Computation of net rental income

	£	£
Rent received		11,550
Expenses		
Agent's fees (10% of rental income)	1,155	
Mortgage interest (£125,000 loan at 5% interest)	6,250	
Insurance	475	
Repairs and maintenance	280	
Other costs	110	
Total expenses		8,270
Net rental income		3,280

Rental yield

Rental yield is a key measure in assessing a potential or existing buy-to-let investment. Agents often measure it as follows:

$$\text{Agent rental yield }(\%) = \frac{\text{Annual rental income}}{\text{Cost of the property}} \times 100$$

The agent rental yield is the figure often quoted by letting agencies and property developers, but it does not measure the true rental yield achieved by a buy-to-let investor, as it calculates the yield based on the whole cost of the property rather than the actual amount that the buy-to-let landlord has invested.

The annual rental income used in the calculation of the agent rental yield is often the gross amount and does not allow for the costs that are likely to be incurred. A more meaningful measure of the rental income is net rental income, which is the income net of all the costs incurred in maintaining and running the property.

Instead of comparing the net rental income to the cost of the property, it is more meaningful to compare it to the amount the landlord has invested in the property. This will comprise the deposit plus all the one-off purchase costs including stamp duty, surveyor's fees, and conveyancing fees.

To assess a potential buy-to-let investment or one made recently, a more appropriate and meaningful rental yield measure would be as follows:

$$\text{Rental yield }(\%) = \frac{\text{Net rental income after all costs are deducted (for the year)} \times 100}{\text{Deposit + All the one-off purchase costs}}$$

Notice that the one-off costs have to be paid when the property is purchased (stamp duty, legal fees, conveyancing fees, repairs), and are not deducted in arriving at the net rental income for the year. They are part of the amount the landlord has to invest to acquire the property.

Over a period of the time the property value may well increase or decrease and then the best way to measure the rental yield would be as follows:

$$\text{Rental yield }(\%) = \frac{\text{Net rental income after all costs are deducted (for the year)} \times 100}{\text{Equity invested in the property}}$$

The equity is the amount that would be released if the property were sold. That is, it would be the current property value less the amount owed to the mortgage lender.

When a potential buy-to-let investment is being appraised, the possibility of vacant periods should be taken into account in arriving at the expected rental income for a property. Anticipating receipt of eleven months' rental income in any one year is a reasonable approach to take account of vacant periods.

Example 10.2

The property rented out by the landlord in Example 10.1 originally cost a total of £155,000, including all purchase costs, and has a current valuation of £185,000. The mortgage on the property is for £125,000.

The rental yield would be 5.5% $\left(\dfrac{3,280}{60,000} \times 100 \right)$

The numerator is the net rental income from Example 10.1. The denominator is the equity in the property which is the difference between its current value and the mortgage owed, £185,000 – 125,000 = £60,000.

Case study—Imran (Town Close)

Imran lives and works in central London. He earns £40,000 per annum and usually receives an annual bonus of at least £6,000. He is keen to join the property ladder but cannot afford to buy a property in the area in which he wishes to live in London. He is considering investing in a buy-to-let property in Town Close, Hertfordshire, where he comes from and where his parents still live. Imran anticipates that he is likely to own the property for approximately five years at which point he plans to move out of London.

The property he has found is a leasehold flat costing £190,000, in perfect order. Imran has £68,000 in savings which have been boosted by an inheritance he recently received. He has a friend who is a property lawyer who has agreed to do the conveyancing for him; the structural survey and valuation will cost £1,000 and Stamp Duty Land Tax will amount to £7,000. From his savings £8,000 will be used to cover the purchase costs and the remainder put down as a deposit.

Details of the expected rental income, mortgage, and anticipated running costs are as follows:

- The agents advise that the rent should be set at £1,100 per month.
- Agent's fees will amount to 10% of rental income per annum. They will find suitable tenants and manage the property.
- Imran will take out an interest-only buy-to-let mortgage from Sox Bank at the rate of 6% per annum, fixed for five years.
- The service charge on the flat will be £250 per annum. This is a contribution towards maintaining the common areas, such as halls, stairways, and the exterior.
- Insurance on the flat is estimated at £500 per annum.
- Imran estimates that repairs and maintenance will amount to between £200 and £300 each year.

Required:

a) Calculate the monthly and annual cost of the mortgage with Sox Bank, for the first three years of the property ownership.

b) Calculate the net rental income that Imran will receive in each of the first three years, (assume that the flat will be rented out for eleven months each year and the rent will remain unchanged over that time, and ignore any income tax.)

Property prices are predicted to remain static for the next three years and to increase by approximately 3% per annum thereafter.

c) Calculate the rental yield for the first three years.

d) Discuss your findings based on the calculations you have done and advise Imran as to whether he should consider investing in this property. Identify possible benefits and possible risks attaching to this opportunity. (Interest of 2.4% is currently available on fixed term building society accounts.)

Taxation of buy-to-let properties

Income tax

The owner of a buy-to-let property will be liable to pay income tax on the net rental income from that property. The net rental income is arrived at after deducting all allowable expenses which were incurred 'wholly and exclusively' for the purposes of running that property. Allowable expenses include costs such as insurance, agent's fees, and service charges. In the past, mortgage interest payments were also a fully deductible expense for tax purposes. However, by 2020 mortgage interest payments will only be fully deductible by basic rate taxpayers as the mortgage interest relief will be restricted to 20%. Examples 10.3 and 10.4 illustrate this effect.

Legal and professional costs incurred in buying the property are not an allowable expense for income tax purposes. (The legal and professional costs can be included as part of the cost of the property for capital gains tax purposes.)

Example 10.3

A property generates rental income of £27,900, mortgage interest amounts to £12,000 per annum, and other allowable expenses amount to £3,000 per annum.

If the landlord is a basic rate taxpayer, Table 10.3 shows how the income tax payable would be calculated.

Table 10.3 Income tax computation (Basic rate taxpayer)

	£
Rental income	27,900
Allowable expenses (excluding mortgage interest)	3,000
Net rental income	24,900
Income tax @ 20%	4,980
Less: tax relief on mortgage interest (£12,000 × 20%)	2,400
Income tax payable	2,580

Example 10.4

Using the same details as in Example 10.3 but assuming that the landlord is a higher rate taxpayer, Table 10.4 shows how the income tax payable would be calculated.

Table 10.4 Income tax computation (Higher rate taxpayer)

	£
Rental income	27,900
Allowable expenses (excluding mortgage interest)	3,000
Net rental income	24,900
Income tax @ 40%	9,960
Less: tax relief on mortgage interest (£12,000 × 20%)	2,400
Income tax payable	7,560

The two tax computations in Tables 10.3 and 10.4, show how much more income tax has to be paid by buy-to-let landlords who are higher rate rather than basic rate tax-payers. This occurs as a result of relief for mortgage interest only being given at the basic rate because mortgage interest is usually the biggest expense a landlord incurs.

Capital gains tax

When individuals sell their own home, then any gain arising is not subject to capital gains tax. However when a buy-to-let property is sold, any gain arising is subject to capital gains tax.

The gain is calculated by comparing the proceeds of the sale, after all selling costs have been taken into account, less the purchase cost, after all the costs of purchasing have been taken into account. Costs incurred when purchasing a property (Stamp Duty Land Tax, legal fees, and survey fees) would not be allowable for income tax purposes but would be taken into account as part of the original cost of the property for capital gains tax purposes, when it is sold. Any such costs increase the original cost of the property thereby reducing the capital gain.

Example 10.5

A buy-to-let property was purchased for £190,000 a few years ago and at the time legal fees of £1,500 were incurred together with surveyor's fees of £800 and Stamp Duty Land Tax of £7,000.

The property was sold for £249,000. Legal fees and estate agent's fees amounted to £9,500.

The capital gain is calculated in Table 10.5.

Table 10.5 Capital gains tax computation

	£	£
Property disposal proceeds:		
Selling price		249,000
Less: costs of selling		9,500
		239,500
Property cost		
Purchase price	190,000	
Add costs of acquisition (1,500 + 800 + 7,000)	9,300	
		199,300
Capital gain		**40,200**

Capital gains tax (at the residential rate) would be payable on the gain after the annual exemption has been taken into account.

Example 10.6

If the individual in the Example 10.5 is a higher rate taxpayer and had no other capital gains or losses in the year, Table 10.6 shows how the capital gains tax payable would be calculated.

Table 10.6 Capital gains tax

	£
Capital gain (from Table 10.6)	40,200
Less: annual exemption	12,000
Taxable capital gain	28,200
CGT payable at 28%	**7,896**

Risks faced by buy-to-let investors

The main risks faced by landlords can be summarized under three headings: those that relate to house price movements, tenant issues, and cost control.

House price movements

Negative house price movements represent a real risk to investors, as falling prices will reduce the value of their investment. Poor market conditions will also make it very difficult for the buy-to-let investor to sell the property when they are ready to.

Tenant issues

Tenants may prove hard to find and empty properties will greatly reduce the rental income as well as presenting potential security issues for the landlord. The mortgage payments have to be paid whether or not the property is occupied and tenant-free periods can impose a considerable strain on the landlord's finances. Once the property is occupied, there will be normal wear and tear on the buildings, plus the possibility of accidental damage. Tenants may abscond from the property without paying all the rent that is due. Agents will hold a deposit against damage and unpaid rent, but the deposit may not be sufficient to cover all such costs.

Cost control

Costs incurred in running the property can increase. In particular, interest rate rises will cause mortgage payments to increase, when the buyer is not on a fixed rate mortgage, or when a fixed rate mortgage comes up for renewal.

Case study—Imran (Station Heights)

Imran is also looking at an alternative to the Town Close property as a buy-to-let investment. He is considering a newly built flat, in a development called Station Heights, which costs £200,000 and he would use £60,000 of his savings as a deposit. The remainder of his savings would be used to cover stamp duty and other purchase costs:

- The mortgage interest rate that Sox Bank would charge on this loan would be 6.5%, which is higher than on the previous loan he considered. There would be no arrangement fee for this mortgage.
- Stamp Duty Land Tax would be £7,500 and no surveyor's or legal fees would be payable.
- The agent's fee would be 10% per annum for finding tenants and managing the rental.
- Insurance would cost £520 per annum and Imran estimates that repair and maintenance costs would be £nil in the first year and a maximum of £200 per annum in the subsequent two years.
- The service charge will be £400 per annum.
- The property developers who built the flat are guaranteeing to cover any tenant-free periods during the first three years, provided an agent is used and the rent asked is no more than £1,100 per month during that time. Imran plans to set the rent at £1,100 per month.

Required:

a) Appraise this buy-to-let proposal for the first three years and compare it to the Town Close flat considered earlier. (Ignore income tax.)

b) What will be the tax implications for Imran, a higher rate taxpayer, of investing in a buy-to-let property?

Conclusion

The popularity of property as an investment has grown as a result of many factors, including a loss of confidence in other forms of investment and the degree of control over an investment which owning a buy-to-let property allows. In addition, demand for rental property is rising as the number of households in the UK continues to rise. Changes in 2016 to the amount of stamp duty that buy-to-let investors have to pay when investing in property, coupled with less generous allowances for income tax purposes, may reduce the popularity of this type of investment.

Investors aim to achieve an annual return on their property in the form of the net rental income they receive. They will also be hoping that, in the long term, the value of the property will increase enabling them to benefit from a capital gain. There can never be any guarantee of achieving a gain and it would certainly be unwise to plan to invest for a short period of time.

When assessing buy-to-let investments, it is important to identify all of the costs that are likely to be incurred in order to purchase the property, and to ensure the investor can cover all the costs plus the deposit.

Rental yield should be based on the net rental income after all the running costs have been met, divided by the total amount the landlord has invested in the property.

Buy-to-let investors become the landlords of their properties with responsibilities to manage the flat or house and with responsibilities to their tenants. Landlords will be subject to income tax on their annual net property income, after allowable expenses are deducted, and to capital gains tax on any gains arising when the property is sold.

Buy-to-let investing is likely to remain popular with some investors who appreciate being able to choose and manage their property investments in a way that other investments do not allow.

Useful websites

The website for the Association of Residential Lettings Agency publishes up-to-date reviews on the buy-to-let market:
https://www.arla.co.uk
For regular surveys of house price movements:
http://www.nationwide.co.uk

The website for the National Landlords Association is a membership body that provides up-to-date information for residential landlords:

http://www.landlords.org.uk

The Residential Landlords Association is a membership body that aims to campaign on key issues and support its members:

http://www.rla.org.uk

 ## References

Nationwide Building Society (2015a) *First time Buyer Affordability Measure*. Available at: http://www.nationwide.co.uk (accessed on 1.12.2015)

Nationwide Building Society (2015b) *UK House Prices since 1952*. Available at: http://www.nationwide.co.uk (accessed on 1.12.2015)

Office for National Statistics (2010) *Communities and Local Government, Household Projections, 2008 to 2033*. Available at: https://www.gov.uk/government/uploads/system/uploads/attachment_data/file/6395/1780763.pdf (accessed on 4.4.2013)

 ## Practice Questions

Question 1 Quick Questions TRUE OR FALSE?

10.1   Property is an asset that over time is certain to yield a capital gain.

10.2   Becoming a buy-to-let landlord carries with it legal and ethical responsibilities.

10.3   Property is a very flexible investment.

10.4   Buy-to-let mortgages usually demand a relatively small percentage deposit.

10.5   Interest rates charged on buy-to-let mortgages are usually higher than on mortgages for homeowners.

10.6   The gross rental income received from a tenant is subject to income tax.

10.7   Capital gains arising on buy-to-let properties are subject to capital gains tax.

10.8   The rental yield is a measure of the net rental income received as a proportion of the cost of the property.

10.9   Mortgage interest payable on buy-to-let properties is an allowable expense for income tax purpose, but it can only be offset at the basic rate of tax, regardless of whether the landlord is a basic or a higher rate taxpayer.

10.10   When calculating the capital gain arising on the disposal of a buy-to-let property, the cost of the property can include all the professional fees and Stamp Duty Land Tax paid when the property was bought.

*Question 2 William

William, aged forty-five, has built up a reasonable level of savings over many years but is concerned at the very low interest rates that his savings accounts are currently paying. He has seen an advertisement placed by a local estate agent that promises:

'Rental properties for sale from £99,000. Guaranteed rental yield of 7% for the first two years. 80% mortgages available.'

William has total savings of £45,000 and after seeing the advert, he is giving serious consideration to buying two of the flats and using most of his savings to do so. The guaranteed return is significantly better than the low interest rates he is currently earning.

Required:

Discuss the issues that William should be aware of before embarking on buying the two buy-to-let flats.

Question 3 Anton

Anton bought a buy-to-let flat for £90,000 some years ago and has an interest-only mortgage for £70,000. The flat is currently worth £100,000. The flat is rented out furnished and he has long-term tenants in the flat who pay a monthly rental of £800 per month. The tenants plan to move out in twelve to fifteen months' time. Over the last year, he has incurred the following costs in connection with the flat:

- Agent's fees at 11% of rental income
- Mortgage interest at £350 per month
- Insurance of £290 per annum
- Property maintenance costs of £800 per annum
- Service charge of £500 per annum
- Replacement furniture at £900

Required:

a) **Calculate Anton's net property income for the year.**
b) **Assuming Anton is a higher rate taxpayer, how much income tax will he have to pay on his property income?**
c) **Anton plans to sell the flat in a year's time when his current tenants move out. He estimates the sale price will be approximately £103,000 and the costs of selling are expected to amount to £5,000. Estimate the CGT that would be payable on the sale.**

* Question 4 Christoph

Christoph is considering investing in a buy-to-let property for £125,000 using an interest-only mortgage for £105,000. He has received the following estimates for the estimated income and costs:

- Rental income of £850 per month.
- Christoph plans to manage the property himself and to pay an agent a one-off fee of £500 to find a tenant. He expects that most tenants will stay for one year and to have an average one month gap between tenants.
- A mortgage arrangement fee of £950 would be payable and mortgage interest of £620 would be payable each month.
- Legal fees and surveyor's fees are estimated at £750. Stamp Duty Land Tax of £3,750 will be payable.
- Insurance on the property will amount to £340 per annum.
- Repairs and maintenance are estimated at £650 per annum.

Christoph plans to sell the property in three years' time and hopes that its value will have increased by at least £5,000 during that time.

Required:

a) Calculate the net property income for three years assuming that the estimated income and costs remain unchanged throughout that time.

b) What is the rental yield for each of the three years?

c) Given Christoph's longer-term plans for the property, advise him on making this buy-to-let investment.

 Visit the Online Resource Centre that accompanies this book for additional material: www.oxfordtextbooks.co.uk/orc/king_carey2e/

11 Using insurance to manage your risks

 Learning Objectives

After studying this chapter, you should understand:

- The importance of insurance in personal financial planning
- The meaning of the terms *uberrima fides*, moral hazard, and adverse selection in the context of insurance
- The difference between the two main types of life assurance
- The circumstances when life assurance should be in place
- How to be a discriminating purchaser of insurance

Introduction

Insurance is a major part of personal financial planning; life assurance and income protection in particular are types of insurance that should be considered at certain stages in life. Life assurance is insurance against loss of life and income protection is insurance against losing the capacity to earn due to illness or an accident. Some forms of insurance are a legal requirement, some are a sensible option, and some do not represent good value for money. The aim of this chapter is to ensure a sound understanding of what insurance is, when some form of cover is essential, when it represents a sensible option, and when it might be better to self-insure.

 Key terms

Self-insurance is when an individual decides to carry the risk personally of suffering a potential loss. If a loss does occur there is no compensation to cover it.
Assurance is a specific type of insurance that relates to insuring against loss of life.
An **insurance premium** is the payment that a policyholder makes in order to buy the insurance cover.

What is insurance?

Insurance is a contract or policy whereby an insurance company agrees to provide compensation or a payout in the event of the policyholder suffering loss, damage, illness, or death. It covers risks from events that might cause a financial loss, where there is no possibility of any gain. If there were the possibility of a gain as well as a loss, then the contract would be described as a form of gambling, rather than insurance. In return for the cover, the insured person pays a premium, which is a payment to the insurance company to buy the insurance policy. Insurance is a form of protection against risk. The policyholder is prepared to pay a relatively small premium in order to receive compensation should they suffer some form of loss. Some types of insurance are a legal requirement but for many, whether or not insurance is taken out depends to some degree on an individual's attitude to risk. A risk averse person may be prepared to buy many insurance policies to avoid the possibility of suffering a loss.

 Ponder point

How many different types of insurance can you think of?

There are many, many different kinds of insurance. You could spend a lot of money insuring against a multitude of risks. Some of the most common ones are:

- Travel
- Mobile phone
- Buildings
- Extended warranty on home appliances
- Car
- Wedding
- Private medical treatment
- Laptop
- Life assurance
- Identity fraud
- Pet
- Accidental death
- Dental care
- Critical illness

The majority of households in the UK will have a number of insurance policies in place. Figure 11.1 shows the percentage of households with different types of insurance products for 2013 and the average annual expenditure on insurance products.

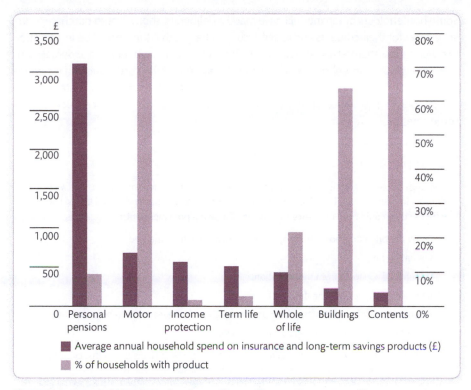

Figure 11.1 Household holdings of, and annual expenditure on, insurance and long-term savings products, 2013

Source: Association of British Insurers analysis, based on ONS data.

There are so many different types of insurance available, it can be difficult to know whether to take out a particular insurance policy or not. It may be possible to self-insure against certain risks. To self-insure means to carry the risk of suffering a loss yourself. If a loss does occur, there is no compensation to cover it and you meet the costs of the loss yourself. Instead of paying a regular premium to an insurance company, the money can be paid into a savings account so that there is a fund available if a loss occurs. Alternatively, a person with sufficient savings can use those to cover the loss.

The average expenditure on personal pension insurance looks high in comparison to other insurances, but it represents the contribution made by individuals towards a personal pension plan. A pension is a particular kind of insurance policy, discussed later in the chapter.

 Ponder point

Figure 11.1 shows that only 76% of households purchased contents insurance in 2013. Why do you think 24% of households chose not to purchase such a policy?

Some householders or tenants will have made a deliberate choice not to purchase insurance cover for their contents and to self-insure, believing that they would be in a position to cover the loss themselves from savings, in the event of a fire, robbery, or accidental damage. Some poorer householders or tenants will have found the cost of such an insurance policy to be prohibitive and as a result will not have been able to purchase contents cover.

Example 11.1 provides an illustration of how difficult the insurance decision can sometimes be.

Example 11.1

A young couple are getting married and have been advised that they should consider wedding insurance. They are both feeling very anxious about the big day and would like to know whether they could have insurance to cover the following possible events:

a) Either the bride or groom changing their mind about getting married.

b) Losing the rings.

c) Presents being stolen from the reception.

d) Rain falling on the wedding day.

e) Parents of the bride contracting food poisoning, causing the wedding to be postponed.

f) A guest falling over a marquee rope and breaking a leg.

After some research they discover that it is not normally possible to insure against circumstances a) or d) but that it should be possible to take out insurance against all of the other events, and indeed many more besides. The more risk averse the couple is, the more policies they can choose to buy. It can be difficult to decide just how much wedding insurance to purchase and what risks could be covered by self-insurance.

Insurable interest

In order to be able to take out an insurance policy, it is necessary for the policyholder to have an insurable interest in the subject matter of the policy. An insurable interest exists where a loss will be suffered if the insured event occurs. For example, footballers can insure their legs or feet or other limbs against injury, because if such an injury occurred they would not be able to earn their living. In contrast, it would not be possible for a football fan to insure a player's legs, because they would not suffer a financial loss if the player were injured.

Many things can be insured against, the principle being that as long as there is an insurable interest and a willing insurance company, it is possible to buy insurance. If the event occurs which the insurance covers, then the policy should pay out. For example, unlikely as it may seem, in America it is possible to buy insurance against alien abduction. If the insured person were to be abducted by aliens, then the insurance company would pay compensation to the policyholder, or perhaps to their beneficiary if the aliens had held onto them!

Key term

Excess is the portion of any insurance claim that would be met by the policyholder. The higher the amount of excess on the policy, the cheaper the policy should be.

To insure or not to insure?

There are some factors to consider when making a decision about whether to take out an insurance policy or not:

- First, consider the chances or probability of a loss occurring. For example, the chances of identity theft occurring are statistically very low. If the chances of such an event happening are statistically very small, it might not be necessary to purchase an insurance policy to provide cover against the very small chance of a loss. According to CIFAS (2016) identity theft is still a comparatively rare crime, with 170,000 cases being reported by their members in the UK in 2015.

- The next step is to consider the amount of any potential loss arising. Where the potential loss is significant it is sensible to consider insuring against the possibility of the loss. For example, buildings insurance usually represents good value for money. The risk is usually quite low, but the potential loss is likely to be high and most people cannot self-insure against this type of risk. According to the Association of British Insurers (2015) the average compensation paid to households suffering a fire in 2013/14 was £11,000. On the other hand, the probability might be higher that a new dishwasher could go wrong within three years, but the potential cost of any repair is likely to be quite low and this is the kind of risk that many people can self-insure against.

- Having considered the probability of a particular event occurring and the potential amount of any loss, the next step is to consider the cost of the policy. The cost of some policies can be out of all proportion to the cover provided. For example, payment protection insurance and extended warranties, discussed later in the chapter, often fall into this category. The insurance cover is expensive compared to the potential amount of compensation. On the other hand, the cost of life assurance is usually small compared to the level of cover provided.

- A final decision is to consider the amount of any excess on the policy. It is possible to reduce the cost of a policy by increasing the amount of any excess. The excess is the portion of any insurance claim that will have to be met by the policyholder and the higher the excess, the cheaper a policy should be. It is in effect an element of self-insurance and a policy might include a compulsory level of excess and then the opportunity to increase that, known as voluntary excess, in order to reduce the premium.

Ponder point

Should a young man going on holiday to America take out travel insurance?

The probability of a loss occurring is quite small for a young man going on holiday to America, but the range of risks covered is wide and includes cancellation, loss of luggage, and medical costs. The loss arising from cancellation and losing luggage can be significant but could possibly be managed. However, the major risk with travel to America arises from falling ill or having an accident and incurring medical costs. The potential loss is enormous and, in that context, the cost of a travel insurance policy represents good value for money. It would not be sensible for this young man to travel to America without travel insurance.

It is important to think rationally before taking out an insurance policy. Over the years the insurance industry has been very good at selling insurance policies on the basis that they will provide 'peace of mind'. If there is a reasonable probability of suffering a loss, the premium is acceptable, and the potential loss is high, then it might be wise to take out a policy. If the risk is low, the premium expensive, and the potential loss manageable, it might be better to self-insure.

Uberrima fides or utmost good faith

 Key term

Uberrima fides means utmost good faith, meaning that all parties to an insurance contract must make a full declaration of all the material facts, otherwise the policy becomes invalid.

Uberrima fides has been a very important legal principle that has underpinned insurance contracts for many years. It means that all parties to an insurance contract must deal in utmost good faith, making a full declaration of all the material facts, when an insurance proposal is being considered. In certain instances there could be a temptation to not be completely honest when seeking insurance. For example, car insurance is very expensive for young people and there may be a temptation to conceal some of the essential facts from the insurance company when taking out a policy. It may be considerably cheaper to declare a parent as the main driver, rather than the young driver who is going to be driving the vehicle. However, because the principle of *uberrima fides* governs all insurance contracts, the policy would be invalid if the insurance company was not in possession of all the material facts. It is a legal requirement to give the insurance company all of the facts so that a proper risk assessment can be made.

There have been cases in the past where insurance companies have invoked the principle of *uberrima fides* to avoid paying out on a claim. For example, on critical illness insurance, there have been cases where insurers have refused to pay compensation when a claimant has been diagnosed with cancer, because a very minor ailment had not previously been disclosed. As a result the law has changed to require insurance companies to ask the right questions, rather than requiring applicants to make a full disclosure of possibly relevant matters. Whilst this should simplify matters for the applicant, it will remain a requirement that all questions should be answered completely and truthfully in order for the insurance policy to be valid.

Moral hazard

 Key term

Moral hazard in insurance occurs where the existence of an insurance policy leads to a person taking greater risks or being less careful than they might have been without insurance.

Moral hazard can occur in insurance as once an individual has an insurance policy in place they may be less careful than they would have been without insurance. Policyholders know that any loss suffered should be covered by their policy. There might be a tendency to take undue risks because any costs would not be suffered by the policyholder. For example, a person with insurance against mobile phone theft may be less careful about the exact location of their phone, because the negative consequences of mobile phone theft are now the responsibility of the insurance company. If the policyholder had been careless in looking after their phone, and that behaviour had contributed to its loss, the insurance company may refuse to meet the claim.

One way to reduce the impact of moral hazard is to have an excess on the policy. Where there is an excess, the first part of any claim has to be met by the policyholder. For example, with a £100 excess on a mobile phone insurance policy, the policyholder would have to meet the first £100 of any claim for loss or damage. This might help to ensure that the policyholder's interests were more closely aligned with those of the insurance company, with both parties having a financial interest in ensuring that the mobile phone is kept safe. Another way in which the risk of moral hazard can be reduced is through the terms and conditions of an insurance policy, where the insurance company may set out certain requirements under the contract. For example, a home insurance policy might require the fitting of window locks or a security alarm, in order to provide cover against the risk of burglary. It is very important that the policyholder understands the terms and conditions of any insurance policy and is able to comply with them in order for a policy to be valid.

Adverse selection

 Key term

Adverse selection in insurance occurs where only high risk individuals take out a specific type of insurance cover, until it reaches the point where it is no longer worthwhile for an insurance company to offer the policy.

In order for insurance to work there must be a pooling of risks. Some people will represent quite high risk and others much lower risk. An effective insurance market requires both types of people to take out policies to spread the risk. If mainly high risk individuals take out policies then the premiums will become more and more expensive, as more and more of the income from premiums has to be paid out to cover the cost of claims. This is likely to result in fewer low risk people buying policies, until eventually the insurance companies stop offering the cover. This is known as 'adverse selection' meaning that only those people who are high risk will take out the policy. In the UK we are approaching this situation in some areas that are at risk of flooding. In England and Wales one in every six homes is at risk of flooding (Association of British Insurers, 2015). Flood insurance is usually a fundamental part of both buildings and contents insurance, but if a home is at particular risk of flooding it will not be covered by a standard insurance policy. These householders need specialist insurance to cover the very real risk of flooding, but because the cost of flood insurance is expensive, only high risk households are prepared to take out the policies. As the likelihood of having to pay out is so high, more and more insurance companies are withdrawing their policies and the government has had to intervene to ensure the continued provision of specialist flood insurance.

Compulsory or required insurance

Motor insurance

Some types of insurance are a legal requirement, the most common example of this being motor insurance. In the UK it is a legal requirement that a vehicle owner must take out a motor insurance policy. The only way to avoid this is to complete a form declaring that the vehicle is not in use. The insurance cover can be third party only, which means that the vehicle owner is only covered for injury to other people or damage to another person's property. The policyholder's own car or personal loss would not be covered by their insurance policy should they suffer an accident. The insurance company would cover the losses of any third party or other person involved, but not that of the policyholder. Third party insurance is the cheapest form of car insurance available, but obviously means that the policyholder is carrying a large amount of the risk themselves, and effectively self-insuring against part of the risk of driving. If they were to be involved in an accident, where they were at fault, they would receive no compensation for the loss or damage to their own vehicle or themselves.

A more expensive form of car insurance is a fully comprehensive policy which covers the policyholder for risks to their own vehicle and themselves as well as to third parties. In the event of an accident or theft of the vehicle, the insurance company would compensate the policyholder for the loss suffered.

The risk of needing to make a claim on a motor insurance policy is relatively high with £27 million paid out every day on motor insurance policies with an average claim amounting to £2,649 (Association of British Insurers, 2015). According to the Association of British Insurers (2015) insurance companies have made a loss on private motor insurance for the past twenty-one years, paying out more in customer claims and expenses than they receive in premiums.

Buildings insurance

The majority of people buying their own home need a mortgage to enable them to make the purchase. It is usual for the bank or building society to require buildings insurance to be taken out, to meet the cost of damage or a rebuild of the property in the unfortunate event of a fire or other accidental damage. This protects the bank and the homebuyer against potential damage or loss of a major asset.

Once a home is fully owned, the homeowner would be unwise not to continue to protect the property by arranging house insurance.

Example 11.2

An elderly widow was finding it difficult to meet all of her living costs from her relatively small pension. She lived in a very attractive thatched cottage that she owned. She decided that she could cut costs by cancelling her buildings insurance policy. Unfortunately, soon afterwards, the chimney caught fire, the house was engulfed in flames and the fire service was unable to prevent the cottage from burning down completely. The widow lost her entire home and all her possessions and without an insurance policy she received no compensation to cover her loss. Although the probability of having to make a claim on a buildings insurance policy is quite low, because the potential loss is so high, it is a key form of insurance and cover should be maintained.

Contents insurance is available to cover the goods that are inside the home, from accidental damage or theft. It can be sold separately to buildings insurance. Both homeowners and tenants should consider whether or not they should take out contents insurance. Some people take out buildings insurance but choose to self-insure the contents.

Life assurance

Life assurance is a key part of personal financial planning. It is an insurance policy that will pay out on death. In order to establish whether there is a need for life assurance, also known as life cover, it is helpful to consider the question of what would happen to a person's dependants following the death of that person. If the answer is that there would be negative financial consequences (apart from the obvious personal ones), then life assurance should be purchased to protect against these consequences. This is a subject that many people do not like to think about and therefore they may choose not to consider it.

It is comparatively straightforward to buy life assurance, unless there are health problems. The potential purchaser decides on the level of cover that is required, the sum assured, and obtains quotations for the cost. Employees may have an element of life assurance included in their remuneration package at work, often as part of a pension scheme. For example, life cover of three times salary might be offered. The pension scheme would pay out a lump sum of that amount on death to the beneficiaries of the insured.

There are two main kinds of life assurance that serve very different purposes. They are:

- Term assurance
- Whole of life assurance

Term assurance

Term assurance lasts for a limited time period (the term) and is most useful for insuring against loss of life whilst paying off a mortgage or raising a family. It is a comparatively cheap form of insurance and once a person has dependants and/or significant borrowings they should consider taking out a life assurance policy to protect their family financially if one or other parent lost their life. According to a Scottish Widows report, in 2015 only 37% of adults in the UK had any life assurance (Scottish Widows, 2016). It would be interesting to know what proportion of the percentage without life assurance had dependants or a mortgage and thus were in need of some form of life assurance.

The usual term of a policy would be for the term of a mortgage, often twenty-five years, or until any children are financially independent, which may be set at eighteen or other agreed age. However, the actual term of the policy can be anything between five and forty years.

There are many different types of term assurance, but three of the main options are as follows:

1. Level term assurance provides a level of cover that remains the same throughout the term of the policy. These policies are normally used to cover an interest-only mortgage or to provide for compensation to dependent family members, in the event of death of the policyholder.

2. Decreasing term assurance provides life assurance where the level of cover reduces each year, decreasing to nil by the end of the term. The cover can reduce by a fixed amount each year, or in line with the outstanding balance on a repayment mortgage, to match the reducing debt. This type of life assurance is cheaper than level term assurance. When taking out a repayment mortgage most lenders will strongly recommend that a policy of this type is taken out.

3. Family income benefit provides dependants with replacement income if the policyholder dies during the term of the policy. A regular annual income would be paid to the dependants, but only for the remainder of the term of the policy. The income would normally be paid annually, although some policies can pay out monthly or quarterly. Some policies provide an income that would increase each year at a fixed rate, such as 3% or 5%.

 Ponder point

Should a young single man, with no dependants, recently graduated from university, take out a life assurance policy?

In most cases the answer is no; a single man with no financial dependants does not need life assurance. Life assurance is very important once a person has dependants, but this young man would be better off considering an income protection policy (discussed later) if he is considering insurance at all.

Before taking out any life assurance, any cover that is available as part of a remuneration package through employment should be taken into account. It is possible that further life assurance would be thought necessary, but the sum assured could perhaps be reduced as a result of the life cover available through work.

 Ponder point

Would it be possible to take out a life assurance policy on your wife, your civil partner, or your best friend?

It is possible to insure another person's life, but only if there is sufficient insurable interest. In the case of husband and wife or civil partners, each spouse is deemed to have an insurable interest in each other's life. It would not be possible to take out a life assurance policy on your best friend, as there is not an insurable interest.

Example 11.3

A young woman has recently married. She and her husband are buying their house together, with the help of a twenty-five-year repayment mortgage for £200,000 from the Southern Building Society. They have a one-year-old child and the mother is the main earner. Under her employment package she has life assurance cover of three times her salary, which amounts to £150,000. The father stays at home to look after the child.

The couple should consider the following when assessing their insurance needs:

- Buildings insurance to cover the cost of repairing any damage caused to their home, including the cost of any rebuild if it was destroyed by fire or other catastrophic event.

- Contents insurance to protect their possessions against fire, theft, or damage.

- Level or decreasing term life assurance for the young mother. If anything happened to the main earner it would be important that the mortgage was paid off and that there was also a lump sum for the family to ensure some financial security. Although part of the mortgage would be paid off by the life assurance from work, the whole of the mortgage would not be covered by that insurance alone. The family would need compensation for loss of earnings and therefore further life cover is needed. A decreasing term assurance policy would probably have been strongly recommended by the building society at the time the mortgage was agreed.

- Level or decreasing term assurance for the husband. As the child's main carer, if anything happened to him, there would be a significant financial impact on the mother, who would either have to give up work or pay for a carer or nursery to look after the child.

Whole of life assurance

Whole of life assurance is a very different kind of policy to term assurance. Essentially it is a savings product, designed to pass wealth or savings onto the beneficiaries under a person's will, to pay for funeral costs, to provide a fund to meet any inheritance tax liabilities, or to reduce a potential inheritance tax liability. In order to reduce any potential inheritance tax the policy must be written in trust and specialist advice would be needed. Whole of life assurance is a policy that will definitely pay out at some point, when the policyholder eventually dies. It is not an appropriate policy for a person needing term life assurance to cover the costs of a mortgage or childcare, because it is an expensive way of obtaining life cover. This form of life assurance can be effective for individuals with spare disposable income whose estate will be liable to inheritance tax. The policyholder pays a premium, some of which goes into a savings pot and some of which goes to cover the cost of the life assurance. There are various different kinds of policies with different costs. Any payout under the policy will usually be a combination of the sum assured and the accumulated investment pot. Unless there is likely to be a significant inheritance tax liability, or a need for a savings policy to cover the costs of a funeral, this type of life assurance is very unlikely to be useful. It is a much more expensive form of life assurance than term assurance.

Ponder point

Would whole of life assurance be an appropriate form of life assurance for a forty-year-old family man with a mortgage, dependants, a small amount of savings, and no other life assurance?

In this case, whole of life policies would not be appropriate. This family man would need term assurance because he has a mortgage and dependants, but unless he is particularly wealthy and worried about inheritance tax, it seems unlikely that a whole of life policy would be the best option for him.

Case study—Imran and Theo

Imran is a commercial lawyer living alone in London. He is an adventurous person who loves adrenaline sports, including skydiving, hang-gliding, bungee jumping, and white-water rafting.

Theo is married and lives in Liverpool with his wife and three young children. He has a secure job and enjoys swimming and gardening but prefers not to fly anywhere because of the risks involved. He would describe himself as a risk averse person.

Required:

Discuss whether either Imran or Theo or both should consider taking out life assurance?

Income protection insurance

After life assurance, income protection is the next most important type of insurance in personal financial planning. In order to establish whether or not there is a need for income protection, it is useful to consider the question of what would happen to a person and their dependants if they became unable to work. Many companies and employers provide a certain amount of sick pay and in the UK there is the possibility of limited state benefits in the form of statutory sick pay, but this might not be sufficient to replace lost income resulting from illness. Income protection is an insurance policy which provides a regular income if the policyholder cannot work as a result of illness or injury. The income received under such a policy would be a percentage of earnings, which could be 50% or more. Some employers offer this type of cover as part of the pension scheme or contract of employment, in which case the cover represents a significant benefit to the employee.

Most income protection policies pay out after the policyholder has been unable to work for a period of time known as the 'deferred period'. They would continue to pay out until the policyholder was able to return to work or until the policy came to an end, which may be at retirement. The deferred period can vary from a few weeks in length to up to a year. The policyholder makes a choice depending on how long they could manage without an income or on the entitlement to sick pay from their employer. The longer the deferred period, the lower the premium is likely to be.

Whilst this form of insurance may be desirable, it is expensive and for many people it is a luxury item that they cannot afford. Before purchasing an income protection policy it would be important to establish whether there was any existing cover within a remuneration package and the amount of any sickness cover provided by an employer.

 Ponder point

What sort of person would benefit from having income protection insurance?

Most working adults would benefit from having income protection insurance, including even those without dependants or a mortgage. Most people need to earn their living and as none of us is able to predict the future with certainty, some form of protection that would provide an income if we were unable to work would be a valuable insurance. However, anyone already covered through a work scheme would be unlikely to need an individual policy.

Critical illness insurance

Critical illness insurance is different to income protection insurance, because it is designed to pay out a lump sum if the policyholder develops a serious illness such as cancer or heart disease. It would provide a lump sum rather than an income and it would only pay out if the illness that developed was on the list of illnesses covered by the policy. Critical illness insurance may provide useful additional cover because it could be used to pay off a mortgage or other large debts if the insured person became seriously ill. In an ideal world this might be the type of policy that everyone would like to have in addition to income protection.

As with all insurance policies, the principle of *uberrima fides* is important and it is necessary to ensure that full disclosure of any medical conditions is made to the insurance company. If full disclosure is not made, the insurance company may refuse to compensate the policyholder, even if a serious illness develops.

A significant drawback of critical illness policies is that even though the policyholder may develop an illness and become unable to work, unless the illness is on the list of conditions covered by the policy, the insurance company will not pay compensation. Thus, although critical illness cover can provide useful additional protection for those who can afford it, it should not be taken out at the expense of a general policy that would provide income protection or life assurance.

 Ponder point

How would an employee know if they had any entitlement to life assurance, income protection insurance, or sick pay through their employment?

An employee would be able to ascertain any entitlement to life assurance, income protection insurance, or sick pay through examining their contract of employment. Any such entitlements would be set out under the terms and conditions of employment in their contract.

Case study—Rachel and her partner

Rachel is twenty-five years old and in a long-term relationship. She is a graduate trainee with a large retail company and is thinking of taking on a substantial repayment mortgage with her partner. Rachel is the main earner.

Required:

Consider the insurance needs of Rachel and her partner and identify any specific types of insurance they may need to take out.

Payment protection insurance (PPI)

Payment protection insurance should cover debt repayments if a borrower with a policy is unable to work. For example, if the person becomes ill, has an accident, or is made redundant. This sounds like a very useful type of insurance policy and one that would give many people peace of mind at the time that they are taking on debt. However, in the UK PPI has been subject to mis-selling, mainly because some of the high street banks sold PPI on mortgages, credit cards, and credit agreements to some individuals who would never have been able to claim against the policy.

PPI policies were sold to people with pre-existing medical conditions that would preclude the policyholder from making a claim. Some were sold to people who were already retired and therefore unable to claim. Some were sold to self-employed people who were not covered under the terms of the insurance. The policies were very expensive in relation to the level of cover provided, often adding a further 25% to the cost of a loan repayment. Many individuals taking out loans or credit cards were under the misapprehension that the PPI was either compulsory or a legal requirement. Many were not clearly advised of the true costs of the policy and many did not understand what they were buying. The banks are in the process of compensating those to whom the policies were mis-sold.

 Ponder point

Are there any actions that might have prevented or reduced the mis-selling of payment protection insurance?

The best way to prevent the mis-selling of financial products is for consumers to become more financially literate, more careful in buying financial products, more willing to understand the nature of those products, and more able to make informed decisions. Consumers would then be less likely to fall prey to the mis-selling of financial products and services.

 Ponder point

How many types of insurance offering financial protection against death, illness, and inability to work can you list?

The list should include:

- term life assurance
- whole of life assurance
- income protection insurance
- critical illness insurance
- payment protection insurance (PPI).

You may also have thought of others.

Assessing the need for life assurance and income protection

It is important to carefully assess the need for life assurance and/or income protection before purchasing this type of insurance. The factors to be considered are:

- The number and age of any dependants; once a person has dependants, life assurance and income protection become important to provide financial support in case of death or illness.
- The amount of financial liabilities or debts; the greater the amount of debt taken on, the greater the need for life assurance or income protection. If a person or family has very limited debt, then the level of required cover may be reduced.
- It is important to establish whether any existing life assurance cover is provided through employment, sometimes through a pension scheme, because this can reduce the amount of cover that individuals need to arrange on a personal basis. Similarly there might be some income protection cover associated with the pension scheme, which would provide some income in case of illness or disability.
- In assessing the need for insurance cover against illness or disability, consideration should be given to any potential sick pay provided by an employer, any statutory sick pay arrangements or further state benefits, some

or all of which might be available to a person unable to work through illness or disability. Although such payments are limited they would provide a measure of support.

Example 11.4

A couple are both aged fifty-five. The husband is the main earner and the wife has taken early retirement and receives a small pension. They still have £50,000 outstanding on their mortgage. In assessing their life assurance and income protection needs, they should consider the following:

1. First, they should consider the fact that the wife is dependent upon the husband and his earnings to provide an income and meet the mortgage payments. Also important is the fact that they still have a significant amount of debt with £50,000 outstanding on their mortgage.

2. The next step would be to establish whether the husband is entitled to any life cover or income protection under his contract of employment. If there is sufficient life assurance to pay off the mortgage and provide a reasonable lump sum in the event of his death, then further life assurance might not be necessary. If the life cover provided by the employer is inadequate or non-existent, then term assurance should be arranged.

3. If there is no income protection cover through the husband's employment, it would be useful to establish any sick pay arrangements or statutory sick pay that might be available, should he be unable to work through illness or disability. These might offer some measure of support but the couple might decide that further income protection insurance is needed.

Table 11.1 provides a simplified summary of the main uses of the different life assurance and income protection policies that are available.

Table 11. 1 Comparison of life assurance and income protection insurance products

Type of policy	Usual period of cover	Appropriate for:
Whole of life	Until death	Covering inheritance tax and/or funeral costs.
Term assurance	For any mortgage term or until dependants are likely to have reached independence	Providing a lump sum if someone dies leaving a mortgage and/or dependants.
Critical illness	Useful to have in place whilst significant debts exist	Useful to pay off mortgage and/or loans and/or provide a lump sum if illness strikes.
Income protection	Throughout working life	Provides an income if the insured is unable to work for a period of time.
Payment protection insurance	The period of a loan or any debt	Covers debt to ensure loan repayments are met should the person be unable to work for a period.

Case study—Oliver

Oliver is a struggling actor living in London who has received some brochures through the post concerning life assurance and income protection. He lives in a rented flat in South London when he is not in a touring production. He believes that the brochures are aimed at people in his age group, so he is considering taking out a life assurance policy. The premium would be £5 per month for a twenty-five-year term assurance policy. He is worried about how he would pay the bills if he was unable to work due to ill health, so he is also considering critical illness insurance.

Required:

Advise Oliver on his need for life assurance and income protection insurance.

Case study—Tian and Brian

Tian is fifty-two and runs her own business with her husband Brian. They manufacture organic pies which are sold to shops and cafes. The business is successful and they each earn a salary of £30,000 per annum and receive dividends from their family business of £20,000 each per annum. One of their close friends has recently become quite ill, which has prompted Tian to review their insurance cover on all aspects of their life and business. Their three children are all adults and living independently. Tian and Brian are both in reasonable health and have not smoked in the last ten years. At the moment they have one term life assurance policy for £100,000 on each person, due to expire in seven years, but no other life assurance or income protection. They have a small amount left to pay on their mortgage of £25,000.

Required:

What factors should Tian and Brian consider in assessing their life assurance and income protection needs?

Pensions

A pension is a type of insurance policy, effectively against 'living too long'. Most people understand the need to save for their retirement and if they knew how long their life in retirement was likely to be they might choose to save exactly the right amount to meet their income needs. This could be achieved through matching spending to savings in retirement, so that by the time of death all the savings were used up. In view of the fact that none of us is capable of this kind of foresight, together with the tax effectiveness of making pension savings and the savings discipline they encourage, many people are prepared to consider buying a pension policy to provide an income in retirement. According to the Association of British Insurers (2015) 50% of the population in the UK contributes to a workplace pension scheme and 33% to a private pension. A pension should continue to pay out, irrespective of whether retirement lasts for two years or thirty years and thus ensures that a person receiving an income in retirement should not run out of income from that policy. Whether that pension is adequate or not will depend on a number of factors. The issue of providing for retirement is discussed in detail in Chapter 12.

Other insurance policies

As discussed already, there are many, many different insurance policies that can be purchased. Here we discuss just three different types of insurance where self-insurance might be considered to be a reasonable alternative.

An **extended warranty** is an insurance contract that covers repair costs on a new product after any initial manufacturer's guarantee has expired. Retailers often promote them enthusiastically. Before buying such a policy, it is important to consider the cost of the policy, the likelihood of something going wrong with the product, and any free warranty period included with the purchase price. Many policies are very expensive compared to the purchase price of the product. In some cases it can be better to self-insure and take on the risk that the product might go wrong, on the basis that then the consumer is only paying for repairs if it does go wrong, rather than paying whether it goes wrong or not. Any loss could be covered by existing savings, or the consumer might choose to save an amount equivalent to the cost of the warranty to provide a fund that would be available to meet the costs of any repairs, should that be necessary.

Identity theft occurs when a criminal steals an individual's personal information and uses that to obtain a loan or credit in their name, or when a criminal gains access to an individual's bank account by obtaining their PIN number. Identity theft insurance only covers the cost of sorting out problems arising from identity theft; it does not cover any money lost through an identity theft fraud. Where a bank account holder suffers a loss as a result of identity theft, there is already an element of cover from most banks, providing the account holder has not been negligent. Very few claims are ever made on this type of policy and therefore some insurance companies are particularly interested in selling identity theft insurance because the risks are very low compared to the premiums. Some banks have been criticized by the regulator for involvement in the mis-selling of identity theft policies and compensation is due to those who were mis-sold such policies. The best insurance against identity theft is prevention, through taking safeguards, choosing unique and unpredictable passwords, carefully checking privacy settings on social media, and regularly checking bank account and credit card statements.

Mobile phone insurance covers the cost arising from damage, loss, or theft of a mobile phone. It is a form of insurance that is often very expensive and it may be that a mobile phone is already covered by an existing insurance policy, such as a home contents policy. Alternatively it may be worth considering the option to self-insure.

Example 11.5

Two students buying the same mobile phone are offered mobile phone insurance at a cost of £6.99 per month. A new phone would cost £170. One student decides to self-insure and puts the £6.99 into a savings account. After eighteen months her phone is stolen from her backpack at a railway station, by which time the cost of a new phone has fallen to £130. She has £125.82 plus a small amount of interest in her savings account, which she uses to purchase a new phone.

Her friend takes out the insurance, but fortunately for him, his phone is not stolen, lost, or damaged. After two years he will have paid almost £170 in insurance premiums.

The risk of loss, theft, or damage to a mobile phone is quite high, but the potential loss is relatively small and this type of insurance is expensive, so self-insurance can be a good option.

 Ponder point

The regulator has found instances of mis-selling of insurance policies in the past. Do you think this indicates a need for discrimination when purchasing insurance?

It has often been the case that policies subject to mis-selling had a very low rate of pay-out for the insurance company, so they were very profitable policies, which may have increased the pressure on sales. From a consumer's point of view there may be little point in having such a policy if the risk is very small or the chance of suffering a loss and requiring compensation is remote. The sale of such products may have been driven by the commission that was earned. However the history of compensation payouts to consumers who have been mis-sold such products suggests that consumers should be discriminating and make sure that any decision to purchase insurance is both rational and considered.

Case study—Imran

Imran is a young single man living in London. He is reviewing his spending as he is trying to save for a deposit on a flat. He is considering potential insurance policies and trying to work out which ones are good value and which ones he could manage without. He has established that he has life cover of three times salary through work. Having carried out some research on the internet he has obtained the quotations set out in Table 11.2, mainly for annual cover:

Table 11.2 Imran: insurance policy premiums

	Annual premium payable
Identity theft	£100
Extended three-year warranty on new washing machine (machine has 12-months' free warranty, from the manufacturer)	(Single premium only) £180
Whole of life assurance	£500
Critical illness insurance	£475
Annual travel policy	£94
Contents insurance	£200
Mobile phone insurance	£84

Required:

Advise Imran on the advisability of taking out each of the above policies.

Conclusion

Insurance can be a thought-provoking business. On the one hand, it is reassuring to be able to reduce the level of personal risk, to know that if a loss is suffered then some compensation will be received. On the other hand, there are so many possible insurance policies that one could take out an insurance policy to cover each and every potential loss.

In personal financial planning, once a person has dependants and/or financial liabilities, it is important to consider life assurance and income protection. Buildings insurance is usually compulsory where there is a mortgage and car insurance is a legal requirement. Some insurance policies are a sensible option, such as contents or travel insurance, and others, such as extended warranties or identity theft, often represent poor value for money. In many cases self-insurance would be a better option.

A decision on whether or not to purchase an insurance policy should begin with an assessment of the likely risk and the amount of any potential loss. This should be followed by consideration of the cost of the premium and the ability to cover any potential loss oneself. In life assurance or income protection decisions it is important to take into account any insurance cover provided through work or other sources. Once the issues have all been considered, then a rational decision can be made on whether or not to buy a particular policy.

Useful websites

The Association of British Insurers provides useful information on insurance:
http://www.abi.org.uk

Which, the consumer organization, provides advice on insurance and whether or not to take it out:
http://www.which.co.uk

References

Association of British Insurers (2015) *Key Facts on the UK Insurance Industry.* Available at: http://www.abi.org.uk (accessed 22.6.2016)

CIFAS (2016) *Fraud Scape 2016.* Available at: https://www.cifas.org.uk/secure/contentPORT/uploads/documents/CIFAS%20Reports/160616_cifas_

fraudscape_FINAL%20PRINT.pdf (accessed 7.7.2016)

Scottish Widows (2016) *Press release.* Available at: http://reference.scottishwidows.co.uk/docs/2016-02-national-heart-month.pdf (accessed 7.7.2016)

Practice Questions

Question 1 Quick Quiz

Which of the following risks can be insured against?

11.1   Conceiving twins.

11.2   Kidnap and ransom.

11.3   Incurring legal fees in a dispute with your employer.

11.4   The legal costs of arranging a divorce.

11.5   Being made redundant.

11.6   Photographer not showing up on a wedding day.

11.7   Being unable to work as a result of a serious illness.

11.8   Loss of a limb.

11.9   Accidental damage to carpets.

11.10   Being struck by an asteroid.

Question 2 To insure or Not to Insure?

Given that there are so many different types of insurance available, how can a rational decision be made on whether or not to buy a particular insurance policy?

* Question 3 Insurance Terms

Explain the following terms in the context of insurance:

a) *Uberrima fides.*

b) Moral hazard.

c) Adverse selection.

* Question 4 Mavis

Mavis is a young single woman with no dependants living in rented accommodation in Manchester. She is about to go on holiday with a tour company to China. She is considering the insurance policies set out in Table 11.3.

Table 11.3 Mavis: insurance policy premiums

	Annual premium payable
Pet insurance for budgerigar	£250
Extended five-year warranty on hair straighteners (manufacturer provides 12-months' free warranty)	(single premium only) £70
Buildings insurance	£175
Level term life assurance for £70,000	£600
Travel insurance (single trip) for tour of China	£70
Contents insurance	£150
Laptop insurance	£84

Required:

Advise Mavis on whether to buy the various insurance policies that she is examining.

* Question 5 Richard

Richard has just bought an expensive new bicycle in order to be able to cycle to work. He is a homeowner with a contents insurance policy with a well-known insurance company. The cycle shop suggested that he take out a policy to cover the potential theft or damage to his bicycle. They were able to offer him a comparatively cheap policy, but only if he was able to sign up for the insurance at the same time as purchasing the bike.

Required:

Advise Richard on whether it would be sensible to take advantage of the cycle shop's insurance offer.

 Visit the Online Resource Centre that accompanies this book for additional material:
www.oxfordtextbooks.co.uk/orc/king_carey2e/

12 Planning for your retirement

Learning Objectives

After studying this chapter, you should understand:

- Why financing pensions has become an increasing problem for individuals, government, and for many businesses
- The need for individuals to plan for their retirement
- The range of possible sources of income in retirement
- The distinction between a defined-benefit and a defined-contribution pension scheme
- The ways in which workplace and personal pension schemes can operate
- The tax benefits of making pension contributions
- The importance of reviewing and adapting a retirement plan

Introduction

Retirement is a period of life that many people look forward to but often with some anxiety as to how they will be able to afford their desired lifestyle and whether they will be able to travel to all the places and do all the things that they did not have time to do during their working lives. With the UK population experiencing increasing longevity, many people can look forward to two decades or more of retirement.

The importance of planning ahead for your retirement is often not understood. When you are in your twenties and thirties, you may consider that retirement is a very long way off and that you do not need to concern yourself with saving for it until you are older.

Background

 Key term

A **pension** is a regular amount paid to an individual who is in retirement.

Pensions are a complex subject and one that has been, and remains, a topical area of debate. Pension provision affects individuals on a personal level but it is also an issue of major concern to successive governments and to many employers. The government provides a basic state pension for most people, as long as they are eligible, and it provides some additional financial support to disabled pensioners. In doing so, it can be argued that it provides a disincentive for people to plan and save for their retirement. However, government provision in the form of the basic state pension only provides a minimal income and, unless you want to spend many years struggling to live on a very low income, then planning for your retirement should feature prominently when personal finances are being considered.

 Key term

A **private pension** is any pension not paid by the state. Workplace pensions and personal pensions are both private pensions.

The problem with pensions

The issue of pensions has become an increasingly problematic area for individuals, the government, and for many employers. The current situation is often described as a pensions crisis. There are numerous factors that have led to this situation and it is useful to understand how this has arisen and what the key issues are.

Life expectancy

Life expectancy in the UK has been on an upward trend for many years now and, whilst this is good news, it does mean that the number of years people spend in retirement has increased and hence the period over which pensions are drawn continues to increase. This has greatly increased the cost to the government, who have to pay state pensions, and has had a significant impact on private pension funds.

Investment performance

Most pension funds have relied on growth in their share portfolios to help fund their pension obligations. The stock market has been very volatile in the years since 2000 and UK share prices have shown little overall growth in the years since. Prior to this, shares had performed more strongly and provided pension funds with relatively good returns that enabled them to meet their pension obligations. Poor investment performance has led to pension fund growth being low, and at times negative. This has led to either smaller pensions being paid and/or pension fund deficits, where employers find they have to pay large sums into their workplace pension schemes in order that the fund can meet its pension obligations.

Lack of confidence

Public confidence in pension schemes has been severely dented as a result of some high profile pension fund collapses, and a well-publicized pensions mis-selling scandal. Two of the most high profile pension fund disasters include the Maxwell case and that of Equitable Life. In the Maxwell case, pension fund money was illegally used to prop up the share price of an ailing company, Mirror Group Newspapers. When the company collapsed, the employees and existing pensioners were either left with much lower pensions or no pension at all (Ringshaw, 2011). Equitable Life gave its pension savers misleading information that encouraged many people to save with them. The company nearly collapsed when the House of Lords ruled in 2000 that it would have to fulfil its obligations, and this subsequently resulted in significant financial losses for those who had saved with it (Parliamentary and Health Service Ombudsman, 2007).

The pensions mis-selling scandal happened during the 1980s and 1990s, when many people were wrongly advised to move funds from their workplace schemes into a personal pension. As a result, these pension savers found that their pension entitlements were significantly reduced. Pension savers did eventually receive some compensation but, in most cases, it did not fully compensate them for the loss suffered.

It is not entirely surprising that following these events, some people began to mistrust the whole pensions industry and chose not to join pension schemes at all. They may be under a misapprehension that the state pension will be adequate, when a glance at its current level would soon persuade them otherwise.

Some people are reluctant to save for their retirement because it seems a long way off and they consider that it is an issue they need not worry about until they are older. Others consider that they would rather not rely on a traditional pension provider to manage their pension savings and instead prefer to make alternative arrangements to provide them with an income when they are no longer working. This might be income from savings and investments or rental income from property.

Many people may plan to have some combination of pension and other income in retirement. Paying into a pension fund will usually be a key element of retirement planning because of the discipline of saving it requires and the way that the tax system boosts pension savings. Pension savings can be inaccessible and this ensures that there is less temptation to use pension savings prior to retirement.

 Ponder point

It can be said that saving for a pension is an insurance policy against living too long. Do you agree with this?

There is certainly an underlying truth to this statement because if an individual knew how many years of retirement they would have, they could ensure that they saved exactly the right amount in order to fund their retirement and would not need a pension fund.

Ponder point

Pensioners frequently have more than one source of income. What sources might they have?

Pensioners in the UK will usually receive a state pension. They may also receive a private pension they have built up personally and possibly a workplace pension arising from an employer's scheme that they belonged to. They may have income from savings and investments and income from property. Some people will continue to work past their retirement age and this can provide a very useful supplement to their income and allow them to delay the point at which they start to rely on their pension.

If a pensioner's overall income is low or if they are disabled, there may be entitled to state benefits.

The basics of retirement planning

One of the first steps to take in retirement planning is to decide at approximately what age you would like to retire and what level of income you will need in retirement. The answer to these two questions will determine the pension savings that you need to build up over your working life.

 Ponder point

Pensioners tend to have different spending habits from people of working age. What are pensioners likely to spend more money on and what are they likely to spend less money on?

Some of the things pensioners in the UK are likely to spend more on include heating and, with more free time available, they may want to spend more on travel, holidays, and leisure activities. This is likely to be partially offset by their use of travel passes and their ability to take advantage of off-peak deals. Some are likely to buy fewer clothes, no longer needing specific clothing for the workplace, and they will no longer incur commuting costs. Pensioners will usually have paid off their mortgages, something that represents a very significant expense for younger homeowners. As a result of changes in spending habits after retirement, most people's income needs are reduced and an estimated income of one-half to two-thirds of pre-retirement income is a realistic starting point in pension planning.

Example 12.1

A twenty-five-year-old male who makes pension contributions of £200 per month during his working life will build up pension savings of £156,000 by the age of sixty, assuming that the fund can generate a return of 3% per annum. An estimate of the projected pension that amount might provide is £6,700 per annum.

(continued...)

If that same individual waited five years until he was thirty before starting to pay any contributions, the pension savings would reach an estimated £123,000 by the age of sixty and pay a projected pension of £5,300 per annum.

If that same individual left it until he was forty before starting to pay any contributions, the pension savings would reach an estimated £71,000 by the age of sixty and pay a projected pension of £3,050 per annum.

 Ponder point

Looking at the above example, what advice would you give to the twenty-five-year-old?

Looking at the figures, one would surely advise the twenty-five-year-old to start saving for his pension now rather than in the future and to consider saving more if possible. The principle of starting to save for a pension as soon as possible in your working life is widely supported. Most younger people may have only a vague notion as to when they would like to retire but in order to give themselves the most flexibility and the greatest income in retirement, they should start saving as soon as they possibly can. Sums invested into a pension fund are allowed to build up tax-free.

Example 12.2

A twenty-five-year-old man would like to retire on an income of £25,000 per annum at age sixty-eight. He estimates that his state pension will be approximately £8,000 per annum and hence he will need a private pension of £17,000 (at today's prices). To achieve this, he would need to contribute £600 per month from the age of twenty-five, after allowing for tax relief.

If the pension saver was earning £50,000 per annum, the contributions would comprise 14% of his gross income.

(From Hargreaves Lansdown pension calculator.)

Pension forecasts usually give the expected pension income in today's prices, because although the actual pension received might be more in money terms, it will not be worth more in real terms. After taking into account the effect of inflation its purchasing power will not be any greater. Many pension providers offer pension calculators on their websites and the user has to be aware that the results are based on certain assumptions regarding returns that can be earned and rates of inflation. These forecasts are useful but as the results are so dependent on assumptions, they need to be revisited at regular intervals.

Pension saving—a rule of thumb

The age at which a person starts saving for their pension determines the amount they should save. A very general rule of thumb is that individuals should, as a minimum, save at a rate that represents half their age when they start saving. A person who starts saving for their pension at thirty years of age should make pension contributions of at least 15% of their earnings each year. A person who starts saving at forty, should contribute at least 20% each year. Contributions made by an employer can be included in arriving at contributions made. This is a very general guideline but nonetheless a useful indication of the impact of time on pension savings. The earlier a person starts saving, the lower the level of contributions required. Clearly much will depend on an individual's current and likely future incomes and their required retirement income.

The state pension

Most people in the UK will be eligible to receive a basic state pension on reaching the state retirement age as entitlement is based on having made sufficient National Insurance (NI) contributions. To receive the full state pension you need to have made National Insurance contributions for a specific number of years. From 2017, thirty-five years' worth of NI contributions are required for a full state pension. The majority of people in employment and self-employment will make National Insurance contributions and credits are often given when people are ill, unemployed, or have caring responsibilities. It is likely that most individuals who spend their working lives in the UK will make adequate contributions. An individual who makes contributions for less than the qualifying number of years will receive a smaller basic state pension.

> **🔑 Key term**
>
> The **basic state pension** is a pension payable to anyone who has paid sufficient National Insurance contributions over their working life.

The amount of state pension receivable can vary from person to person according to the amount of National Insurance contributions made. The state pension is very modest and provides for a very low standard of living.

In 2016, the government introduced a flat rate state pension, of £156 per week, which is payable to everyone who has made thirty-five-years' worth of National Insurance contributions. Anyone who has paid fewer years NI contributions or has paid a reduced rate of NI contributions will receive a scaled down state pension and if fewer than ten years of contributions have been made, then no state pension will be payable.

The state pension is not funded from any giant pot of savings that has been set aside by governments over decades. Current pensioners are funded by today's taxpayers; people in employment or self-employment pay taxes, including National Insurance, that enable the government to pay state pensions. The Office for National Statistics publishes data on the age distribution of the population and produces predicted distributions for the future.

Ponder point

Looking at Figure 12.1 showing predicted age distributions in the UK up to 2081, what impact will this have on the ability of the government to fund state pensions in the future?

Figure 12.1 shows that the proportion of the population aged sixty and over is expected to increase whilst the proportion of the population under sixty is expected to decline. This will mean that the capacity of future governments to raise the sums needed to fund state pensions from those in work is going to be reduced and potentially places a heavy burden on the working population.

The state pension becomes payable at the state pension age which historically was age sixty for women and age sixty-five for men. Women's retirement age is being brought into line with men's and the state retirement age is set to rise to sixty-eight for both sexes. It is liable to rise further in the future.

Given the inadequacy of the basic state pension, it is essential that anyone wishing to have a reasonable standard of living in retirement or wanting to retire before the state pension age, should make other arrangements that will provide them with additional income when they finish working.

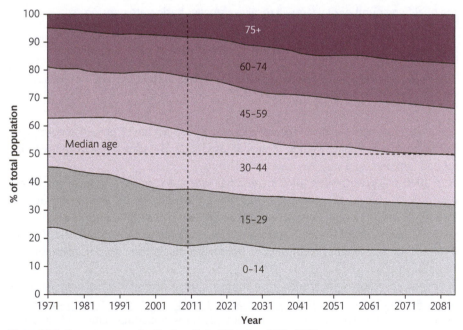

Figure 12.1 Percentage age distribution, United Kingdom 1971–2085

Source: Office for National Statistics, 2010.

This will often be achieved by joining a pension scheme or a number of schemes, and/or by building up savings, investments, and property to provide an income in retirement.

There are many different types of pension scheme and they can all be classified according to whether they are:

- defined-benefit schemes (also known as salary-related) schemes, or
- defined-contribution schemes (also known as money purchase) schemes.

Defined-benefit (salary-related) pension schemes

 Key term

A **defined-benefit pension scheme** is one where the pension payable is determined according to a formula based on the number of years the person has been a member of the scheme and the salary received, often linked to the final salary received, or a career-average salary. This type of scheme is often known as a salary-related scheme. Whilst this type of scheme is common in the public sector, few of these schemes remain open to new members in the private sector.

Defined-benefit schemes have only ever been offered by workplace pension schemes. With a defined-benefit scheme, the pension entitlement is based on the number of years someone is a member of the scheme and the salary earned, often based on the final salary paid or a career-average salary. This type of pension usually increases in line with inflation.

Example 12.3

The pension payable under a defined-benefit scheme is n/80ths of final salary, where n is the number of years that the employee has been a member of the pension scheme. An employee expects to work for the business for thirty-five years and be a member of the pension scheme throughout that time. He anticipates that his final salary will be £50,000. His expected pension would be as follows:

$$\text{Expected pension} = \frac{35}{80} \times £50{,}000 = £21{,}875 \text{ per annum}$$

Defined-benefit schemes provide members with some security in knowing how much they can expect their pension to be. If, for example, the economy is in recession and share prices are very low near the time of an employee's retirement, this will have no impact on their expected pension. The employer bears the risk of ensuring that there are adequate funds in the scheme to pay the pensions.

Most public sector pension schemes are defined-benefit schemes and historically many large companies offered such schemes. The number of companies offering membership of this type of scheme to new employees is now very few.

Ponder point

Why do you think that companies have been closing defined-benefit (salary-related) schemes?

From an employer's perspective, these schemes have proved very expensive to finance. The total amount that has to be paid out to pensioners in a salary-related scheme is determined by salary levels and by the number of years, on average, that pensioners draw their pension. Increasing longevity has meant that pensions have to be paid for many more years than was perhaps anticipated when contribution levels were set. The pension funds available to meet these obligations will also be subject to the influence of fluctuating investment returns. This has made defined-benefit schemes increasingly expensive for employers as, when the value of a pension fund is inadequate to meet its obligations, the company often has to pay additional money in to 'top up' the fund. As a result, financing these schemes can be unpredictable and expensive and companies have responded by closing their salary-related schemes and not allowing newer employees to join.

Defined-contribution (money purchase) pension scheme

 Key term

A **defined-contribution pension scheme** is one where a pension pot is built up over time and the pot is used to finance a pension income on retirement. The pension pot comprises contributions made, plus any returns on investments, less annual pension fund charges.

When an individual is a member of a defined-contribution scheme, the pension contributions accumulate over time to form a pension pot of accumulated contributions. This pot of funds will usually be invested in a range of shares, bonds, and deposits. As a result, the overall value of the pot will vary over time and the exact value of the pot at retirement will be very hard to predict. There will also be pension fund charges that will reduce the size of the pot. The pension saver in this type of scheme bears all the risk of ensuring that the pot is adequate to meet their needs.

Following sweeping changes to pensions in 2015, savers are now faced with a wide range of choices when it comes to using their pension pot. Because the size of the pension pot at retirement cannot be accurately predicted and the ways that a pensioner can access that pot are so varied, a member of a defined-contribution scheme will always find it difficult to predict their income in retirement. This compares to a member of a defined-benefit scheme who will have far greater certainty over their likely pension.

There are two common ways that members of defined-contribution schemes can draw an income from their pot: they can buy an annuity and/or use income drawdown. Alternatively, lump sums or the entire pension pot can be withdrawn.

Annuities and income drawdown

 Key terms

An **annuity** is an annual income purchased with a lump sum, usually an individual's pension pot. The annuity provides an income for the rest of that person's life.
Income drawdown allows a pension pot to remain invested and the pensioner can withdraw variable amounts from the pot, often on a regular basis.

Annuities are usually purchased from an insurance company and there are many different options for the type of annuity that can be purchased. An annuity can be purchased that will provide one or more of the following income streams until the pensioner dies:

- A regular flat rate income
- An income that increases by a fixed percentage each year
- An income that increases in line with RPI or CPI each year
- An income that is guaranteed to be paid for a certain number of years, even if the pensioner dies during that time
- An income for the pensioner plus a reduced income for their spouse, or nominated partner, after their death

The above are examples of some of the most common types of annuity that can be purchased. There are other options regarding the income stream that an annuity can buy.

Annuity rates vary considerably over time and as a result have a major impact on the level of pension income for those purchasing them on retirement. The rates are linked to longevity data, inflation, and the return on gilts, as the insurance company often buys gilts to finance the regular payments it has to make.

Income drawdown allows far more flexibility than annuities, but it also carries far more risks. The pension pot remains invested which may lead to greater returns but if markets fall, it will result in the value of the pension pot being reduced.

With income drawdown, pensioners can choose to vary the amount they withdraw from their pot according to their personal situation but they need to constantly be aware of the remaining size of their pension pot, the likely number of years of retirement remaining, and allow for possible falls in the value of their pot. Income drawdown requires the pensioner to be far more involved in managing their retirement income.

It is possible for retirees to use a combination of annuities and drawdown, or to use income drawdown in the first years after retirement and then to buy an annuity later.

All personal pension schemes and most workplace pension schemes are defined-contribution schemes. This means that the amount of pension that a person may be entitled to is very difficult to predict in advance, as the value of a pension pot is likely to be constantly changing and annuity rates change as well. Members of a defined-contribution scheme carry all the risk as to whether the resulting pension will be adequate or not. Any employer making contributions on an employee's behalf, has no responsibility to ensure that the pension payable is adequate.

Workplace pensions

 Key term

A **workplace pension scheme** is a scheme offered by an employer to some or all of its employees. The scheme often carries other benefits in addition to a pension entitlement.

Workplace pensions are pension schemes run by employers, where usually both the employee and the employer make regular contributions into the pension fund. The schemes frequently offer other benefits to members in addition to the pension, including life assurance, a lump sum payment if the employee has to retire early due to ill health, and, sometimes, other benefits as well. Although employees are likely to have to contribute to the scheme, they benefit from contributions that the employer makes on their behalf.

Most workplace pension schemes are defined-contribution schemes although many public sector workers still have the benefit of salary-related schemes. Historically, employees who had worked for an employer for a certain period of time were offered the opportunity to join a workplace scheme where one existed. Employees then had to make the positive choice to join the scheme. With the introduction of compulsory workplace pensions, employees not wishing to join a workplace scheme have to opt out.

Example 12.4

A twenty-five-year-old, on a salary of £30,000 per annum, is offered the opportunity of joining her employer's pension scheme, a defined-contribution scheme, to which she would be required to contribute 5% of her salary and her employer will contribute an amount equivalent to 8% of her salary. If the employee joins the scheme, then contributions amounting to 13% of her salary will be made to the scheme on her behalf, each year that she is a member. As a result of the employer's contributions, in addition to the employees, her pension pot will build up far more rapidly. She may well also have life assurance cover under the scheme. In general, the employee would be wise to join the scheme unless there were very good reasons not to do so.

> ### ❓ Ponder point
>
> Can you think of any circumstances when an employee might opt not to join a workplace pension scheme?

In general, most employees offered the opportunity to join a workplace scheme would be wise to accept, especially if it is either a salary-related scheme or a defined-contribution scheme where the employer will make a reasonable level of contributions in addition to the employee's contributions.

If the employee knew that he planned to leave that employment in the near future and hence would be a member for a very short time, he might consider declining the chance to join. There may be charges involved in withdrawing money from a scheme.

There might be circumstances when an individual chooses not to join a workplace scheme because they feel that they cannot afford to make their share of the contributions. In such a situation, every effort should be made to find the necessary funds to do so.

Automatic enrolment

Offering a workplace pension has historically been an option that many, especially smaller, employers have chosen not to take. The Pensions Act 2008 established the principle that all employers are required to automatically enrol eligible employees onto a workplace pension scheme. The scheme offered by an employer must be one to which both employers and employees contribute.

Employers are required to enrol all employees who earn more than £10,000 per annum and are between the ages of twenty-two and the state pension age. Younger and older employees can ask to join the scheme if they wish. Table 12.1 gives indicative rates for minimum levels of contributions from both employers and employees.

Table 12.1 Minimum pension contributions (applied to earnings between £6,000 and £43,000). Indicative figures only (For up-to-date figures, see http://www.nestpensions.org.uk)

	Minimum employee contributions	Minimum employer contributions
Up to 5 April 2018	1%	1%
6 April 2018 to 5 April 2019	2%	3%
6 April 2019 onwards	3%	5%

Note that the above amounts are indicative of the minimum permissible contributions and both employers and employees can make higher percentage contributions. It is also possible for employees and employers to pay contributions based not just on the employee's earnings between £6,000 and £43,000, but on all of, or a greater part of, their earnings.

Example 12.5

An employee earning £70,000 per annum is auto-enrolled into their employer's pension scheme in 2017. The minimum permissible pension contributions would be:

Employee contributions: (£43,000 – 6,000) × 1% = £370 per annum
Employer contributions: (£43,000 – 6,000) × 1% = £370 per annum
Total minimum contributions = £370 + £370 = £740 per annum

 Ponder point

Do you consider that the above minimum employee and employer percentage contributions are likely to be adequate to generate a reasonable pension for most employees?

The minimum percentage contributions are very low and are highly unlikely to generate an adequate pension. Hopefully most scheme members and their employers will contribute a higher percentage and make contributions based on all of their earnings.

A young person aged twenty-five, wishing to retire on a pension of half their salary, should be contributing between 10% and 15% of their income in order to achieve this. The total contributions of 2% per annum required under auto-enrolment, are well below this amount.

Example 12.6

An employee earning £70,000 per annum joined his employer's pension scheme in 2017. The scheme requires the employee to contribute 5% and the employer to contribute 7% per annum of the employee's salary in its entirety.

Employee contributions: £70,000 × 5% = £3,500 per annum
Employer contributions: £70,000 × 7% = £4,900 per annum
Total contributions = £3,500 + £4,900 = £8,400 per annum
This compares to the minimum required under auto-enrolment of £740, calculated in Example 12.5.

Leaving an employer–workplace pension scheme

There are a variety of options that may be open to an employee who leaves a workplace pension scheme. If they are leaving a defined-benefit (salary-related) scheme, then it will usually be advisable to leave the benefits in that scheme, as it will provide a guaranteed income on retirement.

Where the scheme is a defined-contribution one, then depending on the terms and conditions of the particular scheme, there may be a number of possible options available, including:

● leave the pension pot in that scheme, so that it can continue to increase as a result of investment returns

- transfer the pension pot to a personal pension scheme (see following section)
- continue contributing to the scheme even though the employment has ceased.

Personal pensions

Personal pensions can be taken out by anyone and can be taken out on behalf of another person. They are always defined-contribution schemes and other benefits, like life assurance, will only be included if they are chosen as an added extra, at extra cost.

 Key term

A **personal pension scheme** is a scheme into which contributions can be made by or on behalf of an individual in order to provide a pension in retirement. These schemes are always defined-contribution schemes.

Personal pensions are suitable for use by people in a wide variety of circumstances, including:

- people in self-employment
- people in employment, when they have opted not to join the workplace scheme
- people in employment, who are members of a workplace scheme, but wish to top up their pension savings
- people who are not working but want to save for a pension in retirement. (They may make the contributions or a partner, parent, or other person could make the contributions on their behalf.)

Employers can contribute into personal pension schemes for a number of employees to avoid the necessity of setting up a workplace pension scheme. This is known as a group personal pension scheme.

Personal pensions suffer from all the drawbacks of defined-contribution schemes; the amount of the final pension will be uncertain until the individual actually starts to draw that pension. One advantage of a personal pension is that the arrangement does not come to an end when jobs are changed; pension savers can continue to pay into the fund whether they change jobs, become self-employed, or even unemployed.

Self-invested personal pension (SIPP)

Self-invested personal pensions (SIPPs) give the person saving for their pension much greater control over the way that their pension contributions are invested. Whilst a traditional personal pension may offer the saver a choice of a few funds to invest in, a SIPP allows the saver the opportunity to invest in a much wider range of investments. The actual range will be determined by the SIPP provider chosen but can include: shares, bonds, gilts, unit trusts, OEICs, investment trusts, commercial property, and cash. (Many of these investments are discussed in Chapter 8.)

 Ponder point

Should anyone who is considering taking out a personal pension give serious consideration to opening a SIPP because of the greater choice of investments that it gives to savers?

SIPPs will not be an appropriate choice for many people wishing to save for their retirement. Anyone seriously considering opening a SIPP needs to understand the investment choices available to them, the risks involved, and be confident that they have the time and expertise to manage the investments in their SIPP. It is not merely about making choices when the investments are made but also about constantly reviewing the portfolio and making changes in the light of varying circumstances.

It is possible to pay an investment manager to manage a SIPP for you but the costs involved will be much greater than one that is self-managed, and will only be worthwhile when the sums involved are relatively large.

There are a number of costs that SIPPs may charge, including set-up costs, contribution costs, dealing costs, and an annual management charge. These costs can vary widely between providers, often according to the range of investment products available, the extent to which investment advice is given, and whether the fund is managed on the saver's behalf.

Pension scheme charges

 Key term

The **annual management charge (AMC)** is a percentage amount deducted from every pension scheme member's fund (when the scheme is a defined-contribution one), that is charged each year until retirement. The AMC can have a significant impact on the eventual pension pot at retirement.

Pension fund charges are often disclosed as the annual management charge (AMC) and the rate can vary a great deal between different schemes. The AMC is expressed as a percentage of the fund value and whilst the charges often seem very low, even seemingly very small charges can have a significant impact on the eventual size of a pension pot. (Salary-related pensions will not be affected by charges as the pension payable is not linked to a pension pot.)

Thurley (2012) in a House of Commons Note dealing with the issue of pension scheme charges included a graph of the pension pot that would result for an individual

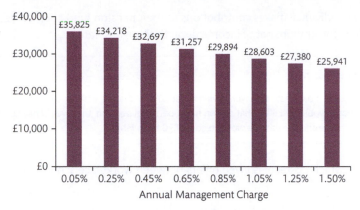

Figure 12.2 Pension fund value by annual management charge

Source: Thurley, House of Commons Note, 2012.

saving £50 per month over forty years, where the fund earns a real rate of return of 2%. The graph is shown in Figure 12.2.

Figure 12.2 shows that the size of the final pension fund varies a great deal according to the level of charges made, and an AMC of 1.5% leads to a fund that is 28% smaller than the fund would be if the AMC is 0.05%. This large difference arises because the AMC is charged as a percentage of the pension pot and although 1.5% is a small percentage, it has a very significant impact when it is charged over forty years.

Tax relief on pension contributions

In order to encourage people to save for their retirement, successive governments have given incentives by way of tax relief on any pension contributions that an individual makes. The maximum pension contributions on which an individual can obtain tax relief for any one tax year is the lower of 100% of earnings or £40,000 (including tax relief).

Non-taxpayers or those with taxable income of less than £3,600 can get tax relief on contributions up to £3,600 (including tax relief) each year.

> ## Example 12.7
>
> An employee earning £34,000 per annum could, in theory, contribute that entire sum into their pension scheme or schemes and it would all be eligible for tax relief. Their partner, who has no earnings, could contribute £2,880 per annum (£3,600 gross) into their own pension scheme.

There are limits on the annual contributions that can be made and the size of a fund that an individual can build up, but these limits are unlikely to affect all but very high earners. The allowances are generous enough not to cause any issues for an average individual.

When an individual makes contributions to their pension fund, then the real cost to them will be the amount net of income tax at their highest rate.

> ### Example 12.8
>
> The real cost to a basic rate taxpayer, paying tax at 20%, of making £100 (gross) of pension contributions, would be £80. If that person had a personal pension, they would pay £80 to the pension scheme and the scheme would recover £20 from HMRC.

The way in which tax relief is given differs between workplace schemes and personal pensions.

Tax relief for contributions to workplace schemes

Members of a workplace scheme have their contributions collected by their employer. The contributions are deducted from their gross pay and they are then taxed on this lower amount, and hence pay less tax than they would have done without the contributions.

> ### Example 12.9
>
> An employee earning £27,500 gross per annum would pay basic rate income tax of £3,000 on that amount. (Remember a tax-free personal allowance of £12,500 means that not all of the £27,500 is taxable.)
>
> If that employee made £4,000 (gross) of contributions to a workplace pension scheme, she would be taxed on £23,500 (£27,500 – £4,000) and she would pay £2,200 of income tax that year.
>
> The difference in tax payable of £800 means that the actual cost to the employee of making £4,000 (gross) of contributions into her pension scheme would be £3,200 (£4,000 less the tax saving of £800).

The employee in Example 12.9 would not have to do anything in order for that tax relief to be obtained. If the employee is a higher or additional rate taxpayer, then she will be given tax relief at her highest rate of income tax.

> ### Example 12.10
>
> An employee earning £75,000 gross per annum would pay income tax of £18,600 on that amount. (Some would be taxed at the basic rate of 20% and some at the higher rate of 40%.)
>
> If that employee made £4,000 of contributions to a workplace pension scheme, he would be taxed on £71,000 (£75,000 – £4,000) and he would pay £17,000 of income tax that year.
>
> The difference in tax payable of £1,600 means that the actual cost to the employee of making £4,000 (gross) of contributions into his personal pension scheme would be £2,400 (£4,000 less the tax saving of £1,600).

In Example 12.10, the higher rate taxpayer gets relief at the higher rate of 40% on contributions made, whereas a basic rate taxpayer gets relief at the basic rate of 20%.

Tax relief for contributions to personal pensions

When a person makes contributions to a personal pension they will be making the contributions out of their income, which has already been taxed. In this situation, the contribution is treated by the pension scheme as having been paid net of basic rate tax and the scheme reclaims the tax that the pension saver would have paid on the amount of the contribution.

Example 12.11

If a basic rate taxpayer pays £3,200 into her personal pension scheme one year, then the scheme will recover £800 from HMRC. The amount recovered from HMRC represents the tax she would have suffered in order to receive £3,200. The total contributions into her personal pension in that year would be £3,200 + £800 = £4,000 (gross).

(Note that if the basic rate of tax is 20%, then the tax suffered on £4,000 of income would be £4,000 × 20% = £800.)

The relief is always given at the taxpayer's highest rate of taxation. The way in which tax relief is given to members of workplace and personal pension schemes means that, in both situations, the member making the contributions should not have to take any action to ensure the basic rate relief is obtained. Higher rate taxpayers can claim relief at the higher rate for pension contributions made, by submitting a self-assessment tax return.

It is also possible for non-earners to make pension contributions up to a limit of £3,600 (gross) per annum. Even though the individual may not have paid income tax during the year, the personal pension scheme can recover tax at the basic rate on any contributions made.

Example 12.12

If an individual with no taxable income pays £2,880 into her pension scheme one year, the scheme will recover £720 from HMRC, even though in this situation no tax has been paid. The total contributions into her personal pension in that year would be £2,880 + £720 = £3,600.

(Note that if the basic rate of tax is 20%, then the tax suffered on £3,600 of income would be £3,600 × 20% = £720.)

? Ponder point

Can you envisage any circumstances where a non-taxpayer, not in employment or self-employment, might want to make pension contributions?

There are many circumstances when an individual might wish to do so, provided they have the funds available to make pension contributions. Individuals on career breaks, those with caring responsibilities, those temporarily out of employment, those starting up a new business who have not yet made any profits, those who have taken early retirement, and many other situations. By making contributions, they will build up a bigger pension pot.

 Ponder point

The grandfather of a student has offered to make contributions into a pension scheme on the student's behalf, for the three years he will be at university. Do you consider this would be a worthwhile thing to do?

From earlier discussions, it is clear that the younger a person is when the pension contributions are made, the more valuable those contributions will be. The grandfather would be wise not to exceed the contributions limit of £3,600 (gross), as above that amount, no tax relief is available. This would be a very helpful start to the student's pension fund.

Options at retirement

Pension savings carry generous tax reliefs and are built up in order to fund an income in retirement. In recent years, the options available to people at retirement as to how they choose to use their pension funds, have greatly increased.

Retirement age

The age when an individual chooses to retire is likely to be the point at which they can start to receive a pension. However, it is perfectly permissible to be in receipt of a pension and continue to work, either full-or part-time.

The state pension age has changed in recent years and for anyone born after 6 April 1978, their state pension will be payable from the age of sixty-eight as the rules currently stand. It is possible to defer drawing your state pension at that point and if an individual chooses to start drawing their state pension after their official pension age, then a higher state pension will be paid.

Workplace and private pensions cannot be taken until the age of fifty-five and individual schemes may set an older age for pension eligibility. The minimum age of fifty-five is set to rise for younger people. There is often some flexibility and the later someone chooses to retire, the greater their annual pension is likely to be. However, this cannot be guaranteed where defined-contribution schemes are concerned as stock market movements and changes in annuity rates could adversely affect anyone choosing to retire later.

The pension pot

As with most other aspects of pension regulation, the rules that apply to pension savers when they retire are constantly changing. The options that may be available to the retiree depend on whether the scheme is a defined-benefit or defined-contribution scheme.

For defined-benefit schemes, the two main options available to the retiree are:

- to take a tax-free lump sum followed by a pension for the retiree and any surviving spouse, or
- to take no lump sum and an increased pension for the retiree and any surviving spouse.

There are other options open to a member of a defined-benefit scheme, but as these schemes offer a pension linked to salaries, it would be unwise for the vast majority of their members not to take the pension offered by the scheme.

For defined-contribution schemes, sweeping pension changes introduced in 2015 means that there are a number of decisions that have to be made by anyone taking retirement about how they will utilize their pension pot. The options available to them include:

Buy an annuity

Convert the entire pension pot into an annuity that will provide a reliable income stream until death.

Take a lump sum and buy an annuity with the remainder

Take up to 25% of the pension pot tax-free on retirement and then utilize the remainder of the pot to buy an annuity.

Use income drawdown

Use the entire pension pot to provide an income during retirement, using income drawdown. Income drawdown means that the pension pot can remain invested and on a regular basis, the saver can withdraw an amount from the pot to provide them with an income.

Take a lump sum and use income drawdown with the remainder

Take up to 25% of the pension pot tax-free and then use income drawdown on the remaining balance to provide an income during retirement.

Take the whole pot as cash

Draw out all the funds from the pension pot, with 25% of the total being allowed tax-free. The remainder would be taxed and would then be available to spend or invest.

Some of the above options can be combined, for example taking a lump sum, buying an annuity with part of the pot, and using income drawdown with the remainder.

Income drawdown is a higher risk option than buying an annuity and it is considered advisable that only savers with significant pension pots or other income streams, should consider taking this option. The option remains available to purchase an annuity with the remaining pension pot at any point. Income drawdown might be used, for example, where pensioners at retirement do not wish to buy an annuity because annuity rates are particularly low.

The two most significant disadvantages of income drawdown are: first, that the pension pot remains subject to fluctuating asset prices that could lead to a smaller pension pot; secondly, there is a risk that too much is taken from the pot in the early years after retirement and the pot becomes too depleted to provide an adequate income in the later years.

The major advantage of income drawdown is that the pension pot remains invested and is able to benefit from any investment growth. Another benefit is that the pension pot remains as an asset that can be passed on to the pensioner's heirs when they die. Tax charges can apply to the inheritance depending on the age at which the pensioner dies. Table 12.2 compares the pros and cons of buying an annuity and utilizing income drawdown.

Table 12.2 Comparing buying an annuity versus using income drawdown

	Annuity	Income drawdown
Guaranteed income amount	Yes	No
Income stream guaranteed for life	Yes	No
Income stream can be flexible	No	Yes
The pension pot will continue to benefit from (or suffer as a result of) market movements	No	Yes
Pension pot can be passed onto heirs	In some rare instances	Yes

Example 12.13

Twin sisters, A and B, retired at age sixty-five and both had a pension pot valued at £250,000. They both opted to take the maximum tax-free cash lump sum. With the remainder, sister A decided that she would like the certainty provided by buying an annuity whereas sister B preferred to leave her pot invested and opted for income drawdown.

Both sisters received a tax-free lump sum of 25% × £250,000 = £62,500. This left each sister with a pot valued at £187,500.

Sister A used the pot remaining to buy a flat rate annuity of £9,300 per annum, where no second pension was provided for. Sister B decided to take an identical amount per annum, by way of income drawdown.

Five years after retiring, sister B decided that she would prefer the certainty that an annuity brings. In the four years since they retired, her pension pot had experienced negative returns and annuity rates had fallen. Her pension pot stood at approximately £135,000 and this would buy her an annuity of £8,200 per annum at age seventy. Sister B's pension pot, after four years of income drawdown and poor investment returns, has been depleted and as annuity rates have deteriorated, the annuity she could buy was lower than previously.

Example 12.13 highlights the risk of using income drawdown rather than buying an annuity at retirement. However, in situations where good investment returns are made, income drawdown would represent a more attractive option. It will always be a more risky option.

Other income streams in retirement

There are many other sources of income that individuals may plan to use in retirement, some of which are as follows:

Income from own home

Many people on or after retirement choose to downsize to a smaller property, thereby releasing equity that can provide them with useful income. This also has the benefit of reducing many household bills. Where people wish to stay in their own home, it may be possible to use equity release schemes to raise funds and/or generate an income. These schemes, which are expensive and restrictive, are discussed in Chapter 9.

Savings and investment income

Income from savings and investments can be a very useful source of revenue in retirement. Most people should consider holding these in ISAs as far as possible. ISAs are discussed in Chapter 8.

Buy-to-let income

Where individuals have a buy-to-let property or properties, the net rental income will provide a very useful source of income in retirement.

Employment or self-employment

Working, at least part-time, during the early years of retirement can be a very useful strategy. As well as providing income, it may allow pension benefits to be deferred for a few years that would result in a greater pension amount becoming payable, when it is drawn.

Pension income, whether from state or private pensions, rental income, and any income from savings and investments (where they are not held in an ISA or covered by allowances), are all liable to income tax. Anyone older than the state retirement age does not have to pay National Insurance contributions.

Ponder point

Pensions income is liable to income tax. Income from savings and investments held in an ISA is receivable tax-free. Should this encourage pension savers to reduce the amount they contribute to their pension fund and build up their ISA savings instead?

A key benefit of saving into a pension fund is that it is very tax effective. For every £100 added to a pension fund, the cost to a basic rate pension saver is £80. If a basic rate saver pays £80 into an ISA, then that £80 is not topped up in the same way as pension contributions. Keeping some savings in an ISA is a sensible strategy as most people will need to have some readily accessible savings for known commitments and especially for emergencies. Income arising from ISAs can also provide a useful boost to retirement income.

Planning for retirement

As explored earlier in the chapter, significant amounts of pension savings need to be accumulated in order to secure a moderately comfortable retirement. The generous tax reliefs given on pension scheme savings mean that for most individuals, saving in a pension scheme will form a large part of their savings for retirement. Many people may plan to have additional income streams to supplement this.

The earlier that an individual starts saving for their pension, the better; £1,000 saved at age twenty-five will grow to be far more valuable than £1,000 saved at age forty-five. Retirement planning should be an integral part of everyone's financial planning and, just as for other personal finance issues, a systematic approach should be used.

Set your objectives

The first step in retirement planning should be to identify when you would like to retire and the income that you would like to receive when you retire.

Measure your position

The second step is to ascertain how much income you expect to receive when you retire, from any existing arrangements:

- You can get a state pension forecast by requesting one from the Gov.uk website.
- Any workplace or private pension will provide an annual statement that gives you an illustration of how much pension you can expect to receive, based on certain assumptions. These illustrations give expected pension incomes in today's prices, which are arrived at after taking account of the likely effect of inflation.

- There may be other investments and savings held, perhaps in ISAs, that will be expected to generate an income and/or some individuals may expect to receive rental income from buy-to let properties.

Research your options

By comparing your required income with your expected income, any expected short-fall can be calculated and possible steps to remedy it can be researched. To undertake the research, you need to understand the options available and take time to fully consider the advantages and disadvantages of the various courses of action.

Act

Having done your research and identified your possible options, decisions will need to be made and it is vital that you act on those decisions.

Review regularly

This whole process of retirement planning should be undertaken at regular intervals, at least every three years and certainly after any significant personal event such as marriage, divorce, birth of a child, or receipt of an inheritance.

Example 12.14

An individual, aged fifty-three, who has been contributing to workplace pension schemes during most of his working life, has calculated that he would like to receive an income of £18,000 (before tax) per annum in retirement. He has researched his state and private pensions and the following are estimates for his income at age sixty-eight, when he plans to retire:

i.   A state pension of £156 per week.

ii. A pension scheme run by his current employer that anticipates paying him £2,080 per annum.

iii. A workplace pension from a previous employment that predicts paying £3,480 per annum.

iv. Cash ISAs that, based on current interest rates, should provide a tax-free income of £800 per annum.

This individual has an estimated retirement income of £14,472 per annum, (£156 × 52 weeks + £2,080 + £3,480 + £800). He has an expected shortfall in his retirement income of £3,528 (£18,000 − £14,472).

  He spends time researching how best to fill this gap and narrows it down to two options that he prefers:

- By using a pension calculator, he discovers that in order to generate extra income of £3,500 per annum at age sixty-eight, he would need to save another £350 per month from now on

(continued...)

- On retirement, he could downsize his property and release capital of at least £90,000 that should enable him to fund his required level of income

He decides that downsizing his property at retirement is the route he will opt for and hopes that nothing untoward happens to property prices in the meantime.

Example 12.15

A self-employed builder, aged fifty-five, has had a private pension for a few years but has struggled to contribute a great deal into it. He identifies that he would like to have an income of £20,000 per annum in retirement. He has researched his state and personal pension and the following are estimates for his income at age sixty, when he would like to retire:

i.   His state pension will not be payable until he reaches the age of sixty-eight and his forecast shows an amount of £156 per week being payable from that age.

ii. His personal pension shows a predicted annual pension of £1,000 per annum payable from age sixty.

iii. He owns one buy-to-let property from which the net rental income is £6,000 per annum.

Using the figures given, his pension shortfall between the ages of sixty and sixty-eight would be very substantial at £13,000 per annum (£20,000 – (£1,000 + £6000)). From age sixty-eight onwards, when his state pension will be received, the shortfall would be £4,888 per annum. The predictions alert the builder to the fact that, as his finances currently stand, he will not be able to afford to retire at the age of sixty and, in addition, he needs to consider saving a great deal more towards his retirement.

Based on his findings, the builder decides to take a phased retirement starting at sixty-five and working part-time until he reaches sixty-eight. His personal pension will pay him £1,500 per annum if he starts to draw it at age sixty-five. A pension fund calculator forecasts that if he starts paying an extra £220 per month into his pension from now on, this should generate an extra £5,000 per annum income on full retirement at age sixty-eight.

Case study—Rachel

Rachel has been in full-time employment since leaving university and having risen quickly through the ranks she is now, aged twenty-five, a manager in a large retail company earning £45,000 per annum. She has student debt and a small car loan outstanding. She has some savings but plans to use them as a deposit on buying her own home, in a few months' time.

Her employer has offered her the chance of joining a defined-contribution workplace pension scheme into which employees are required to contribute 5% of their salary and the employer contributes 5% as well. Rachel is reluctant to join the scheme at this point. She plans to stay with this employer but wants to use all of her current resources towards having enough savings to put down as a deposit on a property. She would prefer to join the scheme in five years' time.

Required:

a) **Identify for Rachel the real cost to her of making 5% pension contributions when her salary is £45,000 per annum. (Assume that all of Rachel's income would be taxed at the basic rate.)**

b) How much will be invested in her pension pot in the first year, if she joins the scheme at this point?

c) How much will be invested in her pension pot over the next five years, assuming her average salary over that time is £47,500 per annum. This will represent the size of Rachel's pension pot when she reaches thirty, after five years of contributing. (For simplicity, assume that the investment returns earned are 0%, over those five years.)

d) When £100 is invested for thirty years and earns a return of 2% per annum throughout that time, then that £100 will be worth £180 at the end of thirty years. Using this information, how much would Rachel's 'five-year pot' be worth by the time she is sixty, assuming a modest growth rate of 2% per annum?

e) If a pension pot of £100,000 belonging to a healthy sixty-five-year-old would buy an annuity of £4,600 per annum, how much pension will Rachel's five-year pot buy?

f) Discuss Rachel's dilemma over whether to join the workplace scheme and advise her on whether or not to defer joining the scheme.

Case study—Theo

Theo, aged forty, has worked for the last fifteen years as a biomedical scientist in the health service. His current remuneration package includes a salary of £29,000 per annum and membership of a final-salary pension scheme. The scheme provides life assurance of two times annual salary.

In recent years, the percentage contributions that Theo has to pay to the pension scheme have been rising and currently stand at 8%. Theo's wife, Kate, runs her own small business from which she receives a small income each month. As they have three young children, they find it increasingly difficult to manage financially and the couple have run up a significant overdraft and credit card debts.

Theo considers that he cannot afford to make pension contributions at the moment and is considering leaving the scheme. He intends to leave his current pension entitlement in the fund and is prepared to draw a smaller NHS pension when he retires based on his fifteen years membership of the scheme. His other plan is to start saving into a personal pension, where he can pay a smaller amount of contributions.

Theo's wife, Kate, has made no pension savings.

Required:

Discuss Theo's pension plans, in the light of the financial difficulties that he and his family are facing.

Conclusion

Retirement planning should be an essential part of any individual's financial arrangements. The earlier that a person starts to save for their retirement the better, as sums saved at a young age are far more valuable than those saved closer to retirement age.

The basic state pension entitlement is very low and will always be subject to regular political change. For most people, it will be a very useful source of income in retirement but should not be relied upon as the main or only source of income. Entitlement to receive the state pension depends on having paid sufficient National Insurance contributions.

Pension schemes can be categorized as being either defined-benefit or defined-contribution schemes. Defined-benefit schemes, also known as salary-related schemes, are ones where an individual's pension entitlement is linked to their salary and the number of years they have been members of the scheme. These schemes are becoming increasingly rare and membership of them should be highly prized as they lead to pensions that are automatically linked to salaries and hence are more predictable.

Defined-contribution schemes are schemes where the final pension payable is notoriously difficult to predict because of variable investment returns. Charges can have a very significant negative impact on the amount of the final fund. There is also the risk of the pension payable being low due to poor annuity rates when the pension pot is converted into an income. If income drawdown is used as an alternative to buying an annuity, it needs to be very carefully managed.

All employers are required to offer workplace pensions, whereby employees are automatically enrolled into the scheme unless they choose to opt out. Many workplace schemes involve reasonable contributions being made by pension scheme members and by the employer. The minimum rate of contributions set by the government are very low and use of a scheme where the minimum contributions are made will provide a very small pension.

Personal pension schemes allow people to save for their retirement by building up a pension pot and then using this pot to fund their pension income. The amount of pension that they might generate will always be hard to predict.

Pension saving has long been encouraged by allowing tax relief on pension contributions made. This makes the real cost of pension saving lower than it would otherwise be.

For many people, the inflexibility of pension saving causes them to plan to generate a retirement income from a range of different sources. The starting point will usually be a pension, or pensions, and other possible sources of income include income from savings and investments, rental income from property, or income from capital released by downsizing their property.

Each individual should on a regular basis, at least a three-yearly cycle, review their retirement plans to ensure that their savings and investments are likely to provide the income they require. Whilst this is difficult for young people to do, it does not mean that it should not be attempted. As retirement approaches, many decisions need to be made: when to retire, whether to take a tax-free lump sum, whether to buy an annuity, or use income drawdown. Every individual should consider their needs and ambitions and plan accordingly.

Useful websites

A government-backed site that has information on state pensions, workplace pensions, and personal pensions:

http://www.pensionsadvisoryservice.org.uk

For information on state pensions and retirement planning, including getting a state pension forecast:

http://www.gov.uk

A useful website for advice on pensions and retirement planning:

http://www.themoneyadviceservice.org.uk/en

Useful websites for advice on pensions and retirement planning:

http://www.hl.co.uk

http://www.pensioncalculator.org

References

Hargreaves Lansdown *Pension Calculator*. Available at: http://www.hl.co.uk/pensions/interactive-calculators/pension-calculator (accessed 19.7.2016)

Office for National Statistics (2010) *Chapter 2: Results, 2010-based NPP Reference Volume*. Available at: http://www.ons.gov.uk/ons/dcp171776-253934.pdf (accessed 19.7.2016)

Parliamentary and Health Service Ombudsman (2007) *A Decade of Regulatory Failure*. Available at: http://www.ombudsman.org.

uk/__data/assets/pdf_file/0010/1252/equitable_life_part_1_main_report.pdfhttp (accessed 19.7.2016)

Ringshaw, G (2011) *Mirror Pension Warnings Ignored*. Available at: http://www.telegraph.co.uk/finance/4487800/Mirror-pension-warnings-ignored.html (accessed 14.5.2016)

Thurley, D (2012) *Pension Scheme Charges*, House of Commons Standard Note 6209. Available at: http://www.parliament.uk/briefing-papers/SN06209 (accessed 16.4.2016)

Practice Questions

Question 1 Quick Questions TRUE OR FALSE?

12.1 An individual's entitlement to the state pension is dependent on having paid income tax over many years.

12.2 A defined-benefit scheme is also known as a salary-related scheme.

12.3 A defined-contribution scheme builds contributions and investment returns into a 'pension pot'.

12.4 Pension savings can be withdrawn from a pension fund at any time.

12.5 Purchasing an annuity is a way of converting a lump sum into an annual income.

12.6 An individual can continue to pay into a personal pension scheme if they move from self-employment to employment.

12.7 It is possible for an individual to get tax relief on contributions to a personal pension scheme even if they have no income and pay no income tax.

12.8 The state retirement age is the minimum age at which all private pensions can be drawn.

12.9   All employers must offer a workplace pension for employees aged between twenty-two and the state retirement age, and earning over a specified sum.

12.10   Income drawdown is a lower risk way of using pension savings as it avoids having to buy an annuity.

* Question 2 Shirley

Shirley, aged thirty-five, is carrying out a review of her pension arrangements, as three months ago she was made redundant from K plc where she had been working since graduating. She has found a new job at L Ltd but on a salary of £30,000 per annum, lower than she was paid in her previous job.

Her current pension arrangements include the following:

i.   She was a member of K plc's defined-benefit pension scheme and she had made twelve years' worth of contributions. A recent statement from the scheme shows an expected pension of £3,400 per annum payable to her from the age of sixty-five.

ii.   She expects to make National Insurance contributions for at least thirty-five years and her state pension forecast expects her to receive £156 per week, from the age of sixty-eight. Shirley plans to work until she is sixty-eight.

iii. Her new employer, L Ltd, is about to auto-enrol her onto a workplace pension that is a defined-contribution scheme. Shirley will contribute 3% per annum and her employer will contribute 5%. A forecast shows that if she were to stay in this scheme, to age sixty-eight, it is predicted she could receive a tax-free lump sum of £22,500 and a pension of £3,500 per annum.

iv.   Shirley received a considerable redundancy payment when she was made redundant and she has used this to reduce the size of her mortgage loan.

Required

a) **Explain to Shirley how a defined-contribution scheme works, and how it differs from K plc's defined-benefit pension scheme that she belonged to previously.**

b) **Prepare a statement that shows Shirley's expected retirement income from age sixty-eight. If Shirley would like to retire at sixty-eight on an income of a minimum of £15,000 per annum, what steps would you advise her to take?**

Question 3 Zola

Zola, aged twenty-eight, has recently joined a workplace pension scheme to which she will contribute 3% per annum and her employer will contribute another 3%. She has not made any previous pension contributions and has savings, all held in cash ISAs, that amount to £8,000.

Zola's salary is £35,000 per annum and because she manages her finances carefully, she can afford to save £120 per month, even after allowing for her pension contributions. She is considering whether she should pay this monthly amount into a pension scheme or make further savings into her ISA accounts.

Zola and her partner hope to buy their own home when they can raise the deposit required. Zola's share of the deposit is estimated at £12,000.

Required:

Discuss the advantages and disadvantages to Zola of making pension savings or ISA savings with her spare income.

* Question 4 Nicholas

Nicholas is sixty-four years old and plans to retire when he reaches sixty-eight. He has an interest-only mortgage of £21,000 outstanding and hopes to be able to pay it off at retirement. He will be entitled to a basic state pension of £156 per week but he would like to have an income of £300 per week in retirement. He also has a personal pension and he estimates that the pension pot will be worth £145,000 in four years' time.

Nicholas is aware that there will be choices that he will need to make when he reaches retirement age as to how his pension pot is used. He has heard of annuities, lump sums, and income drawdown but does not understand what these terms mean.

Required:

a) Explain the terms annuity and income drawdown.

b) How much of the pension pot can be taken as a lump sum? Advise Nicholas as to whether he should consider taking a lump sum.

c) Discuss the advantages and disadvantages of buying an annuity over income drawdown.

d) Would you advise Nicholas to use an annuity or income drawdown if you were aware that:

   i.   he received net rental income from buy-to-let properties amounting to £10,500 per annum, or

   ii. he had a life limiting illness, or

   iii. he had a young family and a wife who earned very erratic income from self-employment.

 Visit the Online Resource Centre that accompanies this book for additional material:
www.oxfordtextbooks.co.uk/orc/king_carey2e/

13 Making your will

 Learning Objectives

After studying this chapter, you should understand:

- The reasons why it is important to make a will
- Essential elements of writing a will
- The rules of intestacy that will apply if you do not make a will
- The family provision legislation that allows the court to make limited provision for family or dependants, whether or not a will is made

Introduction

A will is a legal declaration of how an individual wishes their property to be distributed when they die. It is very tempting to put off making a will because no one likes to think about dying but, as Benjamin Franklin said: 'In this world nothing can be said to be certain, except death and taxes' (Franklin, 1789). This chapter considers the possible financial implications of death upon family and friends and Chapter 7 covers inheritance taxes that may arise. Many young people believe that they do not need to make a will, but in the unlikely event of an early death, the existence of a will would significantly ease the burden on their family at a very difficult time. Once you have some assets of value or have a partner or dependants, making a will becomes more important, whatever your age. The information in this chapter is specific to England and Wales. The law and terminology in Scotland and Northern Ireland are slightly different. Information on intestacy rules in Northern Ireland can be found at http://www.nidirect.gov.uk and in Scotland at http://www.gov.scot

The number of people in the UK who have made a will is surprisingly low. According to the BBC: 'Only three in ten people in the UK have a will' (BBC, 2011). Making a will is usually quite a straightforward process but there is generally a cost involved. The most common route for preparing a will is to use a solicitor who will charge a fee but will also provide advice. It is possible to write a will without a solicitor but it is also easy to make a mistake and hence invalidate all or part of it. Solicitors sometimes say that they make more money from sorting out problems when wills have not been properly drafted, than they make from preparing wills in the first place.

Ponder point

Why do you think a significant number of people in the UK do not make a will?

Many people believe that if they die without making a will their partner will inherit all of their assets, and therefore they do not see any benefit in making a will. This is not necessarily the case; the intestacy rules that apply in the absence of a will can result in a surprising outcome that may not have been what was anticipated or desired.

Making a will requires people to think about their own mortality and this is not a thought process that comes easily.

Some people will be discouraged from making a will because of the cost involved. However, the cost is usually small compared to the benefits derived from having a properly drafted will in place.

Reasons for making a will

Key terms

Estate means the total value of any money, property, or possessions left when a person dies. It includes all property, investments, and anything of value after deducting any liabilities.
Intestate refers to the situation where a person has died without making a will. They are said to have died intestate and the rules of intestacy are applied.
A **testator** is a person who has made or is making a valid will.
A **legacy** is a gift under a will, usually of money or personal property.
A **guardian** is someone who is appointed to take responsibility for a child in the event of the death of the child's parents or other carers.

Ponder point

Can you think of several different reasons for making a will?

For most people the main reason for making a will is to ensure that their estate is distributed in accordance with their wishes. A will enables you to make sure that your estate is distributed amongst your family, friends, and charities in the way that you wish and not according to the intestacy rules.

Making a will should provide clarity about your intentions for your estate and avoid any disputes amongst relatives, although this is not guaranteed. Many a good novel or news story centres entirely around a family disputing a will. Charles Dickens' *Bleak*

House, for example, tells the story of a long-running court case concerning several conflicting wills.

In today's society many people have complicated family lives and this means that making a valid will is essential to ensure that the estate is distributed in accordance with a person's wishes. It is very important for couples who are not either married or in a civil partnership to make a will. If there is no will, then under the current rules of intestacy the unmarried partner will not inherit and this can cause major financial difficulty.

Once a person has children then a will should be made to set out who should look after the children if both parents were to die. A will allows the testator to appoint guardians for their children.

If a person dies intestate their children will inherit at the age of eighteen, or on earlier marriage or civil partnership. Many people would consider that eighteen is too young an age for children to inherit and the terms of a will can set out a later age at which the children will inherit.

Making a will provides an opportunity for tax planning in order to minimize the amount of inheritance tax that will become due on death, particularly where significant estates are likely to be involved. (Inheritance tax is discussed in Chapter 7.) A will can make provision for specific legacies, such as leaving particular items to a friend or relative. It also allows the will-maker to set up a legacy to a charity. The will can set out details about how a funeral should be carried out, including any wish to be buried or cremated.

Misconceptions concerning wills

There are some long-established myths when it comes to wills and inheritance. First of all there is the idea that if a person dies intestate, the person's spouse or civil partner automatically inherits everything. This may not be the case under the rules of intestacy, which will be explored in more detail later in the chapter.

Some people may believe, perhaps from watching American TV programmes, that wills can be made on video or film. This is not the case in the UK, as all wills must be in writing in order to be valid.

There is often a misunderstanding about the position of an unmarried partner or cohabitant, sometimes known as a 'common-law spouse', under the laws of intestacy. Many people believe that if you have a live-in partner they will automatically inherit everything if you were to die without making a will. The fact is that the laws of intestacy are based on very old principles and as they currently stand they only recognize the claims of relatives.

Another misconception is the belief that you do not need to make a will if you do not have children. Whilst it is true that having children increases the need for a will to be in place, anyone with some assets of value should make a will to ensure that, in the event of their death, their property goes to the people they would choose.

Some people believe that making a will is morbid, difficult, time-consuming, expensive, involves lots of paperwork, and is stressful, none of which is necessarily true.

Example 13.1

Samirah had been living with her partner in London for four years, although her partner was not divorced from his wife. He died unexpectedly when he was only forty-five. Samirah's partner died intestate as he had not made a will and the rules of intestacy were applied. Under these rules, even though Samirah was his live-in partner, she was not entitled to inherit anything and his wife inherited the house that he had been living in with Samirah.

If Samirah's partner had made a will, he could have ensured that she was financially secure after his death.

The practicalities of writing a will

A solicitor can be engaged to draw up a will and this is probably the safest option to ensure that the will is valid and accurately reflects the wishes of the testator, but the solicitor will charge a fee. Solicitors are familiar with drawing up wills and can spot pitfalls that are not always obvious to the lay person. There are also specialist will-writing firms who will prepare a will for a fee and some banks offer help and advice with writing wills.

It is possible to download information on writing wills from the internet, to purchase will-making software, or to purchase 'will forms' from a stationers. Do-it-yourself wills are the cheapest option but also the most risky because it is possible to overlook important considerations that could make the will invalid.

Many charities offer a free will-writing service in the expectation that the will-maker will leave a legacy to the charity that provides the service.

 Key terms

A **beneficiary** is a person or entity entitled to receive funds or other property under a will.
An **executor** is the person appointed to carry out the provisions set out in the will. There can be more than one executor appointed.
A **trust** is an arrangement whereby a trustee (or trustees) holds assets for the benefit of those entitled to the assets, namely the beneficiaries.

 Ponder point

Before drawing up a will what factors should you consider?

Prior to drawing up a will the first step is to consider what assets the testator possesses which are likely to be available for distribution under the terms of the will. Having established the assets, the next step is to consider whom the testator would wish to benefit from those assets. The list of beneficiaries is likely to include family and may also include friends. Many people take the opportunity to leave a specific legacy to a charity or charities.

It is possible to make a specific legacy of a particular asset or assets, for example jewellery, or of a specific sum of money, known as a pecuniary legacy. It is also possible to make a will such that one or more beneficiaries each receive a percentage of the estate, often the estate remaining after specific legacies have been made.

If the testator has children, then an important question to consider is who should be appointed as guardians for the children. The appointment should be discussed with the proposed guardians to ensure that they would be willing and able to act in that capacity, should the need arise.

If the testator has children, then another decision that needs to be considered is the age at which they should inherit. If the testator dies before they reach the appointed age, their inheritance can be held in trust.

If there are any offshore assets, such as a holiday home abroad, specialist advice would be needed to consider how the law of the relevant territory would be applied.

A will needs at least one executor to carry out the terms of the will, so consideration would need to be given as to whom that person or persons should be.

Important elements of writing a will

The legislation relating to wills is set out in the Wills Act 1837, supported by a significant amount of case law relating to the interpretation and validity of wills. The following are key components of a valid will:

- A will must be in writing.
- The person making the will must be 'of sound mind' and not under duress or pressure when making the will.
- The will must be signed by the testator and the signature must be witnessed and signed by two witnesses; these witnesses cannot be beneficiaries, nor can they be blind, and they must be capable of understanding what they are doing. The witnesses' spouses or civil partners cannot be beneficiaries either. The witnesses do not need to read the will, but must see the will being signed and then sign it themselves.
- The will must appoint at least one executor who will administer the estate of the person who has died, in accordance with the will. Any executor must be over eighteen and it is quite normal for an executor to be a beneficiary under the will.
- The person making the will must be over eighteen.
- The will should ensure that all of the assets are distributed, not just part of the assets. Failure to distribute all of the assets under the will causes a partial intestacy and the rules of intestacy will apply to the undistributed assets. This is a common reason for partial failure when wills are written without professional help.
- The beneficiaries must not be present when the will is being signed.

- If there are children, the will should set out details of guardians to be appointed in the event of the death of both parents.
- Jointly held assets such as joint bank accounts and some jointly owned property do not need to be included in a will as, on death, they will pass automatically to the joint owner.

Example 13.2

A wealthy widower has no close living relatives and wishes to leave his entire estate to two friends living nearby. He asks both their wives to witness his will. Unfortunately the will would not be valid because the witnesses are both partners of the beneficiaries. In this case the will would be disregarded and the widower's estate would be distributed according to the rules of intestacy.

Example 13.3

A mother asks her daughter to witness her signature to her will and the daughter readily agrees.

This could be a cause for some concern, because if the daughter is named as a beneficiary under the will, she should not act as a witness. If she is a beneficiary and witnesses the will then she will not be able to receive her inheritance and there will be a partial intestacy.

Reviewing and updating wills

 Key term

A **codicil** is a legal document that makes minor changes or amendments to a will.

Wills should be regularly reviewed and updated to reflect changes in personal circumstances.

 Ponder point

Can you think of specific circumstances or events that should prompt a person to review their will?

There are many key events in a person's life that should prompt anyone who has made a will to review it and update it if necessary. If a person having made a will subsequently marries, any existing will is invalidated and a new will should be made. Going through a divorce should prompt a review of a will, to reflect the change in circumstances. A divorce does not necessarily cancel a will, but nevertheless it would be sensible to draft a new will or amend an existing one at such a point. The birth of a child is a significant change in circumstances and a will should be updated or rewritten to reflect such a change and to consider the appointment of suitable guardians. The arrival of a new grandchild may prompt an amendment to a will to add a new beneficiary. If a testator suffers the loss of a partner, child, descendant, or any beneficiary under the will, then the will should be reviewed and revised.

Sometimes a significant event occurs in a person's life that may encourage the testator to leave a legacy to a particular charity, which would require the will to be updated.

Cancelling or updating a will

A will can be cancelled at any time by physically destroying it. Alternatively the testator may decide to make a new will, which would cancel all previous wills. If there are some small changes to be made, then a codicil can be added to the will, which must be signed and witnessed in the same way as a will. A codicil does not usually cancel the will but should be read in conjunction with the will.

Assets that do not form part of an estate

 Key terms

Beneficial joint tenancy is where two, or more, people jointly own a property. If one of the owners dies, the property passes to the remaining owner or owners.

Tenants in common is where two, or more, people jointly own a property and each owner can pass on their share of the property to a beneficiary in their will. The surviving owner does not automatically inherit the deceased's share.

Jointly held assets

Before looking at the rules of intestacy, it is necessary to understand the treatment of jointly held assets and, in particular, property, if one of the owners dies. For the majority of people in the UK, their home is their most valuable asset. If the property has been purchased in joint names, as beneficial joint tenants, then upon the death of one of the owners, the property automatically passes to the other joint owner or owners. Beneficial joint tenancy is the most common way of jointly owning a home in the UK.

An alternative way of jointly owning a property is known as tenants in common, which has different legal implications upon the death of one of the owners. In this situation a surviving partner does not automatically inherit the other person's share. Instead it forms a part of the deceased's estate, similar to any other asset.

In general, when a person dies, any jointly held assets such as bank accounts, normally pass to the other joint owner and do not form part of the deceased's estate.

Example 13.4

Bill is married to Helen and they own their home as beneficial joint tenants. They also have one joint bank account and Bill has a variety of other assets and savings accounts in his sole name. Bill dies intestate.

Helen becomes the sole owner of the property and the joint bank account, as the surviving joint owner. Bill's other assets and savings would be subject to the rules of intestacy.

Pensions

The question of what happens to a person's pension fund on death is a complex one because it depends on several different factors: whether the person was still contributing to the scheme or had retired at the time of death, the type of pension scheme, and its terms and conditions. The general principle is that any sums payable to beneficiaries from a pension fund pass directly to them and do not form part of the deceased's estate.

If a person dies whilst still working and contributing to a pension fund, the pension scheme may provide for a death in service benefit to be paid out. This is usually a multiple of annual salary, such as two or three times salary. With some schemes this is automatically paid to a partner or spouse. With other schemes, at the time of joining the pension scheme, the member must nominate one or more beneficiaries to receive the benefit in the event of their death. Should they die whilst working and contributing to the pension fund, the lump sum benefit would normally be paid out to their nominated beneficiary or beneficiaries, subject to the discretion of the fund's trustees. This payment would not form part of the deceased's estate.

Some types of pension scheme in certain situations will also refund the deceased's pension contributions to the nominated beneficiary. In some situations, the spouse or civil partner of the deceased may be entitled to a pension from the fund. Any such payments would not form part of the deceased's estate.

Example 13.5

Jani and Stieg have been long-term partners and they own their home as beneficial joint tenants. Jani also owns a holiday home in Devon. They have a joint bank account and Jani has been contributing to a workplace pension scheme for many years which includes a death in service benefit of four times annual salary. Jani has nominated Stieg as the beneficiary for her pension fund. Jani dies intestate aged fifty-four, whilst still a contributing member of the pension scheme.

(continued...)

Following Jani's death, Stieg would become the sole owner of their home and the joint bank account, as the surviving joint owner. The death in service benefit of four times Jani's annual salary would be paid out to Stieg as her nominated beneficiary. Jani's pension scheme might (depending on the terms of the scheme), also refund Jani's pension contributions directly to Stieg as her beneficiary. Jani's estate would consist solely of her holiday home that would be distributed according to the rules of intestacy.

Introduction to the rules of intestacy

A person can save a small amount of money by not making a will, but it is likely to prove a false economy. The lack of a will can lead to major problems for the family left behind and especially for an unmarried partner. It may result in the need to go to court to prove a claim against the estate. To die without leaving a valid will that effectively disposes of all property is to die intestate and in the UK the law decides who will benefit from the assets. This distribution of a person's estate might not be in line with their wishes. This chapter considers the law as it currently stands in England and Wales, according to the Inheritance and Trustees Powers Act 2014.

The Law Commission presented a major report in 2011 that proposed changes to the laws of intestacy to reflect modern life in Britain. Some, but not all, of these were accepted and enacted by the government in 2014. The current situation is as set out in Figure 13.1.

Intestacy can be total or partial. Total intestacy occurs if the deceased did not make a will, or made one that was invalid for some reason, or was cancelled. Partial intestacy also occurs if there was a will but somehow it did not dispose of any of the assets in the estate. This can happen, for example, if the will leaves everything to someone who has already died and the will made no provision for such an event. There is a partial intestacy if there is a will that details how some of the deceased's assets are to be distributed, but not all of them.

The intestacy rules determine the distribution of the deceased's estate after any debts and liabilities, funeral expenses, and costs of the administration of the estate have been paid. If the intestacy is partial, the distributions under the will take priority; once those distributions have been made the intestacy rules take effect, regardless of whether any of the beneficiaries under those rules have already received anything under the will.

The rules of intestacy differ depending on the deceased's marital status and whether the deceased had children or not. There is a greater probability that a will exists when larger estates are left, and intestate estates tend to be smaller. However, this is not always the case and some very large estates have been distributed according to the rules of intestacy.

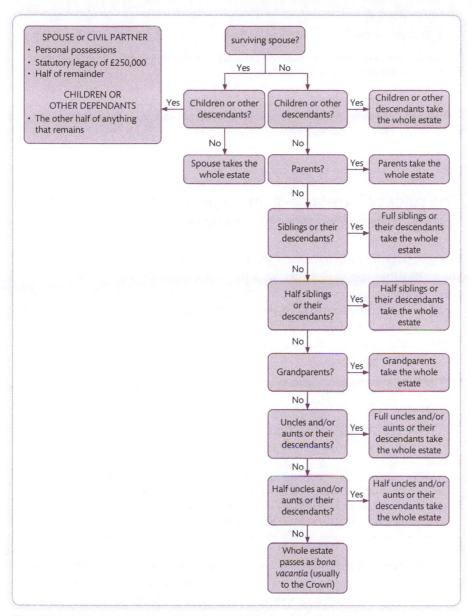

Figure 13.1 Diagram summarizing distribution under the intestacy rules

Source: Adapted and updated from the Law Commission Report 2011, *Intestacy and Family Provision Claims on Death.*

Key terms

Spouse means a legally married partner. A divorced partner is no longer a spouse. The term spouse as used in this text includes civil partner.

Civil partner means someone in a same-sex relationship who has entered a registered civil partnership, designed to give comparable rights to marriage.

Hierarchy is the term used to describe the order in which an estate must be distributed if someone dies without making a will.

The rules of intestacy—general principles applied when the deceased is survived by a spouse

The general principle of the rules of intestacy is that a spouse will inherit all or part of the estate if their spouse dies intestate. If the deceased has children as well as a spouse, then they too could be entitled to a share of the estate. The term children includes legally adopted children and adult sons and daughters, but does not include stepchildren, unless they have been adopted. If a child of the deceased has already died but has living children of its own, then they step into the shoes of their parent and are entitled to receive their parent's share.

Example 13.6

John died intestate, leaving a large estate. John had been married to Mary and they had three children; one of their children, Peter, had pre-deceased John. Peter had one child of his own, Paul.

Mary would inherit most of the estate but the remainder of the estate would be divided between John and Mary's three children in accordance with the rules of intestacy. The three children would each be entitled to receive equal shares; Paul, Peter's son, would step into his father's shoes and inherit Peter's share of the estate.

Children under eighteen do not receive their inheritance immediately. They receive it either when they reach the age of eighteen, or marry, or form a civil partnership under this age. Until then, a trust is established to manage the inheritance on their behalf.

Example 13.7

In the previous example, if Peter's son, Paul, was aged eleven when his grandfather John died intestate, then he would be entitled to receive his father's share of the estate but it would be held in trust until he reached eighteen. The person administering the estate would establish a trust and trustees would be appointed to manage the funds on behalf of Paul.

The spouse must survive the deceased by twenty-eight days in order to inherit under the rules of intestacy. If there is an accident in which a married couple or civil partners both die and it is not clear which person died first, it will not affect the intestacy rules, because neither can inherit from the other.

Applying the intestacy rules

Before considering the specific rules in detail, it is important to clarify again the situation with regard to jointly held property. Where this is held in joint names as beneficial joint tenants, the surviving owner would be entitled to the joint property, whether or not a will has been made. Assets held jointly in this way do not form part of an estate for intestacy purposes.

Similarly, death in service benefits and refunded pension contributions pass directly to the nominated beneficiary or beneficiaries and do not form part of the estate for intestacy purposes.

Using the left-hand side of Figure 13.1 the rules of intestacy can be explored in more detail.

Deceased is survived by a spouse, plus children or other descendants

If the estate is worth less than £250,000 then the spouse inherits everything.

If the estate is worth more than £250,000 then the spouse would receive £250,000, personal possessions, and half of the remainder. The children would be entitled to receive the remaining half of the estate over £250,000 immediately. This can cause difficulties, particularly where the family home forms a major part of the estate.

Example 13.8

A man died intestate leaving an estate of £500,000, consisting mainly of the family home, solely owned by the deceased. The home was worth £450,000 and the deceased also had savings of £50,000. The deceased was survived by a spouse and twins aged eighteen. The man believed that his wife would inherit the family home under the rules of intestacy and that was what he wished to happen.

In this situation, the spouse would stand to inherit £250,000 plus half the remainder, amounting to £125,000, and the twins would be entitled to inherit £125,000 immediately. As the family home was solely owned by the deceased and it was the biggest part of the estate, it would be necessary to sell the home to provide the twins with their inheritance. This was not what the deceased had anticipated or wished for. He should have made a will leaving the family home to his wife to ensure that she would inherit the property.

Deceased is survived by a spouse, had no children but is survived by parents or brothers and sisters

Whatever the estate is worth, the spouse inherits everything once the intestacy has gone through the due process of administration. This is one of the significant changes to the legislation introduced in 2014. Previously, part of the estate would have gone to the parents or brothers and sisters, but this is no longer the case.

Example 13.9

Pippa died intestate leaving an estate worth £600,000, survived by her husband. Pippa did not have any children. Her parents had died some time previously and she was very close to her two young half-sisters with whom she was brought up and who are both still alive. She had always promised them a legacy.

Under the rules of intestacy Pippa's husband will inherit everything. Her half-sisters will not receive anything under the intestacy rules. If she had made a will, she could have left her estate to be shared between her family as she wished.

Example 13.10

Michael dies, leaving an estate of £1m but without having made a will. He leaves behind a civil partner, a half-brother in some financial difficulty, and an aunt.

Under the rules of intestacy, Michael's civil partner will inherit the whole estate of £1m; the other relatives will not inherit anything.

The rules of intestacy—general principles applied when the deceased is not survived by a spouse

If there is no surviving spouse then any children or their descendants inherit the whole estate. This follows the right-hand side of Figure 13.1. A general principle is that only blood relatives can inherit; relatives through marriage, such as in-laws, are not entitled to inherit under the rules of intestacy.

If there is no spouse, children, or descendants, then the hierarchy applies. If there are any relatives in a category, then those relatives will inherit the whole estate. If one of them has died before the deceased but has left surviving children, the children step into their parent's shoes and take the share their parent would have been entitled to. Only if there are no relatives in a particular category would the estate pass to the next category.

A simple summary of the rules where there is no surviving spouse would be to say that the estate will pass in the order **down, up**, then **sideways**. First the estate will pass **down** through the family to any children of the deceased. If there are no children or

Table 13.1 Hierarchy of distribution

If the deceased had no spouse then the hierarchy of distribution is as follows:	
Children or other descendants	Everything to the children in equal shares
Parents	Everything to the parents in equal shares
Brothers or sisters	Everything to brothers or sisters in equal shares
Half-brothers or sisters	Everything to half-brothers or sisters in equal shares
Grandparents	Everything to grandparents in equal shares
Uncles or aunts	Everything to uncles and aunts in equal shares
Half-uncles or half-aunts	Everything to half-uncles or half-aunts in equal shares.

descendants, then the estate will pass **up** to the parents. If there are no surviving parents then the estate will pass **sideways** to brothers and sisters (Table 13.1).

Deceased had no surviving spouse, but was survived by children or other descendants

The estate will be shared equally between the children. Should any of the children have died before their parent, then their children (the deceased's grandchildren), will inherit in their place.

Example 13.11

Alex and Georgie were married and had two children, Ed and Annie, before eventually getting divorced. Alex then had another child, Matthew, with his new partner Sally. Alex and Sally never married. Several years later Alex died without ever making a will.

Under the intestacy rules, Georgie will not inherit because she is divorced from Alex and neither will Sally because she has not married Alex. Because Alex had no spouse or civil partner at the time of his death, under the rules of intestacy the three children, Ed, Annie, and Matthew, will inherit all of Alex's estate in equal shares.

Deceased had no surviving spouse and no children, but was survived by parents or other relatives in the hierarchy

The estate will be distributed according to the hierarchy.

Example 13.12

A wealthy, young, single man died unexpectedly. He had a brother with whom he was on very good terms. They were very close, having been brought up by their mother on her own, as

(continued...)

she divorced their father when the children were small. The father had chosen not to have any contact with the boys since his divorce. He did not even send the boys cards on their birthdays. The young man had not left a will, so he died intestate.

The rules of intestacy dictate that his estate should be shared equally between his mother and father, as both parents are still alive. The mother has to locate and contact the absent father who will be entitled to receive an equal share of his son's estate, despite his lack of contact. In this case the father accepts his full share of his son's estate and the brother receives nothing.

If the young man had made a will then he could have left his estate to his brother and his mother if he so wished.

Deceased had no surviving spouse and no other relatives in the hierarchy

 Key term

Bona vacantia means ownerless property. If a person dies intestate and there is no one entitled to inherit under the laws of intestacy, then the estate passes to the Crown as *bona vacantia*.

The entire estate will generally go to the Crown, which essentially means the government or Treasury. This is known as *bona vacantia*, meaning 'ownerless property'. The assets would be collected by the Treasury Solicitor and used for general public spending. Although the estate is described as ownerless property it may only be 'ownerless' in the sense that any remaining family members are unable to qualify under the rules of intestacy.

 Ponder point

Can you think of any people or family members who may feel they should be entitled to a share of an estate, but who would not inherit under the rules of intestacy?

There could be many different examples of people or family members excluded by intestacy who feel they should have a share of the estate. The main example would be an unmarried partner or cohabitant. Stepchildren may also believe an entitlement to inherit should exist. Relatives through marriage are excluded by the rules of intestacy; for example a daughter-in-law or a sister-in-law would not be able to inherit, even if there were no other surviving relatives. Carers are not recognized by the rules of intestacy and they too cannot inherit.

The Treasury Solicitor has discretion to make grants from the estate for dependants of the deceased and others who might have had a reasonable expectation of inheritance. These might include, for example, unmarried partners, stepchildren, friends or neighbours, or other relatives through marriage or civil partnership who are not entitled to an inheritance under the rules of intestacy. The Treasury Solicitor's Department publishes guidelines as to the way in which this discretion will be exercised and information on how to make a claim. These can be found at http://www.bonavacantia.gov.uk.

The Treasury Solicitor will make efforts to trace relatives and if they are found or come forward after the estate has been acquired under the *bona vacantia* regulations, the Treasury Solicitor will make payment, with interest, if the claim is received within twelve years from the death. The Treasury Solicitor will consider claims received up to thirty years from the date of death.

The Treasury Solicitor is not responsible for all *bona vacantia* estates in England and Wales. There are separate but similar processes for the Duchy of Cornwall and the Duchy of Lancaster.

Example 13.13

Mary and Michael invite Michael's infirm but wealthy unmarried brother, Victor, to come and live with them. Michael dies, but Mary continues to look after her sickly brother-in-law. Eventually Victor dies without leaving a will. Victor has no other relatives who would qualify under the rules of intestacy.

Mary is unable to inherit because she is not a blood relative, being only related to Victor through marriage. The estate will go to the Crown as *bona vacantia*. Mary can make a claim to the Treasury Solicitor for a grant from the estate on the grounds that she looked after Victor for many years.

Deed of family arrangement or variation

Whether or not there is a will, it is possible to rearrange the way property is shared out when someone dies, provided this is done within two years of the death. This is known as making a deed of family arrangement or variation. All the people who would inherit either under the will, or under the rules of intestacy, must agree to the change.

If all of the existing beneficiaries agree, the property can be shared out in a different way so that the beneficiaries receive different amounts, or people who would not have inherited under the will or intestacy rules can receive some of the estate.

 Ponder point

Given that it is possible to apply for a deed of family arrangement or variation, do you consider that this means it is less important for an individual to make a will?

The possibility of applying for a deed of family arrangement does not take away the importance of making a will. Such a deed can only be made if all of the beneficiaries agree, which can cause conflict in itself. A will is not only about families but also about other legacies, charitable donations, the appointment of guardians, and funeral arrangements. A deed of family variation can be a useful mechanism for varying a will or inheritance, but it is not a substitute for making a will.

 Key term

Mirror wills are the wills of a couple which are identical, except that each leaves the same gifts to the other, and each names the other as executor.

Case study—Tian and Brian

Tian and Brian are a married couple aged fifty-two and fifty-eight respectively. They have three adult children, the eldest of whom is Tian's daughter and Brian's stepdaughter. Tian and Brian own their own home, worth £750,000.

Tian and Brian made their wills many years ago, first leaving everything to each other in mirror wills, to be followed on the death of the second person by an equal distribution of their assets between the three children.

Since making their wills they have set up their own business, which has become very successful. Their son has played an important part in setting up and running the business and has been an instrumental part of its success. He continues to work with his parents in the business.

In contrast to their son, Tian's oldest daughter has deliberately removed herself from any involvement in the family firm. As she has grown up she has regularly asked her parents for money, which has then been spent on extravagant projects. She has proved very unreliable when it comes to her finances.

Tian's other daughter has not worked in the family firm but she has a well-paid job and she has proved responsible with her personal finances.

Tian and Brian's mirror wills were made some years ago and they are now considering altering their wills.

Required:
Discuss the issues that Brian and Tian should take into consideration when amending their wills.

The law of family provision

 Key term

A **cohabitant** is someone who lives with their partner as man and wife or as civil partners, without being married or having entered into a civil partnership.

It has long been a principle of the law in England and Wales that a person can dispose of their property as they wish, even if this leaves their family and dependants destitute. This is different to more general principles of inheritance in much of European Law, where the right to inherit is set out within the Law (European Commission, 2010). However, in 1938, Parliament decided to allow certain dependants, including cohabitants, to make a claim on the estate of a deceased person. This legislation is now contained in the Inheritance (Provision for Family and Dependants) Act 1975.

This law of family provision supplements legislation on wills and intestacy, by enabling a limited range of potential applicants to apply to the court for an inheritance from the estate of someone who has died. This can be done on the basis that reasonable provision was not made for them either by the will, or by the rules of intestacy.

Thus although cohabitants have no entitlement to inherit under the intestacy rules, they are able to apply to the courts for family provision by virtue of the fact that they were living with the deceased as a cohabitant. The only grounds for a claim for family provision is that the way in which the deceased person's estate is to be distributed, either under the will or the intestacy rules, does not make reasonable financial provision for the applicant. The family provision legislation cannot be used to redistribute the estate on the basis of fairness or what the deceased is supposed to have wanted.

In general, claimants have only six months from the death in which to pursue their claim. If an application is successful, the court can make orders for various types of financial provision from the estate, including regular payments, lump sum payments, the transfer of particular property in the estate, such as a house, or the purchase of property for the applicant.

The Act only considers four types of claimant:

1. The surviving spouse of the deceased, or even former spouse provided that they have not remarried or entered into a new civil partnership.

2. Any person who lived with the deceased, as cohabitant, for a period of at least two years up to the date of death. They must have been living with the deceased at the time of death.

3. Children, including stepchildren, treated as a child of the family.

4. Other dependants, whether members of the family or not.

If the applicant qualifies under one of the above categories, then the court will decide whether reasonable financial provision has been made, either by the will or the rules of intestacy. If reasonable financial provision has not been made, then the court can decide whether such a provision should be made and if so, what that provision should amount to.

Example 13.14

Bella and Euan, who were engaged, had been living together for three years when Euan died without leaving a will. Euan had owned the house that they lived in. Because they lived together they had assumed that each of them would be provided for, should anything happen. However, according to the rules of intestacy, everything that Euan owned, including his house, his savings, and all his possessions went to his surviving parents, meaning that Bella received nothing.

Bella took a claim to the court under the family provision legislation hoping to obtain the whole value of the estate. The court found that she was only entitled to a proportion of Euan's estate and she had to pay significant legal costs in making the claim. If Euan had made a will, he could have left everything to Bella, in accordance with his wishes.

It is possible for a testator to limit or prevent this Act from having an effect by stating in the will that the testator has considered the question of reasonable provision and he or she feels that there is no need to make provision, since the individual is already adequately provided for. It would then be for a judge to consider the statement as a matter of fact.

The administration of an estate

 Key term

Probate is the process of officially proving the validity of a will, which allows the executors the power to administer the will.

When someone dies, the estate must be 'administered'; this is the term used for the process of dealing with the deceased's property and carrying out their wishes. This may involve paying whatever inheritance tax is due, paying any outstanding debts, and then distributing the rest of the estate according to the deceased's will or the rules of intestacy. Sometimes this can be done informally, for example where the assets are of low value and comprise only cash or personal effects. Where the estate is more valuable or comprises assets such as land that cannot be transferred informally, a grant of representation is required. A grant of representation is a formal authorization to deal with the estate. There are two kinds of grant: a grant of probate and a grant of letters of administration.

If the deceased left a will appointing an executor or executors, they have to apply for a grant of probate to the probate registry. Otherwise, in the case of intestacy, an application for a grant of letters of administration has to be made, usually by the deceased's relatives. Those to whom letters of administration are granted are known as the administrators. Once the grant of representation has been made, the executors or administrators will be able to manage and distribute the estate, using the grant of representation to prove their entitlement to do so where necessary.

Case study—Imran

Imran is a successful young lawyer, living and working in London. He has some savings and investments and he is concentrating on building these up because he is looking to purchase his first property. His parents are both working and they are financially secure, having a reasonable amount of accumulated wealth in savings and investments, as well as owning a substantial property in Hertfordshire.

Imran has a sister who has recently married and is expecting her first baby. Imran's sister and her husband are struggling financially with the demands of a very large mortgage and significant other debts.

Imran discovers that neither of his parents has made a will. This prompts him to ask his sister about her will and she admits that she has not made a will. Imran confesses to his sister that despite being a lawyer he has not found the time to make a will either.

Required:
Discuss the different reasons why it might be important for Imran's parents, Imran's sister, and Imran to make a will and consider what would happen to Imran's estate under the rules of intestacy.

Conclusion

The cost and effort involved in making a will is small, particularly in comparison to the benefits it can bring. Making a will ensures that a deceased person's assets will be distributed according to their wishes. A will can set out provisions for looking after children, clarify wishes concerning burial or cremation, and ensure that an unmarried partner is properly provided for. A will can also avoid family disputes, reduce inheritance tax liabilities, and provide for specific legacies.

There are some important considerations when it comes to writing a will, including the need to appoint executors and to have the will properly witnessed. If the will is not properly written or witnessed then it becomes invalid. For this reason it is usually worth using specialist help in drawing it up. Once a will has been made it should be regularly reviewed and kept up to date, because significant events such as marriage will invalidate a will.

Property or assets that are beneficially jointly owned cannot be given away in a will. Property that is owned by beneficial joint tenants, such as a joint bank account, automatically passes to the surviving owner. Assets held jointly in this way do not form part of the estate for intestacy purposes. Similarly, death in service benefits, any refund of pension contributions, or spouse pension entitlement, will pass directly to the beneficiary or beneficiaries and do not form part of the deceased's estate.

If a will has not been written or the will is invalid, then a person is said to die intestate and the laws of intestacy are applied. In England and Wales this generally means that a spouse or civil partner will inherit all or part of the estate, but an unmarried partner or cohabitant would not inherit anything. Children of the deceased may be entitled to a share of the estate depending on its size. If there are no direct descendants of the deceased then parents or brothers and sisters may be entitled to a share of the estate. A hierarchy of inheritance follows. If there is a relative or relatives in any of the categories then the whole estate would be taken by the relatives in that category. If there are no qualifying blood relatives then the estate falls to the Treasury Solicitor as *bona vacantia*, and becomes available for public spending. The Treasury Solicitor has the ability to make grants from the estate to potential claimants.

Regardless of whether or not a will has been made, if reasonable financial provision has not been made for family members or dependants, there is the possibility of making a claim under the law of family provision. The classes of applicant are limited and there is only a six-month period from the death in which to make a claim. If reasonable financial provision has not been made, then the court has the power to award a range of financial settlements.

The intestacy rules are not a substitute for putting careful thought into making a will that is right for a particular individual's circumstances. The main conclusion of this chapter is that it is important to make a will and to keep it under review, because the consequences of not doing so can cause significant anxiety to close family members at a time when they are mourning a death. Unmarried partners or those not in a civil partnership could find themselves in severe financial hardship if a will has not been made.

Useful websites

Citizens Advice has a comprehensive website on wills and intestacy:
http://www.citizensadvice.org.uk/
A guide to who will inherit under the intestacy rules can be found at:
https://www.gov.uk/inherits-someone-dies-without-will
The government provides a useful guide to making a will:
http://www.gov.uk/make-will
The up-to-date laws of intestacy in England and Wales can be found at:
http://www.justice.gov.uk
For Northern Ireland the up-to-date laws of intestacy can be found at:
http://www.nidirect.gov.uk
For Scotland the up-to-date laws of intestacy can be found at:
http://www.gov.scot

References

BBC (2011) *News Magazine.* Available at: http://www.bbc.co.uk/news/magazine-15368029 (accessed 25.10.2012)

Benjamin Franklin (1789) *Quotation from Letter to Jean-Baptiste Le Roy.* Available at: http://www.quotationspage.com (accessed 1.5.2013)

The European Commission (2010) *Successions in Europe.* Available at: http://www.successions-europe.eu/en/home (accessed 1.5.2013)

The Law Commission (2011) *Report on Intestacy and Family Provision Claims on Death.* Available at: http://lawcommission.justice.gov.uk/docs/lc331_intestacy_report.pdf (accessed 25.10.2012)

Practice Questions

Question 1 Quick Quiz

Who would inherit in the following situations of intestacy?

13.1 A dies, survived by his only grandchild and his own brother.

13.2 B dies survived by his divorced parents and three sisters.

13.3 C dies survived by a sister and two half-brothers. He was much closer to his half-brothers than his sister, who has no contact with the family.

13.4 D dies survived by her stepdaughter and two aunts.

13.5 E dies survived by his grandparents, his aunt, his stepson, his half-sister, and the son of his half-brother.

13.6 F died aged 100, having had four daughters. Each of the daughters had had two sons. Two daughters had pre-deceased F and two had survived her.

13.7 G dies leaving a nephew (his brother's son) and grandparents.

Question 2 Benefits of Making a Will

Describe five possible reasons why it is advisable to make a will.

Question 3 Susan

Susan is in a civil partnership with Jia and they have adopted a daughter Ali, who is sixteen. Susan dies without leaving a will. Her estate is worth £450,000. How will the estate be distributed under the rules of intestacy?

Question 4 Frank

Frank was not married and had no children. Frank died without leaving a will and with an estate worth £750,000. Frank's brother and parents had died some time previously. Frank was survived by his two young half-sisters and his two nieces, who are his brother's daughters, aged twenty and twenty-two. Frank had always promised his half-sisters a legacy but had never discussed this with his nieces. How would the estate be distributed according to the rules of intestacy?

* Question 5 John

John and Cathy lived together as man and wife, but were not married.
John died intestate, leaving an estate worth £240,000. John had had three children with his former wife. The children were called Peter, Monica, and Philip. Peter and Monica had died in a tragic accident, Peter leaving behind a wife and three small children; Monica was survived by a husband but they had had no children. Philip has no children. How would the estate be distributed?

* Question 6 Anish

Anish dies intestate survived by an elderly aunt and uncle, and his mother. Anish was brought up by his aunt and uncle when his mother married again and had a second family. Anish had had little contact with his mother and her new family for many years. Under the rules of intestacy, who would inherit Anish's estate?

* Question 7 Bertie

Bertie and Jayne had been living together for five years in Bertie's house. Bertie had two grown-up children from a previous marriage, who did not approve of their father's relationship with Jayne. Jayne had two small daughters from a previous relationship who lived with them and were supported financially by Bertie. Bertie died suddenly from a heart attack without having made a will.

Required:
a) Under the rules of intestacy who would be entitled to inherit Bertie's estate?
b) Is there any course of action available for Jayne?

 Visit the Online Resource Centre that accompanies this book for additional material:
www.oxfordtextbooks.co.uk/orc/king_carey2e/

14 Coping in a crisis

 Learning Objectives

After studying this chapter, you should understand:

- The need to recognize and act upon debt problems
- The main options available to people with debt problems

Introduction

There will be times when some people will be faced with a financial crisis. Their financial difficulties may arise as a result of failing to live within a budget, a sudden unexpected large expenditure, a change in personal circumstances, or a change in the cost of borrowing. Typical changes in personal circumstances that lead to financial problems include long-term illness and the loss of a job. Crises can also arise where individuals are the victim of a share scam or a mis-sold financial product; these events are likely to lead to a loss of savings and a lower income than anticipated.

One common impact of a financial crisis where action is not taken promptly is that people find themselves with debts that they can no longer manage. Once significant events such as redundancy or long-term illness have occurred, it can be difficult to adjust personal circumstances, and subsequent outgoings, quickly. Sometimes the crisis could have been avoided if some savings had been in place.

This chapter's focus is on discussing the options available to individuals who have a debt problem; individuals, who as a result of a crisis or poor financial management, have debts on which they can no longer afford the repayments. There are often various options available to a borrower and advice should always be taken from a suitable independent organization, such as the Citizens Advice or Step Change Debt Charity, before deciding on which option to take.

Background

 Key term

A **creditor** is a bank, business, or individual to whom money is owed.

There are a range of options available to anyone with debt problems and most people with a debt issue will need to take some advice before deciding on which actions to take.

One very important point in relation to debt is that the sooner action is taken the better. Ignoring statements and letters from creditors will lead to bigger debts and a more difficult problem to deal with. There is perhaps an understandable temptation to avoid opening and reading letters that remind borrowers of the money that is owed, and they may decide to put off facing the problem until another day. The result of such actions is that more and more interest will be added to the amounts owed, significant charges may be incurred, and ultimately they may be faced with court action taken against them, the possibility of losing their home, and in some rare instances, a prison term.

Debt problems can cause a great deal of personal misery but there is no debt problem that does not have some solution. That solution will usually involve a change of lifestyle and the need to live within a carefully defined budget. It may involve moving home, entering into a formal arrangement with creditors, or being declared bankrupt. The peace of mind that will result from regaining control of personal finances, however that is achieved, will make those changes worthwhile.

Facing a debt problem

A key principle to follow in managing problem debts is to keep creditors informed. Most creditors will be prepared to work with a borrower once they understand that the borrower wants to take control of their liabilities and to begin paying back at least some of the amounts owing. If creditors do not know a borrower's circumstances, they will not be able to understand why their debts are not being repaid and will continue to charge interest and keep contacting the borrower to try and get their balance settled. Informing creditors may be the first signal to them that there is a debt problem, but it also indicates to creditors that the problem has been recognized and that steps are being made to bring those debts under control.

Priority debts

 Key terms

Priority debts are debts that if they remain unpaid, may lead to the borrower losing their home or to the borrower losing an essential service, such as electricity or gas.

Repossession of a property may occur if the mortgage payments due on a loan have not been made for a period of time. After a certain period of non-payment, the lender can force the house-buyer to move out of the property so that the lender can then take ownership of the house and arrange for it to be sold in order that the loan can be repaid.

There are certain debts, known as priority debts, where if no action is taken, the borrower may end up losing their home through eviction or repossession or losing an essential service such as electricity. Certain creditors, such as local councils, take non-payers to court and the borrowers can end up facing a prison sentence. Some utility companies will halt the supply of their service when a customer's account remains unpaid for a period of time. For this reason, it is crucial that the creditors for priority debts are made aware when a debt problem has arisen.

Example 14.1

A twenty-six-year-old, who lost his job three months ago, owes the following amounts:

- Student debt £31,000
- Bank overdraft of £1,200
- Council tax for six months of £600
- Rent for two months of £800

This twenty-six-year-old has two priority debts: the council tax owed and the rent owed. If he does not pay, or make arrangements to pay, the amount owing for council tax, he will be taken to court and could end up in prison. If he does not pay his rent, his landlord will probably have him evicted from the property. Repayments on his student debt will only be required once he is working again and although the overdraft will need to be repaid at some point, the priority debts need to be dealt with first.

In dealing with any debt problem, priority debts should be identified at the outset and contact made with the relevant creditor to explain the problem and let them know that steps are being taken to tackle the issue.

Case study—Theo and Kate (cash budget)

Theo is forty years old, married to Kate, and has three young children. He is employed by the National Health Service and earns £29,000 per annum. His take home pay after deducting tax, National Insurance, and pension contributions, amounts to £21,000 per annum. Kate runs a small business from home from which she draws an income of £500 each month.

Theo and his family live in a detached house worth £220,000 that Theo and Kate are buying with the help of a £150,000 repayment mortgage repayable over twenty-five years. It is a fixed rate mortgage at an interest rate of 4%, which costs £780 per month. They have no savings.

Theo and Kate have three credit cards that have reached the credit limit of £3,000 on each of them and they are only making the minimum payment of £75 on each card per month. Credit card interest is running at £1,800 in total per annum.

Theo and Kate have a joint bank account with an authorized overdraft limit of £4,000 and this is the balance on the account on 1 January. Interest and charges on the overdraft are expected to amount to £50 per month.

(continued...)

Food costs the family £600 per month. The total amount payable monthly for all the other household costs is expected to be £800 and this includes council tax, electricity, gas, water, broadband, telephone, and car costs.

Required:

a) Based on the information given, prepare the cash budget for Theo and Kate's household for the next three months to 31 March.

b) Suggest changes that the household might make in order to start reducing the overdraft month by month.

c) Calculate Theo and Kate's total borrowings at the beginning of the period. Do they have any priority debts?

d) Do you consider that Theo and Kate have a debt problem?

Options for homebuyers with debt problems

When the borrower facing a debt crisis is a homebuyer, there are likely to be a range of possible options open to them for resolving their debt problem. It is useful to estimate the equity in the property; equity is the difference between the likely sale price (the property's current valuation) and the amount outstanding on the mortgage and any other loans secured against it.

 Key terms

Equity in a property is the amount by which the property's current valuation exceeds the amount owing on the mortgage plus any other loans secured against it.

A **secured debt** is one where the lender is given security over an asset, usually the borrower's home. If the borrower fails to meet their mortgage or other loan payments, then after a period of time, the lender can repossess the property and arrange to sell it in order to try and recoup the amount they are owed.

An **unsecured debt** is one where the lender is not given any security for a loan advanced.

Example 14.2

A homebuyer bought a flat six years ago for £185,000 and, to finance the purchase, he took out an interest-only mortgage for £165,000.

- If the current valuation of the flat is estimated at £195,000 then the equity would be £30,000
- If the current valuation of the flat is estimated at £170,000, then the equity would be £5,000
- If the current valuation of the flat is estimated at £150,000 then the homebuyer would have negative equity of £15,000 in the flat

There are several possible ways of resolving a problem with mortgage arrears. The borrower might seek to:

- extend the mortgage term, so that the mortgage is repaid over a longer period, and/or
- request that any mortgage arrears be capitalized, that is the arrears are added to the loan, and/or
- move to an interest-only mortgage for a specified period, and/or
- request a mortgage holiday, a short period when mortgage repayments do not have to be made.

The lender is only likely to consider the above options if they are convinced that in the long term, the borrower will be able to meet their mortgage commitments. All of the above options will cost the borrower more in the long run and hence are steps that should only be considered when absolutely necessary.

Releasing equity in a home

Where homebuyers have a reasonable amount of equity in their home, then there are two options that may be open to them, both of which would release some of the equity in the home, in the form of cash.

Remortgaging

Remortgaging is the process of replacing an existing mortgage with a new mortgage product and a homebuyer with debt problems may be able to raise a new mortgage for a sum greater than the amount owing on their existing mortgage. The extra loan raised would be received as cash and could be used to pay off some or all of their debts. This could enable a borrower to replace expensive debts that carry a high rate of interest with money borrowed on a mortgage at a lower rate of interest. This should enable the borrower to reduce their monthly debt repayments. However, although the monthly outgoings would be reduced, the total cost of the extra mortgage borrowing taken over the life of the mortgage, may be more than it would have been had the borrower been able to repay their more expensive debts over a shorter time.

Lenders are only likely to consider making such a remortgage loan where there is adequate equity in the property. There are also many costs associated with remortgaging including the cost of having the property valued, legal fees payable, and sometimes there are costs associated with ending the old mortgage and an arrangement fee payable for setting up the new mortgage.

Downsizing

An option open to homebuyers with adequate equity in their property could be to sell their existing home and buy somewhere that is cheaper; often a smaller property and sometimes it may be in a less desirable location. In downsizing, the homebuyer should be able to release some of the equity in their home, which then becomes available to pay off some or all of their debts.

Example 14.3

A married couple have accumulated bank overdrafts, loans, and credit card debts that total £21,000. They are buying their own home and the mortgage outstanding is £95,000.

The couple sell their home and realize £165,000, after meeting all the costs of selling, and buy a much smaller home for £120,000 with a £75,000 mortgage.

Their old home had equity in it of £70,000 (£165,000 – £95,000). When this property is sold, the cash raised is used as follows:

- Pay the deposit on the new home of £45,000 (£120,000 – £75,000)
- Pay off their overdrafts, loans, and credit card debts of £21,000
- Open a savings account with the money left after meeting any moving costs

This couple have a lower mortgage on the new home which will reduce their monthly repayment obligations in the future. Sensible advice would be that they avoid using their overdraft facility in the future, cut up their credit cards, and budget carefully to live within their means.

Example 14.3 demonstrates how downsizing to a smaller, less expensive, property can provide a solution to debt problems, where the borrower is a homeowner with reasonable equity in their property.

Other options for dealing with debt problems

There are many other options available to borrowers with debt problems and before any particular option is chosen, the advantages and disadvantages of each one should be carefully considered. This chapter considers some of the main options but is not an exhaustive list of options.

Negotiate with creditors

Contacting creditors and arranging to repay debts at a negotiated amount per month is a strategy that creditors will often respond to. The creditors will want to see details of the borrower's personal budget and have an understanding of all the debts that they owe. The borrower should ensure that they will be able to meet the repayments agreed. On occasions, it may not be possible for the borrower and the creditors to agree on how the debts will be repaid.

Debt consolidation loan

 Key term

A **debt consolidation loan** is a loan that is taken out to replace multiple, smaller loans and this reduces the number of repayments that the borrower has to make each month and if chosen wisely, will reduce the monthly cost of the borrower's debts. Debt consolidation loans often require that security is provided for the loan.

A debt consolidation loan is a way that borrowers can reorganize their debts. A borrower with multiple debts, who takes out a debt consolidation loan, can transfer all the amounts they owe into one loan. This makes managing the debt much simpler as only one monthly repayment will be due instead of multiple payments and if the right product is chosen, the monthly outgoings should be lower.

As with all financial products, the terms and conditions of the consolidation loan should be carefully checked. There may be arrangement fees for setting up the loan, the interest rate charged may be relatively high, the repayments may be payable over a long period, and the lender may demand security on the borrower's property if they are a homeowner.

If taking out a debt consolidation loan means that the borrower is changing unsecured debt into secured debt, this will significantly increase the risk to the homeowner of losing their home if they find they are unable to keep up repayments on the loan.

Example 14.4

A homebuyer with a mortgage has three credit card debts that amount in total to £6,000. He currently makes monthly repayments on the credit cards of £180, the minimum sum allowed, and hence the debts are reducing very slowly as interest charged on the balances exceeds £100 per month.

Taking out a debt consolidation loan for £6,000, secured on his property, enables him to pay off his credit cards. The borrower now owes one creditor, Pitt Bank, in place of the three credit card companies. The monthly cost of the loan is £200 per month and the loan will be repaid over four years. He also cuts up his credit cards to avoid running up any further debts on them in the future.

 Ponder point

What do you consider to be the major risk to the borrower in Example 14.4 of taking out the debt consolidation loan?

The main risk is that if the borrower fails to keep up his monthly repayments on the loan, for whatever reason, then his home will be at risk of being repossessed by the lender.

Individual voluntary arrangement (IVA)

 Key term

An **individual voluntary arrangement (IVA)** is an agreed plan drawn up by an insolvency practitioner, whereby a borrower with unmanageable debt makes regular payments over a period of time, typically five years. These payments are distributed to the lenders and, at the end of the IVA term, the remaining debts covered by the IVA are written off. An IVA may require the borrower to release equity in their home.

An individual voluntary arrangement (IVA) is a formal agreement to pay back creditors but it is usually arranged to cover unsecured debt: this would include overdrafts, unsecured loans, credit card debts, and hire purchase debts. The arrangement does not usually include secured debts, for example, amounts owing on a mortgage. There are certain other debts that an IVA cannot cover, including student loans.

To set up an individual voluntary arrangement, it is necessary to engage an insolvency practitioner, authorized to act in that capacity. The insolvency practitioner will explore the individual's circumstances, their personal budget, and their outstanding debts and then negotiate with the creditors concerned as to how much they will be repaid and how often. The insolvency practitioner will charge a fee for this service.

If the borrower is a homeowner, then in the final year of the arrangement, the borrower will usually be required to establish whether there is equity in their home. If there is equity in their home, they may be required to remortgage the property in order to raise more funds for their creditors. The IVA does not force borrowers to sell their homes.

Example 14.5

A borrower with £45,000 of unsecured debts enters into a five-year IVA. After four years, the remaining debts amount to £25,000. The borrower is required to have her property valued and its valuation at that time is assessed to be £220,000 whilst the mortgage owing is £180,000. The borrower might be required to increase her mortgage by up to £25,000 (the amount of the outstanding debts), and to pass over the £25,000 cash generated for the benefit of the creditors who are still owed money.

IVAs are an alternative to bankruptcy and avoid the stigma that bankruptcy carries. Certain occupations and professions will not accept individuals who have been declared bankrupt. An IVA is also a way that may enable those with significant debts to hold onto some of their important assets, including their home. However, it will impact on an individual's credit rating and their ability to obtain credit in the future.

Bankruptcy

For individuals with significant debts, little available income with which to repay them, or any likelihood that their circumstances will change, bankruptcy may be a possible way forward. Being declared bankrupt means that the borrower is required to hand over control of their assets, including their home (if they are a homeowner), which will usually be sold.

Individuals can apply to the court to declare themselves bankrupt or a creditor may make the application. Once the bankruptcy declaration has been made, then the Official Receiver, acting on behalf of the court, takes control of all the borrower's bank accounts, property, and other assets and uses the funds raised from these assets to pay the creditors who are owed money. Each creditor usually only receives a portion of the sum they are owed. The borrower is allowed to hold onto certain key assets, for example household goods, and to continue to receive a reasonable income to live on.

> **Key term**
>
> **Bankruptcy** is a legal process whereby individuals who cannot afford to repay their debts, can have many of their debt obligations settled. The process, which usually lasts for one year, involves the borrower handing over control of their assets. Bankruptcy will not necessarily remove all of the borrower's debts.

Bankruptcies usually last for one year, at the end of which time the remaining debts are usually written off. However, any amount owing for student loans is not written off by the bankruptcy. The borrower may well have lost their home and other assets as a result of the bankruptcy and it could have a significant impact on their choice of career. A bankrupt is not allowed to act as a company director or manage a business without informing the directors that he is a bankrupt. The details for anyone declared bankrupt are recorded on an insolvency register, and the information is publicly available. Becoming a bankrupt remains on that person's credit reference for six years.

Example 14.6

A borrower owes £90,000 on a mortgage and £32,000 to three credit card companies. As well as buying her own home, she owns a car, household furnishings, and three electric guitars. Her available income is £450 per month once all essential bills have been paid. She applies to the court and is declared bankrupt.

   The Official Receiver would take control of her house and non-essential assets, including the guitars, and would probably sell them all in order to repay her creditors. One year after being declared bankrupt, the credit card companies are still owed £19,000 and these debts would be written off.

 Ponder point

Being declared bankrupt would provide the above borrower with the opportunity to write off all her debts after one year and start afresh. What would be the main drawbacks to becoming a bankrupt?

The main drawbacks would include the loss of the borrower's home and significant personal assets, which may be irreplaceable. The bankruptcy will show up on the borrower's credit record for six years and it will be very difficult for them to obtain credit during that time and possibly after that period has elapsed. There are certain employers that will not employ anyone who has been declared bankrupt and certain statutory restrictions placed on the jobs that a bankrupt can undertake. It may therefore prevent the individual from pursuing the career path that they had hoped for.

Debt relief order

A debt relief order is an alternative to an IVA (individual voluntary arrangement) or bankruptcy for people with small amounts of debt (less than £20,000), where the borrower has a very low income and minimal assets.

Managing a debt problem

There are certain steps that anyone facing a debt problem will need to go through:

- They will need to establish exactly how much they owe and to whom. A schedule of debts should be prepared that also identifies repayments due and interest rates charged. Priority debts need to be identified so that they are acted upon first.

- A personal or household budget should be prepared that identifies the expected income and expenditure over the coming months and the amount of funds, if any, that will be available to pay creditors.

- Options for dealing with the debts should be explored. This chapter and reputable online resources can be referred to in order to understand some of the potential options. However before deciding on which option to go for, one of the independent debt advice agencies should be consulted to help confirm that all options have been considered and understood.

- Once a plan of action has been decided upon, it needs to be acted upon.

Case study—Theo and Kate (resolving a debt problem)

Theo and Kate are married with three dependent children. Following the cash budget they prepared in January (in the earlier case study), the bank offered them a secured loan for £5,000 to pay off their overdraft, which they took out. The bank then reduced their authorized overdraft limit to £2,000. Theo and Kate were aware that the loan was a short-term solution to their debt problem.

Theo works for the NHS and Kate has a small income from her own business. She has found a Saturday job with a local boutique that has added a small amount, £250 per month, to the family income. Theo was unable to secure any paid overtime with the Health Service.

Theo and Kate realize that they need to make some major changes in order to bring their debts under control as their personal circumstances are going to change later in the year, when they are expecting their fourth child. Kate's Saturday job is expected to end in July but she is confident that she can continue to run her small business even after the new baby arrives. They are aware that their car needs a major service and its tyres need replacing in the next few months.

Table 14.1 shows a summary of their debts as they expect them to stand as at the end of March.

Table 14.1 Theo and Kate: summary of outstanding debts

Lender	Amount £	Interest rate	Secured/unsecured
Mortgage	£150,000	4%	Secured
Credit card 1 (limit £3,000)	£2,880	20%	Unsecured
Credit card 2 (limit £3,000)	£3,000	17%	Unsecured
Credit card 3 (limit £3,000)	£2,750	18%	Unsecured
Bank loan (5 year)	£5,000	10%	Secured
Bank overdraft (authorized overdraft limit £2,000)	£200	14%	Unsecured

Because of earlier difficulties in Theo's credit history, mortgage lenders are unwilling to allow the couple to remortgage and increase the size of their mortgage.

(continued...)

Required:

a) Describe Theo and Kate's current financial position and identify the steps that they could have taken earlier that may have prevented their current debt problem.

b) Theo has started to research some of the options and has read a little about IVAs (individual voluntary arrangements). Do you consider that an IVA may be an appropriate option for Theo and Kate?

c) Discuss possible steps that Theo and Kate might consider taking to ensure that they can manage their debts in the short to medium term. Identify any advantages or disadvantages of the measures you suggest.

d) Kate's preferred option would be to move house to a mid-terrace, smaller property in a less desirable street than where they currently live. Kate has worked out that their existing house would raise £213,000 after meeting all the costs of selling. The new house would cost £175,000 including all the costs of buying it. The monthly outlay on utilities will fall as the new house is smaller and far better insulated than their existing home. Theo and Kate's existing mortgage is for £150,000 (cost £780 per month) and this will be replaced with one for £130,000 (cost £680 per month.)

Calculate how much cash Theo and Kate could raise from the move and suggest how it should be utilized.

e) Draw up a revised cash budget for the couple for the nine months from April to the end of the year, assuming that the move goes ahead on 1 June, based on your suggestions above and the following additional information:

- Theo's take home pay is £1,750 per month and Kate's business generates an income for her of £500 per month.
- Kate's Saturday job pays her £250 per month but this will finish on 30 June.
- The house move will happen on 1 June.
- The food bill will amount to £550 per month from 1 April. Other household expenditure will reduce from £800 to £700 per month after the house move.
- The credit card repayments will total £225 per month, until the balances are paid off
- The bank loan has to be repaid at £110 per month.
- The major car service and tyres will cost £1,200 and be payable in July.

f) Assess whether you consider that Kate's idea of downsizing will resolve their debt problem in the short to medium term. What other actions would you recommend that they take before embarking on a house move?

Conclusion

Most people will have significant debts that they take out and slowly pay off over their working lives. Most people will manage their debts, make repayments when they are due, and benefit from the assets those debts have financed; for example, a university degree or the purchase of a home. Problems arise when debt repayments cannot be afforded and/or household bills cannot be paid. This may arise from a failure to live within a budget, or when personal circumstances change unexpectedly. Debt problems can cause a great deal of personal anxiety and stress but there are many agencies where specialist help and advice can be obtained. The worst thing that someone facing a debt crisis can do, is to ignore it, as that will allow interest and charges to grow and a bigger problem to be created.

For many people with a debt problem, there may be several options for dealing with the problem, and they should explore and understand the implications of each option before deciding on appropriate action to take. Where the borrower is a homebuyer with equity in their home, then there are likely to be a greater range of options available to them.

No matter how big a debt problem is, there is always a solution. It may be a painful solution that involves moving, working long hours, living on a very tight budget, or even being declared bankrupt. However, all solutions offer a way forward for borrowers and a future in which their personal finances are under control.

Useful websites

The Citizens Advice website provides a great deal of useful information about managing debts. Their bureau and telephone helpline provide free and independent debt advice:
http://www.citizensadvice.org.uk

The Step Change Debt Charity website provides much useful information on the different options available to borrowers struggling with debt problems. They operate a telephone helpline that provides free and independent advice:
http://www.stepchange.org.uk

Practice Questions

Question 1 Quick Questions TRUE OR FALSE?

14.1 Mortgage arrears would be a priority debt.

14.2 An amount owed to a credit card company would be a priority debt.

14.3 The equity in a property is the difference between the current valuation and the cost of the property.

14.4 A lender will only consider a remortgage loan where there is adequate equity in the property.

14.5 Moving from a repayment to an interest-only mortgage will reduce the amount of the monthly mortgage payments.

14.6 A debt consolidation loan is one loan taken out to replace multiple smaller loans.

14.7 A debt consolidation loan never requires security for the loan.

14.8 The bankruptcy process usually lasts for one year.

14.9 Being declared bankrupt is an easy way of clearing personal debts.

14.10 Student loans are not written off as a result of being declared bankrupt.

Question 2   Zachary

Zachary, aged twenty-five, graduated four years ago and has a well-paid job working in Liverpool as a software engineer. He enjoys a good standard of living and over the last three years he has built up a sizeable credit card debt and an overdraft, mainly through spending on clothes and his social life. He recently took out a car loan as he needed to buy a car to get to work. He has produced a schedule of his debts, shown in Table 14.2.

Table 14.2 Zachary: schedule of debts

Lender	Amount owed £	Monthly repayment £	Interest rate
Student loan company	31,000	75	5%
Express credit card	7,400	220	19%
Bank overdraft	800	–	14%
Car loan	7,000	200	12%

Zachary's take home pay is £3,100 per month, after all deductions, and his essential outgoings amount to £1,900 per month. He always makes the debt repayments due but often only repays the minimum due on his credit cards, usually amounting to approximately £220.

Required:
Discuss Zachary's outstanding debts and the actions you would suggest that Zachary takes in order to improve his debt situation.

* Question 3   Zola and Tim

Zola and Tim have one child and they are both in full-time employment. They started buying their own flat four years ago and, after running into some debt issues, three years ago they took out a consolidation loan for £5,000, secured on their flat, to pay off all their credit card balances. The family have recently taken an extended holiday to Australia to visit Zola's twin brother. Having arrived back home and received all their latest statements, they realize that they need to do something about their mounting debts. Table 14.3 shows a schedule of their debts that Zola has prepared.

Table 14.3 Zola: schedule of debts

Lender	Amount owed £	Monthly repayment £	Details
Shopnonstop credit card	2,000	60	Only minimum monthly repayments being made
Impress credit card	1,490	50	
Mortgage	135,000	770	Last month's mortgage payment is still owing
Consolidation loan	2,000	110	Two years of the loan term remain

Zola and Tim have a combined net income of £3,280 per month and their essential expenditure amounts to £2,000 per month, before any loan repayments are taken into account. They have savings of £5,000 in cash ISAs and they estimate that the value of their flat has fallen since they purchased it and is now valued at approximately £140,000.

Required:

a) Identify Zola and Tim's priority debts and explain the significance of recognizing them.

b) Discuss the steps that the couple might consider taking in order to deal with these debts.

c) Tim would like to take out another consolidation loan to raise enough to cover the two credit card debts. Do you consider that the couple would be likely to be able to raise such a loan?

d) Calculate the couple's net income after all essential expenditure and monthly debt repayments. Outline at least four actions that they might consider taking to help deal with their debt liabilities.

Visit the Online Resource Centre that accompanies this book for additional material:
www.oxfordtextbooks.co.uk/orc/king_carey2e/

15 Bringing it all together

 Learning Objectives

After studying this chapter, you should understand:

- The usefulness of personal financial planning at all stages in your life

Introduction

This book has considered some important areas of personal financial planning and explored the major financial decisions that most individuals will encounter at some point during their lives. Our world is exciting because it presents us with opportunities and choices, but it increases the complexity of our decisions. Young people may have aspirations that include obtaining a good education, having a successful career, and owning their own home. In order to meet these aspirations many financial decisions will need to be taken. Significant debts are likely to be built up to achieve a university degree; these will be repayable over a very long period of time. Housing is expensive relative to earnings and mortgages can be difficult to obtain; a considerable deposit is needed and a reliable income is required to ensure the mortgage payments are met. In fact, affording the mortgage payments may require two incomes. Increased longevity may lead to a longer time spent in retirement and require greater provision for income during that time.

To a certain extent previous generations were able to depend on their employer or the government to help meet their financial needs. This is no longer possible and as a result we need to take responsibility for our personal finances, and that requires regular financial planning.

The planning decisions that affect your financial position

A significant goal of personal financial planning is to become financially secure. A financially secure person is someone who is financially literate, is in control of their financial situation, and takes the time to undertake a regular review of their finances and put their plans into action.

In Chapter 1 we considered the variety of financial decisions that a person is likely to make during their lifetime that will impact upon their financial position and potential. These are likely to include:

- How to balance their personal budget
- When to take on debt and how to manage it
- How much to save so as to have cash available for unforeseen problems
- What taxes will have to be paid and how much will have to be paid
- Whether to buy or rent a home
- Whether to use property as a form of investment
- Whether to put money into investments (directly or indirectly), appreciating the potential risks and returns involved
- How much to save and when to start saving for retirement
- Which types of insurance to take out
- When and how to make a will

These kinds of financial decisions are made throughout a person's life.

The requirements of successful financial planning

In order to become financially secure it is necessary to understand the benefits of financial planning, believe that it is possible to take control of personal finances, take the time to understand and research issues, plan and implement decisions, and regularly review the situation. Successful personal financial planning requires information, understanding, confidence, and actions based on informed decisions.

It is essential to change plans as life events unfold and to keep informed on government legislation, inflation, and other economic conditions to ensure that financial goals can be met.

The case studies

This book has looked at different financial decisions that need to be made over an individual's lifecycle and has introduced the knowledge and tools to enable sensible financial decisions to be made. Theo and Kate have reached a crisis point and their situation is reviewed and possible solutions discussed in Chapter 14; they are not considered further in this final chapter. We return to the other four case studies to examine their various financial situations, reflect on the decisions taken, and consider what further financial decisions they need to make.

Case study—Oliver

Oliver is a young man living in London working hard to make a living as an actor. When we met him in the budgeting chapter, he was unable to make ends meet and had to ask his parents for a loan in order to be able to pay his next month's rent. His parents were willing and able to help him, on condition that he took on some extra shifts at work and prepared a sound budget so that they could see when they would be repaid. Following some negotiation, a budget was agreed and Oliver's parents lent him £4,500 to help him over a difficult period. Oliver then went on tour with a production of *As You Like It* for which he was well paid. During the tour he paid attention to his budgeting, was careful with his expenditure, and repaid the loan to his parents. By the end of the tour he had managed to save £3,600, which surprised him somewhat. He knows that as he is self-employed he will need some of those savings to pay his income tax liability.

Since that time Oliver has been working as a children's entertainer whilst he auditions for his next acting role. The work as an entertainer is hard but it is well paid and Oliver has had lots of recommendations and repeat bookings which have kept him busy and he has not had to use any of his savings for his day-to-day living expenses. His student loan is slowly being repaid.

Oliver and his partner have been offered the chance to go and work for a gorilla conservation charity in Africa for a year. This is something that they have been hoping to do for some time and they are very excited at the prospect. The job will commence in four months' time. Their transport, food, and accommodation will be paid, but they will need to fund their own social activities, local trips, and personal expenditure whilst in Africa. The charity has been organizing this type of trip for the past three years.

The younger Oliver would have asked his parents for a loan, to be repaid at some point in the future. The new Oliver, having learned about personal financial responsibility, decides to work things out for himself and see if he really needs help or if he can manage without relying on his parents. He is grateful that he built up his savings whilst he was on tour and that he has managed to hold onto these savings, following his return to London.

Oliver and his partner take a systematic approach to preparing for their trip to Africa.

They decide to set their goals, prepare a budget, and then implement the budget for four months to save as much as possible before the start of the trip. They establish a forecast for the time they will spend in Africa and produce their best estimate of expenditure. The charity is able to give them some idea of what their expenditure might be and Oliver uses his forecast to ensure that his savings will be adequate to cover all of the anticipated costs of the trip to Africa. The couple prepare a realistic budget to help them control expenditure for the next four months in order to save as much as possible to enable them to fund their trip.

Oliver has learned some key things about personal financial planning that have helped to put him in a position to achieve this goal. With the help of his parents, Oliver has learned to budget and this technique has enabled him to build up his savings. By ensuring that he paid back his loan quickly and built up savings whilst on tour, he has become more financially independent and secure. He has become more careful with his expenditure, understanding that his hard-earned money can only be spent once. He has learned the value of saving and realizes that sacrificing current consumption to fund future spending can open up opportunities. If he had not learned to budget and save, it is unlikely that he would have been able to take advantage of this opportunity without resorting to his parents for help once again.

Case study—Imran

Imran is a lawyer living in London just beginning to make his way in his career. When we met Imran in the budgeting chapter, he was not very careful with his spending and needed to make some changes to build up his savings. He was keen to buy his first property, but as he was unable to afford somewhere in London he decided to look in a cheaper housing market, for a buy-to-let property. He reorganized his budget and realized that small changes could have a significant impact on his financial position. He bought a flat in Hertfordshire for £190,000 which he has successfully rented out. The rental income is now covering the mortgage and generating a small surplus.

Imran has made a will. Having considered the laws of intestacy, he decided that should he die without a wife and children, he would like to leave a substantial legacy to a charity for the homeless in London. He has arranged to leave the largest part of his estate to his sister and an amount in trust for her children. He knows that any changes in his personal circumstances, such as getting married, would require him to rewrite his will.

Imran has considered his insurance needs and as he does not have any dependants he has decided against taking out any life assurance or critical illness insurance at this point. He is choosing to focus instead on his property investments and putting any surplus income towards his next investment property.

He is thinking about the future and considering how he will ensure that he has sufficient income in his retirement. He estimates that he will retire at the age of sixty-seven and is investigating the possibility of investing in property rather than a traditional pension scheme, to accumulate savings for his retirement. Imran's firm provides a contributory pension scheme which is a money purchase (defined-contribution) scheme. So far Imran has not joined the scheme, but should he do so he would be required to make contributions of 5% of his salary and the firm would make a similar contribution of 5% into the scheme. Imran's pension contribution would be tax deductible and would save him tax at his marginal rate of 40%.

As an alternative to this, Imran is considering putting his savings into a second buy-to-let property and developing a property portfolio to fund his retirement. This is his preferred option, because he likes the idea of keeping control over his investments and he is rather pessimistic about the long-term prospects for the stock market.

We can consider a list of factors to help compare and contrast the two options for his retirement income provision, considering which of these factors might be contributing to his preference for property.

There are a number of key factors that should be considered before deciding on whether to choose property or a pension scheme to fund income in retirement:

Tax on contributions: contributions into a pension fund are tax deductible, which means that the contributor does not pay any tax on that income, up to certain limits. This significantly increases the value of any contributions. By way of contrast, there are no tax deductions for investing in property, so all investment will have to be made from after-tax income. For Imran, any pension contributions would save him tax at 40%, so a £10,000 pension contribution would only cost him £6,000. Alternatively he would need to earn £10,000 before tax, to make an investment of £6,000 after tax, into his property portfolio. The tax effectiveness of pension contributions is a powerful argument for having a pension fund and is a factor that Imran needs to take into account.

Employer contributions: increasingly employers are required to contribute towards an employee's pension fund. There is no requirement or expectation that an employer would make any contribution towards a property portfolio, even though it might be building up an income for retirement. For Imran, his employer is prepared to contribute an amount equivalent to 5% of his salary into the scheme, providing Imran also contributes 5%. This increases the value of the pension fund option and is another powerful argument in favour of Imran joining the pension scheme.

Control: in general when contributions are made into a pension fund, control of those funds is lost to the individual and they become subject to many rules as to when an income can be taken and what happens to those funds on death. A measure of investment control can be retained through choice of funds or by using a self-invested personal pension (SIPP) plan. By way of contrast, any investment into property remains within the control of the individual. For Imran this is a significant factor in persuading him that a property portfolio is an attractive option for provision of his retirement income; he likes the idea that he retains control of his investments and he can choose to buy and sell them as he wishes, taking an income at any point and leaving the properties to the beneficiaries in his will.

Charges: over the years pension funds have been criticized for charging significant fees for managing pensions, which have significantly diminished investor returns. A SIPP provider will charge fees and these can be significant. A property portfolio can be managed by an individual and charges avoided or kept to a minimum, but if an agent is used they will charge a fee for managing the property. One of the things that Imran objects to about his employer's pension fund is the high level of charges it is subject to. He finds the option of managing his property portfolio himself more appealing, believing that he has the time and skills to do this. He is aware that this has its own costs, but he likes to think that those costs would be within his control.

Income: the income that accrues within a pension fund, such as dividends and interest, is tax-free and depends on stock market returns and interest rates. The income from a property portfolio is taxable on net income after allowable expenses. The net income generated will depend on the rental market and how the property is managed. Imran believes that a well-managed property portfolio will generate enough income to cover the mortgages and costs, including any tax liability.

Capital growth: capital growth is not guaranteed with any type of investment. However, capital growth may be expected to build up within a pension fund, if the value of investments increases over time. If those investments are sold and capital gains are realized, there is no tax to pay. A property portfolio might increase in value, depending on the state of the property market, but this is by no means guaranteed. If a property is sold and a capital gain is made then capital gains tax will be payable. To a certain extent Imran is relying on increases in property values over a long period of time to increase the value of his portfolio. Imran feels more positive about the prospects for the property market than he does for the stock market and this encourages him to turn towards property rather than a pension fund.

Inflation: it is generally felt that investing in the stock market via a pension provides some hedging against inflation. If inflation is running at high levels then it might be expected that the stock market would rise accordingly. A property portfolio should also provide a hedge against inflation as the value of property might be expected to keep pace with inflation. Imran is concerned about the impact of inflation upon any savings and investments and he believes that property provides a better hedge against inflation at the present time.

Risk: stock market investment involves risk because of the underlying riskiness of the investments. Most pension funds are invested in equities and bonds on the stock market. The property market is generally, but not always, considered to be less volatile than the stock market, but nevertheless investing in property carries risk. Property values may fall leaving an investor with negative equity. Investing in property involves borrowing large amounts of money and there is always the risk that income might not be sufficient to cover the mortgage payments. If rental income falls and mortgage payments cannot be met, then the lenders can repossess the properties. Imran has seen the value of his stock market investments fall as a result of the world financial crisis, yet at the same time there has been a small increase in the value of his rental property.

Personal time invested: a pension can be managed by a pension fund entirely or can be self-invested. A property portfolio can be managed by an agent for a fee or can be managed by the owner, requiring a significant investment of time.

Flexibility: once funds are invested in a pension fund they cannot be accessed until retirement and even in retirement there are limits on what can be withdrawn from the fund. As such, a pension represents a rather inflexible investment. In contrast a property portfolio is flexible in that the investor has control and properties may be bought and sold at will, but such actions are dependent upon the state of the market and selling property can often take time. Furthermore, properties are large indivisible, illiquid investments; for example, it is not possible to withdraw £10,000 from a property (which in contrast can easily be done with shares or savings accounts).

Case study—Imran continued

We can identify the systematic steps that Imran should take to ensure adequate income in his retirement, assuming he chooses to develop his property portfolio, rather than contribute to his occupational pension scheme.

Imran has decided on an approximate retirement age and he needs to consider what would be a reasonable income in retirement to establish his objectives. Then he should review his current position, and see where he stands with regard to his potential income in retirement at this point. Once he has established his current position, he should research his options and see how he will be able to generate the required income in retirement. That will be followed by making a detailed plan and subsequent action to implement the plan. This might include establishing how many properties he needs in his portfolio and then some thought as to where these should be. It will be necessary to work out how much he will require for each deposit and how he will be able to save and reach these amounts. He will need to consider the risk of taking on a substantial amount of debt. His plans should be subject to regular review to check whether he is likely to achieve his goals.

Case study—Imran continued

Imran has considered the two options for his retirement income. In an ideal world he should consider building up both a pension and a property portfolio and spreading his risk. However, Imran's income is limited and he is unable to contribute to both property and a pension fund, so he is seriously considering the property portfolio option. He is concerned at the amount of risk this would expose him to, both in terms of a large amount of borrowing and dependence on the property sector, so before he makes his decision he is considering the possibility of building up savings for retirement within a cash ISA instead. He is only considering a cash ISA, rather than a stocks and shares ISA, because he is generally not very confident about future stock market performance.

We can consider a brief comparison of the major differences between these two options for his retirement income provision.

There are a number of key factors that Imran should consider before deciding on whether to choose property or cash ISAs to fund his income in retirement:

Tax on contributions: contributions to both the property portfolio and a cash ISA would be made from after-tax income.

Employer contributions: an employer would not contribute to a property portfolio or a cash ISA, even if it was a vehicle for providing retirement income.

Control: both a property portfolio and a cash ISA are within the control of the investor.

Charges: Imran would have control over any charges involved in managing his property portfolio. There would be no charges for a cash ISA.

Income: the advantage of an ISA is that interest is received free of any tax. The net income arising on the property portfolio would be subject to taxation.

Capital growth: a property portfolio would be expected over time to provide some capital growth. This is a major drawback with a cash ISA as no capital growth can occur.

Inflation: another major drawback with a cash ISA is the danger of inflation eroding the value of the capital. It is difficult to find an account that keeps pace with inflation, so real returns can be negative, even taking into account the favourable tax status of an ISA. A property portfolio would theoretically provide a better hedge against inflation and inflation would reduce the value of the mortgages in real terms over time.

Risk: a cash ISA is not risky in the sense that the capital cannot be lost, but a cash ISA is in danger of inflation risk. Although property investments are generally seen as less volatile than stock markets, nevertheless property values can fluctuate and the large amounts borrowed via mortgages increase the risk of the property option.

Limits: another major drawback of ISAs is the limits on annual contributions into an ISA. This would restrict the amount that Imran can invest. There are no such limits with the property portfolio.

Case study—Imran continued

We can consider which might be the better option between investing in a property portfolio or a cash ISA as a means of providing a retirement income for Imran.

If Imran has to choose between a property portfolio and a cash ISA, he might wish to consider the major drawbacks and benefits of both options. There are three major drawbacks of the ISA which are:

- the difficulties of keeping pace with inflation
- there is no possibility of capital growth
- there are limits on annual contributions.

The benefits are:

- the tax-free status of the income
- the flexibility it offers
- the fact that control remains entirely with the account holder.

The major difficulties with the property portfolio are:

- the amount of risk linked to the high borrowing
- reliance on the property market
- the time or costs involved in managing the portfolio
- the illiquid nature of the investments.

The positive aspects are:

- the potential for capital growth
- the inflation hedging benefit of property
- the tangible nature of the investments.

There is no ideal method of providing for Imran's retirement, but most advisers would recommend a combination of all three methods that Imran is considering, in order to reduce risk and reliance on one particular type of investment. Given that Imran cannot afford this, the cash ISA is unlikely to grow sufficiently to provide enough income, unless he is prepared to consider a stocks and shares ISA as well. Therefore he has a choice between the property portfolio or the pension scheme and that comes down to personal preference and an informed decision.

Case study—Rachel

Rachel is twenty-five years old and in a long-term relationship. She is a graduate trainee with a large retail company and has risen to the position of manager of the food hall in a large store, now earning £50,000 per annum. She has joined the workplace pension scheme and her remuneration package includes life assurance of three times salary. When we met Rachel in the property chapter she and her partner were considering buying a four-bedroom town house, as beneficial joint tenants, which they were able to do, having taken out a mortgage for £210,000. Rachel is paying off her student debt and she no longer has any other debts. She is the main earner and her partner earns £25,000 per annum. Rachel and her partner have written their wills to ensure that each would be properly provided for in the event of an untimely death. They are aware of the particular importance of making their wills in view of the fact that they are not married.

Rachel has been thinking seriously about her career prospects, having been employed by the same organization for six years, and she has decided that she would benefit from a masters degree in logistics if she wants to make further progress. She feels she is not in a position to take a year off work to attend a full-time course, due to her mortgage commitments, but she has been offered a place on a part-time course at her local university. Her employer has agreed that she may take one afternoon per week to attend the course but she will have to pay for it herself. The fees for the part-time course are £5,500 per annum for each of the two years. The university allows the fees to be paid via a monthly standing order, spread over the two years of the course, at £459 per month.

Since they have a large mortgage, Rachel's budget is very tight and she does not have spare income. She has been looking at some different options to establish the best method of paying the £5,500 per annum for her course.

She has come up with the following alternatives:

- Take out an unsecured personal loan from the bank at an interest cost of 8% per annum to be repaid over five years, at approximately £225 per month.
- Rent out a room in her house for £350 per month and take a pension contributions holiday for two years. Her pension contributions of 5% of salary amount to £2,500 per annum but as she is now a 40% taxpayer, her tax bill would increase by £1,000 per annum (£2,500 @ 40%)

if she stopped the contributions. The net after-tax increase in her income from taking a contributions holiday would be £1,500 per annum or £125 per month.

- Rent out the whole house for £1,500 per month and Rachel and her partner move back in with her parents; they would pay a nominal rent of £400 per month to her parents to cover expenses. Their current mortgage payments are £1,200 per month and their utility bills are usually £160 per month.

Rachel is considering which of these options might be best for her to enable her to afford her masters course. We can reflect on the following points.

It would be difficult for Rachel to find the £225 per month to repay the loan, without taking some other action as well, so taking a loan out does not seem to be a feasible option for funding the course.

Renting out the room and taking the pensions contribution holiday would generate £5,700 per annum and would seem to be a reasonable option. The rent-a-room scheme is tax-free as long as the rent is less than £7,500, so there would be no tax to pay on the income generated. The pensions contribution holiday would impact on her retirement income but she is young enough to be able to catch up with contributions and the potential for increased earnings as a result of her masters degree would increase her future pension.

However, the tax impact would be significant and it would possibly be better for Rachel to continue with her pension contributions and rent the room out, finding economies to make up the difference. If she could find a tenant to pay £400 per month she would only need another £59 per month to make up the fees.

The option of moving back in with her parents would save Rachel and her partner the most money and would enable Rachel to easily meet the costs of the course. Instead of paying £1,360 (£1,200 + £160) to live in their house each month, they would only be paying £400 to live with her parents. Their house would be rented out, and even if they used an agent to manage the property, the rent should cover the costs of the mortgage. They would need to consider the potential financial impact of any tenant-free periods and advise the building society and insurance company of their plans, which might increase the mortgage and insurance costs. Whilst this option might be financially attractive, the practicalities of Rachel and her partner moving in with her parents after many years of living independently would need some consideration.

In summary, the personal loan is not a feasible option; the rent-a-room scheme would provide a tax-free income, making good use of their major asset and, together with some economies or a small loan, should enable Rachel to take the course. It would be less disruptive a measure than moving back to her parents' house.

The final decision will be determined by Rachel and her partner's personal preferences, taking into consideration the benefits and drawbacks of each option.

Case study—Tian and Brian

Tian is now fifty-six years old and her husband Brian is sixty-two. Their children are grown up and independent. For many years Tian and Brian have been running a successful family business. They own their own house valued at £750,000, as beneficial joint tenants, having paid off the mortgage several years ago. Neither Tian nor Brian have made any significant pension contributions as they have been relying on the sale of their business to provide their pension income. Over the years they have put almost all of their savings into the business, and reinvested all of the profits in order to build up the business. Their only savings are £15,000 each, saved within an ISA, and a small pension entitlement for Tian, from an earlier employment, of £2,500 per annum. Having worked long hours and six days a week for many years, Tian is ready to retire at this point and spend more time on her hobbies of walking and riding. She would like to buy a horse.

Tian and Brian have made their wills with the help of a solicitor, so they are clear what will happen when one or other of them dies. They have left legacies to their children and various charities. Two years ago their son decided to set up his own business, rather than take on the family business, and they were able to lend him some money to help with the start-up.

Tian will not be entitled to receive the state pension until she is sixty-six.

The couple have just sold their business. The sale of the business has realized £550,000 each, after taxes. Tian is going to buy a horse and build some stables, using £50,000. She has decided to use the remaining capital sum to provide her retirement income and has split it 40:60 between fixed rate savings certificates, currently providing an income of 3%, and higher risk investments expected to yield 5%. This will provide her with an income of £21,000, without drawing down the capital. This income can be added to her occupational pension of £2,500, providing an annual income of £23,500, before tax. This is an income that is equivalent to somewhat less than half of her pre-retirement income, which she thinks will be more than adequate for her needs. At the moment Tian and Brian plan to stay in their house but a longer-term plan is to sell the house and move into something smaller, releasing capital, should it be needed.

It is useful to reflect on what changes in Tian's life mean that £23,500 might be a sufficient income in retirement and to consider how Tian and Brian have achieved a comfortable retirement despite having no formal pension provision.

We can also consider what effect inflation might have upon Tian's retirement income and suggest ways of reducing the impact.

Tian no longer has a mortgage, which consumes a major part of most peoples' disposable income. The children are grown up and independent, and do not require financial support. She has no expenses linked to work such as commuting, and no major capital expenditure, apart from a horse and stables. Brian and Tian can take off-peak holidays and travel to take advantage of cheaper deals. It is likely that her expenditure in retirement will be less than her expenditure when she was working.

Brian has received the same amount as Tian from the sale of the business and therefore is likely to have a retirement income similar to Tian's. He will receive the state pension in four years' time at age sixty-six.

They have achieved a comfortable retirement by working hard in their business and ploughing back profits into the business to build it up. They have been rewarded with a successful business that they have been able to sell for a significant sum. They have used this sum to generate an income in retirement. They own their house outright; this is a substantial asset that could be sold in the future should they wish to downsize and release some equity to increase their retirement income.

The state pension will provide a welcome supplement to their retirement income but cannot be relied upon to provide sufficient income in retirement. Neither Tian or Brian will receive it until they reach sixty-six and this does not fit in with Tian's wish to retire ten years earlier than that, aged fifty-six. It is apparent that she needs to make her own pension provision to ensure that she can retire when she wants to, on a reasonable income.

Inflation will be a potential problem for Tian. She is very young to be retiring, aged fifty-six, and life expectancy rates indicate that she can expect to spend thirty years or more in retirement. Over that time inflation will reduce the buying power of her income, whatever rate it is running at. As the real value of her pension decreases, she will need to consider ways of making sure her income keeps pace with inflation. Instead of buying fixed income bonds, she could consider using some of her capital to buy an indexed annuity that will increase with inflation, to provide a measure of protection. The amount of the state pension is linked to inflation and will provide a small element of protection against inflation. Tian and Brian also have the possibility of downsizing and releasing some capital from their property, which may become a more attractive option as their retirement progresses. Finally, as they get older, at some point they may consider drawing down on the capital to increase their disposable income. For many pensioners being on a fixed income exposes them to the dangers of inflation, but Tian and Brian are fortunate in having plenty of options available to reduce its impact.

Conclusion on the cases

Although the cases cover a range of different scenarios, they each illustrate the importance of knowing your financial position and understanding your options in order to make informed personal financial planning decisions, at different stages of the lifecycle.

Conclusion

The aim of this book has been to provide the knowledge, tools, and confidence for an individual to take an interest in and responsibility for their personal finances. It might have been possible in the past to rely more on the government or on an employer to look after your financial needs but this is no longer the case. Taking the time to understand your personal finances and the products and decisions that need to be taken is empowering. Some people will decide to use a personal financial adviser or other specialist to advise them on their choice of products but it is still crucial that no product should be chosen unless the person signing up to it understands exactly what risks, responsibilities, potential returns, and potential losses they may be subjecting themselves to.

Having control of their personal finances should enable most people to move towards achieving their ambitions. Knowledge and control bring security even in difficult personal circumstances. When financial difficulties arise, the sooner the problems are identified and steps taken to improve the situation, the shorter and smaller the crisis is likely to be. The worst possible approach in troubled times is to ignore the problem.

Understanding your financial situation will enable you to respond more swiftly and effectively to any unexpected crisis that may arise, whether the crisis is of a personal nature or arising from national or international events. Failure to engage with your personal financial situation is liable to lead to anxiety and no real understanding of what the future holds for you from a financial perspective.

Personal financial planning is not always straightforward and it is rarely an exact science as there will often be many uncertainties. However, this should not be a barrier to planning; on the contrary it should provide the impetus to review your plans on a regular basis. Creating flexible plans and revising them on a regular basis is part of the key to building a sound financial future. Engaging with personal financial planning can result in an improved standard of living, sensible spending habits, and a more financially secure position with conscious use of resources.

As we have seen, a financially secure person is someone who is financially literate, is in control of their financial situation, and is someone who takes the time to undertake a regular review of their finances and to put their plans into action. The aim of this book has been to ensure that readers recognize the importance of becoming financially secure and have the knowledge and confidence to achieve this.

 Visit the Online Resource Centre that accompanies this book for additional material: www.oxfordtextbooks.co.uk/orc/king_carey2e/

Solutions to chapter questions

Solutions to asterisked questions are only available to lecturers online.

Chapter 1

Case Study Suggested Solutions

Suggested solution—Oliver

There is no one definitive answer to this case. You might expect Oliver's personal finance goals to include:

1. Reducing his overdraft and credit card debts. (Paying off his student debt will happen once his earnings reach a certain amount and it is unlikely to be a priority at this time.)
2. Ensuring that he builds up some savings whilst on tour, when he will be earning a reasonable salary.
3. Arranging insurance cover for his personal possessions, including his guitar and laptop.

Suggested solution—Rachel

a) To pay off her overdraft and make substantial savings, she will have had to control her spending very carefully. This is likely to have involved very careful budgeting with Rachel choosing to be a saver rather than spender. She is fortunate to be employed in a well-paid job and it is likely that she has worked hard to gain rapid promotion.

b) Rachel's financial objectives might include:
- to continue to save carefully in order to have enough for a deposit when buying a property
- to purchase her own property
- to start making savings that will provide her with an income on retirement, either by joining a pension scheme or saving in some other way.

Rachel may have other ambitions:
- to take a masters course
- to take unpaid leave and have an extended holiday.

Rachel would need to identify her main objectives, both in the shorter and the longer term and match her aims and ambitions to her current position and likely future earnings.

Suggested solution—Imran

Imran is in a well-paid job and clearly using a significant proportion of his income to fund his lifestyle. Whilst no doubt he is enjoying life, in a few years he may well regret not having given some time to looking at financial planning matters.

The process of identifying his goals and ambitions would serve to focus his thoughts as to how he can achieve those goals. His disposable income is high at the moment and it may well be that, with some budgeting, he can save a great deal more of this. Failing to make savings might be something he regrets in a few years' time when his personal circumstances may have changed.

The more that is saved at a young age, the more valuable that sum becomes. Imran should not disregard making any provision for his pension. If he chooses to avoid pension schemes, he should consider other means of securing a suitable income in retirement.

Imran is undoubtedly busy but he should set aside a specific time when he will start to look at his personal finances. If he waits for an opportunity to arise when he will suddenly find himself with a few hours to spare, it will probably not happen. If he plans a time into his diary, he is far more likely to actually do it.

Carrying out a personal financial review would give him control over his finances and a better understanding of his situation. He should feel more secure with that knowledge. If any unexpected event impacts on his situation or his assets, he will be able to act in a considered way rather than potentially making a poor decision as a result of acting in haste or acting on poor or incomplete information.

As Winston Churchill said during World War II: 'He who fails to plan, is planning to fail.'

Suggested solution—Theo and Kate

a) Personal financial planning is not simply concerned with advising people as to where and how they might save or invest money. It is also concerned with managing money by careful planning and budgeting, with reducing debt, and minimizing interest suffered. It also involves taking steps to ensure that provision is made for any dependants, just in case that individual is unable to work or dies.

Longer-term planning needs to be looked at as well, so that adequate steps are taken and savings made to ensure a reasonable income can be expected in retirement. Merely knowing that you belong to a pension scheme is not enough. Theo needs to find out how much retirement income the pension scheme expects to provide.

b) The potential benefits to Theo and Kate from financial planning might include:
- the creation of a family budget that enables them to have better control over the family finances
- a schedule of debts that enables Theo and Kate to understand how much they owe, the relative cost of each debt, and possibly to rearrange some debts so that the interest they have to pay is reduced
- consideration of the arrangements that would be in place if Theo or Kate were to die whilst the children were still dependent on them. This would involve creating a will and ensuring adequate insurance is in place
- a review of their pension arrangements to understand whether they can expect to receive a reasonable pension in retirement
- finally, as a result of all of the above, Theo and Kate should feel far more in control of their situation and less anxious about how the family is going to cope financially in the future.

Practice Question Solutions

Solution 1 True or False?

1.1   False. Personal financial planning is a process that should be carried out on at least a two- or three-yearly basis.

1.2 False. It is important for young people to engage with personal financial planning.

1.3 True

1.4 True

1.5 True

1.6 True

1.7 False. The RPI and the CPI are both separate measures of inflation.

1.8 True

1.9 True

1.10 False. State benefits are limited and would provide a very low income.

Chapter 2

Case Study Suggested Solutions

Suggested solution—Imran

a)

Table 2.4 Imran: cash budget for the four months to 30 April

	Jan £	Feb £	Mar £	Apr £
Income	1,800	1,800	1,800	1,800
Salary (net)				
Bonus (net)		4,000		
Total income	1,800	5,800	1,800	1,800
Expenditure				
Rent	870	870	870	870
Utilities	80	80	80	80
Groceries etc	200	200	200	200
Entertainment etc	250	250	250	250
Travel	180	180	130	180
Mobile phone	40	40	40	40
Gym	75	75	75	75
Holiday	850		400	
Clothes	300	60	60	60
Total expenditure	2,845	1,755	2,105	1,755
Net income / (expenditure)	(1,045)	4,045	(305)	45
Balance at beginning of month	400	(645)	3,400	3,095
Balance at end of month	(645)	3,400	3,095	3,140

b) Imran's cash budget reveals an expected overdraft of £645 at the end of January. To avoid this, Imran could transfer an amount in from his savings account in order to cover the shortfall. Alternatively, he could try and negotiate delaying payment for his skiing holiday, postpone buying a new suit, and/or reduce the amount he plans to spend on non-essential spending such as entertaining and eating out. There are possibly other expenses he could reduce as well.

c) From Imran's cash budget, we can see that even in a month without any unusual expenses, April, he plans to spend nearly all of his income. There are many steps that Imran could consider taking in order to reduce his expenditure and increase the amount he saves each month. Steps that could be suggested relate to both non-essential and essential expenditure and include:

- cancelling his gym membership and perhaps taking up running or cycling
- reducing his use of taxis and using public transport instead, or perhaps cycling to work
- spending less on entertainment and eating out
- choosing less expensive holidays
- finding a better mobile phone deal
- looking for special offers when food shopping.

You may be able to make other suggestions for ways Imran can cut his expenditure.

Suggested solution—Oliver

a)

Table 2.5 Oliver's cash budget for nine months to 30 September—after parent review

	Jan £	Feb £	Mar £	Apr £	May £	Jun £	Jul £	Aug £	Sep £
Income:									
Net earnings	1,000	1,000	1,000	2,500	2,500	2,500	2,500	2,500	2,500
Loan from parents	4,500								
Total income	**5,500**	**1,000**	**1,000**	**2,500**	**2,500**	**2,500**	**2,500**	**2,500**	**2,500**
Expenditure:									
Rent/theatrical lodgings	600	600	600	450	450	450	450	450	450
Utilities	150	150	150	–	–	–			
Phone	35	35	35	35	35	35	35	35	35
Travel	120	120	120	100	100	100	100	100	100
Food	300	300	300	300	300	300	300	300	300
Entertainment	100	100	100	100	100	100	100	100	100
Clothes	30	30	30	75	75	75	75	75	75
Sundry	70	70	70	70	70	70	70	70	70

(continued...)

Table 2.5 (*continued*)

	Jan £	Feb £	Mar £	Apr £	May £	Jun £	Jul £	Aug £	Sep £
Pay off credit card	2,000								
Loan repayment to parents	–	–	–	500	500	500	500	500	500
Savings	–	–	–	600	600	600	600	600	600
Total expenditure	3,405	1,405	1,405	2,230	2,230	2,230	2,230	2,230	2,230
Net income/ (expenditure)	2,095	(405)	(405)	270	270	270	270	270	270
Balance at beginning of month	(1,000)	1,095	690	285	555	825	1,095	1,365	1,635
Balance at end of month	1,095	690	285	555	825	1,095	1,365	1,635	1,905

b) Oliver's parents will have lent him £4,500 (including £2,000 to pay off his credit cards) of which he will pay back £3,000 during the period to 30 September. As his cash budget shows that he will have a substantial bank balance at the end of that time, it appears that he could agree to repay them at a faster rate. If he repaid them £750 per month from April to September, he would have fully repaid them by the end of that period. (£750 × 6 months = £4,500.) Assuming his budget is reasonably accurate, it shows that even with a monthly repayment of £750 he should still have a positive bank balance throughout the nine-month period.

c) It is a good discipline to keep savings separately from a current account. Not only should the savings account pay better interest than a current account, it makes the savings less accessible and Oliver would be less tempted to spend them.

Practice Question Solutions

Solution 1 True or False?

2.1   False. A budget is useful in many circumstances, not least to ensure that personal expenditure does not exceed income.

2.2   True

2.3   False. A budget can be prepared using pen and paper, a spreadsheet, or an app.

2.4   True

2.5   False. The more accurate a budget is then the more useful the information it provides.

2.6   False. An exceptionally tight budget will not help a potential saver. A budget should be as realistic as possible to allow a saver to meet their goals. An unrealistic budget will be demotivating and difficult to follow.

2.7   True

2.8   False. Unarranged overdrafts are an expensive form of emergency borrowing, because the bank will charge fees, high rates of interest, and may refuse to honour payments made.

2.9 False. If there is a shortfall in the budget then ways of increasing income should also be considered.

2.10 True

Solution 2 Sam

a) Essential expenditure: housing, phone, utilities, food (but excluding bought lunches). All other expenses could be classed as non-essential.

b)

Table 2.6 Sam's cash budget for three months—first draft

	Month 1 £	Month 2 £	Month 3 £
Income: Net earnings (take home pay)	1,766	1,766	1,766
Expenses:			
Rent	500	500	500
Utilities	100	100	100
Mobile phone	35	35	35
Food	250	250	250
Total essential expenditure	**885**	**885**	**885**
Beer and wine	80	80	80
Theatre	150	150	150
Clothes	50	50	50
Lunches	50	50	50
Holiday fund	200	200	200
Car costs, including petrol	267	267	267
Total non-essential expenditure	**797**	**797**	**797**
Total all expenditure	**1,682**	**1,682**	**1,682**
Net income/(expenditure)	**84**	**84**	**84**
Balance at beginning of month	150	234	318
Balance at end of month	**234**	**318**	**402**

a) There are a variety of changes that Sam could make to his spending in order to save more. If Sam is to save £15,000 within two years he needs to save £625 per month (15,000/24). Sam could give up his holiday fund, lunches, and coffees at work and reduce his food spending. He could choose to use the car as little as possible and cycle more to reduce petrol costs. If he reduces his leisure expenditure in the ways suggested in Table 2.7 as well, then he can save £644 per month which will allow him to save £15,000 within two years. Within his revised budget there are different choices to be made, beer or theatre for example, or the choice of giving up the car altogether. Having set out his cash budget he can see more clearly the choices to be made, what he can spend on each category and still meet his savings target.

Table 2.7 Sam revised cash budget for three months

	Month 1 £	Month 2 £	Month 3 £
Income: Net earnings (take home pay)	1,766	1,766	1,766
Total essential spending but reducing food spending by £40	845	845	845
Beer and wine reduced and no lunches/coffees	20	20	20
Theatre reduced	40	40	40
Clothes reduced	20	20	20
Car costs reduced	197	197	197
Total non-essential expenditure	277	277	277
Total all expenditure	1,122	1,122	1,122
Net income/potential savings	644	644	644
Balance at beginning of month	150	794	1,438
Balance at end of month	794	1,438	2,082

Chapter 3

Case Study Suggested Solutions

Suggested solution—Tian and Brian

a) Tian and Brian could have been more careful at the time of taking out the endowment policy, making sure that they were fully aware of the implications of taking on an interest-only mortgage, with an endowment policy as the vehicle for repaying the mortgage. They should have considered the implications of the growth projections shown in the forecast and established what would happen if the forecast growth did not materialize. Even so they might have decided that the endowment policy was a good option for them as it allowed them to afford a larger property than would otherwise have been the case; they might have been prepared to accept the risk that the policy would not cover the outstanding mortgage.

b) In 2005, having been advised of the potential shortfall in their endowment policy Tian and Brian could have switched part of their mortgage to a repayment mortgage to make sure their mortgage would be repaid at the end of its term. Alternatively they might have decided to increase their regular savings to cover the shortfall, building up funds in a savings account or an ISA. They could have considered the nature of the advice they had been given at the time of taking out the endowment and reflected upon whether the risks linked to an interest-only mortgage had been fully explained by their financial adviser. If the advice given had not set out the risks associated with such a course of action, they could have made a claim for compensation.

Practice Question Solutions

Solution 1 True or False?

3.1   True

3.2   False. Financial services are the services provided by financial institutions, not just the banks. Although the term includes the provision of bank accounts, it also relates to insurance policies, investment advice and management, pension funds, loans and mortgages, and financial advice.

3.3   True

3.4   False. During 1997–2013, when the FSA was the regulatory body responsible for financial services, there were many instances of mis-selling.

3.5   True

3.6   True

3.7   False. The pensions advisory service provides independent advice to a person in connection with their pension that is entirely free of charge.

3.8   False. Since 2013 financial advisers charge fees for their advice, and no longer receive commission, but the fees do not have to be paid upfront and can be collected from any sums invested.

3.9   True

3.10   True

Solution 2 Financial Regulation

Since 2013 the regulatory framework consists of the Financial Conduct Authority (FCA) and the Prudential Regulation Authority (PRA) who are the main bodies responsible for regulating financial products and services. Banking is regulated via the independent Financial Policy Committee (FPC) at the Bank of England and also the Prudential Regulation Authority (PRA) as a subsidiary of the Bank.

The main role of the FPC is to contribute to the Bank of England's financial stability objective by taking action to remove or reduce systemic risks with a view to protecting and enhancing the resilience of the UK's financial system as a whole.

The PRA has a general objective to promote the safety and soundness of the firms that are regulated, including banks, insurance companies, and certain investment firms. The Authority also has a specific objective to secure an appropriate degree of protection for insurance policyholders.

The FCA is the organization responsible for regulating financial services in the UK, ensuring that financial markets and firms operate fairly and that consumers are protected. The organization is responsible for regulating financial services, markets, and exchanges and preventing unauthorized firms taking advantage of consumers by taking enforcement action against such firms.

Solution 3 Retail Distribution Review

Since 31 December 2012, instead of receiving commission on new investments made by their clients, an adviser must clearly explain how much the advice will cost and agree how it will be paid with his client. This could be a set fee paid upfront or the client may agree with the adviser that they can take the fee from the sum invested. This should ensure that individuals know exactly what they are paying and that the advice they receive is not influenced by how much an adviser could earn from the choice of product.

Financial advisers either advise on all products that may be right for a client or provide advice on certain areas, such as life assurance. Financial advisers that provide independent advice consider all types of financial products. They can also consider products from a wide variety of firms across the market. An adviser who has chosen to offer restricted advice will only consider certain products, product providers, or both. An adviser must clearly explain what they are able to advise their clients on.

Chapter 4

Case Study Suggested Solutions

Suggested solution—Oliver

Oliver's three debts will carry very different rates of interest. His student debt will carry relatively low interest charges but his unarranged overdraft and his credit card debts will both attract relatively high rates of interest, possibly around 16% to 20%. He is unconcerned about his debts but he is incurring unnecessarily high interest and bank charges as a result of his situation. With more careful planning, he can take steps to reduce the interest and charges in the future.

Student loans

Oliver has student debt that will attract a relatively low rate of interest. According to his income levels, he will be required to make repayments at a set rate—9% of his earnings in excess of £21,000 per annum. He does not need to take any action in relation to this debt.

Bank overdraft

By exceeding his arranged overdraft limit, Oliver will be incurring higher interest charges than if his account balance stayed within it. Most banks also charge for transactions made whilst the amount overdrawn is in excess of its agreed limit. Even when his overdraft is within the arranged limit, he will be incurring interest charges.

One step Oliver could take is to try and negotiate with the bank to arrange a higher overdraft limit so that his actual overdraft remains within it. The bank may not agree to this.

The other action Oliver should take is to try and reduce his expenditure wherever possible and to keep spending to essential items only. When he is not earning, he cannot afford to attend as many concerts and festivals as he would like. When he is next in work, he should aim to pay off his overdraft and to build up some savings to carry him over future periods when his income is reduced.

Credit card debts

By making the minimum monthly payments on his credit card liability, Oliver will be incurring significant interest charges. He should try and find a balance transfer deal that offers zero, or a very low, interest rate for a period of time. He can then transfer his existing credit card debt across to the new card and continue to reduce the liability but without incurring any further interest charges. Oliver will need to be careful to ensure that as the interest-free period draws to a close, he aims to find another similar offer and transfer the debt remaining to yet another credit card provider.

Whilst he is using zero interest deals in this way, Oliver should not add any further liabilities to his credit card, however tempting that might be. He should be advised that a credit card should only be used for payments that he can afford to make.

Suggested solution—Rachel

a) It is likely that in order of increasing APR, Rachel's borrowings will be as follows:

Increasing APR		
	Mortgage*	£210,000
	Student loan	
	Interest at RPI + 3% as Rachel is earning £45k	£28,000
	Personal loan	£4,500

* *Mortgages could at times carry a higher APR than student loans.*

b) Mortgages are secured debts and, for that reason, tend to have a low rate of interest. (In Rachel's case, the LTV of her mortgage would be 87.5% (210k/240k × 100) which would attract a higher APR than mortgages with lower LTVs.) Her home could be at risk if she does not keep up the payments on her mortgage and so she should ensure that she meets her monthly payments on time.

Her student debt attract interest at 3% above RPI, which means that it will take Rachel many years to pay this loan off. Based on her current salary, she would be making repayments of £2,160 per annum ((£45,000 − 21,000) × 9%). It is, however, not a debt that Rachel should worry unduly about because if her income were to fall or cease, so would her student loan repayments. In addition, any amount remaining unpaid after thirty years will be written off.

Rachel's personal loan is likely to be the borrowing that carries the highest APR. If she could afford to pay this loan off sooner, so much the better, but as long as she keeps up her repayments, it will be repaid in two years.

There are many forms of borrowing which carry much higher APRs and which Rachel has wisely avoided taking on, as there is no mention of credit card debt in her case summary. Rachel will have high levels of personal borrowing but from the information given, these are debts that have been taken on for a specific purpose and they all carry a low to moderate rate of interest. She has clearly managed her financial affairs well during her early working life and she should not be unduly worried about her debts especially as she considers her job to be secure.

Practice Question Solutions

Solution 1 True or False?

4.1   True

4.2   True

4.3 True

4.4 False. Graduates who are self-employed make student loan repayments to HMRC via the self-assessment system.

4.5 False. Outstanding student loans will be written off thirty years after graduation.

4.6 False. Personal loans usually carry a lower rate of interest than overdrafts.

4.7 False. An arranged bank overdraft will not usually be interest-free. On occasions they can be interest-free; for example, for students or recent graduates.

4.8 True

4.9 True. A personal loan would also be appropriate.

4.10 False. The limit set on a credit card is not an indication of the amount it is wise to borrow. It is set by credit card companies to encourage the user to spend more.

Solution 2 Robin

a) As Robin will not earn more than £21,000 during the five years after graduating he will make no student loan repayments during that time. The debt will attract interest at a rate equal to the RPI.

Estimate of Robin's student debt five years after graduating

$$= £46,000 \times (1.03)^5 = £53,327$$

b) Robin should not be unduly alarmed about the size of his student debt. If he continues to take low paid work after his PhD, then he will probably only have to make very small repayments on the debt. If he secures a better paid job, then he will start to repay the student debt more quickly. Student loans do not attract a very high rate of interest, they are not secured debt, and the way in which the loans are repaid is linked to the individual's income. If after thirty years he has not repaid all of the debt, the remaining balance will be written off.

In Robin's particular situation, making voluntary payments to reduce his student debt is unlikely to be a sensible course of action.

Solution 3 Ulrika

a) Table 4.5 shows the total interest payable on Ulrika's loan options.

Table 4.5 Ulrika's loan options: calculation of total interest payable

	Option (i)	Option (ii)	Option (iii)
Monthly repayment (£)	£159	£161	£229
Number of repayments	60	36	36
Total of repayments made (£)	9,540	5,796	8,244
Loan (£)	7,000	5,000	7,000
Total interest (£)	2,540	796	1,244

b) Assuming that Ulrika can afford to make the repayments under each of the options:

Option (i) is the most expensive as the loan is repaid over five years. If she can afford a shorter-term loan, she should avoid this option.

Option (ii) is the cheapest option but it does mean that she would use up all her savings. She would probably be wise to hold onto her savings so that she has some spare funds for any unforeseen events that might arise.

Option (iii) would allow her to hold onto her savings and because the loan is repaid over three years, the total interest that she would pay would be considerably cheaper than under option (i). This is an option she could explore further.

Option (iv) would mean that Ulrika would be left with no savings and would have large credit card debts and a large overdraft. These debts could indeed be repaid as quickly as she wishes, but in the meantime, they would attract very high rates of interest. The bank could change Ulrika's arranged overdraft limit with very little notice. Overall, this is not a suitable means of funding the purchase. If she thinks she could pay off a loan more quickly, she could look at taking out a loan repayable over a shorter term.

All in all, she would probably be best exploring option (iii).

c) Ulrika could look at the terms offered by peer-to-peer lending.

d) Ulrika can look to improve her credit rating by not moving home too frequently, making sure that she is on the electoral roll, and continuing to make sure that she makes all debt repayments on time.

Chapter 5

Case Study Suggested Solutions

Suggested solution—Rachel (1) (Uses iR)

a) Rachel's salary, interest received from Bing Building Society, and dividends received will all be subject to income tax. However the PSA and DA mean that the rate of tax applying to interest and dividends received, will be 0%.

The interest received in her ISA account is exempt from tax.

b) Rachel would be a higher rate taxpayer.

Rachel's total income = £45,000 + £400 + £200 = £45,600.

When her PA of £12,500 is deducted, that leaves £33,100 which would make her a higher rate taxpayer as this amount exceeds the basic rate band.

c) Rachel would be entitled to a PSA of £500 and a DA of £5,000.

d) Table 5.15 illustrates Rachel's income tax computation.

e) Rachel's tax computation shows that she has another £100 tax to pay, as the amount deducted from her employment earnings does not quite cover her full liability for the year.

Table 5.15 Rachel—income tax computation

	Total £	Earned income £	Interest £	Dividends £
Employment income (gross)	45,000	45,000		
Interest received	400		400	
Dividends	200			200
Total income	**45,600**	**45,000**	**400**	**200**
Less: personal allowance	(12,500)	(12,500)		
Taxable income	**33,100**	**32,500**	**400**	**200**
Income tax liability:		**£**		
Earned income—at basic rate:	32,000 × 20%	6,400		
Earned income—at higher rate:	500 × 40%	200		
Interest: (PSA)	400 × 0%	–		
Dividends (DA)	200 × 0%	–		
Total tax liability		6,600		
Less: tax paid on employment earnings		(6,500)		
Income tax payable		£100		

Suggested solution—Imran (Uses iR)

a) Imran's taxable benefits would be the company car he is provided with plus the fuel benefit. In addition, the private medical insurance cover would give rise to a taxable benefit. The benefit of having a subsidized staff restaurant does not give rise to a taxable benefit as long as it was available to all employees.

b) Car benefit = £21,000 × 19% = £3,990

Fuel benefit = £22,500 × 19% = £4,275

Private medical insurance = £900 (the cost to his employer)

Total taxable benefits = £9,165

c) Imran is a higher rate taxpayer.

Imran's total income = £40,000 + bonus £6,000 + benefits £9,165 + interest £3,100 = £58,265.

After deducting his PA of £12,500, his taxable income will exceed the basic rate band (Table 5.16).

d) See Table 5.16 for Imran's tax computation.

e) The taxable benefit arising from the car and the fuel benefit is a total of £8,265 (3,990 + 4,275). As Imran's highest rate of tax is 40%, the cost to him is £8,265 × 40% = £3,306.

If he rarely uses the car for any private journeys, he would be well advised to give up the benefit in kind and avoid being taxed on the car and fuel benefit.

Table 5.16 Imran—income tax computation

	Total £	Earned Income £	Interest £
Employment income			
Salary	40,000		
Bonus	6,000		
Car benefit (21,000 × 19%)	3,990		
Fuel benefit (22,500 × 19%)	4,275		
Private medical insurance	900		
Total employment income	55,165	55,165	
Interest	3,100		3,100
Total income	58,265	55,165	3,100
Less: personal allowance	(12,500)	(12,500)	
Taxable income	45,765	42,665	3,100
Income tax liability:	£		
Earned income			
Basic rate: 32,000 × 20%	6,400		
Higher rate: 10,665 × 40%	4,266		
Interest (all in higher rate band)			
500 × 0% (PSA for HR taxpayer)	—		
2,600 × 40%	1,040		
Total income tax liability	11,706		

Suggested solution—Rachel (2) (Uses iR)

a) Table 5.17 shows Rachel's income tax calxulation for next year.

Table 5.17 Rachel—income tax computation for next year

	Total £	Earned income £	Dividends £
Employment income	48,000	48,000	
Dividends	220		220
Total income	**48,220**	**48,000**	**220**
Less: personal allowance	(12,500)	(12,500)	
Taxable income	**35,720**	**35,500**	**220**

Rachel's expected total taxable income for the year would be £35,720.

b) Table 5.18 shows Rachel's income tax liability.

Table 5.18 Income tax liability

	£
Earned income—basic rate: 32,000 × 20%	6,400
Earned income—higher rate: 3,500 × 40%	1,400
Dividends: 220 x 0% (PSA)	–
Income tax liability	7,800

c) Rachel will have to pay class 1 NI contributions.

d) Annual salary = £48,000

Monthly salary = £48,000/12 = £4,000 per month

Class 1 NI contributions per month

First £700: no NI contributions

Next £3,000: £3,000 × 12% = £360

Next £300: £300 × 2% = £6

Total = £360 + £6 = £366 per month

Class 1 NI contributions for the year:

£366 × 12 = £4,392

Suggested solution—Kate (Uses iR)

a) Table 5.19 illustrates Kate's income tax calculation.

Table 5.19 Kate—income tax computation

	Total £	Earned income £
Self-employed income	15,000	15,000
Total income	**15,000**	**15,000**
Less: personal allowance	12,500	12,500
Taxable income	**2,500**	**2,500**
Income tax liability: £2,500 × 20%		500

b) Classes 2 and 4 NI contributions on self-employed income

Class 2: £3.00 × 52 = £156

Class 4: (15,000 – 8,000) × 9% = £630

c) Income tax, class 2, and class 4 NI contributions are collected by self-assessment.

d) As a self-employed person, Kate should complete a self-assessment tax return. The deadline for online submission of this is 31 January following the end of the tax year.

If Kate waits for a few years, then she will miss this deadline and start incurring penalties for late submission of the return and interest and penalties for late payment of tax. She must ensure that she meets the deadlines for submission of the return and payment of the tax due.

Practice Question Solutions

Solution 1 True or False? (Uses iR)

5.1   True

5.2   False. If an individual does not use all of their personal allowance in one tax year, then the unused allowance is lost.

5.3   True

5.4   True

5.5   True

5.6   True

5.7   False. Only certain taxpayers have to complete a self-assessment tax return: for example, the self-employed.

5.8   True

5.9   False. Class 1 National Insurance contributions are based on an individual's gross income.

5.10   True

Solution 2 Vikram (Uses iR)

a) Vikram's income that will be subject to income tax includes:

- his salary
- the interest received from the savings account that is not an ISA, but only to the extent that it exceeds his PSA
- the dividends he received, to the extent that they exceed his DA

The interest arising in the ISA is exempt from income tax and the provision of a workplace gym is not taxable.

b) Table 5.20 shows Vikram's income tax calculation.

Table 5.20 Vikram—income tax computation

	Total £	Earned income £	Interest £	Dividends £
Employment income	24,000	24,000		
Interest received	500		500	
Dividends	480			480
Total income	24,980	24,000	500	480
Less: personal allowance	(12,500)	(12,500)		

(continued...)

Table 5.20 *(continued)*

	Total £	Earned income £	Interest £	Dividends £
Taxable income	12,480	11,500	500	480
Income tax liability:				
Earned income: 11,500 × 20%	2,300			
Interest: 500 × 0% (PSA)	–			
Dividends: 480 × 0% (DA)	–			
Total tax liability	2,300			
Less: tax paid at source	(2,300)			
Income tax due	£nil			

c) Vikram has paid the correct amount of tax for the year.

Solution 4 Amas and Amat (Uses iR)

a) Amas would have to pay class 1 National Insurance contributions.
   Monthly salary = £42,000/12 = £3,500
   NI contributions = (£3,500 − 700) × 12% = £336 per month, £4,032 per annum.

b) Amat would have to pay class 2 and class 4 National Insurance contributions.
   Class 2: £3.00 × 52 weeks = £156
   Class 4: (£42,000 − 8,000) × 9% = £3,060
   Total class 2 and class 4 NI contributions = £3,216 per annum

c) Amat who is self-employed pays significantly less NI contributions than Amas, who is an employee. This difference exists because class 1 contributions entitle the payer to a greater range of social security benefits.

Solution 6 Rex (Uses iR)

a) Table 5.21 illustrates Rex's income tax calculation.

Table 5.21 Rex—Income tax computation

	Total £	Earned income £	Interest £	Dividends £
Self-employed profits	46,400	46,400		
Interest received	1,000		1,000	
Dividends received	6,200			6,200

(continued...)

Table 5.21 (*continued*)

	Total £	Earned income £	Interest £	Dividends £
Total income	53,600	46,400	1,000	6,200
Less: personal allowance	(12,500)	(12,500)		
Taxable income	41,100	33,900	1,000	6,200
Income tax liability:				
Earned income:				
At basic rate: 32,000 × 20%	6,400			
At higher rate: 1,900 × 40%	760			
Interest (all in HR band):				
500 × 0% (PSA)	–			
At higher rate: 500 × 40%	200			
Dividends (all in HR band):				
5,000 × 0% (DA)	-			
At higher rate: 1,200 × 32.5%	390			
Income tax liability	**7,750**			

b) National Insurance Contributions

Class 2: £3 per week × 52 = £156

Class 4: (£44,000 – £8,000) x 9% = £3,240

Plus £2,400 × 2% = £48

Total NI contributions = £3,444

c) If Rex transfers all his shares to his wife, she will receive the dividends in the future. Assuming dividends received remain the same in future years, then Rex will no longer be liable to pay any tax on the dividends. (In the above computation, the tax arising on those dividends was £390 because Rex is a higher rate taxpayer.)

If his wife is a basic rate taxpayer and assuming that, even when she receives these dividends, she will remain so, then she too will be liable to pay tax on the dividends received in excess of the Dividend Allowance. As a BR taxpayer, she would be liable to pay tax of £90 (£1,200 × 7.5%) on the dividends.

The optimum solution as regards minimizing the couple's tax liability would be to transfer a proportion of the shares so that both Rex and his wife make use of their Dividend Allowances. There may of course be other factors that will influence the couple's decision as regards the shareholdings.

Chapter 6

Case Study Suggested Solutions

Suggested solution—Rachel and her partner

a) For Rachel and her partner the change from spenders to savers occurred when they decided that they were ready to settle down together and buy a house and they realized that they would need a significant deposit to achieve their aim. They decided to sacrifice some current spending in order to achieve a longer-term goal.

b) The systematic steps for Rachel and her partner to build up the deposit began with setting their objectives. This required clarification of the amount needed for the deposit and a timescale for reaching that amount. Having established their goal, it was necessary to measure their financial position and prepare a careful budget to identify where savings could be made. Savings accounts were researched for the best rates, terms, and conditions to meet their needs, taking into account any tax payable on interest. Action was taken to open an account and set up a standing order to put the money beyond everyday spending. Throughout the time of saving for their deposit, they reviewed the position regularly and ensured they were getting the best possible rates of interest and were on schedule to meet their target. They took control of their personal finances.

Taking control included preparing a cash budget, which limited the amounts they could spend on non-essential items such as entertainment and holidays. They would have looked at ways in which they could reduce their other expenditure, sharing lifts to work, cutting out sandwiches and coffees, buying discount cinema tickets, and getting better deals on their phones. They each opened a savings account and set up a regular standing order into the account, so that the money was removed from their current accounts early on in the month, and the temptation to spend it was reduced.

They may have found it difficult to change their spending habits but statements showing the accumulated funds in the savings accounts and knowing that they were taking steps to achieve their long-term goal would have motivated them and helped to keep them on track. In the end the long-term reward of being able to buy their own property outweighed any short-term sacrifice.

Suggested solution—Imran

Imran should consider risk and return when making his decision, taking into account both the interest rate offered and the level of risk attached to each option. Given the Personal Savings Allowance he should not be paying tax on any interest received, as long as the amount is below his Personal Savings Allowance of £500.

The cash ISA is tax-free and is therefore worth 2.5% per annum. The regular savings account looks attractive at 2.8%, but the return would be lower than on the ISA because the full rate is only paid on the first month's saving. The second month's saving would only earn $11/12 \times 2.8\%$ and so on.

A good option for Imran's regular savings plan would be to set up a standing order into the cash ISA. If he opened the regular savings account instead, the return would be lower and he would need to move his savings after a year, as the rate becomes uncompetitive.

The two-year bond requires a lump sum to be placed in the account, so that is not particularly of use to him at this point.

Imran could decide to set up a regular standing order to buy premium bonds, and take the risk that his return in the form of prizes might be higher or lower than the 2.5% in the cash ISA, but with reasonable rates of tax-free interest available to him, this looks to be a less attractive option.

The National Savings index-linked savings certificate would be an attractive option, as it would be tax-free and guaranteed to keep pace with inflation as measured by the retail prices index, but it too would require a lump sum for Imran to invest.

Although the peer-to-peer lending site offers the highest potential return it carries a much higher level of risk than any of the other options. It is not covered by the FSCS and Imran would need to consider the possibility of a borrower defaulting, which would cause the loss of some of his savings. This level of risk is unlikely to be acceptable to Imran, as he cannot afford to lose his savings.

Overall the cash ISA looks to be the best choice at this stage for Imran's regular savings.

Suggested solution—Oliver

a) Oliver needs to save for several reasons. First of all so that he has some money put aside to meet his tax liability. Secondly, Oliver needs savings to cover the times when he returns from the tour and he is looking for work. Thirdly, he needs savings for emergencies, savings for holidays and larger purchases, and savings towards meeting his longer-term goals.

b) First of all Oliver should establish his savings objectives. They might be to have enough savings to meet his tax liabilities, to cover some work-free periods, for emergencies, and for a holiday. This should be followed by measuring his financial position by preparing a cash budget for the six months whilst he is on tour, so he can see how much he can save per month. Then he should carry out some research into the best savings accounts available, and open an account setting up a standing order into the account. This should be followed by regular review to ensure that he is still receiving a good rate of interest on his savings and that he is on target to meet his goals.

Practice Question Solutions

Solution 1 True or False?

6.1 False. There are many good reasons for saving; they can be summarized as the precautionary motive, the transactions motive, and the speculative motive. Saving for a 'rainy day' would be part of saving driven by the precautionary motive.

6.2 True

6.3 True

6.4 True (see Example 6.7).

6.5 True

6.6 True

6.7 False. The FSCS guarantees accounts up to £75,000 per person, not £30,000.

6.8 False. The main risk associated with savings accounts is the risk that the rate of interest will not keep pace with inflation, and the real value of the savings will fall. Furthermore, the FSCS only covers savings up to £75,000 per person per institution. Savings greater than that held with one institution are at possible risk of loss of capital.

6.9 False. Any premium bond prizes are tax-free.

6.10 False. An account with an interest rate of 5% paid monthly will have a higher AER than an account with an interest rate of 5% paid annually, because the interest will be compounded more frequently.

Solution 2 Savings Account Risks

The main risk associated with keeping savings in a savings account is the inflation risk. It is important for savers to keep an eye on rates of inflation and rates of interest on their savings and to be prepared to move savings regularly to obtain rates of interest above inflation. Index-linked savings certificates are a good option, when they are available.

The risk of loss of capital resulting from the collapse of a financial institution has been much reduced following the introduction of the FSCS, which covers deposits in the UK up to £75,000. Savers might wish to consider limiting their deposits with any one institution to £75,000 to ensure full protection from the scheme.

The risks arising from information asymmetry include adverse selection and moral hazard. Savers should always carry out plenty of research before placing any savings with a particular bank or institution. To reduce risk they should consider whether or not a return offered seems 'too good to be true', and if it does seem too good to be true then to treat it with suspicion.

Solution 3 Olga

Olga, although a basic rate taxpayer, will not suffer tax on interest received because her interest will not exceed the Personal Savings Allowance.

The rate of interest on her new account is 7%.

At an interest rate of 7% the savings in Olga's account, assuming no withdrawals and the benefits of compound interest, will double in ten years to approximately £24,000

$12,000 \times (1 + 0.07)^{10}$

$12,000 \times 1.9672$

$= £23,606.$

This is not enough to fund Olga's expedition. She will need to consider ways to make up the shortfall.

Solution 4 Callum and his partner

The first step for Callum and his partner is to set their objectives and establish the likely costs of travelling for six months. They should investigate the costs and prepare a budget to include all the different costs they are likely to incur whilst travelling. This will enable them to set their savings goal. They should be able to identify how much they need to save over a particular timescale, so that they can see whether their goal is achievable.

With a savings goal in mind to allow them to go travelling, Callum and his partner should prepare a detailed cash budget to measure their financial position for the next few months. This will help to control their expenditure and build up their savings.

They should research the various savings accounts available and then act upon the research, opening a savings account and setting up a monthly standing order into this account.

During the next few months they will need to review their progress to check that they are on target to meet the objectives.

In order to achieve their goal they will need to take control of their joint finances. They will probably have to accept any overtime offered and cut down on their social activities and music festivals. They will need to be prepared to sacrifice their current consumption in order to save up for their future benefits, but with a goal in mind, a budget to keep them on track, and a savings account to remove their savings from the temptation of day-to-day spending, they should be on the way to achieving their goal.

Chapter 7

Case Study Suggested Solutions

Suggested solution—Tian (1)

Note that the restoration fees are included as part of the cost of the antique table when working out the gain because the value of the asset was enhanced by the French polishing. The repair costs are considered to be maintenance and do not form part of the cost. All of Tian's gains are taxed at 20% because she is a higher rate taxpayer (Table 7.13).

Table 7.13 Tian—Capital gains tax computation

		£
Proceeds from selling table		87,200
Less: auctioneer's fee		17,440
Net proceeds		69,760
Cost	23,000	
Restoration fees	1,000	
Less: total cost		24,000
Capital gain		45,760
Less: annual exemption		12,000
Taxable capital gain		33,760
		£
Capital gains tax thereon at 20%		6,752

Suggested solution—Tian (2)

Table 7.14 shows Tian's capital gains tax calculation.

Table 7.14 Tian (2)—Capital gains tax computation

	£	Total gains/ (losses) £
Shares		
Proceeds from selling shares (net of dealing fee)	740	
Cost plus dealing fee	1,512	
Loss (shares)		(772)
Antique necklace		
Proceeds from antique necklace	20,000	
Less: original cost	11,000	
Capital gain (necklace)		9,000
Unit trust		
Proceeds from selling unit trust	37,000	
Less: original cost	10,000	
Capital gain (unit trust)		27,000
Total gains net of losses		35,228
Less: annual exemption		12,000
Taxable capital gains		23,228
Capital gains tax payable		
Capital gains tax at 10% (£10,000 × 10%)		1,000
Capital gains tax at 20% (£13,228 × 20%)		2,646
Total capital gains tax payable		3,646

Note that the fine wines are excluded from the computation under the chattels exemption, but this does not apply to the shares or the antique table.

Tian had £10,000 remaining in her basic rate band, and hence £10,000 of the gain is taxed at 10% and the remainder, which would fall into the higher rate band, is taxed at 18%.

Suggested solution—Tian (3)

Tian could transfer some of her assets to her husband Brian. These would take place at a 'no gain/no loss' value. For example, Tian could transfer the antique necklace to Brian. In this case the transfer value would be £11,000, equal to the original cost of the necklace. Brian now has a cost on disposal of £11,000 so the calculation of the gain remains the same, except that now Brian has his own annual exemption of £12,000 to offset against the gain of £9,000 on the necklace. Therefore, assuming Brian has no other capital gains arising in that year, there would be no tax to pay on the disposal of the necklace. The total capital gains tax would be reduced by £1,800 (£9,000 @ 20%). Similarly, some of the units in the unit trust could be transferred to Brian before disposal.

Alternatively, Tian could delay selling the antique necklace until the following tax year, when she would have her own annual exemption to set against the gain.

Suggested solution—Tian (4)

Table 7.15 shows Tian's capital gains tax calculation.

Table 7.15 Inheritance tax computation—Tian's uncle

	£
Nil rate band	325,000
Less PET made 3.5 years previously	90,000
Remaining nil rate band	235,000
Value of estate (400k + 240k + 30k)	670,000
Less: nil rate band	235,000
Taxable estate	435,000
Inheritance tax on estate at 40%	174,000
Less: taper relief on PET 90,000 @ 40% × 20% taper relief	7,200
Inheritance tax due	£166,800

Note that the estate of Tian's uncle cannot benefit from the main residence nil rate band because he had no direct descendants to leave the property to.

Practice Question Solutions

Solution 1 True or False?

7.1   False. There are many assets that are exempt from CGT including cars and principal private residences.

7.2   False. The £6,000 exemption is for chattels that are 'tangible, movable property'. Shares are not chattels.

7.3   False. Transfers of assets between spouses are at a 'no gain/no loss' valuation.

7.4   True

7.5   True

7.6   False. Once an estate has a value greater than £2.35 million, the maximum nil rate band available will be limited to £650,000 for a couple.

7.7 False. Any disposal of an asset two years or less prior to death will not reduce the inheritance tax payable.

7.8 True

7.9 False. Gifts up to £3,000 per year are exempt.

7.10 True

Solution 2 Fred

a) Table 7.16 shows Fred's capital gains tax calculation.

Table 7.16 Fred—Capital gains tax computation

	£	Estimated gains £	Total gains/losses £
Proceeds from selling stamp collection		295,000	
Less: selling costs		5,000	
Net proceeds		290,000	
Cost	150,000		
Buying costs	2,000		
First day covers	10,000		
Less: total cost		162,000	
Capital gain		128,000	
Half gain (jointly owned with wife)			64,000
Proceeds from selling shares			
		50,000	
Less: selling costs		1,500	
Net proceeds		48,500	
Cost	30,000		
Buying costs	250		
Less: total cost		30,250	
Capital gain			18,250
Proceeds from selling painting		10,000	
Less: auctioneer's fee		2,000	
Net proceeds		8,000	

(continued...)

Table 7.16 (*continued*)

	£	Estimated gains £	Total gains/losses £
Less: cost		20,000	
Capital loss			(12,000)
Total net gains			70,250
Less: annual exemption			12,000
Taxable capital gains			58,250
Capital gains tax thereon at 20%			£11,650

Note that the antique chair would be covered by the personal possessions exemption. The capital gain on the stamp collection is split between Fred and his wife, as they are joint owners.

b) **Some tax planning steps to reduce liability:**

1. As both Fred and his wife have high capital gains for the year, both will be paying CGT at 20%. There is no benefit in transferring any gains to his wife this year.

2. Delaying the disposal of the shares to the following tax year and giving half of the shares to his wife would ensure that both annual exemptions are used (to some extent) and no CGT would be payable on the share disposal. There may be other reasons for wanting to sell the shares in the current year, which could outweigh any tax saving considerations.

3. Had the shares been held in an ISA, no CGT would be due on the disposal of the shares at all.

4. Consider whether they have any other assets standing at a loss, which they might wish to dispose of in the current year, to offset the large gain on the stamp collection.

Solution 3 Maurice

Table 7.17 shows Maurice's capital gains tax calculation.

Table 7.17 CGT calculation—Maurice

	£
Nil rate band	325,000
Less PET made 3.5 years previously $50,000 - (5,000 + 3,000 + 3,000) = 39,000$	39,000
Remaining nil rate band	286,000
Main residence nil rate band	175,000
Total available nil rate band	461,000
Value of estate	575,000

(continued...)

Table 7.17 (*continued*)

	£
Less: nil rate band	461,000
Taxable estate	**114,000**
Inheritance tax on estate at 40%	£45,600
Less: taper relief on PET	
39,000 @ 40% × 20% taper relief	3,120
Inheritance tax due	**£42,480**

Note: as the gift to the daughter was made more than ten years before the death, it has no effect on the inheritance tax computation. As no other gifts were made, two years' worth of annual exemptions can be set against the PET. £5,000 can be deducted from the gift to the son, as it was in consideration of his marriage, together with two years' annual exemptions.

Chapter 8

Case Study Suggested Solutions

Suggested solution—Tian and Brian

Review of Tian and Brian's investments

a) Table 8.17 shows the dividend yields of Tian and Brian's investments.

Table 8.17 Dividend yield calculations

Company	Dividend yield	Working
Beech	1.8%	7/400 × 100
Oak	6.0%	9/151 × 100
Elm	—	No dividends paid

Total shareholder return calculations		
Company	Total shareholder return	Working
Beech	4.4%	(7 + 10)/390 × 100
Oak	0%	(9 − 9)/160 × 100
Elm	6.25%	(0 + 8)/128 × 100

Although the dividend yield for Oak plc appears to provide a good return for their shareholders, the total shareholder return is 0% over the year because of the fall in the share price. By contrast, Elm plc did not pay a dividend but the rise in its share price led to a total shareholder return of 6.25% over the last year. Beech's dividend yield at 1.8% coupled with the increase in the share price, gave a total shareholder return of 4.4%. Both Beech plc and Elm plc provided better total shareholder returns than the quoted 4.0% average returns.

b) The following table shows what the current P/E ratios reveals about the future prospects for each company.

P/E ratio calculations		
Company	P/E ratio	Working
Beech	16.2	400/24.7
Oak	7.6	151/19.8
Elm	12.4	136/11.0

The P/E ratios reveal that the market is most optimistic about the future prospects for Beech plc, in terms of expected increases in profitability. The higher P/E ratio reflects the relatively high share price for the company. The P/E for Elm plc is rather lower and lower still at 7.6 for Oak plc. The market could be said to have lower expectations for profit growth in Oak plc. Lower P/E ratios are not necessarily a negative indicator; if, for example, a company has a really profitable year, and the share price stays at roughly the same level, the P/E will fall.

c) If Tian and Brian decide to adopt a strategy whereby they sell shares that have a low P/E ratio, this will mean that they will be selling those shares when their price is relatively low. This might prove to be a sensible strategy but only if the share price continues to fall. Many investors would see a low P/E as a sign of good value and perhaps a good time to invest because the share represents good value. Buying when the P/E is high would mean that they have to pay a high price for the shares.

Tian and Brian should investigate Oak plc more fully before deciding to sell at a low price. They should research the company's prospects before deciding whether it is a company that they want to remain invested in.

Suggested solution—Imran

Review of Imran's portfolio

Imran's portfolio is a mix of inherited investments, shares in a company, Rosier plc, that he chose, and two collective investments held in ISAs. The comments made take into account Imran's attitude to risk and the fact that he is keen to have saved enough for a deposit on a property in a couple of years' time.

The ISA holdings take advantage of the tax efficiency of ISAs but Imran has not used his ISA allowances in full for last year or this year. Last year's unused allowance is now lost but he has £14,500 (£20,000 – £5,500) of unused ISA allowances available for the current tax year.

As Thyme plc has experienced a surge in share price recently, Imran might consider selling some or all of the shares as he is hoping to use the proceeds of those shares towards a deposit on a property. It is possible that the share price could fall again and reduce his ability to raise the deposit. There is, of course, the possibility that the share price of Thyme plc may continue to rise and that if he sells, Imran could miss out on that gain.

His choice of ISA investments shows that he chose a low cost tracker fund last year and a lower risk bonds and gilts fund this year. However, he would be best advised not to invest his £3,000 of savings into the bonds and gilts fund as the value of that fund could fall whereas the capital would be safe in a bank deposit. It is useful for an individual to have some accessible savings in case of an emergency.

Overall, his current portfolio has significant sums tied up in individual company shares, which is a high risk strategy. Imran is prepared to take some risks but he should consider making greater use of his ISA allowances, and having less dependence on the performance of a few companies. This could be achieved by the greater use of collective investments.

Practice Question Solutions

Solution 1 True or False?

8.1   True

8.2   False. Companies do not have to pay dividends to their shareholders and many do not do so.

8.3   True

8.4   True

8.5   True

8.6   False. Bonds are long-term loan contracts that are usually repayable.

8.7   False. A company with an AAA credit rating is considered to be very safe.

8.8   False. '4% Treasury Stock 2020' is a description of government bonds (gilts) that pay interest at 4% on nominal value and are repayable in 2020.

8.9   True

8.10   True

Solution 2 Sandy

a) Pepper plc's eps has increased significantly over the last four years, particularly between years 2 and 3, when it increased by 36%. The growth in eps, or profit per share, over the four years means that the company's profitability has shown significant growth over the four-year period.

b) The P/E ratios are as follows:

P/E (Year 1)	= 36.0/4.0	= 9.0
P/E (Year 2)	= 40.5/4.5	= 9.0
P/E (Year 3)	= 66.4/6.1	= 10.9
P/E (Year 4)	= 65.1/7.1	= 9.2

The P/E ratio remained static at 9.0 over years 1 and 2 and then showed an increase in year 3 indicating that by the end of that year the market's expectations for future profit growth in the company had improved and this led to a big increase in the share price over that year. By the end of year 4, the P/E fell to close to the level it was at in years 1 and 2.

c) Note: The TSR includes no figure for dividends as none were paid.

$$\text{TSR (year 4)} = \frac{(65.1 - 66.4)}{66.4} \times 100 = -2.0\%$$

$$\text{TSR (year 3)} = \frac{(66.4 - 40.5)}{40.5} \times 100 = 64.0\%$$

The TSR (total shareholder return) for year 3 was an extremely high (64.0%) as a result of the huge increase in the share price during the year. In year 4, the price levelled off and a small negative TSR was generated. Overall the TSR over those two years would represent a very good rate of return for shareholders.

d) Sandy may be disappointed to have not received any dividends over the last four years but the company's share price has risen from 36.0 to 65.1 pence over that time, an increase of 81%. This is a very good rate of return and if he needs the cash that he thought the dividends would provide, he could sell a few of the shares.

Chapter 9

Case Study Suggested Solutions

Suggested solution—Rachel

a) The issues that Rachel and her partner should consider before choosing the type and amount of mortgage include:
- How secure are their jobs? Are they planning to move jobs/change location/take a course?
- What is predicted for interest rates? This will influence their decision concerning fixed or variable rate mortgages.
- Have they saved enough of a deposit to secure a reasonable mortgage offer?
- Overall, how affordable will their mortgage be?

b) A repayment mortgage, rather than interest-only, would be the sensible choice for the couple. Then there is the question of whether to go for a fixed or variable rate mortgage.

A fixed rate repayment mortgage would give them certainty over costs in the initial years and ensure that the loan is paid off over the term of the mortgage. It is likely to be more expensive than a variable rate mortgage, but it will provide some certainty in the early years that the repayments can be met. They could also consider a tracker mortgage, depending on predictions for interest rates. This would carry more risk, but could be a cheaper option.

c) LTV: $210/240 \times 100\% = 87.5\%$

d) Interest per annum: £210,000 × 4% = £8,400

Over twenty-five years: £8,400 × 25 years = total interest of £210,000

The £210,000 interest-only mortgage would cost £210,000 in interest over the term of the mortgage and they would still owe the original £210,000 at the end of the twenty-five years.

e) Total mortgage payments: £1,120 × 12 months × 25 years = £336,000

Less: mortgage loan	= £210,000
Interest payable under the repayment mortgage	= £126,000

Interest payable under the repayment mortgage is less than under an interest-only mortgage because with the former option, the capital is gradually being paid off over the period of the loan. With an interest-only mortgage, none of the capital is paid off during the term of the mortgage, which makes it a much more expensive option.

f) Using the rule of thumb, they can afford £42,000/3 = £14,000 per annum or £1,167 per month.

g) One-off costs would be likely to include: survey fee, legal fees, Stamp Duty Land Tax, mortgage arrangement fee, removals costs, furniture, carpets, any maintenance or renovation work required on property.

h) Inflation at 5% will gradually reduce the real value of their mortgage, and will make it more affordable. Inflation is generally beneficial for borrowers.

However, inflation could possibly lead to an increase in interest rates.

i) Interest payable (tracker mortgage) = £210,000 × 3.39% = £7,119

Interest payable (fixed rate) =	£210,000 × 4.99% = £10,479
Add fee =	£995
	£11,474
Difference =	£4,355 in the first year

There is no easy answer as to which mortgage they should take. The fixed rate looks expensive and has high fees and early repayment charges, but if mortgage rates start to increase it could become worthwhile. Do Rachel and her partner need the security of a fixed rate mortgage or can they take the risk that interest rates might rise and benefit from taking out the cheaper tracker?

j) The advice would be very different; Rachel and her partner should not consider buying a house if she is thinking of retraining. Their joint income will go down and they could be unable to pay the mortgage. They could be forced into a sale at a reduced price.

Suggested solution—Oliver

Oliver and his girlfriend need flexibility. Buying a property would not be a sensible option in their situation, even if Oliver's parents were prepared to lend him the deposit. They have no savings and considerable debt, so they would not be in a strong position to take on a mortgage. Oliver would not be sensible to take on a mortgage in London at a time when he might be offered work in other parts of the country.

Oliver should bear in mind the benefits of renting a property, rather than buying, such as:

- flexibility to move if circumstances change
- short-term commitment only

- repairs and maintenance are the landlord's responsibility
- low risk in comparison to the risks and responsibilities of a mortgage.

Suggested solution—Theo and Kate

a) Table 9.5 shows the calculation for Theo's income after tax and other deductions and Table 9.6 illustrates the joint calculation for Theo and Kate.

Table 9.5 Theo: calculation of income after tax and other deductions

	£
Theo salary	29,000
Less: pension contributions (29,000 × 8%)	2,320
Less: income tax	3,300
Less: National Insurance	2,280
Available income	21,100

Table 9.6 Theo and Kate: calculation of joint income after tax and other deductions

Kate business income £500 × 12	£6,000 (no tax or National Insurance)
Theo available income	£21,100
Total net annual income	£27,100
Available income per month (27,100/12)	£2,258

b) Table 9.7 lists Theo and Kate's assets and liabilities.

Table 9.7 Theo and Kate: assets and liabilities

Assets	£	Liabilities	£
House	220,000	Mortgage	150,000
		Credit card debts	9,000
		Bank overdraft	4,000
Total	220,000	Total	163,000

Although Theo and Kate have a reasonable amount of equity in their property of £70,000 (£220,000 – £150,000) they have also accumulated some debts and this has increased their liabilities and their costs. They are unable to reduce their debts at the moment, and if their expenditure consistently exceeds their income, their debts will be increasing.

c) Table 9.8 illustrates the mortgage payments Theo and Kate can afford.

Table 9.8 Theo and Kate: affordability of mortgage payments

Theo and Kate	£
Available income per month	2,258
1/3 available income	752
Mortgage payment	780

Although Theo and Kate's mortgage does not seem excessively large in relation to their available income, we should look at their monthly income and expenditure to see whether they are able to meet all their commitments (Table 9.9). The fact that they have accumulated some debts is contributing to their difficulties.

Table 9.9 Theo and Kate: available income per month

Monthly income	£	Monthly expenditure	£
Available income	2,258	Mortgage	780
		Credit card payments (minimum)	225
		Bank interest on overdraft (600/12)	50
		Utilities, etc.	700
		Car running costs	100
		Food	600
Total available income	**2,258**	**Total expenditure**	**2,455**

The fact that Theo and Kate's monthly expenditure is exceeding their income is a problem for them, as they have no immediate access to further sources of borrowing. This issue is addressed further in Chapter 14, Coping in a crisis. The major risk in their situation is that they may fail to keep up the mortgage payments, with the potential threat of repossession of their home.

d) Theo and Kate's house is their major asset but it is an inflexible one. The house cannot be sold off in parts to release any capital, unlike other investments that could be partially sold. They also have significant liabilities. Their normal monthly expenditure exceeds their income, before taking into account any unforeseen expenditure. They are unable to pay off their credit cards that are costing them £1,800 in interest each year and this amount will be increasing. Similarly with their overdraft, they cannot afford to reduce it and the interest charge is likely to increase as the debt rises.

Theo and Kate could try and sell their house and buy a smaller one to release some capital. They could consider renting out one of the rooms, taking in a lodger and benefiting from tax-free income under the rent-a-room relief. Kate could try and find a job in addition to running her business and Theo could consider taking a second job.

Practice Question Solutions

Solution 1 True or False?

9.1   False. A useful rule of thumb is not to commit more than one-third of income after income tax, National Insurance contributions, and student loan repayments to mortgage payments.

9.2   True

9.3   True

9.4   False. With an interest-only mortgage, none of the capital will be repaid at the end of the mortgage term.

9.5   False. A repayment mortgage will have higher monthly payments than an interest-only mortgage, because the capital is being repaid as well as the interest charge.

9.6   False. Taking on a mortgage is a significant responsibility, with many one-off costs involved, and should not be taken on unless financial circumstances are settled. History suggests that property prices are not guaranteed to rise.

9.7   True

9.8   True

9.9   False. The APR is a useful starting point in considering a mortgage but other costs, terms, and conditions should be considered.

9.10   True

Solution 2 Elliott

a) Elliott has a reasonable deposit of approximately 18.6%. The decision as to which mortgage to choose revolves around whether to opt for a lower interest rate variable mortgage, with high arrangement fees and low early repayment charges, or to opt for a fixed rate mortgage at a higher rate of interest with low arrangement fees but higher early repayment charges. The APR is calculated over the twenty-five years of the loan and depends on the SVR, which will follow on after the initial period. On the assumption that he would be able to remortgage after the initial period, the APR is not a particularly helpful measure. Some simple calculations allow him to make a comparison between the two mortgages (Table 9.10).

Table 9.10 Elliott: comparison of two mortgage products

Costs	Image: tracker mortgage £	Farleys: fixed rate mortgage £
Interest (215,000 – 40,000) × 4.47% or 5.8%	7,822	10,150
Arrangement fee	999	550
Valuation fee	325	145
Total cost year 1	9,146	10,845
Total cost year 2	7,822	10,150
Total interest and charges for two years (ignoring repayments)	16,968	20,995

Over the two-year period Elliott can see that the tracker is considerably cheaper.

b) Elliott should consider the questions set out below. If the answer to each of the following questions is 'Yes', Elliott should consider the tracker mortgage, as it is substantially cheaper than the fixed rate mortgage in the short term. If the answer to some of the questions is 'No', then he should consider paying more for his mortgage and opt for the certainty of a fixed rate mortgage, to eliminate any risk arising from future rises in interest rates.

- Are interest rates relatively stable and unlikely to change significantly in the next two years?
- If interest rates increase quickly and I have taken out a variable rate mortgage, will I still be able to afford the mortgage repayments?
- Am I prepared to take the risk that interest rates could rise quickly?
- If interest rates do rise quickly and I want a fixed rate mortgage in two years' time, am I prepared for it to be substantially more expensive?

c) If interest rates are likely to remain the same or fall then Elliott should definitely consider opting for the variable rate tracker mortgage, otherwise he will find himself with an expensive fixed rate mortgage with some high penalties if he seeks to change his mortgage before the end of the five-year term. Of course, predicting what will happen to interest rates in the future is a difficult exercise as the future course of interest rates is dependent on many different variables.

Solution 3 Ashma

The Hampton mortgage is not available to Ashma as she needs a 90% LTV mortgage product. Her deposit is just over 10% of the price of the property (14,000/134,000).

The Northern mortgage represents the best value for Ashma. Although it has a higher APR than the Eastern mortgage, the high APR is due to the higher follow-on rate. In fact it has a lower rate of interest for the first five years of the mortgage and a lower arrangement fee. If Ashma is prepared to remortgage in five years' time, she should consider the Northern mortgage as her best option.

Chapter 10

Case Study Suggested Solutions

Suggested solution—Imran (Town Close)

a) Years 1 to 3: Annual mortgage interest $= £130,000 \times 6\% = £7,800$

Years 1 to 3: Monthly mortgage interest $= £7,800/12 = £650$ per month

b) Table 10.7 shows a calculation of net property income in the first three years.

c) Deposit plus all the one off purchase costs

$$= 60,000 + \text{SDLT } £7,000 + \text{Survey } £1,000 = £68,000$$

$$\text{Rental yield (years 1, 2, and 3)} = \frac{2,090 \times 100}{68,000} = 3.1\%$$

Table 10.7 Calculation of net property income

	Year 1 £	Year 2 £	Year 3 £
Rental income (1,100 × 11 months)	12,100	12,100	12,100
Expenses			
Mortgage interest	7,800	7,800	7,800
Agent's fees (10% × rent)	1,210	1,210	1,210
Service charge	250	250	250
Insurance	500	500	500
Repairs (average amount)	250	250	250
Total expenses	10,010	10,010	10,010
Net property income	**2,090**	**2,090**	**2,090**

d) The rental yield at 3.1% is slightly better than Imran could currently earn if he deposited his money with a building society but the return on a savings account does not carry the same risks as investing in rental property. If property prices rise, as is expected in the future, then this would make this a more attractive investment.

Investing in property will be much more time-consuming for Imran than investing in stocks and shares or holding a building society account.

There are risks attached to this investment, as there is no certainty that prices will stay stable and then rise, as is expected; they could fall. There is the risk that at the end of five years, if prices have fallen, then his equity in the property will have fallen below the £68,000 he put in. There is also the risk of unforeseen maintenance costs, significant periods when the property is empty, unpaid rents, or damage caused by tenants. If these events were to occur, they could wipe out any expected return completely.

Suggested solution—Imran (Station Heights)

a) Table 10.8 shows a calculation of net property income in the first three years.

Table 10.8 Calculation of net property income

Station Heights	Year 1 £	Year 2 £	Year 3 £
Rental income (1,100 × 12 months)	13,200	13,200	13,200
Expenses			
Mortgage interest (140,000 × 6.5%)	9,100	9,100	9,100
Agent's fees (10% × rent)	1,320	1,320	1,320
Service charge	400	400	400

(continued...)

Table 10.8 (continued)

Station Heights	Year 1 £	Year 2 £	Year 3 £
Insurance	520	520	520
Repairs	-	200	200
Total expenses	11,340	11,540	11,540
Net property income	1,860	1,660	1,660

Total amount invested in the property = deposit + SDLT + suveyors fees + legal fees.

= Deposit 60,000 + SDLT £7,500 + surveyors and legal fees £nil

$$\text{Rental yield (year 1)} = \frac{1,860 \times 100}{67,500} = 2.8\%$$

$$\text{Rental yield (years 2 and 3)} = \frac{1,660 \times 100}{67,500} = 2.5\%$$

The investment in Station Heights would lead to a yield of 2.8% in the first year of ownership and would give a yield of 2.5% for the next two years of ownership. This is very slightly lower than the yield on the Town Close property over the first three years of ownership.

The yield on Station Heights after year one is 2.5% each year, and once the developer's commitment to cover any tenant voids is over after three years, this yield is likely to fall. Covering this to a limited extent, there might be increases in the rent that can be charged by that time.

Based on longer-term expected rental yields alone, Imran might be better opting for the Town Close investment which, based on eleven months a year expected occupancy, would give a rental yield of 3.1% per annum. The long-term rental yield on Station Heights is almost the same as the return offered on bank deposits of 2.4% per annum. The return from the buy-to-let flats carries more risk than a bank deposit, as the rental yields are by no means certain and could be wiped out altogether by unforeseen costs.

Imran does need to be aware that the value of both properties might fall in the future and he could be faced with a capital loss. However, looking back over many decades, housing has proved to be a less volatile investment than stocks and shares. Providing Imran is able to choose the time of sale of the property, he should be able to sell when prices are buoyant.

b) When Imran buys a buy-to-let property he will have to pay Stamp Duty Land Tax on the purchase at rates much greater than a homeowner would have to pay.

As a higher rate taxpayer, Imran will be liable to pay income tax, at the higher rate, on the net property income he earns. He will only be given relief at the basic rate of income tax for the mortgage interest paid.

When the property is eventually sold, he will be liable to pay capital gains tax on any gain arising after allowing for the annual exemption. As a higher rate taxpayer, he will be liable to pay capital gains tax at the higher rate for residential property.

Practice Question Solutions

Solution 1 True or False?

10.1 False. There is no guarantee that property prices will rise over time.

10.2 True

10.3 False. Property is a very inflexible investment. It is not easy to realize your investment as you can only sell the whole property at once and it can be difficult to find a buyer for a property.

10.4 False. Buy-to-let mortgages usually demand a relatively high percentage deposit.

10.5 True

10.6 False. The rental income received, net of allowable expenses, is subject to income tax.

10.7 True

10.8 False. The real rental yield is a measure of the net rental income received as a proportion of the equity invested in the property.

10.9 True

10.10 True

Solution 3 Anton

a) Table 10.9 shows Anton's net property income in the year.

Table 10.9 Calculation of taxable property income

	Year 1£
Rental income (800 × 12 months)	9,600
Expenses	
Mortgage interest (350 × 12)	4,200
Agent's fees (11% × 9,600)	1,056
Service charge	500
Insurance	290
Property maintenance	800
Replacement furniture	900
Total expenses	7,746
Net property income	**1,854**

Notes on the calculation:
- Twelve months' rental has been used, as Anton has tenants who plan to be in the flat for at least twelve months more.

b) As a higher rate taxpayer, the income tax payable on this property income is shown in Table 10.10.

Table 10.10 Anton—income tax computation

(Higher rate taxpayer)	£
Rental income	9,600
Allowable expenses (excluding mortgage interest)	3,546
Net rental income	6,054
Income tax @ 40%	2,422
Less: tax relief on mortgage interest (£4,200 × 20%)	(840)
Income tax payable	1,582

c) Table 10.11 shows the calculation for capital gains tax should Anton sell the flat in twelve months' time.

Table 10.11 Anton—capital gains tax (estimated)

	£
Proceeds from flat sale (103,000 − 5,000)	98,000
Cost of flat (this could be increased by any purchase costs)	90,000
Capital gain	8,000
Annual exemption (max of 12,000 available)	8,000

Assuming that Anton does not have any further gains in the next tax year, the gain on the sale of the flat will not be liable to CGT because it will be less than the annual exemption.

Chapter 11

Case Study Suggested Solutions

Suggested solution—Imran and Theo

As a single person Imran does not have an obvious need for life assurance, even though his hobbies are quite risky. He does not have any dependants who would be financially affected by his death.

Theo, although much more risk averse, needs life assurance, to cover the mortgage and loss of income in the event of his death because of his dependent family and the level of borrowing.

Suggested solution—Rachel and her partner

Rachel should identify if any life assurance cover is available through her remuneration package. If she has a reasonable amount of life assurance provided through work, she might not need a further policy. She should also find out whether she has any income protection cover through her employer. As she works for a large employer it is quite possible that her remuneration package includes these elements. She should also enquire into the sick pay arrangements offered by her employer.

As the couple are considering taking on a large mortgage, they should be considering taking out term assurance, particularly for Rachel as she is the main earner. It would also be important to consider life assurance for her partner, as he will be contributing towards the mortgage.

Any mortgage lender is likely to insist on buildings insurance along with the mortgage, but Rachel should shop around to find a good policy. The insurance does not have to be purchased through the mortgage provider.

Rachel and her partner should consider contents insurance to protect against theft, fire, or accidental damage to their possessions.

Suggested solution—Oliver

Oliver is not in a position where he needs life assurance as he does not have any dependants. He could consider an income protection policy but he would be likely to find the premiums rather too expensive for his circumstances. As a young man in good health, the chances of becoming unable to work through illness or disability are relatively small, so it might be a level of risk that he is prepared to take.

Suggested solution—Tian and Brian

There are some important questions that Tian and Brian need to consider. What would happen to the business if one of them became ill or died? They have no other dependants now that their children are all adults, so they only need to consider each other and they only have a small amount of outstanding debt.

There is a type of cover called 'key person insurance' that would compensate the business for the financial losses arising from the death or incapacity of a person key to the business, that they might consider.

They should think about what might happen if one or other of them became ill or died, because if the other party were forced to sell the business, the price it could fetch might be reduced. With only one income coming in, would £100,000 compensation be enough to enable the current standard of living to be maintained? It seems unlikely, given that their joint current income is £100,000 (before tax) per annum.

Tian and Brian should consider increasing their term life assurance cover and make sure they have a good level of cover until their expected retirement dates. They might also consider whole of life assurance for inheritance tax planning purposes and take specialist advice on this.

Income protection insurance would potentially be valuable for them, but it comes at a high price and the risk of being unable to work through illness or disability might be a risk they are prepared to take.

Critical illness insurance would be another possibility to consider, that would pay out a lump sum, but only in relation to the development of specific illnesses.

Suggested solution—Imran

Identity theft: providing Imran is not negligent in protecting his identity, has set strong PIN numbers, does not reveal his PIN numbers, is careful about his privacy settings on social media, and does not carelessly dispose of important documents, he should be covered by the bank for any fraud on his accounts. Identity theft insurance only covers the cost of sorting out the problem, it does not cover any money lost through an identity theft fraud and therefore Imran should be advised to think very carefully about the need for this type of insurance.

Extended warranty: the extended warranty on the washing machine does not represent good value for money. The machine has a twelve-month warranty anyway and as Imran has some savings he will probably be able to self-insure and cover the costs himself if the machine does go wrong.

Whole of life assurance is not relevant to Imran, as he has no dependants, no potential inheritance tax liability, no significant savings, and substantial life cover through work.

Critical illness insurance might be a policy Imran should think about, to meet his debts in case he cannot work due to illness, but the policy is expensive. Again this might be a risk he chooses to carry himself at a time when he is trying to build up savings.

The annual travel policy at £94 looks like good value for money and should be taken out to provide general cover for Imran's holidays, assuming he intends to take holidays in the coming year. It is extremely unlikely to cover any adrenaline sports, as most travel insurance policies would exclude those potentially dangerous hobbies.

The contents insurance would cover Imran's possessions in the event of fire, theft, or damage. This should be a policy for serious consideration. Although the chances of loss are quite small, the consequences of the loss would be serious and the loss could be substantial.

The cost of the policy is small relative to the potential level of loss. If Imran does purchase the policy he should make sure that he complies with any terms and conditions attached to the policy, to ensure that the insurance cover is valid.

Mobile phone insurance is expensive and Imran would probably be better to self-insure, saving the cost of the premium and covering any potential loss himself.

Practice Question Solutions

Solution 1 Quick quiz

It is possible to insure against all of these potential problems, and some of the policies are discussed here. The insurance company will need to assess the risk in each case in order to determine the premium. For example, if twins run in the family then there is quite a high risk of conceiving twins and the premium will reflect this. The principle of *uberrima fides* would require the policyholder to disclose whether or not twins run in the family.

Divorce insurance can be taken out to meet the costs of any divorce proceedings, but this would need to be taken out before there was any likelihood of a divorce. By the time a divorce became likely, it would be too late to take out the insurance.

Wedding insurance to cover the photographs is quite common, and can extend to covering the costs of reassembling the main wedding party (close family and bride and groom) to reshoot the photos.

Solution 2 To insure or Not to Insure?

In a number of circumstances, having insurance is a legal requirement and it must be purchased. If it is not a legal requirement to have insurance, then the following factors should be considered before deciding on whether to purchase a policy:

- The chances or probability of a loss occurring. If the chances of such an event happening are statistically very small, it might not be necessary to purchase an insurance policy to provide cover against the very small chance of a loss.
- The next step is to consider the amount of any potential loss arising. Where the potential loss is significant, it is sensible to consider insuring against this possibility, even if the probability of the event occurring is small.
- Having considered the probability of a particular event occurring and the potential amount of any loss, the next step is to consider the cost of the policy. The cost of some policies can be out of all proportion to the cover provided. If the insurance cover is expensive compared to the potential amount of compensation it might be better to consider self-insurance. If, on the other hand, the cost of insurance is small compared to the level of cover provided, then the policy might be worthy of further consideration.
- The cost of the policy can be reduced by the amount of any excess agreed to.

If the risk exists, the premium is reasonable, and the potential loss high, then it may be wise to take out insurance. If the risk is low, the premium expensive, and the potential loss manageable, it may be better to self-insure. In all circumstances the above factors should be reflected upon in order for a rational decision to be made on whether or not to purchase the policy.

Chapter 12

Case Study Suggested Solutions

Suggested solution—Rachel

a) The real cost to Rachel of her pension contributions will be:

Gross amount of contributions = £45,000 × 5% = £2,250

Her taxable income will be reduced by £2,250.

As a basic rate taxpayer, she will pay £2,250 × 20% = £450 less tax.

Real cost to her of 5% contributions = £2,250 − 450 = £1,800 per annum.

b) The amount invested in her pension pot in the first year would be (5% from Rachel + 5% from her employer) × £45,000 = £4,500.

c) The amount that would be invested in her pension pot in the first five years would be ((5% + 5%) × £47,500) × 5 years = £23,750. (This ignores any investment gains or losses that may be made.)

d) Rachel's 'five-year pot' would be worth £23,750 × 180/100 = £42,750 in thirty years' time.

e) The amount of annuity that her 'five-year pot' would buy would be 42,750/100,000 × £4,600 = £1,970 per annum.

f) Rachel's personal finances are clearly at full stretch at the moment as she is trying to build enough savings to enable her to buy her own home.

She should be made aware of the benefits of joining the workplace scheme as for a cost to her of £1,800 in the first year, her pension pot will receive contributions of £4,500. Contributions made when she is twenty-five will have forty years to increase in value (if Rachel retires at sixty-five), as a result of any investment gains made. These contributions are likely to prove extremely beneficial when she reaches retirement age. Based on the workings above, a conservative estimate of the income that her five-year pot might buy is £1,970 (£4,600 × 42,750/100,000) per annum.

Another factor for Rachel to consider is that many workplace schemes often carry other benefits such as life assurance. Rachel should be advised to try to do whatever she can to enable her to afford to join the scheme as it is a very cost-effective way for her to start saving for her retirement.

Suggested solution—Theo

Theo is currently a member of a workplace final-salary pension scheme. These schemes are becoming increasingly rare as they are expensive for employers but offer many benefits to employees who are fortunate to be members of such schemes. A final-salary scheme has many benefits over a personal pension. Being a member of a final-salary pension, Theo will always be able to have confidence that his pension will be linked to salary rates when he retires. As he approaches retirement, he will be able to predict the amount of pension that he will receive in retirement, as it will be a multiple of his final salary.

This contrasts with membership of a personal pension scheme which would be a defined-contribution scheme where the eventual pension payable will be difficult to predict and often of a disappointingly low amount. If he joined a defined-contribution scheme, Theo's pension would depend on the returns earned on his pension savings, and probably on annuity rates at the point when he eventually decides to buy one. Personal pensions carry an annual management charge that will reduce the size of any pension pot. When investment returns are weak or even negative, the pension payable may be very low.

Another real benefit to Theo of the workplace scheme is the life cover it provides. As he has a wife and three dependent children, it is clearly very important that there is life assurance in place in case he dies young, whilst the children and his wife are still dependent on his financial support. If he leaves his workplace scheme, he will need to ensure that he organizes life cover both for himself and his wife.

Many final-salary schemes allow the scheme member to opt for a pension that remains payable, at least in part, if the member dies before their spouse. It is possible that Theo's workplace scheme may provide Kate with the comfort of knowing that she could receive a pension from the scheme throughout her retirement even if Theo dies before she does.

Theo should do everything that he can to remain in the final-salary scheme. This is likely to involve reorganizing his debt. He should try to cut household spending and look at ways to increase the household income. Perhaps he may be able to take on overtime or his wife might be able to grow her business or take on a part-time job. Leaving a final-salary scheme would mean some extra income now but, in all likelihood, a significantly lower pension in the future.

Practice Question Solutions

Solution 1 True or False?

12.1   False. An individual's entitlement to the state pension is dependent on having paid National Insurance contributions over many years.

12.2   True

12.3   True

12.4   False. Pension savings cannot be withdrawn from a pension fund at any time.

12.5   True

12.6   True

12.7   True

12.8   False. The minimum age at which all personal pensions can be drawn depends on the scheme but it is usually lower than the state retirement age.

12.9   True

12.10 False. Income drawdown is a higher risk way of using pension savings as the pension pot remains vulnerable to fluctuating asset prices and there is the risk of drawing too much too soon and having an inadequate income in later years.

Solution 3 Zola

- If Zola makes pension savings with her spare income, then it will attract tax relief at the basic rate. Savings into an ISA will not attract such tax relief.
- Savings in a cash ISA earn interest which is free of tax, as do savings in a pension fund. As a basic rate taxpayer, Zola is entitled to a PSA of £1,000, which means she can earn this amount free of tax.
- Zola would not be able to withdraw any sums from her pension until she reaches a minimum retirement age (currently that age is fifty-five, but this earliest retirement age is increasing to sixty), whereas she could withdraw funds from her ISA at any time, assuming the terms of the ISA allow instant access.

Given that Zola and her partner are saving for a deposit on a house, she should consider putting her savings into a cash ISA so that she can access the savings in order to raise the deposit. (A Help to Buy or Lifetime ISA would attract a government bonus when Zola and her partner's savings are withdrawn to buy their home.)

Chapter 13

Case Study Suggested Solutions

Suggested solution—Tian and Brian

The issues to be taken into consideration by Tian and Brian when revising their wills include:

- Do they still wish to share their estate equally between all three children?
- Do they want to reflect their son's role in the business?
- Should they take account of the money already received by Tian's oldest daughter in working out the distribution of their assets after death?

- Is it sensible for Tian's daughter to inherit outright a potentially substantial amount of money if she has not proved financially responsible?
- Are they prepared to discuss their will and any different distribution arrangements with their family, to explain their reasons and avoid potential family disputes after their death?
- Are there any inheritance tax planning measures they might consider?
- Will they rewrite their wills completely or just add a codicil?

It is extremely important that they explore all the potential changes they might wish to make and discuss them with a solicitor for advice. Solicitors have experience in dealing with this type of family situation and can provide appropriate advice and solutions.

It is equally important if they decide to amend their wills to alter the distribution of their assets that they should discuss this openly with their family to avoid damaging family disputes after their deaths.

Suggested solution—Imran

Imran's parents

The main reason for Imran's parents to make their wills is to ensure that their estate is distributed in accordance with their wishes, rather than the intestacy rules. On the death of one or other parent the intestacy rules could force the sale of the family home to provide Imran and his sister with their share of the estate, assuming their estate is worth in excess of £250,000. A will enables Imran's parents to make sure that their estate is distributed amongst their family, friends, and charities in the way that they wish.

Making a will should provide clarity about their intentions for their estate and avoid any disputes amongst their family, although this is not guaranteed.

For Imran's parents, who have substantial assets, making a will provides an opportunity for tax planning in order to minimize the amount of inheritance tax that will become due on death.

Their wills can set out details about how their funerals should be carried out, including any wish to be buried or cremated.

Imran's sister

As well as the reasons set out above, Imran's sister and her husband should make their wills because it will allow them to set out who they wish to look after their child (or children) if both parents were to die. A will allows them to appoint guardians for their children.

If they were to die intestate their children would inherit at the age of eighteen, or on earlier marriage or civil partnership. They might consider that eighteen is too young an age for children to inherit and the terms of their wills can set out a later age at which the children will inherit.

Imran

The same reasons for making a will apply to Imran as to his parents. In addition, if Imran does not make a will and dies intestate, his estate would go to his parents, who are described as financially secure. He might prefer to leave his estate to his sister or to other beneficiaries, including a charity for the homeless that he supports.

Practice Question Solutions

Solution 1　Quick quiz

13.1　The grandchild would inherit the estate and nothing would go to the deceased's brother.

13.2　The parents would inherit in equal shares. The divorce would not affect the inheritance.

13.3　The sister would take precedence over the half-brothers and, despite having no contact with the family, she would inherit the whole estate.

13.4　The aunts would inherit in equal shares and the stepdaughter would not inherit anything.

13.5　E's half-sister and half-brother would be entitled to equal shares. They are above grandparents and aunts in the hierarchy. As his half-brother has already died, the son of his half-brother would be entitled to his father's share.

13.6　The estate would be divided into four equal parts for F's four original children. The two surviving daughters would each inherit one-quarter of the estate. The children of the two deceased daughters would inherit their mothers' share. Each grandson would inherit one-eighth of the estate, as they step into the shoes of their mother.

13.7　The nephew would step into his father's shoes and inherit G's estate.

Solution 2　Benefits of Making a Will

There are many potential benefits of making a will, including:
- It allows the testators to leave their estate to the people that they choose.
- It allows the testator to make sure that any unmarried partners are looked after. The rules of intestacy do not recognize unmarried partners.
- The intestacy rules might force the family home to be sold. A will can avoid this situation arising.
- It allows testators to appoint guardians for their children.
- It allows testators to set an age for their children to inherit. Under the rules of intestacy, they would inherit at eighteen.
- It allows testators to make clear their wishes re burial or cremation and any funeral arrangements.
- It allows the testator to make a specific legacy (for example of jewellery or artwork) to a particular person.
- It allows testators to make specific bequests to charities.
- It allows testators to minimize the impact of inheritance tax.
- It reduces the potential for family disputes at a stressful time.
- It allows a testator to choose their executor or executors, who will administer their estate.

Solution 3　Susan

Table 13.2 shows how Susan's estate will be distributed.

Table 13.2 Distribution of Susan's estate under the rules of intestacy

Name	Inheritance	
Jia (civil partner)	Personal possessions	
	First	£250,000
	Half of the remainder	£100,000
Ali	Half of the remainder (will be held in trust until she reaches eighteen)	£100,000

Solution 4 Frank

Table 13.3 shows how Frank's estate will be distributed.

Table 13.3 Distribution of Frank's estate under the rules of intestacy

Name	Inheritance	
Niece 1	The estate would be split between the nieces	£375,000
Niece 2		£375,000
Half-sisters	Inherit nothing under the intestacy rules—Frank should have made a will.	

Chapter 14

Case Study Suggested Solutions

Suggested solution—Theo and Kate (cash budget)

a) Table 14.4 shows Theo and Kate's cash budget.

Table 14.4 Theo and Kate's cash budget for the three months to 31 March

	January £	February £	March £
Income:			
Theo—net earnings (21,000/12)	1,750	1,750	1,750
Kate—income	500	500	500
Total income	**2,250**	**2,250**	**2,250**
Expenditure:			
Mortgage	780	780	780

(continued...)

Table 14.4 (*continued*)

	January £	February £	March £
Other household costs	800	800	800
Food	600	600	600
Credit card minimum payments (3 × £75 per credit card)	225	225	225
Bank interest	50	50	50
Total expenditure	2,455	2,455	2,455
Net expenditure	(205)	(205)	(205)
Bank overdraft at the beginning of the month	(4,000)	(4,205)	(4,410)
Bank overdraft at the end of the month	**(4,205)**	**(4,410)**	**(4,615)**

b) Looking at the cash budget in Table 14.4, the overdraft is forecast to increase month by month from January to March because the anticipated expenditure exceeds the income by £205 in each of the months. As their overdraft limit is £4,000, Theo and Kate will incur interest at a higher rate, have to pay extra charges, and the bank is very likely to soon stop meeting payments on the account. This could cause the family real difficulty, as they would not be able to pay their bills, including the mortgage.

Many of the expense payments made in the cash budget cannot be avoided. Perhaps the food bill could be reduced if cheaper choices were to be made. The couple could investigate whether cheaper electricity, gas, or broadband suppliers are available.

Theo and Kate could try to increase the income coming into the household in order to reduce the overdraft. One possible solution would be for Kate to grow her business or try to find a part-time job. Theo could explore whether there are any opportunities to work overtime. Perhaps they could earn some rental income by taking in a lodger.

c) Theo and Kate's total debts at the start of the year are:

Bank overdraft	£4,000
Credit card debts	£9,000
Mortgage	£150,000
Total	£163,000

As Theo and Kate have not fallen behind with their mortgage payments or council tax or utility bills, they do not have any priority debts at this point.

d) Theo and Kate do have a debt problem. They have borrowed the maximum amount on their credit cards and are incurring high interest charges on the balances. They can barely afford to make the minimum payment each month and it would take them many years to pay off these credit card balances. Their bank account has reached its overdraft limit and the cash budget shows that they expect to exceed it in the coming months.

They do not have any priority debts owing as they have not fallen behind with their mortgage payments, or council tax or utility bills, but the cash budget gives an indication that this may be forced upon them soon unless they take some action.

Without any savings, they will be at risk if they have to deal with any unexpected expenses.

Suggested solution—Theo and Kate (resolving a debt problem)

a) Theo and Kate have almost £9,000 of unsecured debt, a £150,000 mortgage, and a secured bank loan for £5,000. Because the household income is low they cannot afford their mortgage repayments and, although the bank loan has reduced their overdraft, they do still have an overdraft and this is likely to increase during the year.

Theo and Kate's biggest debt is their mortgage and this carries a much lower rate of interest rate than their other debts. If they had been allowed to increase the size of their mortgage, this would have reduced the total interest charges that they are having to pay. However, they are struggling to cover their existing mortgage payments and increasing the mortgage would also have increased the repayments required. If in the future, the couple were unable to meet some of the repayments, then their home would be at risk of repossession.

The couple owe nearly £9,000 on three credit cards and these attract very high rates of interest. The couple had an overdraft limit of £4,000 at the beginning of the year and they had not only gone overdrawn to this limit, they nearly exceeded it. The bank overdraft also attracts a high rate of interest. At the end of March, this overdraft balance has fortunately been reduced because the couple took out the bank loan. The bank loan does carry a lower rate of interest but, worryingly for Theo and Kate, it is secured on their home. If they fail to keep up repayments on it, they will put their home at risk.

Steps that the couple might have taken earlier to prevent their current debt problem:

- The couple seem to have a very large mortgage relative to their incomes and it would appear that the house they bought was too expensive as they struggle to meet their mortgage repayments. This is particularly so as they now have a young family and Kate's income is very low.
- The couple have clearly used their credit cards a great deal in the past. It is likely that they were used to buy things that the couple could not afford. Using credit cards for purchases you cannot afford merely creates a bigger problem at a later date and ideally Theo and Kate should have avoided using credit cards.

b) An IVA is an arrangement that is usually made for unsecured debts and as the majority of Theo and Kate's debts are secured, this is probably not a route that it would be helpful for them to consider. It would not cover the secured bank loan or the mortgage and they are struggling to meet the repayments on these. The IVA would last for five years and it is very likely that they would be forced to remortgage their home at the end of that time. (As there would be equity in their home, assuming house prices do not fall in the meantime.) An IVA would impact on their credit rating and limit their capacity to borrow in the future.

c) There are many possible options that could be suggested. The following is a list of some of the options they could consider individually, or a combination could be used:

Extend the mortgage term

Theo and Kate could ask their mortgage lender to extend the term of their mortgage. The advantage is that the monthly repayment would be reduced but the disadvantage is that, over the life of the mortgage, it will cost them more.

Move to interest-only mortgage

They could ask their mortgage lender to make their mortgage interest-only in order to reduce their monthly outgoings. When the family income increases in the future, they could transfer the mortgage back to being a repayment one. The advantage is that the monthly cost would be reduced but the disadvantage is that, in the long run, the mortgage will cost Theo and Kate more.

Help from family

They could ask for help from family members if there was a parent or other relative who might be in a position to make an interest-free or low interest loan so that the credit card debts and maybe the bank loan could be repaid. If they were able to get help in this way, Theo and Kate would also need to make very significant adjustments to their lifestyle to ensure that they live within their means in the future. The advantage of a loan from a family member is that it would be a cheap form of borrowing and the disadvantage is that it might be embarrassing to ask for such help.

Use 0% credit card balance transfers

The couple could explore the possibility of transferring some or all of their credit card balances onto a 0% balance transfer deal. The advantage of this is that they would greatly reduce the interest they are incurring on their cards.

Take in a lodger

Theo and Kate could consider renting out one of the rooms in their home. The advantage is that it would bring in extra income that would be tax-free if less than £7,500 pa and the disadvantage is that they would have to share their house with someone from outside the family.

Downsize their home

The couple could move to a less expensive property and in doing so, release some of the equity in their home. The advantage of this step is that the equity could be used to pay off the loan and credit card debts, and if a smaller mortgage is taken out after the move, it would cost the couple less each month in the future. The disadvantage is that the cheaper house is likely to be smaller and/or in a less desirable location and moving home will give rise to some significant costs.

Less useful suggestions include:

Debt consolidation loan

A less helpful option might be to take out a debt consolidation loan. This should reduce their interest costs but Theo and Kate are still likely to struggle to make their budget balance.

d) The sale of their existing house will release equity of £63,000 (proceeds £213,000 less existing mortgage £150,000).

The new house costs £175,000 and the new mortgage is for £130,000. Therefore the couple need to put £45,000 towards the purchase cost.

The £63,000 raised from the sale could be used to:

- Pay the deposit required to buy the new house (£45,000)
- Pay off all the credit card debts (approximately £9,000)
- Pay off the bank loan (£5,000)
- Have £4,000 left to settle any overdraft and start a savings account.

e) Table 14.5 shows a revised cash budget for Theo and Kate.

Table 14.5 Theo and Kate's cash budget for the nine months to December

	Apr £	May £	Jun £	Jul £	Aug £	Sep £	Oct £	Nov £	Dec £
Income									
Theo net pay	1,750	1,750	1,750	1,750	1,750	1,750	1,750	1,750	1,750
Kate income—own business	500	500	500	500	500	500	500	500	500
Kate net pay—PT job	250	250	250	0	0	0	0	0	0
Total income	**2,500**	**2,500**	**2,500**	**2,250**	**2,250**	**2,250**	**2,250**	**2,250**	**2,250**
Expenditure									
Mortgage	780	780	680	680	680	680	680	680	680
Utilities and car	800	800	700	700	700	700	700	700	700
Credit card min payts	225	225	0	0	0	0	0	0	0
Food	550	550	550	550	550	550	550	550	550
Car service				1200					
Bank loan	110	110	0	0	0	0	0	0	
Total expenditure	**2465**	**2465**	**1930**	**3130**	**1930**	**1930**	**1930**	**1930**	**1930**
Net income/(exp)	**35**	**35**	**570**	**−880**	**320**	**320**	**320**	**320**	**320**
Balance at beg of month	−200	−165	−130	440	−440	−120	200	520	840
Balance at end of month	−165	−130	440	−440	−120	200	520	840	1160

f) Kate's plan for the family to move from their existing house to a cheaper property, pay off their credit card bills and bank loan, and reduce their mortgage will certainly leave the household budget in a far more positive position at the end of the year. Given that the monthly outgoings would then be lower than the couple's income, they should be able to live within their means and avoid debt as long as their circumstances do not change again.

One step they should take before deciding to go ahead with the move is that they should seek independent debt advice to ensure that they have fully explored all the options available to them and that they have chosen the best option for them. Another action they should take, if they have not done so already, is to cut up their credit cards.

Practice Question Solutions

Solution 1 True or False?

14.1   True

14.2   False. An amount owed to a credit card company would not be a priority debt.

14.3   False. The equity in a property is the difference between the current valuation and the borrowings secured against that property.

14.4   True

14.5   True

14.6   True

14.7   False. A debt consolidation loan often requires security for the loan.

14.8   True

14.9   False. Being declared bankrupt will mean that the borrower loses control of their significant assets, will probably lose their home, and being a declared bankrupt may impact on their future career choices.

14.10   True

Solution 2 Zachary

Zachary has total debts of £46,200 that at first sight may appear rather daunting in size. However, a closer look at his personal circumstances and his debts reveals that he has the capacity to bring his debts under control and eliminate his most expensive debts over a period of months. He has no priority debts as none of his debts are secured on his home. He should carry out a personal financial review to establish how best to bring his debts under control.

Set objectives

Zachary could set his objectives: to pay off his credit card debt and bank overdraft, whilst continuing to meet his repayments on the car loan. (He should also have a longer-term objective to build up some savings.)

The car loan will be repaid over the term of the loan at the agreed rate per month. The debt with the Student Loans Company will be collected from his salary each month and his take home pay will be received after his monthly repayment has been deducted. The interest charged on it is relatively modest.

Measure his position

Zachary should draw up a detailed cash budget that lists his essential and non-essential expenditure. From the information provided, Zachary's available monthly income after essential expenditure and the car loan repayment amounts to: £3,100 net income less (£1,900 essential expenditure + £200 car loan) = £1,000 per month. He needs to avoid or greatly limit making non-essential expenditure, including expenditure on clothes and his social life, and could perhaps reduce his essential expenditure. If he can limit his non-essential expenditure to £200 per month, he would have approximately £800 excess of income over expenditure each month and would be able to afford to pay off his credit card balance and his overdraft over a number of months.

Research options

Zachary could explore whether there are any 0% balance transfer deals available that he could transfer his credit card debts to. If he is able to do so, he should ensure that he stops using credit cards and takes a careful note of when the 0% deal expires.

He could research whether he could reduce his utility and other bills by changing suppliers.

Act

Having drawn up a budget and decided on the amounts he can afford to spend, he must then make every effort to keep to the budget. If he has identified any 0% credit card deals, he should act to transfer his balances. If he has identified cheaper deals for electricity, gas, insurance, etc, he should act to change suppliers.

Review regularly

Zachary should check that he is keeping to his budget and that repaying his credit card balances is going according to plan. If not, he may need to reassess his budget and take steps to regain control of his finances.

Index